INTRODUCTION TO BIBLICAL HEBREW

A Workbook and an Answer Key to the exercises in this book
are also available from CPT Press:

Workbook for
Introduction to Biblical Hebrew
ISBN 978-1-935931-76-8

Answer Key to
Introduction to Biblical Hebrew
ISBN 978-1-935931-75-1

INTRODUCTION TO

BIBLICAL HEBREW

FOURTH EDITION

LEE ROY MARTIN

CPT Press
Cleveland, Tennessee USA

INTRODUCTION TO BIBLICAL HEBREW

Fourth Edition

Published by CPT Press
900 Walker ST NE
Cleveland, TN 37311
email: cptpress@pentecostaltheology.org
website: www.pentecostaltheology.org

ISBN-13: 978-1-935931-74-4

Library of Congress Control Number: 2018908336

BWHEBB, BWHEBL, BWTRANSH [Hebrew]; BWGRKL, BWGRKN, and BWGRKI [Greek] Postscript® Type 1 and TrueTypeT fonts Copyright © 1994-2009 BibleWorks, LLC. All rights re- served. These Biblical Greek and Hebrew fonts are used with permission and are from BibleWorks, software for Biblical exegesis and research.

Photo Credits:
Lee Roy Martin, Matthew Holmes, Friedhelm Wessel, and Deror Avi
Cover Design: Lee Roy Martin

To
Karen

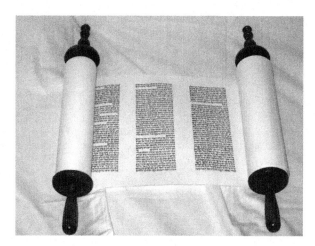

Torah Scroll

CONTENTS

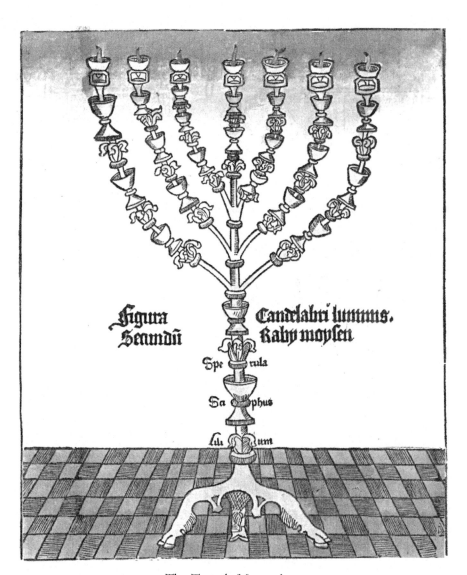

Figura Secundu Candelabri lumins. Raby moysen

Spe rula

Sa phus

fli um

The Temple Menorah

INTRODUCTION

History of the Hebrew Language

Hebrew is one of the world's oldest languages. It has the distinction of being the only language to have been revived as a spoken language after centuries of disuse. The ancient Israelites who lived in Palestine during biblical times spoke and wrote Hebrew. The Bible is the greatest product of Hebrew literature. Today Hebrew still serves as the language of Judaism, and is also the official language of the state of Israel.

The Name of the Hebrew Language

Hebrew is the language of the Old Testament (even though small sections of the Old Testament are written in Aramaic). The people who are the center of God's actions in the Old Testament are called Hebrews. The name of the people and of the language was probably derived from Eber, son of Shem.

In the Old Testament the language of the Hebrews is described as the language of Canaan (Isa. 19.18), or the language of Judah (Neh. 13.24; Isa. 36.11). The first occurrence of the designation Hebrew is in the prologue to Ben Sira, written approximately 130 BCE. The New Testament writers and Josephus used the designation Hebrew to refer both to Hebrew and to the locally spoken Aramaic.

The language of the Jews was finally singled out as Hebrew by the later Rabbinic literature. In Rabbinic literature the Hebrew is often referred to as the sacred tongue.

Historical Periods of the Hebrew Language

The Hebrew language has undergone relatively minor changes throughout history as compared to other languages. Nevertheless, four main phases of Hebrew may be proposed:

1. Biblical Hebrew, also known as classical Hebrew

2. Rabbinical Hebrew, or Mishnaic Hebrew

3. Medieval Hebrew, also called Rabbinic, the Hebrew of the Middle Ages

4. Modern Hebrew

The rabbinical stage of the Hebrew language was used in the composition of theological works after the close of the Old Testament canon. Rabbinical Hebrew was characteristic especially of the Mishna, as well as the Hebrew portions of the Talmud and Midrash.

Rabbinic, the third stage, was the Hebrew of the great theological, philosophical, and poetical works composed during the Middle Ages, mainly in Spain and North Africa. It was also used in translating works from Arabic. During the Middle Ages it served as a *lingua franca* for Jews throughout the world.

The Origin of the Hebrew Language

Hebrew is a member of the Semitic family of languages. Broadly speaking, the Semitic family is divided into East Semitic (Akkadian, Babylonian, Assyrian), South Semitic (North Arabic, South Arabic, Ethiopic), and Northwest Semitic (Canaanite, Aramaic, Syrian, Ugaritic, and Hebrew).

Scholars disagree about the origin of Hebrew. Some suggest that it developed from Canaanite circa 1000 BCE. Others propose that it developed simultaneously with Canaanite, Moabite, and Phoenician at approximately 1500 BCE.

The first canonical reference to spoken Hebrew occurs in Gen. 31.47 where Laban and Jacob refer to a heap of stones in their own native speech. Laban calls it Jegarsahadutha, which is Aramaic, but Jacob calls it Galeed, which is Hebrew. He also calls a nearby pillar by a Hebrew word, Mizpah. By the time of Moses, there were several well established means of written communication. Akkadian was the common language of the times; Egyptian was being written in hieratic script; and Ugaritic cuneiform was being used by the Canaanites. By 1500 BCE the alphabet, as distinct from cuneiform and hieroglyphs, came into use in Palestine. Scholars have adopted the name Proto-Semitic for the parent language that stands behind the Semitic languages.

The first record of Hebrew as a separate language is the 'Izbet Sartah inscription from the eleventh century BCE. It is not possible, however, to know how long Hebrew had existed prior to that time. The various tribes of peoples in Canaan began to grow and develop, and as they grew they became more distinct from one another. As distinctions (and even conflicts) developed, each group also developed its own language based on the Proto-Semitic dialects. Exodus 3.8 lists six separate peoples: Canaanites, Hittites, Amorites, Hivites, Jebusites, and Perizzites. Each one of these groups developed its own language. The languages were close enough, however, that the different peoples could communicate with one another easily.

The Development of the Hebrew Language

The Record of the Inscriptions

With the exception of the Old Testament, very few remains of old Hebrew have been preserved. The inscriptions are brief, but they yield some important results. One of the oldest is the 'Izbet Sartah inscription, dated in the eleventh century BCE It contains around eighty letters.

The Gezer calendar, dated in the tenth century BCE, is a flat limestone tablet that appears to have been used by a student for practicing handwriting. The inscription is in the form of a poem, describing the planting and harvesting cycle.

In 1976 about seventy Hebrew and Phoenician inscriptions were found at Kuntillet 'Ajrud in Sinai, and they are dated in the ninth and eighth centuries BCE. One text refers to God under his covenant name YHWH.

Samaritan ostraca of the ninth century have also been discovered. Although the question of early Hebrew dialects is uncertain, these ostraca seem to show a northern dialect which differs somewhat from the southern dialect of the Gezer calendar.

An inscription of six lines was discovered in the tunnel between the Virgin's Spring and the Pool of Siloam at Jerusalem. It has come to be called the Siloam inscription and dates from the eighth century BCE.

About forty engraved seal stones have been discovered. Some of them are pre-exilic. Other inscriptions, called the Lachish letters, have been found written on potsherds. They are dated at approximately 590 BCE, and consist largely of military communications.

The Development of the Hebrew Script

Although the evidence is scattered both chronologically and geographically, it is sufficient to indicate that the early Hebrew alphabet was constant throughout the millennium of its usage, beginning in the tenth century BCE. The alphabet in use at this time was a cursive script commonly designated as Phoenician script (also called paleo-Hebrew). Hardly any of its letters changed so radically during that time that a layman could mistake its identity. Part of the reason for Hebrew's uniformity may be the fact that it was the vehicle for the sacred writings. The language itself, therefore, came to be considered sacred.

After the Babylonian captivity, modified forms of the Aramaic characters, which had by that time diverged considerably from the Phoenician script, were adopted by the Jews. The Dead Sea Scrolls were written during the transitional period (from 250-100 BCE). Some of the scrolls were written in the cursive script and some in the square script. The Aramaic square script was eventually adopted as the standard Hebrew alphabet, even though the Phoenician forms continued in use to the second century CE.

Apparently, the Aramaic characters had been introduced as the official script for Torah scrolls in the fifth century BCE. No one knows why the Jews changed scripts. It does seem unusual that they would give up the script in which their sacred literature was enshrined, a script they had used for almost one thousand years.

Aramaic was the most important language of the day; therefore, the Jews adopted Aramaic as their common language. They adopted the Aramaic script, however, before they Aramaic as their language. Even after they began to use Aramaic as the vernacular, the Bible remained in Hebrew, but with Aramaic script. Why did they not simply translate the Bible into Aramaic?

Figure 1

The changing of the sacred script must have been a deliberate action on the part of the religious leaders, motivated by religious reasons. This assessment is confirmed by both the Palestinian and Babylonian Talmuds, as well as the Church Fathers. The earliest evidence is from the Talmud, where R. Eliezer ben Jacob (150 CE) wrote: 'Three prophets [Haggai, Zechariah, Malachi] came with them from the exile. One testified that the Torah must be written in square script'. Other references in the Talmud suggest that Ezra was responsible for changing the script. The reason for the change is related to the Samaritans. Among the church fathers, Origen and Epiphanius refer to Ezra's changing of the script. Epiphanius declares:

> The Samaritans, however, retain the [Phoenician script], which form, as we have said, was engraved in older times in the stone tablets. But when Ezra came up from Babylon and desired to make Israel different from the other peoples in order that the offspring of Abraham should not appear to be defiled by the inhabitants of the land—who have indeed the Law but not the Prophets—he changed the previous form, abandoning the [Phoenician script], because that form was already in the hands of the Samaritans.

It seems that the Jews may have changed the script of the Bible in order to erect a wall against Samaritanism. It is possible that Ezra could have instigated the change to the square script.

Historical Divisions of Biblical Hebrew

Notwithstanding the general uniformity of the Old Testament, there is a noticeable progress from an earlier to a later stage. Two periods, with some reservations, may be distinguished. The first period began approximately with Moses and continued until the end of the Babylonian captivity. The second period spanned the years from the captivity to the Maccabees (about 160 BCE).

The majority of the Old Testament books belong in the first period. Even in this period, which embraces about six hundred years, there are some differences in linguistic form and style. These differences are due partly to the individuality of the authors, and partly to the time and place of composition. Isaiah, therefore, writes differently from the later Jeremiah, but he also writes differently from his contemporary Micah. In the historical books differences may be observed when a biblical author uses previously existing sources.

The second period of biblical Hebrew is chiefly distinguished by a closer approximation to kindred western Aramaic. This is due to the influence of Aramaeans, who lived in close contact with the small post-exilic colony in Jerusalem. Aramaic was already important by virtue of its being the official language of the western half of the Persian empire.

The widespread importance of Aramaic caused it to eventually replace Hebrew as the spoken language of Palestine. The incident in 2 Kgs 18.26-36 is clear evidence that Hebrew was the spoken language in Jerusalem when the city was besieged by Sennacherib circa 701 BCE. In Neh. 8.2-8, however, the people needed interpreters when Ezra stood to read the Law. Nevertheless, the supplanting of Hebrew by Aramaic proceeded very gradually. Early writings intended for popular use, such as the Hebrew original of Jesus the Son of Sirach, show that Hebrew was still in use as a literary language at about 170 BCE. They also demonstrate that Hebrew was still understood by the people at that time. When Hebrew ceased to exist as a living language, it was still preserved as the language of the scholars.

Several Old Testament books belong to this second period. Aramaic coloring appears in varying degrees in Ezra, Nehemiah, Esther, Chronicles, Haggai, Zechariah, Malachi, and some of the Psalms. In addition to Aramaic influence, the later books show a development of grammatical forms and a use of particles foreign to the earlier language.

Phonetics

As the Hebrew writing on monuments and coins consisted only of consonants, so also the writers of the Old Testament used merely the consonant signs. Even now the written scrolls of the Law used in synagogues must not contain anything more. The present pronunciation of this consonantal text, its vocalization and accentuation, rests on the tradition of the Jewish schools. This tradition was finally fixed by the system of pronunciation introduced by Jewish scholars about the seventh century CE.

A first step toward vocalization of the consonantal Hebrew was the introduction of *matres lectionis* (Latin for mothers of reading), also called vowel letters. Gradually, the letters *vav, yod, heh,* (ו י ה) and to a lesser extent *alef* (א), began to represent the lengthened vowels. These vowel letters appear at a relatively early date, possibly as a borrowing from Aramaic, but they were used somewhat haphazardly. The Septuagint shows that vowel letters were not used consistently in the Hebrew text from which it was translated. Furthermore, their use in the Dead Sea Scrolls indicates that they were regarded as secondary elements in the text.

Vocalization beyond these vowel letters was not necessary when Hebrew was a living language. As it came to be less and less the language of common discourse, however, it was needful to have some way of indicating more fully the vocalization. This was done by the pointing, that is, providing the consonants with small signs, written above, below, or within them, to indicate the vowels with which they were to be pronounced.

Three such systems of vocalization are known. The system ordinarily used in printed texts of the Old Testament is the Tiberian system worked out by the Masoretes of the School of Tiberias. It is a predominantly infralinear system (The marks are under the consonants.) Two older systems, both supralinear (marks above the consonants), are the Babylonian and the Palestinian, which appear in certain groups of manuscripts. These manuscripts indicate that the pointing systems were introduced gradually, for only ambiguous words were pointed at first. These helps to pronunciation were inserted only where they were felt necessary.

It is probable that the three systems of pointing represent a late tradition as to the pronunciation. When translating the Latin Vulgate, Jerome tried to transcribe in Latin the pronunciation that he heard from his Jewish teachers. From these transcripts of Jerome, along with even earlier transcriptions of the Septuagint and of Origen, it is possible to work back to some understanding of an earlier pronunciation, which seems to be nearer that of classical Arabic.

There was no punctuation in the early Hebrew writing and often not even word division. In some inscriptions, words are separated by a dot or stroke (e.g. the Siloam inscription, an excerpt of which is pictured in Figure 2). The evidence of the Septuagint shows that its translators used Hebrew manuscripts that were sometimes void of word division.

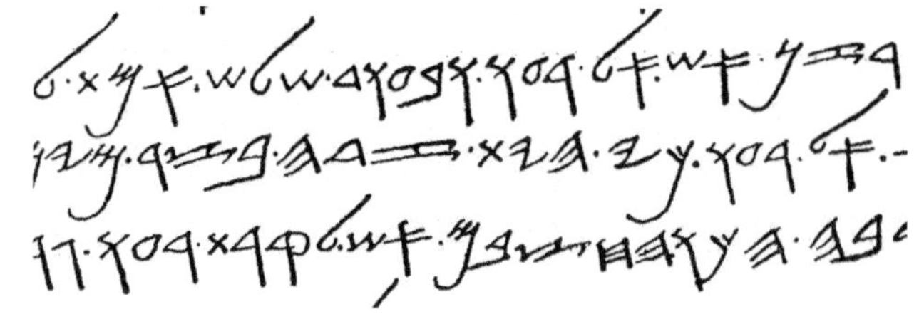

Figure 2—Excerpt from the Siloam Inscription

One attempt at minimizing some elements of confusion arising from the lack of word division was the assigning of a special form of some letters as final letters. These final letters came into use gradually. The Masoretes, who worked out the signs for vocalization, also worked out another set of signs to serve as marks of punctuation, and yet another set of signs to guide readers to the proper cantillation of the text. In the poetical books these signs are somewhat different from the prose books. In addition to vocalization guides to the text, other phonological changes occurred in biblical Hebrew. For instance, the distinction in pronunciation between the two letters *samek* (ס) and *seen* (שׂ) was apparently lost in the northern kingdom quite early. In Judah it faded away by the sixth century BCE. Following the loss of distinction in sound, the spelling of some words began to change. For example, the letter *samek* began to be substituted for the letter *seen*.

It should also be noted that sometime after 500 BCE the letters *beyt, gimel, dalet, kaf, peh,* and *tav* (ב ג ד כ פ ת) became spirantized after vowel sounds unless the consonant was doubled.

Grammar

The early writers of Hebrew would have been little conscious of grammar. As any language, however, comes more and more into use as a literary medium, it tends to become fixed. This is a slow process, and in the case of Hebrew may be considered to have gained impetus when the Jerusalem dialect, perhaps as early as the United Kingdom under David and Solomon, came to be regarded as the standard form of the language.

The body of inscriptional material in Hebrew is so small and fragmentary that any study of the grammatical forms must of necessity be based on the text of the Old Testament. The great number of variants for certain grammatical forms recorded in the Hebrew grammars suggests there may have been a period of considerable uncertainty before a standard form imposed itself. In Ezek. 13.20-22, for example, there are three different ways of forming the suffix for the second person plural, and in Isa. 32.9-11 there are three different ways of forming the feminine plural of the imperative. It is possible that some of the anomalous grammatical forms may be based on dialects, but it is difficult to distinguish in any detail the dialectical strata in the text of the Old Testament.

In the earliest period, the Hebrew nouns possessed short vowel endings to identify the cases. There was also a dual number (especially for bodily parts that exist in pairs). In the course of time the case endings were dropped. The genitive case, therefore, had to be expressed by word position; the possessor always followed right after the thing possessed. The first member of the pair was put in what was called construct state. One other important development ensued upon the loss of case endings, and that was the use of the untranslated sign of the direct object. Interestingly enough, Hebrew was the first of the Canaanite dialects to develop the definite article.

Conclusion

Archaeologists and paleographers continue to work, in order to bring to light more and more of the rich history of the Semitic languages. The computer has brought the ancient Semitic texts into wide accessibility. Scholars are using the computerized Hebrew text as the basis of new studies in phonology, grammar, syntax, and discourse analysis. Some of these studies may influence the dating of biblical texts. The next few years promise to bring new insights into the Hebrew language.

Selected Bibliography

Barr, James. *Comparative Philology and the Text of the Old Testament* (Oxford: Clarendon Press, 1968).

Birnbaum, Solomon A. *The Hebrew Scripts* (2 vols.; Leiden: Brill, 1971).

Diringer, D. 'Early Hebrew Writing', *The Biblical Archaeologist* 13 (October 1950), pp. 80-89.

Encyclopedia Judaica. S.v. 'Hebrew Language', by Charles Black; S.v. 'Semitic Languages', by Chaim M. Rabim.

Harris, Zellig S. *Development of the Canaanite Dialects.* American Oriental Series; 6 (New Haven, CT: American Oriental Society, 1939).

The Interpreter's Dictionary of the Bible. S.v. 'Hebrew Language', by Arthur Jeffery.

International Standard Bible Encyclopedia. S.v. 'Hebrew Language', by Leslie McFall.

Jewish Encyclopedia. S.v. 'Semitic Languages', by George A. Barton.

Kutscher, Edward Yechezkel. *A History of the Hebrew Language* (Jerusalem: Magnes Press of the Hebrew University, 1982).

Psalm 119 from the Dead Sea Scrolls
An Acrostic Psalm

Why should we learn Hebrew?

- Translations are good, but no translation is able to convey all the subtleties of Hebrew.

- Poetry and all figures of speech rely heavily upon the sounds and meanings of the original Hebrew.

- Literary devices and rhetorical structures cannot be interpreted easily from a translation.

- Many commentaries refer to the Hebrew text. An intelligent reading of these commentaries requires a knowledge of the original language.

- Other resources utilize Hebrew words: lexicons, word studies, theological works, grammars, concordances, journal articles.

- Every student of the Bible needs the ability to critique the opinions of others. If the Bible student does not learn Hebrew, s/he will forever be dependent upon the thoughts and ideas of someone else.

- Knowing the original language of the Bible enables more effective original research, utilizing the concordance, lexicon, and/or computer Bible program. Questions not answered in the standard reference works may be researched.

- Knowledge of Hebrew enhances sermon and lesson preparation. Ideas will come from the original language that would otherwise be unnoticed.

- Learning any new language enhances communication skills by adding to the understanding of linguistics in general.

- The ability to study the original language of Scripture raises the student's level of confidence.

- Learning the vocabulary and idioms of the biblical culture leads directly to a greater understanding of that culture.

Silwan Tomb Inscription in Phoenician Script

Study Hints

On the one hand, the learning of Hebrew presents several difficulties to the student whose native language is non-Semitic. These difficulties include the strange shapes of the alphabet, the direction of the writing (right to left), the vowel points in unusual positions, the large number of words that sound similar to each other, and the large number of *hapax legomena*. On the other hand, some elements of Hebrew are rather simple when compared to other languages. For example, Hebrew has only two genders (masculine and feminine), while many other languages have three genders. Furthermore, rules for grammar are consistent, with few irregularities. Also, sentence structure is relatively simple.

The study of Hebrew requires some memory work. The effectiveness of your study time will depend upon several factors, including the following:

Repetition

The human brain stores short term memories fairly easily, but in order to remember any facts over the long term, you must repeat those facts throughout a period of months. Also, short study periods are more effective than lengthy ones. For example, you should break up your study into three one-hour periods, rather than attempt a single three-hour period. If it is to be successful, this repetition must include times when you lay aside the book and recite the facts that you have been studying. This technique is called forced recall. In summary, the best method for memorizing new information includes many short study periods conducted over a long term, which include forced recall.

Association

Associate new concepts with ones that you already know. Associate Hebrew with verbal, visual, and auditory cues. Try to use as many mnemonic devices as possible.

Motivation

Your interest level helps to determine how easily you learn. Memory is affected by your attention span. You must learn to concentrate all your energy toward your study. Avoid all distractions while studying.

After becoming acquainted with the Hebrew Language, you will be better equipped to read and study the Hebrew Bible.

Psalms Scroll fragment from the Dead Sea area.

Chapter 1

The Hebrew Alphabet

In this chapter you should learn:

- The Hebrew alphabet and vowel symbols
- How to write the Hebrew letters and vowels
- How to pronounce the Hebrew letters and vowels

1.1   The Hebrew Letters

Ancient Hebrew was written from right to left (opposite to English). It had no vowels, no capital letters; and often there were no spaces between words. Consider the following sentence:

> Robert said to his brother Bruno, 'Let's go ride the horses'.

If we use the rules of ancient Hebrew, the sentence (but still in English letters from left to right) might look something like this:

RBRTSDTHSBRTHRBRNLTSGRDTHHRSS.

Today's Hebrew Bible has vowel letters inserted above, below, and between the letters, and it includes spaces between the words. The same sentence might look like this today:

RBRT SiD T HS BRTHR BRuN LTS G RD TH HRSS

You can see why some people find it difficult to read Hebrew!

The Hebrew alphabet consists of twenty-three (23) letters, all of which are consonants. The type of script in use today is called the Aramaic **square script**. Vowel sounds are indicated by a system of diacritical marks called **pointing** (or *nikkud*)

Because Hebrew is a Semitic language, it is not easy for the English speaking student to reproduce the sounds of Hebrew. In fact, Hebrew may be pronounced slightly differently by various groups. We will use the Sephardic pronunciation as it has been modified for Modern Hebrew.

The Hebrew alphabet is listed on the following pages, along with directions for writing each letter and its pronunciation.

1.2   Writing the Hebrew Letters

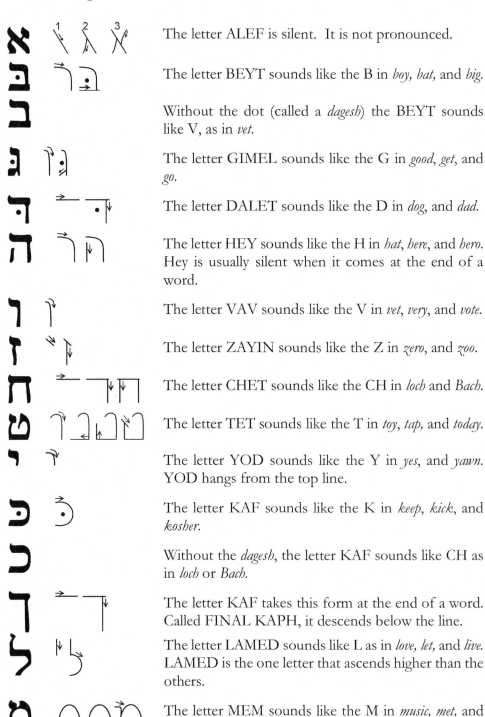

The letter ALEF is silent. It is not pronounced.

The letter BEYT sounds like the B in *boy*, *bat*, and *big*.

Without the dot (called a *dagesh*) the BEYT sounds like V, as in *vet*.

The letter GIMEL sounds like the G in *good*, *get*, and *go*.

The letter DALET sounds like the D in *dog*, and *dad*.

The letter HEY sounds like the H in *hat*, *here*, and *hero*. Hey is usually silent when it comes at the end of a word.

The letter VAV sounds like the V in *vet*, *very*, and *vote*.

The letter ZAYIN sounds like the Z in *zero*, and *zoo*.

The letter CHET sounds like the CH in *loch* and *Bach*.

The letter TET sounds like the T in *toy*, *tap*, and *today*.

The letter YOD sounds like the Y in *yes*, and *yawn*. YOD hangs from the top line.

The letter KAF sounds like the K in *keep*, *kick*, and *kosher*.

Without the *dagesh*, the letter KAF sounds like CH as in *loch* or *Bach*.

The letter KAF takes this form at the end of a word. Called FINAL KAPH, it descends below the line.

The letter LAMED sounds like L as in *love*, *let*, and *live*. LAMED is the one letter that ascends higher than the others.

The letter MEM sounds like the M in *music*, *met*, and *mark*.

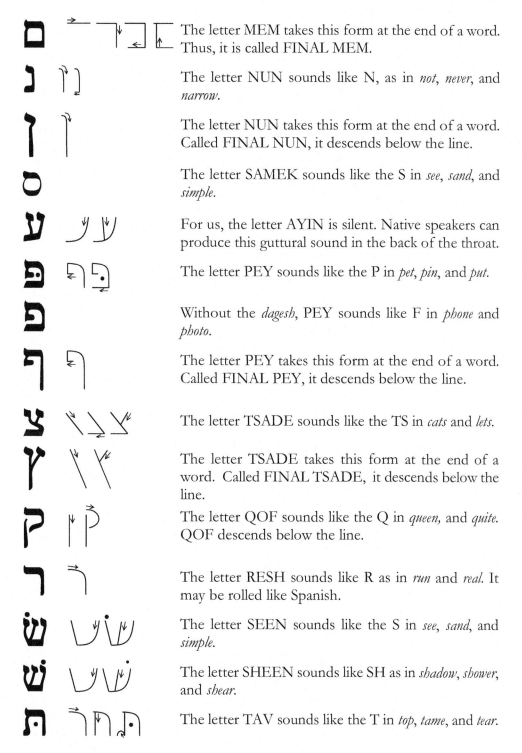

The letter MEM takes this form at the end of a word. Thus, it is called FINAL MEM.

The letter NUN sounds like N, as in *not*, *never*, and *narrow*.

The letter NUN takes this form at the end of a word. Called FINAL NUN, it descends below the line.

The letter SAMEK sounds like the S in *see*, *sand*, and *simple*.

For us, the letter AYIN is silent. Native speakers can produce this guttural sound in the back of the throat.

The letter PEY sounds like the P in *pet*, *pin*, and *put*.

Without the *dagesh*, PEY sounds like F in *phone* and *photo*.

The letter PEY takes this form at the end of a word. Called FINAL PEY, it descends below the line.

The letter TSADE sounds like the TS in *cats* and *lets*.

The letter TSADE takes this form at the end of a word. Called FINAL TSADE, it descends below the line.

The letter QOF sounds like the Q in *queen*, and *quite*. QOF descends below the line.

The letter RESH sounds like R as in *run* and *real*. It may be rolled like Spanish.

The letter SEEN sounds like the S in *see*, *sand*, and *simple*.

The letter SHEEN sounds like SH as in *shadow*, *shower*, and *shear*.

The letter TAV sounds like the T in *top*, *tame*, and *tear*.

Practice writing the Hebrew letters, using the examples above as a guide.

1.3   Reading Hebrew

Now that we have learned the alphabet we can learn the vowel signs and begin reading Hebrew. The following rules apply to reading Hebrew:

1. Hebrew reads from right to left.
2. Each word and syllable begins with a consonant.
3. Every consonant has one and only one vowel (but the last letter of a word may not have a vowel).

1.4   Final Forms

Five letters have a different form when they come at the end of a word. These are called *final forms*:

1. כ becomes ך at the end of a word.

2. מ becomes ם at the end of a word.

3. נ becomes ן at the end of a word.

4. פ becomes ף at the end of a word.

5. צ becomes ץ at the end of a word.

> Five letters have a different shape when they come at the end of a word.

These letters form the mnemonic KeMNeFaTS, representing the letters:

כ מ נ פ צ.

EXERCISE 1-A

- Learn the names of the letters in alphabetical order.
- Practice the following reading drill.

The following verse (Jer. 22.3) from the Hebrew Bible has all the letters of the alphabet. Identify each letter by name, in order, from right to left.

Repeat the drill orally until you can read the letters easily. **Always** read aloud!

1. כה אמר יהוה עשו משפט וצדקה
2. והצילו גזול מיד עשוק וגר יתום
3. ואלמנה אל תנו אל תחמסו
4. ודם נקי אל תשפכו במקום הזה

1.5   Similar Letters

The following letters appear similar in the square script:

בּ   is similar to כּ

ג   is similar to נ, זִ, ו, and ן

ר   is similar to ד and ך

ע   is similar to צּ

שׁ   is similar to שׂ

ס   is similar to ם

ה   is similar to חּ and תּ

1.6   Pronunciation

The alphabet chart lists the Sephardic pronunciation of each letter. The pronunciation of three letters will change when a dot is inside the letter. That dot, called a *dagesh lene*, is explained below.

1.6.1   *Dagesh Lene*

Hebrew has six letters that may have a dot within the letter called a *dagesh lene* (weak *dagesh*). Those six letters are ב ג ד כ פ ת, represented by the mnemonic BeGaD KeFaT. The *dagesh lene* appears in these letters anytime they are not preceded by a vowel (either at the beginning of a word or within a word).

The *dagesh lene* indicates a change of pronunciation. These letters without the *dagesh* are pronounced as spirants, and with the *dagesh* they are stops. A stop is produced by temporarily stopping the flow of breath with the lips, tongue, teeth, or palate. In English the lips produce *b* and *p*. The tongue and teeth produce *t* and *d*. The tongue against the palate produce *k* and *g*. If the vocal passage is left slightly open, the resulting sound is called a spirant. Spirants include *v*, *f*, and *th*.

Modern Hebrew, however, changes only three letters from stops to spirants:

בּ is pronounced like **B**, but ב is like **V**.

כּ is pronounced like **K**, but כ is like **CH**.

פּ is pronounced like **P**, but פ is like **F**.

But,

Both גּ and ג are pronounced like g.

Both דּ and ד are pronounced like d.

Both תּ and ת are pronounced like t.

The *dagesh lene* occurs
in six letters.
It changes the pronunciation of three letters.

1.6.2   *Dagesh Forte*

Other letters may have a *dagesh*, and when they do, it is called *dagesh forte. Dagesh forte* does not change the pronunciation of the other letters; it signifies that the letter is doubled.

1.7   Letters With Similar Sounds

The Following letters are pronounced similarly:

א	ע		(Both are silent)
ב	ו		(Both sound like v)
ה	ח	כ	(h, ch, and ch)
כ	ק		(k and q)
ט	ת		(Both sound like t)
ס	שׂ	שׁ	(s, s, and sh)

Knesset Menorah

1.8   Vowel Points

The vowel points and *sheva* (called *pointing*) are placed under the consonants (except *cholem*, which is placed above and to the left, and *shureq*, which follows to the left of the consonant). In the chart below, the letter בַ is not part of the vowels, but is included here so that the position of the vowels may be visualized.

1.8.1   Pointing

Sign	Name	Sound	Transliteration
בַ	*patach*	a as in father	a
בָ	*qamets*	a as in father	a
בָ	*qamets-qatan*	a as in father	o (see note below)
בֶ	*segol*	e as in bet	e
בֵ	*tsere*	e as in they	ey
בֵי	*tsere-yod*	e as in they	ey
בִ	*chireq*	i as in siesta	i
בִי	*chireq-yod*	i as in siesta.	iy
בֹ	*cholem*	o as in roll	o
בוֹ	*cholem-vav*	o as in roll	o
בֻ	*qibbuts*	u as in rule	u
וּ	*shureq*	u as in rule	u
בְ	*sheva*	no vowel	ᵉ or none
בֳ	chatef-*qamets*	a as in father	ᵒ
בֱ	chatef-*segol*	e as in bet	ᵉ
בֲ	chatef-*patach*	a as in father	ᵃ

Chatefs are a type of *sheva*. They are sometimes called *composite sheva*. When *sheva* is under a guttural letter, it is written as a *chatef*, but it is still a *sheva* and functions like a *sheva*. The guttural letters are א , ע , ה , ח , and ר.

Note concerning *qamets-qatan*: This vowel is identical in form to the *qamets*, but it is a different vowel altogether. *Qamets* is a long a-class vowel and *qamets-qatan* is a short o-class vowel. *Qamets-qatan*, therefore, is designated in the transliterations with an *o* sound but in Modern Hebrew is pronounced like *a* as in *father*. We will discuss the grammatical significance of the two different vowels at a later time.

1.8.2   Full Vowels

Before the vowel points were invented, the scribes used the letters ו א ,י, and ה to indicate vowel sounds. These are called full vowels, or *matres lectiones* (Latin for *mothers of reading*). The ה signified the vowel *a*, the י signified *i* and *e*, and the ו signified the *o* and *u*. Later, these vowel letters were combined with the vowel points to form the *full vowels*. Simple vowels and full vowels represent the same sounds. Full vowels are just a variation in spelling. The chart on the previous page includes the full vowels *tsere-yod* (ֵי), *chireq-yod* (ִי), *cholem-vav* (וֹ), and *shureq* (וּ). In full vowels, the consonants are not pronounced. They are considered part of the vowel. Most words ending with a vowel combine with the vowel letter ה (e.g. הָ , הֶ, and הֵ).

A dot inside a final ה (called *mappiq*, הּ) indicates that the ה is to be considered a consonant. Thus, when ה appears at the end of a word, it will be a part of a full vowel, unless it has a *mappiq*.

1.9   Writing Hebrew Words

> **Hebrew is written from right to left.**

Hebrew is written from right to left.

All Hebrew letters are the same HEIGHT, except for the following letters that may reach above or below the level of the other letters.

> 1. The י is suspended, level with the top of the other letters. E.g. שׂים
>
> 2. The ל projects above the other letters. E.g. מלא
>
> 3. The ן ף ץ ק and ך descend below the line.
>
>   E.g. in the words מן נדף אין קול אך
>
> 4. All of the Hebrew letters are the same WIDTH, except for the following narrow letters: ג נ ו ז י ן

EXERCISE 1-B

- Practice writing the letters in alphabetical order until you can write them fluently.

- Be able to write the letters (including final forms) in order.

1.10 Quiescent *Alef*

Because it is so weak, there are times when *alef* (א) does not accept a vowel. Thus, it represents no sound at all; it is quiescent, e.g.

לֵאלֹהִים	ley-lo-heem
צֹאן	tson
רֹאשׁ	rosh

> Quiescent *Alef* is an *Alef* without a vowel.

EXERCISE 1-C

1. Learn the full vowels and their pronunciation.

2. Practice the following reading drills until you are able to read them easily.

Remember the following rules that apply to reading Hebrew:

- Hebrew reads from right to left.

- Each word and syllable begins with a consonant (except for the vowel וּ, which may begin a word as an attached conjunction).

- Every consonant has one and only one vowel or *sheva* (If the word ends with a consonant, it may have *sheva* but usually does not).

- For example, בָּ is pronunced *ba,* and טֶל is pronounced *tel.* We can combine the two syllables and form the word בָּטֶל, which is pronounced *ba-tel.*

Torah Scroll—Exodus 12.2-4

We will learn to read by focusing on a few letters at a time.

SET 1

Consonants

א   *Alef* is the first letter of the Hebrew alphabet. It is silent.

בּ   *Beyt* is the second letter, and sounds like *b* as in *boy* when it has a dot within it.

ב   *Beyt* without the dot is pronounced *v* as in *vet*.

Vowels

אָ   The vowel qamets (under the *alef* at left) is an *ah* sound, like the *a* in *father*. The *alef* is not part of the vowel. Since *alef* is silent, this combination of letters is pronounced *ah*.

אַ   The vowel patach (under the *alef*) is also pronounced *ah*, like the *a* in *father*. Since *alef* is silent, this combination of letters is *ah*.

Practice reading the following syllables by covering the English transliterations while you recite the Hebrew (remember to start on the right and read toward the left):

בַּא	בָּא	אָב	אַב	בָּ	בַּ	אָ	אַ
ba	*ba*	*av*	*av*	*ba*	*ba*	*a*	*a*

You can now read two words and one complete sentence:

Hebrew Words

אָב   The word *av* means *father*.

בָּא   The word *ba* means *came*.

Hebrew Sentence

אָב בָּא   *Av ba* means *Father came.*

Now we will practice the next two letters and two more vowels.

SET 2

Consonants

גּ   *Gimel* is always pronounced *g* as in *go* (with or without a dot).

דּ   *Dalet* is always pronounced *d* as in *dog* (with or without a dot).

Vowels

בֵּ   *Tsere* is pronounced like the *ey* in *they* or *prey*. The syllable at left would be pronounced *bey* as in *obey*.

בֶּ   *Segol* is pronounced like the *e* in *bet* or *let*. The syllable at left would be pronounced *be* as in *bet*.

Practice the following syllables:

אֵד	גֵּא	גַּב	דַּג	דֵּד	בֵּד	בֵּ	דַּ	דֵּ	גַּ	גַּ
ed	*gey*	*gav*	*dag*	*ded*	*bed*	*bey*	*da*	*dey*	*ga*	*ga*

Hebrew Words

גָּד   The word *gad* means *Gad*, one of Jacob's sons.

דָּג   The word *dag* means *fish* (Jonah 2.1)

גֵּא   The word *gey* means *proud* (Isaiah 16.6)

בַּד   The word *bad* means *portion*, or *linen fabric*.

Hebrew Sentence

גָּד אָב גֵּא   *Gad av gey* means *Gad is a proud father*. The words *is* and *a* must added to the English translation; they are not written in the Hebrew. Also, in Hebrew, an adjective follows the noun it modifies, so the word *proud* follows *father*.

Now we will practice the next two letters and two more vowels.

SET 3

Consonants

ה   *Hey* is pronounced *h* as in *hat*, but it is silent if it comes at the end of a word or syllable.

ו   *Vav* is always pronounced *v* as in *vet*.

Vowels

בִ   *Chireq* is pronounced like the *i* in *siesta*. The syllable at left would be pronounced *bi* (sounds like *bee*).

בִי   *Chireq-yod* is pronounced like the *i* in *siesta*. The syllable at left would be pronounced *bi* (sounds like *bee*).

Practice the following syllables:

דִג	בִינ	בֶּגֶד	וָו	וַד	בַּה	גִיב	הָ	גִד	הִד
dig	big	beged	vav	vad	bah	giv	ha	gid	hid

Hebrew Words

וָו   The word *vav* means *nail, peg*.

בֶּגֶד   The word *beged* means *garment*.

הִגִּיד   The word *higid* (sounds like *hee-geed*) means *told*.

אַבֵּד   The word *abeyd* means *to destroy*.

הִיא   The word *hiy* (sounds like *hee*) means *she*, or *it*.

דָּוִד   The word *david* means *David*.

Hebrew Sentence

דָּוִד בָּא אַבֵּד בֶּגֶד בַּד   David came to destroy a linen garment.

SET 4

Consonants

ז   The letter *zayin* sounds like *z* as in *zero* or *zoo*.

ח   The letter *chet* sounds like *ch* as in *loch* and *Bach*.

Vowels

בֵּי   *Tsere-yod* is pronounced like the *ey* in *they*. The syllable at left would be pronounced *bey*.

בֹ   *Cholem* is pronounced like the *o* in *roll*. The syllable at left would be pronounced *bo*.

בּוֹ   *Cholem-vav* is pronounced like the *o* in *roll*. The syllable at left would be pronounced *bo*.

Practice the following syllables:

בֹז	חֵיב	אוֹח	גֵּז	אָז	בִּז	בַּח	בֵּיד	זוֹח	זֹח
boz	*cheyv*	*och*	*gez*	*az*	*biz*	*bach*	*beyd*	*zoch*	*zoch*

Practice saying these Hebrew words as well:

Hebrew Words

אָז	*az*	The word *az* means *then*.
זֶבֶד	*zeyved*	The word *zeyved* means *gift*.
זָבַח	*zavach*	The word *zavach* means *sacrificed*.
זֶבַח	*zevach*	The word *zevach* means *a sacrifice*.
זֶה	*zeh*	The word *zeh* means *this*, or *these*.
זָהָב	*zahav*	The word *zahav* means *gold*.
חֹב	*chov*	The word *chov* means *shirt-pocket*.
חַג	*chag*	The word *chag* means *festival, feast*.
חָגָא	*chaga*	The word *chagga* means *shame*.
חָגָב	*chagav*	The word *chagav* means *locust*.

Hebrew Sentences

אָז דָוִד זָבַח זֶבַח זֶה   Then David sacrificed this sacrifice.

חָגָב בָּא אַבֵּר הִיא   A locust came to destroy it.

We will now practice the next two letters and two more vowels.

SET 5

Consonants

ט The letter *tet* sounds like *t* as in *toy* and *tap*.

י The letter *yod* sounds like *y* as in *yes* and *yawn*.

Vowels

בֻ *Qibbuts* is pronounced like the *u* in *rule*. The syllable at left would be pronounced *bu* (sounds like *boo*).

בוּ *Shureq* is also pronounced like the *u* in *rule*. The syllable at left would be pronounced *bu* (sounds like *boo*).

Practice the following syllables:

טוּג	יָדָה	בוֹא	הוּט	יוּ	יָה	חֻט	יוּט	אֲבִי	טֻב
tug	*yadah*	*bo*	*hut*	*yuv*	*yah*	*chut*	*yut*	*avi*	*tuv*

Practice saying these Hebrew words as well:

Hebrew Words

טוֹב	*tov*	good		אֹהַב	*ohav*	love gifts
טָח	*tach*	plaster		אֵהוּד	*eyhud*	Ehud
טָח	*tach*	smeared		אוֹ	*o*	or
יָגֵב	*yageyv*	field		אוּד	*ud*	log
יָד	*yad*	hand		אוֹי	*oy*	alas! woe!
יָדִיד	*yadid*	beloved		בָּטַח	*batach*	trusted

Hebrew Sentences

דָּוִד בָּטַח אֵהוּד אַבֵּד חָגָב זֶה   David trusted Ehud to destroy this locust.

טוֹב יָגֵב זֶה   This field is good.

We will now practice the next two letters and *sheva*.

SET 6

Consonants

כּ   The letter *kaf* (with a dot) sounds like *k* as in *keep*.

כ   The letter *kaf* (without a dot) sounds like *ch* as in *Bach*.

ך   The letter *kaf* has this form at the end of a word. Since it has no dot, it
ךְ   sounds like *ch* as in *loch* and *Bach*. Usually, the final *kaf* will have a *sheva*
     inside it (see *Shevas*, below).

ל   The letter *lamed* sounds like the *l* in *love*.

Shevas

בְּ   *Sheva* is a sign placed under letters that have no vowel (Gesenius §10).
     When it appears under a letter that begins a syllable, the *sheva* is usually
     indicated by a very short *e* sound, and it is transliterated with a super-
     script ^{e}.

בֳ   *Chatef-qamets* is now pronounced as an *ah* sound, like the *a* in *father*, but
     it is transliterated with a superscript ^{o}.

בֱ   *Chatef-segol* sounds like the *e* in *bet*. Indicated by ^{e}.

בֲ   *Chatef-patach* sounds like the *a* in *father*. Indicated by ^{a}.

Practice the following syllables:

דֵּךְ	כִּי	חֲגִּד	אֶל	חֲבִי	נֶכֹה	בְּנוּ	לֵךְ	כָּ
deych	*kiy*	*ch^{a}ggid*	*^{e}l*	*ch^{o}vi*	*ga-choh*	*b^{e}nu*	*lech*	*ka*

Practice saying these Hebrew words as well:

Hebrew Words

כִּי	*kiy*	because	לֹא	*lo*	no, not
בָּכָה	*bachah*	wept	הָיָה	*hayah*	was
אֶל	*el*	unto	הָלַךְ	*halach*	went
אֵל	*eyl*	god	הוּא	*hu*	he
כֹּל	*kol*	all	הִנֵּה	*hinneyh*	behold
כָּבוֹד	*kavod*	glory	אָכַל	*achal*	ate

Hebrew Sentences

הִנֵּה גַּד אָכַל חָגָב טוֹב   Behold, Gad ate a good locust.

דָּוִד הָלַךְ אֶל כָּבוֹד   David went unto glory.

We will now practice the next three letters and *furtive patach*.

SET 7

Consonants

מ   The letter *mem* sounds like *m* as in *music* and *met*.

ם   The letter *mem* takes a different form at the end of a word. This is called the final form. It also sounds like *m* as in *met*.

נ   The letter *nun* sounds like *n*, as in *not*.

ן   The letter *nun* has this form at the end of a word.

ס   The letter *samech* sounds like *s* as in *sand* and *sister*.

Vowels

חַ   When the guttural letters ח, ע, or ה stand at the end of a word, they may be preceded by a *furtive patach*. This *patach* is pronounced before the consonant instead of after it. The *furtive patach* is inserted so that the guttural sound will not be neglected. Thus, נוֹחַ (Noah) is pronounced *no-ach*.

Practice the following syllables:

נָא	מָה	סָב	סֹב	בֵּן	גַּם	דָּם	סִן	סֵ	נָ	מַ
na	mah	sav	sov	beyn	gam	dam	sin	sey	na	ma

Practice saying these Hebrew words:

Hebrew Words

לֶחֶם	lechem	bread	מָה	mah	what?
נוֹחַ	noach	Noah	סֹב	sov	to surround
לוּחַ	luach	table	בֵּן	beyn	son
מָן	man	manna	גַּם	gam	also, even
מִן	min	from	דָּם	dam	blood
נָא	na	please	סִינַי	sinay	Sinai

The covenant name of God is יהוה, usually written *Yahweh* and pronounced *Yahveh*. Whenever you see the name of God you may say *Yahveh*, or you may follow the Jewish tradition of not pronouncing God's name and say *the LORD* or *Adonai*.

Hebrew Sentences

יהוה הָלַךְ סֹב סִינַי   Yahweh (the LORD) went to surround Sinai.

דָּוִד אָכַל לֶחֶם מִן אֵל   David ate bread from God.

We will now practice the next three letters.

SET 8

Consonants

ע   For us, the letter *ayin* is silent.

פּ   The letter *pey* (with a dot) sounds like *p* as in *pet* and *put*.

פ   The letter *pey* (without a dot) sounds like *f* as in *phone* and *photo*. It has this form at the end of a word.

ף   The letter *pey* takes this form at the end of a word. Called *final pey*, it descends below the line. Since it has no dot, it sounds like *f* as in *phone* and *photo*.

צ   The letter *tsade* sounds like the *ts* in *cats* and *lets*.

ץ   The letter *tsade* takes this form at the end of a word. Called *final tsade*, it sounds like the *ts* in *cats* and *lets*.

Practice the following syllables:

צֶם	מֵץ	צוּף	פֶּל	אַף	פָּס	פֶּן	עַף	עֵב
tsam	mets	tsuf	pel	af	pas	pen	af	ev

Practice saying these Hebrew words as well:

Hebrew Words

עִם	im	with	עַד	ad	until
עַם	am	people	עֹד	od	again
נוֹעַ	noa	to shake	צֹאן	tson	flock
יָדֹועַ	yadoa	to know	פֶּה	peh	mouth
עָמַד	amad	stood	פֹּה	poh	here
אָדָם	adam	Adam	חַוָּה	chavvah	Eve
עַל	al	upon			

Hebrew Sentences

אָדָם עָמַד פֹּה עִם חַוָּה   Adam stood here with Eve.

גַּם הוּא הָלַךְ מִן יהוה   Also, he went from Yahweh (the LORD).

We will now practice the last five letters of the alphabet.

SET 9

Consonants

ק   The letter *qof* sounds like *q* as in *queen* and *quite*.

ר   The letter *resh* sounds like *r* as in *run* and *real*. Some native speakers roll the *r* like speakers of Spanish.

שׂ   The letter *seen* sounds like *s* as in *see* and *sand*.

שׁ   The letter *sheen* sounds like the *sh* in *shadow* and *shear*.

תּ   The letter *tav* (with a dot) sounds like the *t* in *top* and *tape*.

ת   The letter *tav* (without a dot) also sounds like the *t* in *top* and *tape*. In biblical times it sounded like *th* as in *Ruth*.

Practice the following syllables:

שִׂים	שֶׁל	רַק	רוּת	תֻ	תֹ	שִׁ	שֵׂ	רְ	קָ
siym	*shel*	*raq*	*rut*	*tu*	*to*	*shi*	*sey*	*ra*	*qa*

Practice saying these Hebrew words as well:

Hebrew Words

שָׁם	*sham*	*there*	קָדוֹשׁ	*qadosh*	*holy*
רוּחַ	*ruach*	*spirit*	קַל	*qal*	*easy*
שָׁמֹעַ	*shamoa*	*to hear*	תוֹרָה	*torah*	*Torah, law*
רֵעַ	*reyah*	*friend*	תֵּבָה	*teyvah*	*ark, chest*
שָׁמַיִם	*shamayim*	*heaven*	רָץ	*rats*	*ran*
קוֹל	*qol*	*voice*	רָם	*ram*	*was high*

The following Hebrew scriptures contain the entire alphabet in each verse:

Hos. 10.8 וְנִשְׁמְדוּ בָּמוֹת אָוֶן חַטַּאת יִשְׂרָאֵל קוֹץ וְדַרְדַּר יַעֲלֶה
עַל־מִזְבְּחוֹתָם וְאָמְרוּ לֶהָרִים כַּסּוּנוּ וְלַגְּבָעוֹת נִפְלוּ עָלֵינוּ:[1][2]

Eze. 38.12 לִשְׁלֹל שָׁלָל וְלָבֹז בַּז לְהָשִׁיב יָדְךָ עַל־חֳרָבוֹת
וְאֶל־עַם נוֹשָׁבֶת מְאֻסָּף מִגּוֹיִם עֹשֶׂה מִקְנֶה וְקִנְיָן יֹשְׁבֵי
עַל־טַבּוּר הָאָרֶץ:

---

[1] The symbol ׃ is one of the Hebrew accent marks called *sof pasuq*, which means *end of verse*.

[2] The horizontal mark joining words (such as between מִזְבְּחוֹתָם and עַל) functions much like a hyphen and is called *maqqef*.

Practice reading the verses according to following guide:

Hos. 10.8 *The high places of Aven, the sin of Israel, shall be destroyed:*

וְנִשְׁמְדוּ	בָּמוֹת	אָוֶן	חַטַּאת	יִשְׂרָאֵל
v⁻-nish-m⁻-du	ba-mot	a-ven	chat-tat	yis-ra-eyl
and shall be destroyed	the high places of	Aven	the sins of	Israel

thorn and thistle shall come up on their altars;

קוֹץ	וְדַרְדַּר	יַעֲלֶה	עַל	מִזְבְּחוֹתָם
qots	v-dar-dar	ya-ᵃ-leh	al	miz-b⁻-cho-tam
thorn	and thistle	will come up	upon	their altars

and they shall say to the mountains, Cover us; and to the hills, Fall upon us.

וְאָמְרוּ	לֶהָרִים	כַּסּוּנוּ	וְלַגְּבָעוֹת	נִפְלוּ	עָלֵינוּ
v-am-ru	le-ha-riym	kas-su-nu	v-lag-va-ot	nif-lu	a-ley-nu
and they will say	to the mountains	cover us	and to the hills	fall	upon us

Ezekiel 38.12 To take a spoil, and to take a prey; to turn your hand

לִשְׁלֹל	שָׁלָל	וְלָבֹז	בַּז	לְהָשִׁיב	יָדְךָ
lish-lol	sha-lal	v-la-voz	baz	l⁻-ha-shiyv	yad-cha
to take spoil	spoil	to take prey	prey	to turn	your hand

against inhabited ruined places, and unto the people gathered from the nations,

עַל	חֲרָבוֹת	נוֹשָׁבֶת	וְאֶל	עַם	מְאֻסָּף	מִגּוֹיִם
al	ch⁻-ra-vot	no-sha-vot	v-el	am	m⁻-us-saf	mig-go-yim
against	ruined places	inhabited	and unto	the people	gathered	from nations

who have gotten cattle and goods, dwelling on the highest part of the land.

עֹשֶׂה	מִקְנֶה	וְקִנְיָן	יֹשְׁבֵי	עַל	טַבּוּר	הָאָרֶץ:
o-seh	miq-neh	v-qin-yan	yosh-vey	al	tab-bur	ha-a-rets
making	cattle	and goods	dwelling	upon	highest part of	the land

DO NOT BE DISCOURAGED!

Reading Hebrew requires several weeks of disciplined rehearsal. The unusual script and the placement of vowels make reading Hebrew difficult.

KEEP STUDYING, AND YOU WILL LEARN HEBREW!

1.11   Chart of the Hebrew Alphabet

	Name	Medial Form	Final Form	Hebrew Spelling	Sound	Transliteration In Exercises
1	*alef*	א		אָלֶף	silent	(none)
2	*beyt*	בּ		בֵּית	**b** as in book	**b**
		ב			**v** as in very	**v**
3	*gimel*	גּ		גְּמֶל	**g** as in good	**g**
		ג			**g** as in good	**g**
4	*dalet*	דּ		דָּלֶת	**d** as in door	**d**
		ד			**d** as in door	**d**
5	*hey*	ה		הֵא	**h** as in house	**h**
6	*vav*	ו		וָו	**v** as in very	**v**
7	*zayin*	ז		זַיִן	**z** as in zoo	**z**
8	*chet*	ח		חֵת	**ch** as in Bach	**ch**
9	*tet*	ט		טֵת	**t** as in top	**t**
10	*yod*	י		יוֹד	**y** as in you	**y**
11	*kaf*	כּ		כַּף	**k** as in kitten	**k**
		כ	ך		**ch** as in Bach	**ch**
12	*lamed*	ל		לָמֶד	**l** as in love	**l**
13	*mem*	מ	ם	מֵם	**m** as in man	**m**
14	*nun*	נ	ן	נוּן	**n** as in not	**n**
15	*samek*	ס		סָמֶךְ	**s** as in see	**s**
16	*ayin*	ע		עַיִן	silent	(none)
17	*pey*	פּ		פֵּא	**p** as in put	**p**
		פ	ף		**f** as in phone	**ph**
18	*tsade*	צ	ץ	צָדִי	**ts** as in cats	**ts**
19	*qof*	ק		קוֹף	**q** as in queen	**q**
20	*resh*	ר		רֵישׁ	**r** as in run	**r**
21	*seen*	שׂ		שִׂין	**s** as in see	**s**
22	*sheen*	שׁ		שִׁין	**sh** as in she	**sh**
23	*tav*	תּ		תָּו	**t** as in top	**t**
		ת			**t** as in top	**t**

1.12   Chart of the Hebrew Vowel Signs

Sign	Name	Sound	Transliteration
בַּ	*patach*	a as in father	a
בָּ	*qamets*	a as in father	a
בָ	*qamets-qatan*	a as in father	o
בֶּ	*segol*	e as in bet	e
בֵּ	*tsere*	e as in they	ey
בֵּי	*tsere-yod*	e as in they	ey
בִּ	*chireq*	i as in siesta	i
בִּי	*chireq-yod*	i as in siesta.	iy
בֹּ	*cholem*	o as in roll	o
בּוֹ	*cholem-vav*	o as in roll	o
בֻּ	*qibbuts*	u as in rule	u
וּ	*shureq*	u as in rule	u

1.13   The *Shevas*

בְּ	*sheva*	no vowel	e or none
בֳּ	*chatef-qamets*	a as in father	o
בֱּ	*chatef-segol*	e as in bet	e
בֲּ	*chatef-patach*	a as in father	a

1.14   Other Combinations of Letters

Combination	Sound
יָ as in אֲדֹנָי	ai as in aisle
הֶ as in רֹאֶה	ey as in prey
יָ as in תֵּעֲשֶׂינָה	ey as in prey
יַ as in אָחַי	ai as in aisle
יו as in אֵלָיו	av as in lava
וֹי as in גּוֹי	oy as in boy

Chapter 2

The Noun

In this chapter you should learn:

- Fuller rules for pronunciation
- Gender and number of the noun
- Rules for vowel changes in nouns
- Irregular plurals
- The definite article

2.1 More Rules for Pronunciation

2.1.1 *Dagesh*

2.1.1.1 Dagesh lene

We studied the *dagesh lene* in Chapter One. Six letters may have a dot within the letter called a *dagesh lene* (weak *dagesh*). Those six letters are ב ג ד כ פ and ת, represented by the mnemonic BeGaD KeFaT.

The *dagesh lene* indicates a change of pronunciation. Three letters change from stops to spirants: ב, כ, and פ. Three other letters (ג, ד, and ת) may have a *dagesh lene*, but their pronunciation is not changed. **Dagesh lene occurs ONLY when it is not preceded by a vowel.** For further explanation of this rule see Gesenius, *Hebrew Grammar*, §21b.

2.1.1.2 Dagesh forte

The *dagesh* may also be found in other letters, where it is called a *dagesh forte* (strong *dagesh*). The *dagesh forte* signifies that a letter is doubled, but there is no real change in pronunciation. Similarly, the English words *metal* and *mettle* are pronounced the same. The *dagesh forte* will be important in identifying certain types of verbs. A *dagesh forte* in ב, כ, and פ will be pronounced like the *dagesh lene*. The *dagesh forte* sometimes occurs in the first letter of a word that is closely tied in pronunciation to the previous word. For example: מֹשֶׁה לֵּאמֹר (Exod. 6.10), לְכָה־נָּא (Num. 22.6). For further explanation of this rule, cf. Gesenius, *Hebrew Grammar*, §20c.

2.1.2 Guttural letters

There are five letters that cannot be doubled with the *dagesh forte*. These are called guttural letters (*guttur* is Latin for 'throat').

These guttural letters are א, ה, ח, ע, and ר.

2.1.3   *Sheva*

2.1.3.1 *Simple* sheva

The *sheva* (ְ) is placed under a consonant that does not have a vowel (Gesenius §10). Usually, however, the *sheva* is not found at the end of a word. Whenever two consonants come together, they both are pronounced, even if only one of them has a vowel. A *sheva* that comes at the beginning of a word or syllable is usually transliterated by superscript [e]. Sometimes, *sheva* comes at the end of a syllable, and in that case, it is not transliterated at all. Consider the word נְבִאִים. The letter נ has the *sheva* rather than a vowel sign. Therefore, the word נְבִיאִים is pronounced n[e]-vee-eem.[1] On the other hand, the word מִשְׁפָּט is transliterated *mish-pat*.

2.1.3.2 *Composite* sheva

The composite *sheva* is a combination of the *sheva* with one of the vowel signs *qamets*, *segol*, or *patach*. Guttural letters usually take composite *sheva* rather than simple *sheva*. These *shevas* are pronounced like the corresponding short vowel. They are always vocal *shevas*.

Occasionally, a nonguttural will take a composite *sheva* to indicate the beginning of a syllable, e. g. הַלְלוּ is transliterated *ha-la-lu*, not *hal-lu*.

2.1.4   Determining Syllables

In order to pronounce words correctly, one must be able to divide the word into syllables. The following rules will guide in that process.

- A syllable always begins with one and only one consonant; it cannot begin with a vowel (except when a word begins with וּ, which is a form of the conjunction).

- A syllable always has one and only one vowel, which may be short, long, full, or *sheva*.

- A syllable may end with a consonant or a vowel.

- A closed syllable ends in a consonant and *sheva* (the *sheva* is omitted from most letters at the end of a word). Closed syllables usually have a short vowel, unless they are accented.

- An open syllable ends with a vowel. Open syllables usually have a long vowel, unless they are accented.

---

[1] Vocal *sheva* is not pronounced in Modern Hebrew (Moshe Greenberg, *Introduction to Hebrew* [Englewood Cliffs, NJ: Prentice-Hall, 1965], p. 22).

- A *dagesh forte* always causes the previous syllable to be closed because it doubles the consonant. For example דִּבֶּר is transliterated *dib-ber*.

The words of Exod. 16.16 can serve as an illustration of syllable division.

זֶה הַדָּבָר אֲשֶׁר צִוָּה יְהוָה לִקְטוּ מִמֶּנּוּ אִישׁ לְפִי אָכְלוֹ

The syllables would be divided as follows:

זֶה is one syllable and is open because it ends in ה, which is a vowel letter.

הַדָּבָר is three syllables, transliterated *had-da-var*. The dividing line is drawn through the ד because it has *dagesh forte*, doubling the letter. How do we know that the *dagesh* in the ד is a *dagesh forte* (doubling the letter) and not *dagesh lene* (since d is a *begad kephat* letter)? Because *dagesh lene* only occurs when it is NOT preceded by a vowel. In this case, ד is immediately preceded by the vowel *patach*, so the *dagesh* must be *dagesh forte*. Therefore, הַד is closed (ending in a consonant), דָ is open (ending with a vowel), and בָר is closed (ending with a consonant).

אֲשֶׁר is two syllables. The first syllable is open (ending with *sheva*), and the second syllable is closed (ending with a consonant).

צִוָּה is two syllables. The first syllable is closed, ending with a consonant. The letter ו has *dagesh forte*, causing the ו to be doubled. The second syllable is open, ending in a vowel letter. When ה comes at the end of a word, it is always a part of the vowel, thus signifying an open syllable, unless it has the *mappiq* dot within it (ה). The *mappiq* signifies that the ה is a consonant (see Chapter 1, *Full Vowels*).

יְהוָה is the divine name, whose written form cannot be pronounced.

לִקְטוּ is two syllables, the first being closed with the consonant ק, and the second being left open with the vowel וּ.

מִמֶּנּוּ is three syllables, transliterated *mim-men-nu*, because of *dagesh forte* in both the מ and the נ. The syllables, therefore, are closed, closed, and open.

אִישׁ is only one syllable.

לְפִי is two syllables, both open.

אָכְלוֹ is two syllables, the first closed and the second open.

2.1.5 Stress

Stress (accent) may fall on the last syllable (ultima) or the next to last syllable (penultima) but never on the antipenultima. Stress is usually on the last syllable, but if the last syllable has a short vowel then the accent will be on the previous syllable (except with verbs, which stress the second root letter). In the Hebrew text of the Bible, every word will have an accent mark that indicates which syllable should be stressed. (See the appendix at the end of this chapter for more detailed rules of stress.)

The Hebrew Bible utilizes 48 different accent marks, which function as stress markers, punctuation signals, and cantillation signs. These accent marks are not commonly used outside the Bible text itself (For further explanation of the accent marks, see §9.6 and §28.1).

2.1.5.1 *An important rule of stress*

A closed, unaccented syllable must have a short vowel.

For example, in the word חָכְמָה, pronounced *choch-máh*, the first *qamets* is *qamets qatan*, short *o*, but in Modern Hebrew it is pronounced *a* as in father).

2.1.5.2 *Maqqef*

Maqqef is a mark of punctuation similar to a hyphen. Many Hebrew words are connected by the *maqqef*. Whenever *maqqef* is present, the stress is removed from the word that precedes it. For example, בֶּן אָדָם is two words, pronounced *beyn adam*, and meaning *son of man*. These same two words can be connected by *maqqef*, (בֶּן־אָדָם) and the stress will be removed from בֶּן. Now it is a closed, unaccented syllable and must have a short vowel (בֶּן).

2.1.6　More on *Qamets Qatan*

The *qamets* (ָ) may be long *a* or short *o*. When it is short *o* it is called *qamets qatan* (some scholars prefer to call it *qamets chatuf*). It will be short *o* in a closed, unaccented syllable; otherwise it is long *a*. Whenever there is the possibility of confusion, the long *a* will have a short vertical stroke, called a *meteg*, to indicate that it is an open syllable and should be long *a*, e.g. חָכְמָה (Although we transliterate the *qamets qatan* with an *o*, we pronounce it like *a*). Unfortunately, the use of the *meteg* is not consistent throughout the Hebrew Bible (see Joüon §14).

Examples:

- וַיָּקָם *vay-ya-qom* (the last syllable is closed and unaccented)

- חָכְמָה *choch-ma*, but חָכְמָה is *cha-che-ma* because of the *meteg*.

- חָנֵּנִי *chon-ney-ni* (*dagesh forte* places *qamets* in a closed, unaccented syllable)

- כָּל־אִישׁ *kol-ish* (the *maqqef* has deprived כֹל of its accent, thus it is closed and unaccented. Therefore the word כֹל is changed to כָּל).

2.2   The Noun

2.2.1   Gender and Number of the Noun

Hebrew has two genders: masculine and feminine (There is no neuter gender). The masculine singular has no special ending, but the masculine plural ends with יִם . For example:

	Masculine Singular		Masculine Plural
סוּס	horse	סוּסִים	horses
כּוֹכָב	star	כּוֹכָבִים	stars

Masculine nouns may be changed to their feminine counterpart by adding the feminine endings. The feminine singular is marked by הָ . and the feminine plural is signified by וֹת.

For example:

סוּס horse   סוּסָה mare   סוּסוֹת mares

Most nouns, however, occur only in one gender, either masculine or feminine, and the gender of these nouns must be learned by consulting the lexicon. Nouns that are categorized as feminine in their lexical form do not have the feminine ending. Types of words that are feminine include:

a. Nouns that are neuter in English, e.g.   עִיר city.
b. Nouns of the feminine sex, e.g.   אֵם mother.
c. Parts of the body that come in pairs, e.g.   יָד hand.

In addition to the singular and plural, Hebrew has a *dual*. The dual refers to two of anything, except for certain words that have no apparent relation to number, e.g. מַיִם water, שָׁמַיִם sky.

2.2.2   Noun Endings

	Masculine	Feminine
Singular	no ending	הָ
Plural	יִם	וֹת
Dual	יַ_ִם	תַיִם

Examples:

MASCULINE		FEMININE	
סוּס	horse	סוּסָה	mare
סוּסִים	horses	סוּסוֹת	mares
סוּסַיִם	two horses	סוּסָתַיִם	two mares

2.2.3   Vowel Changes

When letters are added to the end of a noun, one (but only one) of the vowels may reduce:

Qamets or *tsere* in the first syllable will reduce to *sheva* (ֲ in gutturals). For example:

נָבִיא prophet   נְבִיאָה prophetess

לֵבָב heart   לְבָבִים hearts

If there is no *qamets* or *tsere* in the first syllable, but there is a *tsere* in the second syllable that *tsere* will reduce to *sheva*.

e.g.   יוֹשֵׁב inhabitant   יוֹשְׁבִים inhabitants

Other changes may be necessary before adding letters to the end of a noun.

Remove ה ֶ or ה ָ before adding endings,

e.g.   חֹזֶה   seer   חֹזִים   seers

תּוֹרָה   law   תּוֹרוֹת   laws

Segolate nouns have a different (but consistent) form. A *segolate* noun is one whose vowels are two *segols*. In the plural, the *segols* will be replaced by a *sheva* and a *qamets*. Examples:

Masc. Singular   Masc. Plural

מֶלֶךְ   king   מְלָכִים   kings

עֶבֶד   servant   עֲבָדִים   servants

Fem. Singular   Fem. Plural

נֶפֶשׁ   soul   נְפָשׁוֹת   souls

אֶרֶץ   land   אֲרָצוֹת   lands

2.2.4   Irregular Plurals

Some nouns do not follow the prescribed pattern when forming their plurals. These irregulars will be noted when they occur in the vocabulary. We would expect the plural of אָב (father) to be אָבִים, but the plural is אָבוֹת, which looks like a feminine form. The following are some other important examples.

Sing.		Plural		Not
אִישׁ	man	אֲנָשִׁים	men	אִישִׁים
אִשָּׁה	woman	נָשִׁים	women	אִשּׁוֹת
יוֹם	day	יָמִים	days	יוֹמִים

EXERCISE 2-A

Form the plural of the following masculine words.

דָּבָר	word, thing	הַר	mountain
יוֹם	day	אִישׁ	man
מִקְדָּשׁ	sanctuary	מִשְׁפָּט	judgment
נָבִיא	prophet	אָב	father

2.3   Definite Article

Like Greek, Hebrew has no indefinite article. Therefore, מֶלֶךְ can mean either 'king' or 'a king'. Unlike other languages, however, the definite article does not occur as a word in independent form. Rather, it is prefixed to the word that it modifies. The regular form of the definite article is הַ with a *dagesh forte* in the following letter. For example:

מֶלֶךְ	king	הַמֶּלֶךְ	the king
סוּס	horse	הַסּוּס	the horse

The guttural letters present some variation since they cannot accept the *dagesh forte*. The following chart summarizes the form of the definite article when prefixed to a guttural letter.

usual form	before ר, א	before ח, ה	before ע	before עָ, חָ, & הָ
הַ	הָ	הַ	הַ or הָ	הֶ

Because the gutturals do not take the *dagesh*, the *patach* is lengthened to qamats when the article is attached to words beginning with א and ר (and usually ע). This is called **compensatory lengthening**. The rules for attaching the article to the gutturals are detailed in the chart above. Below are some examples of applying these rules:

אוֹר	light	הָאוֹר	the light
חֹשֶׁךְ	darkness	הַחֹשֶׁךְ	the darkness
חַיִל	valor	הֶחָיִל	the valor

Exceptions to the rules in the chart above include the word הַר (mountain). With the article, it becomes הָהָר (the mountain), not הַהַר, which would be expected.

2.4   Vocabulary

אָח   *noun. m.* brother. *plural* אַחִים

אָדָם   *n.m.* man, human

אֲדָמָה   *n.f.* ground, earth

אִישׁ   *n.m.* man, husband. *pl* אֲנָשִׁים

אִשָּׁה   *n.f.* woman, wife. *pl* נָשִׁים

אָב   *n.m.* father. *pl* אָבוֹת

אֵם   *n.f.* mother. *pl* אִמּוֹת

בֵּן   *n.m.* son. *pl* בָּנִים

בַּת   *n.f.* daughter. *pl* בָּנוֹת

אֱלֹהִים   *n.m.* God

אֶרֶץ   *n.f.* land. *pl* אֲרָצוֹת

בַּיִת   *n.m.* house. *pl* בָּתִּים

דָּבָר   *n.m.* word, thing

EXERCISE 2-B

PART 1:

Add the definite article to the following Hebrew words.
For example, אֵם = mother, so הָאֵם = the mother.

דֶּרֶךְ   road, way

חַי   life, living

יָד   hand

יוֹם   day

כֹּהֵן   priest

לֵב   heart

יָם   sea

מֶלֶךְ   king

נֶפֶשׁ   soul, life

מַיִם   water

PART 2:
Translate the following English words into Hebrew:

the brother

the husband

the father

the son

the daughter

the God

the house

the women

the sons

the fathers

the words

Youth Torah Scroll inside
its velvet cover

2.5   Appendix to Chapter 2

2.5.1   Rules of Stress

- If the last syllable has a long vowel, that syllable usually will be accented, e.g. לֵוִי = *le-ví* (On the Hebrew words, the symbol ^ will be used to mark the stress).

- A long vowel in a closed syllable MUST be accented, e.g. צָפוֹן = *tsa-phón*

- A short vowel in an open syllable MUST be accented, e.g. אֶלֶף = *é-leph*

- A closed, unaccented syllable MUST have a short vowel, e.g. חָכְמָה = *choch-máh* (the first *qamets* must be short 'o')

- Although a *sheva* counts as a vowel for purposes of syllable division, it cannot receive an accent because it never bears the stress. e.g. אֲשֶׁר = *a-shér*

- Verbs are usually accented on the middle root letter (except when ending with תֶם־ or תֶן־ or when taking verbal suffixes). e.g. שָׁמַרְתִּי = *sha-már-ti*

2.5.2   Rules for Vowel Changes

When letters are added to the end of a noun, certain vowel changes occur. Some vowels, however, do not change:

      1- Full vowels
      2- *Cholem*
      3- Vowels in closed Syllables

When letters are added to the end of a noun, one (but only one) of the vowels may reduce. The priority for vowel reduction is on reducing the propretonic vowel. (The tonic vowel is the one that is stressed; the pretonic precedes the tonic, and the propretonic precedes the pretonic.)

Vowel reductions:

    ◌ָ → ◌ְ   *Qamets* reduces to *sheva* (◌ֲ in gutturals)
        e.g. נָבִיא prophet   נְבִיאָה prophetess

    ◌ֵ → ◌ְ   *Tsere* reduces to *sheva* (◌ֲ in gutturals)
        e.g. לֵבָב heart   לְבָבִים hearts

If the propretonic vowel cannot be reduced and if the pretonic vowel is *tsere*, then reduce it to *sheva* (no. 2 above).

e.g. יוֹשֵׁב inhabitant   יוֹשְׁבִים inhabitants

Other changes may be necessary before adding letters to the end of a noun.
Remove ה before adding endings,
e.g. חֹזֶה seer   חֹזִים seers
Remove f.s. הָ before adding וֹת,
e.g. תּוֹרָה law   תּוֹרוֹת laws
Change final letters to medials.
e.g. מֶלֶךְ king   מְלָכִים kings

Segolate nouns have a different (but consistent) form. A *segol*ate noun is one whose vowels are two *segol*s. The *segol*s will be replace by a *sheva* and a *qamets*. Examples:

Masc. Singular	Masc. Plural
מֶלֶךְ king	מְלָכִים kings
עֶבֶד servant	עֲבָדִים servants

Fem. Singular	Fem. Plural
נֶפֶשׁ soul	נְפָשׁוֹת souls
אֶרֶץ land	אֲרָצוֹת lands

The Western Wall of the Jerusalem Temple Mount

Chapter 3

The Adjective & Participle

In this chapter you should learn:

- Forms and uses of the adjective
- The verbless clause
- The conjunction
- Forms and uses of the participle

3.1 The Adjective

An adjective modifies a noun and agrees with that noun in gender and number. The noun *daughter* is feminine singular; therefore, any adjective that modifies it will also be inflected as feminine singular.

3.1.1 Inflections of the Adjective

The inflections of the adjective are the same as those of the noun (see Chapter 2), except there is no dual form for the adjective. Example:

טוֹב *good*

	Masculine	Feminine
Singular	טוֹב	טוֹבָה
Plural	טוֹבִים	טוֹבוֹת

3.1.2 Uses of the Adjective

An adjective may function either as an attributive adjective, a predicate adjective, or a substantive. In *the good man*, the adjective *good* is attributive; but in *the man is good*, it is a predicate adjective. In *think on the good, not the bad*, the adjectives *good* and *bad* are substantives (adjectives used as nouns).

3.1.2.1 Attributive adjectives

In Hebrew, attributive adjectives follow the noun they modify, and agree with it in gender, number, and definiteness.[1]

---

[1] There are two exceptions to this rule. The cardinal numbers and the adjective רַב *(many)* can occur before the noun they modify. אֶחָד אִישׁ means *one man,* and רַבִּים אֲנָשִׁים is *many men.*

מֶלֶךְ טוֹב   a good king
מַלְכָּה טוֹבָה   a good queen

מְלָכִים טוֹבִים   good kings
מְלָכוֹת טוֹבוֹת   good queens

> Attributive adjectives agree in definiteness with the noun they modify.

הַמֶּלֶךְ הַטּוֹב   the good king
הַמַּלְכָּה הַטּוֹבָה   the good queen
הַמְּלָכִים הַטּוֹבִים   the good kings
הַמְּלָכוֹת הַטּוֹבוֹת   the good queens

IMPORTANT NOTE: The adjective maintains the regular ending even if the noun is irregular. For example, *fathers* is masculine plural, but it has a feminine plural ending; and *women* is feminine plural, but it has a masculine plural ending. The adjective will agree with the gender of the noun.

אָבוֹת טוֹבִים   good fathers
נָשִׁים טוֹבוֹת   good women

3.1.2.2 Predicate adjectives

A predicate adjective describes the state of a noun. It agrees with the noun in gender and number, but it never takes the definite article. The adjective may either precede the noun or follow the noun. Hebrew does not use the present tense of *to be*, but it is implied. Therefore, it must be supplied in the translation.

הַמֶּלֶךְ טוֹב   The king is good.
טוֹבָה הַמַּלְכָּה   Good is the queen.
הַמְּלָכִים טוֹבִים   The kings are good.
הַמְּלָכוֹת טוֹבוֹת   The queens are good.
הָאִישׁ מֹשֶׁה גָּדוֹל   The man Moses is great (Exo. 11.3).

> A predicate adjective never takes the article.

3.1.2.3 Substantives

A substantive is an adjective or participle that is used grammatically as a noun. It may function as a subject or object of the verb. A substantive will usually have the definite article.

טוֹב good   הַטּוֹב the good one, or the good thing
טוֹב good   הַטּוֹבָה the good woman
חָכָם wise   הֶחָכָם the wise man

EXERCISE 3-A

Part 1: Translate the following Hebrew into English (You should first memorize the vocabulary at the end of the chapter):

1. הָאִשָּׁה הַטּוֹבָה
2. הַסּוּסוֹת טוֹבוֹת
3. מַלְכוֹת טוֹבוֹת
4. אָח טוֹב
5. הַבֵּן טוֹב
6. הַמְּלָכוֹת הַטּוֹבוֹת
7. הַדָּבָר הַטּוֹב
8. הַמְּלָכִים הַטּוֹבִים
9. טוֹבָה הָאָרֶץ   Num. 14.7
10. טוֹב הַדָּבָר   1 Kgs 2.38
11. טוֹב יְהוָה   Ps. 34.8
12. אִישׁ טוֹב   2 Sam. 18.27
13. אֶרֶץ טוֹבָה   Exod. 3.8

Part 2: Translate the following English into Hebrew:

1. Good men
2. The fathers are good.
3. The day is good.
4. The daughter is good.

3.2   Verbless Clauses

A verbless clause is a sentence that contains no written verb, but the verb *to be* is implied. It may be a nominal clause in which one noun functions as the subject and the other as the predicate, or it may be a clause that is formed by a noun and a predicate adjective. The tense is determined from the context, but it is most often present tense.

The standard word order for a *clause of identification* (Who or what is the subject?) is subject→predicate.

אֵלֶּה שְׁמוֹת   These are the names (Exo. 1.1).

אֲנִי יְהוָה   I am Yahweh (Gen. 15.7).

יְהוָה הַצַּדִּיק   Yahweh is the righteous one (Exo. 9.27).

The standard word order for an *clause of classification* (How is the subject described?) is predicate→subject.[2]

אֲשֵׁמִים אֲנַחְנוּ   We are guilty (Gen. 42.21).

טָמֵא הוּא   He is unclean (Lev. 11.4).

צַדִּיק יְהוָה   Yahweh is righteous (2 Chr. 12.6).

3.3   The Conjunction

The conjunction וֹ (translated *and*, or *but*) does not exist as a separate word, rather, it is attached to the beginning of a word as an inseparable particle (similar to the definite article).

The conjunction may be vocalized in different ways:

3.3.1   Most often it is וְ
   דָּבָר a word   וְדָבָר and a word
   הַדָּבָר the word   וְהַדָּבָר and the word

3.3.2   It is וּ before the labials בּ מ and פ, and before strong consonants with vocal *sheva* (strong consonants do not include gutturals, י, or וֹ).
   מֶלֶךְ a king   וּמֶלֶךְ and a king
   דְּבָרִים words   וּדְבָרִים and words

3.3.3   Before a composite *sheva*, it takes the short vowel corresponding to that of the composite *sheva*.[3]
   אֱמֶת truth   וֶאֱמֶת and truth
   אֲגֻדָּה a bundle   וַאֲגֻדָּה and a bundle

EXERCISE 3-B

Part 1: Add the conjunction to the following words and write their translations:

אָדָם

אֲדָמָה

---

[2] Francis I. Andersen, *The Hebrew Verbless Clause in the Pentateuch* (JBL Monograph Series, 14; Nashville, TN: Abingdon Press, 1970). For a fuller description of word order in verbless sentences, see Bruce K. Waltke and Michael Patrick O'Connor, *An Introduction to Biblical Hebrew Syntax* (Winona Lake, IN: Eisenbrauns, 1990), p. 130 ff.

[3] Other rules for the conjunction are found in the appendix at the end of this chapter.

אִישׁ

אִשָּׁה

בֵּן

בַּת

אֶרֶץ

בַּיִת

Part 2: Translate the following Hebrew into English:

וּמְלָכִים רַבִּים	Jer. 50.41
וְיוֹם טוֹב	Esther 8.17
וּמְלָכִים גְּדוֹלִים	Jer. 25.14

3.4   The Participle

The participle is being considered in this chapter because it utilizes the inflectional endings similar to the noun and adjective. In fact, the participle can function as a noun, an adjective, or a verb.

Hebrew participles are formed by taking the root letters (called *radicals*) and adding appropriate vowels and inflectional endings (HVS 12D & 9C).[4] The basic, ground form of the Hebrew verb is called the *qal*, which means light.

For root XXX, the *qal* active participle, masculine singular is XX̣X.

Therefore, the forms of the *qal* active participle of the verb שָׁמַר *to guard, keep* are:

Qal Active Participle of שָׁמַר: *to keep*

	singular			plural	
masculine	שֹׁמֵר	keeping	Masculine	שֹׁמְרִים	keeping
feminine	שֹׁמֶרֶת	keeping	Feminine	שֹׁמְרוֹת	keeping

Qal Passive Participle of שָׁמַר: *to keep*

	singular			plural	
m.	שָׁמוּר	being kept	m.	שְׁמוּרִים	being kept
f.	שְׁמוּרָה	being kept	f.	שְׁמוּרוֹת	being kept

---

[4] See the Chart of Hebrew Verb Slots, column 12, section D, found at the very end of this book.

3.4.1   Uses of the Participle

The participle is a verbal adjective; and, like the adjective, the participle must agree in gender and number with the word that it modifies.

3.4.1.1 *Verbal participle*

The participle may be used as the main verb in a clause. When used as a verb, the participle signifies durative action. The tense may be past, present, or future, as determined by the context.

הָאֲנָשִׁים הֹלְכִים אֶל הַבַּיִת   The men are/were going unto the house.

מֶלֶךְ יֹשֵׁב עַל הַכִּסֵּא   A king is/was sitting upon the throne.

When the participle functions as the main verb of a clause; there will, of course, be no other verb in that clause. Also, watch for a lack of agreement in definiteness that will signal the participle as a verb rather than a noun (first example above). That is, a verbal participle will **never** have the article.

3.4.1.2 *Adjectival participle*

Like the adjective, the attributive participle will agree with the noun that it modifies in gender, number, and definiteness and comes after the noun. The English translation usually includes the relative pronoun *who*.

הָאֲנָשִׁים הַהֹלְכִים   The going men (the men who are going)

מֶלֶךְ יֹשֵׁב   A sitting king (a king who is sitting)

The participle may function as a predicate adjective. In the following example, the word לָבֵשׁ is a passive participle that means *clothed*. (Other biblical examples are Isa. 17.2; Zech. 3.3; Jonah 3.4; and Ps. 111.2.)

הַמֶּלֶךְ הָיָה לָבֵשׁ   The king was clothed

3.4.1.3 *Substantive participle*

Like the adjective, the participle may be used as a noun. Many Hebrew nouns are formed from participles. Like a noun, these may or may not have the article.

יֹשֵׁב   a dwelling one = dweller, inhabitant

שֹׁפֵט   a judging one = judge

הַשֹּׁמֵר   the keeping one = the keeper/guard

An participle may be classified as a substantive when there is already a verb in the clause, and a noun form is needed to complete the syntax of the clause. For example:

הַיּשְׁבִים שֹׁמְרִים הַדָּבָר הַטּוֹב

The inhabitants are keeping the good word.

The verb in the sentence is שֹׁמְרִים (*keeping*). A verbal participle will never have the definite article. The subject of the sentence is הַיּשְׁבִים (*the inhabitants*), which is a substantive participle.

3.5   Vocabulary

הָלַךְ — *verb.* he went[5]

יָשַׁב — *v.* he dwelled, he sat

עָלָה — *v.* he went up

שָׁמַר — *v.* he kept, he guarded, he watched

אֶל — *preposition.* unto

עַתָּה — *particle.* now

אֶחָד — *adjective (cardinal number).* one. Fem. אַחַת

גָּדוֹל — *adj.* great, large

טוֹב — *adj.* good

רַב — *adj.* much, many. Plural, רַבִּים

רַע — *adj.* evil. f. רָעָה m. *pl* רָעִים

הַר — *noun, m.* mountain. w. art. הָהָר *pl* הָרִים

מֶלֶךְ — *n.m.* king

יוֹם — *n.m.* day. *irreg. pl* יָמִים

EXERCISE 3-C

Part 1: Translate the following sentences from Hebrew into English:

1. וְהַמֶּלֶךְ הַטּוֹב שֹׁמֵר הַבֵּן וְהַבַּת

2. רַבִּים אֲנָשִׁים וְרָעִים הֹלְכִים אֶל הַבַּיִת

3. וְעַתָּה נָשִׁים טוֹבוֹת הֹלְכוֹת אֶל הָאָרֶץ

4. אֱלֹהִים הַמֶּלֶךְ הַגָּדוֹל

---

[5] The dictionary form of Hebrew verbs is the third masculine singular because it is the simplest verb form, having no inflectional preformatives or afformatives.

5. מַלְכָּה טוֹבָה הֹלֶכֶת אֶל הָהָר הַגָּדוֹל

6. וְהָאַחִים שֹׁמְרִים הַדָּבָר

7. טוֹבִים הַמְּלָכִים וְגָדוֹל הַבַּיִת

8. הָאֲדָמָה וְהָאָרֶץ שְׁמוּרוֹת

Part 2: Translate the following sentences from English into Hebrew:

1. The good word is being kept.

2. The queen is keeping the word.

3. The big house is being guarded (kept).

4. A good man is keeping the word.

5. Now the king is the one keeping the word.

3.6   Appendix: Rules for the Conjunction

The conjunction ו (translated *and,* or *but*) does not exist as a word, rather, it is attached to the beginning of a word as an inseparable particle (similar to the definite article).

The conjunction may be vocalized in different ways:

1. Most often it is וְ

דָּבָר a word	וְדָבָר and a word
הַדָּבָר the word	וְהַדָּבָר and the word

2. It is וּ before the labials ב מ and פ, and before strong consonants with vocal *sheva* (strong consonants do not include gutturals, י, or ו.

מֶלֶךְ a king	וּמֶלֶךְ and a king
דְּבָרִים words	וּדְבָרִים and words

3. Before a composite *sheva*, it takes the short vowel corresponding to that of the composite *sheva*.

אֱמֶת truth	וֶאֱמֶת and truth

4. It it contacts to וִי before יְ.

יְהוּדָה Judah	וִיהוּדָה and Judah

5. It is וֵ before אֱלֹהִים.

אֱלֹהִים God	וֵאלֹהִים and God

6. It may be וָ before a stressed syllable.

רַע evil	וָרַע and evil

Chapter 4

The Perfect

In this chapter you should learn:

- Forms and uses of the *qal* perfect verb
- The personal pronouns
- Prepositions

4.1   Introduction to the Hebrew Verb

The English verb has tense, voice, and mood. Compare the usage of the verb *cook* in the following sentences:

> John *cooked* the chicken.
> John *should cook* the chicken.
> The chicken *will be cooked.*

In the first sentence, the verb *cooked* is past tense, active voice, indicative mood. In the second sentence, the verb *cook* is present tense, active voice, subjunctive mood. In the third sentence, the verb *cooked* is future tense, passive voice, indicative mood. Greek verbs are parsed according to a similar formula, even though the concept of tense is not equivalent in English and Greek. For example, the aorist is past tense only in the indicative mood. In the other moods, the aorist does not express a particular tense.

In Hebrew, verbs are parsed according to state and stem. *State* corresponds roughly to *tense*, but *state* is broader, and may encompass what is called in other languages *mood*. In Hebrew the states are perfect, imperfect, imperative, participle, infinitive absolute, infinitive construct. There are seven basic Hebrew stems, sometimes representing voice, and at other times expressing types of action that do not exist in the English or Greek verb systems (*Stem* does not refer to the verbal root).

In addition, it is very important that we understand the difference between form and function. In Greek, for example, the form called present tense often functions as past tense in some contexts (called the historical present, e.g., Mk 1.12). English verbs may use helping words to identify tense and mood (e.g., sentences 2 and 3 above).

Parsing, therefore, is a means of identifying the *form*, but not necessarily the *function* of the verb. In Hebrew, the function is often determined by the word order and the context. For example, a participle may express past, present, or future time, depending upon the way that it is used. The usual format for parsing of Hebrew verbs is: Stem, State, Person, Gender, Number, Root.

Hebrew has seven basic stems: *qal, nifal, hifil, hofal, piel, pual,* and *hitpael.* The word *qal* means *light*, and it is the name for the easiest of the seven stems. The *qal* stem presents active voice (except for the passive participle). The other stems will be learned in later lessons.

> **Hebrew verb forms are built from the three root letters, called RADICALS.**

4.2   The Conjugation of the Perfect

There are two finite verb forms in the Hebrew verb system. Their traditional names are the PERFECT and the IMPERFECT. Some scholars prefer the designations SUFFIX CONJUGATION and PREFIX CONJUGATION because the terms *perfect* and *imperfect* may lead to a misunderstanding of the usage of the verb forms. For example, the perfect form is not always perfective in aspect, and the imperfect form is not always imperfective in aspect. However, since most reference works and commentaries still use the traditional terminology, this textbook will do so as well.

In addition to the finite verbs, there are the participle, the imperative, the infinitive absolute, and the infinitive construct.

4.2.1   Inflection of the Perfect

The perfect is formed by the addition of inflectional endings, which are sometimes called *afformatives*. **It is essential that these afformatives be memorized.** These afformatives will be consistent in all seven verb stems (HVS 12A).

Afformatives of the Perfect

	Singular			Plural	
1c	תִּי	I	1c	נוּ	We
2m	תָּ	You	2m	תֶּם	You
2f	תְּ	You	2f	תֶּן	You
3m	(none)	He	3c	וּ	They
3f	הָ	She			

The afformatives of the perfect were probably derived from the personal pronouns (see section 4.3). The similarities are obvious in the first and second persons. The verb will agree with the subject in gender and number. The 2f singular illustrates the fact that the *sheva* is sometimes used at the end of a word.

Qal perfect of שָׁמַר: to keep

	Singular				Plural	
1c	שָׁמַרְתִּי	I kept		1c	שָׁמַרְנוּ	We kept
2m	שָׁמַרְתָּ	You kept		2m	שְׁמַרְתֶּם	You kept
2f	שָׁמַרְתְּ	You kept		2f	שְׁמַרְתֶּן	You kept
3m	שָׁמַר	He kept		3c	שָׁמְרוּ	They kept
3f	שָׁמְרָה	She kept				

The lexical form of the verb (the form found as a dictionary entry) is the *qal* perfect, third masculine singular, e.g.שָׁמַר. This form is sometimes referred to as the *root*, although the root is more often given without vowel points, e.g. שׁמר. Unlike other languages, the root should not be called a *stem*, because in Hebrew *stem* is a designation of a type of verbal conjugation. שָׁמַר is parsed as *qal* stem, perfect state, third person, masculine, singular, from the root שׁמר. Note the *meteg* in the 3f singular and in the 3c plural, which indicates an open syllable (see §2.1.6).

4.2.2 Meaning of the Perfect

When standing alone (that is, without a conjunction attached) the perfect represents action that is completed, either in time or in the mind of the writer. The perfect presents the whole of an event from its inception to its conclusion. Therefore, the simple perfect usually signifies past tense. The subject may come either before or after the verb. The full significance of the perfect and word order will be discussed later. A perfect without the conjunction attached is called a *qatal* form. The word *qatal* is no more than a transliteration of קָטַל, the perfect, third masculine singular, from the root קטל. Since most Hebrew sentences begin with a conjunction, the *qatal* rarely occupies first place in a sentence. In Hebrew narrative, the *qatal* is most often used in subordinate clauses.

הָאֲנָשִׁים הָלְכוּ אֶל הַבַּיִת	The men went unto the house.
מֶלֶךְ יָשַׁב עַל הַכִּסֵּא	A king sat upon the throne.
הַיֹּשְׁבִים שָׁמְרוּ הַדָּבָר	The inhabitants kept the word.

EXERCISE 4-A

Translate the following (Note: The : is called סוֹף פָּסוּק, *soph pasuq*, which means *end of verse*):

1. הָאָרֶץ שָׁמַרְתְּ׃
2. הָאִשָּׁה וְהָאִישׁ שָׁמְרוּ הָאָרֶץ׃
3. אִישׁ שָׁמַר הַבַּיִת׃

4. הָאָרֶץ שְׁמַרְתֶּם:

5. הָאִשָּׁה שָׁמְרָה הָהָר:

6. הַדָּבָר שָׁמַרְנוּ:

7. הַדָּבָר שָׁמַרְתִּי:

8. הַבֵּן שָׁמַרְתָּ:

4.3   Independent Personal Pronouns

The following pronouns are used mainly as subjects of a sentence, especially when a participle is the main verb, or when attention is called to the subject for reasons of emphasis. **These pronouns must be memorized.**

	Singular				Plural	
1c	אֲנִי/אָנֹכִי	I		1c	אֲנַחְנוּ	we
2m	אַתְּ/אַתָּה	you		2m	אַתֶּם	you
2f	אַתְּ	you		2f	אַתֵּן	you
3m	הוּא	he, it		3m	הֵמָּה/הֵם	they
3f	הִיא	she, it		3f	הֵנָּה/הֵן	they

4.4   Prepositions

Hebrew has two types of prepositions, those that stand alone as independent words, and those that are prefixed to the noun they modify.

4.4.1   Prefixed Prepositions

There are only three prepositions that are inseparably prefixed to the noun that they modify. Those three prepositions are:

לְ   to, for

בְּ   in, by

כְּ   like, as, according to

4.4.2   Vocalization of the Prefixed Prepositions

1. The inseparable prepositions are usually vocalized with *sheva*.

דֶּרֶךְ	road	בְּדֶרֶךְ	in a road
מֹשֶׁה	Moses	לְמֹשֶׁה	to Moses
כֹּהֵן	priest	כְּכֹהֵן	like a priest

a. Before a word that begins with *sheva*, the *sheva* under the preposition becomes *chireq*, e.g.

מְלָכִים	kings	לִמְלָכִים	to kings

b. Before a word that begins with composite *sheva*, the *sheva* under the preposition becomes the corresponding short vowel, e.g.

אֲדָמָה   ground   כַּאֲדָמָה   like ground

c. Two exceptions are the word אֱלֹהִים and words beginning with יְ .

אֱלֹהִים   God   לֵאלֹהִים   to God

יְהוּדָה   Judah   לִיהוּדָה   to Judah

2. Sometimes before the tone syllable, when the accent mark indicates heavy stress, the *sheva* becomes a *qamets*.

מַיִם   water   לָמַיִם   to water

3. When the preposition is attached to a word with the definite article, the letter ה falls away, and the preposition takes its place with the same pointing.

הַמֶּלֶךְ   the king   לַמֶּלֶךְ   to the king

הָאָדָם   the man   כָּאָדָם   like the man

4.4.3   Other Prepositions

Prepositions that occur as separate words include עַל, which means *over, upon*, אֶל, which means *unto*, and include מִן, which means *from*.

אֱלֹהִים	God	מִן אֱלֹהִים	from God
אֶרֶץ	land	מִן הָאָרֶץ	from the land
הַר	Mountain	עַל הָהָר	upon the mountain
מֶלֶךְ	king	אֶל מֶלֶךְ	unto a king

4.5   Vocabulary

אָמַר   *v.* he said

זָכַר   *v.* he remembered, he mentioned

יָדַע   *v.* he knew. The perfect of יָדַע is usually translated present tense.

כֹּל   *n.m.* the whole, all, every. *also* כָּל-

דֶּרֶךְ   *n.m. or f.* road, way

כֹּהֵן   *n.m.* priest

לְ   *inseparable preposition.* to, for

בְּ   *inseparable prep.* in, by (*instrumental*)

כְּ   *inseparable prep.* like, as, according to

מִן   *prep.* from

אֲשֶׁר   *relative pronoun.* who, which, that, what, when

מִי   *interrogative pronoun.* who?

לֵאמֹר   *infinitive construct. Translated* 'saying'[1]

אֶת־   *sign of the def. object.* אֶת־ *with the hyphen, which is called* maqqef

EXERCISE 4-B

Part 1: Translate the following Hebrew sentences into English.

1. הַמֶּלֶךְ הַטּוֹב שָׁמַר [2]אֶת־הַבֵּן וְאֶת־הַבַּת:

2. וַאֲנָשִׁים רַבִּים הָלְכוּ אֶל הַבָּיִת:

3. וְהַנָּשִׁים הַטּוֹבוֹת הָלְכוּ מִן הָהָר:

4. אֲנִי יָדַעְתִּי אֶת־הַמֶּלֶךְ הַגָּדוֹל:

5. וְרָחֵל[3] אָמְרָה לֵאמֹר מִי עָלָה מִן הַדֶּרֶךְ אֶל הָהָר הַגָּדוֹל:

6. וְאַתְּ אָמַרְתְּ לֵאמֹר עָלָה הָאִישׁ לֵאלֹהִים:

7. וְהַמֶּלֶךְ הַגָּדוֹל זָכַר אֶת־הַבָּנִים וְהַבָּנוֹת:

8. אַתֵּן זְכַרְתֶּן אֶת־הָאָח אֲשֶׁר בַּבָּיִת:

9. וְיַעֲקֹב[4] יָדַע אֶת־הַכֹּהֵן אֲשֶׁר כְּאָח:

10. הָאִשָּׁה יָשְׁבָה בַּבַּיִת הַגָּדוֹל וְהִיא שֹׁמֶרֶת אֶת־הַדָּבָר:

11. אַתְּ אָמַרְתְּ לֵאמֹר מִי עָלָה אֶל הָהָר:

12. וְהַכֹּהֵן הָרָע זָכַר אֶת־הָאִישׁ הַשֹּׁמֵר אֶת־הַדָּבָר:

13. כַּכֹּהֵן זָכַרְתָּ אֶת־הַדָּבָר וְאַתָּה שֹׁמֵר אֶת־הַדָּבָר:

14. אֲנַחְנוּ זֹכְרִים אֶת־כָּל־הַדְּבָרִים אֲשֶׁר אָמַרְתָּ:

15. וְעַתָּה הוּא יֹשֵׁב בַּבַּיִת הַגָּדוֹל:

16. וְיַעֲקֹב אָמַר לֵאמֹר שֹׁמְרִים אֲנַחְנוּ אֶת־הַדָּבָר הַטּוֹב:

17. הִנֵּה זְכֹרוֹת אֶת־הַדָּבָר אֲשֶׁר אָמַר יַעֲקֹב בַּדֶּרֶךְ:

18. וְאַתָּה שֹׁמֵר אֶת־הַמֶּלֶךְ:

---

[1] This form will be discussed in a later chapter. This particular word is used idiomatically to introduce direct speech, similar to quotation marks. The KJV translates it *saying*, but often it may be left untranslated.

[2] אֶת־ is the sign of the definite object. It is not translated, but it identifies the following noun as an object of the verb rather than the subject of the verb.

[3] Rachel

[4] Jacob

Part 2: Translate the following English sentences into Hebrew.

1. The priest knew the way.

2. And all the priests remembered the good words.

3. The son is remembering the words which the mother said.

4. Who is the man who remembered the king.

5. And the good man went up to the priests who knew the king.

4.6   Appendix to Chapter 4

4.6.1   Terminology

Hebrew scholars often use different terminology to describe the same verb forms. Semitists and linguists often prefer to use *qatal* (קָטַל) rather than *perfect* as the name for the suffix conjugation, because 1) *qatal* reflects the Hebrew spelling of the third masculine singular from the root קטל, and 2) *qatal* describes the form without giving misleading implications regarding function. The following explanatory notes will help you identify the terms as they are used in various reference works:

4.6.2   The Two Finite States or Tenses of the Hebrew Verb

1. The Perfect is also called *qatal* or the Suffix Conjugation

2. The Imperfect is also called *yiqtol* or the Prefix Conjugation

The Arch of Titus in Rome
Depicts the Romans Looting the Jerusalem Temple

Chapter 5

The Imperfect

In this chapter you should learn:

- The imperfect form of the verb
- Negation of the finite verb
- Genitival relationships of the noun
- The imperative state of the verb

5.1 The Imperfect Conjugation

Hebrew has only two finite verb forms, perfect and imperfect. At the risk of over-simplification, we might say that the perfect represents the whole of an action, from beginning to end (completed aspect). The imperfect, however, represents the beginning and the continuance of and action but not the end of the action (incomplete aspect).

While the perfect indicates person, gender, and number through the use of afformatives, the imperfect utilizes both afformatives and preformatives (HVS 4A and 12B).

Important Fact:
In every case, without exception, the imperfect will have a preformative א, ת, י, *or* נ.

In contrast to the perfect, the imperfect distinguishes between the masculine and the feminine in the third person plural.

> **The imperfect will *always* have a preformative.**

5.1.1 Preformatives and Afformatives of the Imperfect

	Singular			Plural	
1c	—א	I	1c	—נ	We
2m	—ת	You	2m	ו—ת	You
2f	י—ת	You	2f	נָה—ת	You
3m	—י	He	3m	ו—י	They
3f	—ת	She	3f	נָה—ת	They

Qal imperfect of שָׁמַר: *to keep*

	Singular			Plural	
1c	אֶשְׁמֹר	I shall keep	1c	נִשְׁמֹר	We shall keep
2m	תִּשְׁמֹר	You will keep	2m	תִּשְׁמְרוּ	You will keep
2f	תִּשְׁמְרִי	You will keep	2f	תִּשְׁמֹרְנָה	You will keep
3m	יִשְׁמֹר	He will keep	3m	יִשְׁמְרוּ	They will keep
3f	תִּשְׁמֹר	She will keep	3f	תִּשְׁמֹרְנָה	They will keep

Note: The 2f plural is also found in this form: תִּשְׁמֹרְן

5.1.2   Meaning of the Imperfect

When standing alone (without the conjunction attached), the imperfect is called the *yiqtol*, and designates an action that is imperfective, either in time or in the mind of the writer. That is, the imperfective verb includes the beginning and progress of an action or state but not the end of the action or state.[1] Remember these important rules of word order for the imperfect as used in direct speech (not narrative):

Important Rule:

When the imperfect is first in the clause, it always denotes a volitive mood (e.g. subjunctive, injunctive, hortatory). This function is often called modal.[2]

When the imperfect is not first in the sentence, it usually denotes simple future, but there are times when a volitive form is not first in the sentence.

Examples:

מֹשֶׁה יִזְכֹּר אֶת־הַדֶּרֶךְ:	Moses will remember the way.
יִזְכֹּר מֹשֶׁה אֶת־הַדֶּרֶךְ:	May Moses remember the way.
אַתְּ תִּזְכְּרִי אֶת־הַדֶּרֶךְ הַטּוֹב:	As for you, you will remember the good way.
תִּזְכְּרִי אֶת־הַדֶּרֶךְ הַטּוֹב:	You shall/may you remember the good way.
אֱלֹהִים יִזְכֹּר אֶת־הַמֶּלֶךְ:	God will remember the king.
יִזְכֹּר אֱלֹהִים אֶת־הַמֶּלֶךְ:	May God remember the king.

---

[1] Some scholars argue that Hebrew once had a preterite conjugation (perfective in aspect) whose form was like the imperfect (*yiqtol*) and that a few of these preterites remain in the Hebrew Scriptures.

[2] Alviero Niccacci, 'A Neglected Point of Hebrew Syntax: Yiqtol and Position in the Sentence', *Liber Annuus* 37 (1987), pp. 7-19. David Kummerow, 'Job, Hopeful or Hopeless? The Significance of גַּם in Job 16:19 and Job's Changing Conceptions of Death', in Ehud Ben Zvi (ed.), *Perspectives on Hebrew Scriptures II* (Piscataway, NJ: Gorgias Press, 2007), p. 275 n63.

EXERCISE 5-A

Part 1: Translate the following Hebrew into English:

1. וְאֶת־הַיּוֹם הַטּוֹב נִזְכֹּר:

2. תִּזְכֹּר הָאֵם אֶת־הַבַּת:

3. אַתֵּן תִּזְכֹּרְנָה אֶת־הַמַּלְכָּה:

4. וְיַעֲקֹב יִשְׁמֹר אֶת־הַדָּבָר:

5. תִּזְכְּרוּ אֶת־הָאָרֶץ:

6. יִזְכְּרוּ אֶת־הַמֶּלֶךְ הַטּוֹב:

7. וֵאלֹהִים אָמַר אֶזְכֹּר אֶת־הַכֹּהֵן:

Part 2: Translate the following English into Hebrew:

1. May Rachel remember the word.
2. Rachel will keep the word.
3. Let us remember the way.

5.2   Negation of the Finite Verb

The negative particle לֹא is used with the perfect and the imperfect.

The negative לֹא always precedes the verb that it negates.

Examples:

וְהָאֲנָשִׁים הָלְכוּ אֶל הַבַּיִת	And the men went to the house.
וְלֹא הָלְכוּ הָאֲנָשִׁים אֶל הַבַּיִת	And the men did not go to the house.
מֶלֶךְ יָשַׁב עַל הַכִּסֵּא	A king sat upon the throne.
לֹא יָשַׁב מֶלֶךְ עַל הַכִּסֵּא	A king did not sit upon the throne.
וְהַיֹּשְׁבִים יִשְׁמְרוּ אֶת־הַדָּבָר	And the inhabitants will keep the word.
וְלֹא יִשְׁמְרוּ הַיֹּשְׁבִים אֶת־הַדָּבָר	And the inhabitants will not keep the word.

5.3   Genitival Relationships

There are no case endings in Hebrew. In most situations, the case of a noun is determined by its position in the sentence. A noun will usually be nominative (subjective) when it follows a verb. A noun will be accusative (objective) when it follows the particle אֶת־.

When two nouns are juxtaposed in a clause the second noun will usually be of the genitive case, even though there may be no change in its form. The genitive can be expressed by the English word *of*, e.g. *man of God*. For example:

הַר אֲדָמָה   a mountain of earth

מֶלֶךְ הָאָרֶץ   the king of the land

אֵם הַמַּלְכָּה   the mother of the queen

Adjectives and participles may also function in the construct state. For example, the adjective טוֹב means *good* or *beautiful*, and טוֹבַת מַרְאֶה means *beautiful of appearance* (Gen. 26.7). The participle יֹדֵעַ means *knowing*, and the phrase יֹדְעֵי טוֹב וָרָע means *knowers of good and evil* (Gen. 3.5). See also Hosea 2.7; 3.1; Gen. 22.12; etc.

5.3.1   Construct State and Absolute State

The first word in a genitive relationship is said to be in construct. Any noun that is not in construct is said to be in the absolute state. In the phrase *the man of God*, the word *man* is in construct, and the word *God* is absolute. This idiom is very common in Hebrew and should be mastered as soon as possible. For example:

הַר אֲדָמָה   The word הַר is construct, and אֲדָמָה is absolute.

מֶלֶךְ הָאָרֶץ   The word מֶלֶךְ is construct, and הָאָרֶץ is absolute.

5.3.1.1 Construct nouns

Sometimes, the form of the noun will change when it is in the construct state (see §5.6.1 for details). Also, the construct and the genitive may or may not be connected by a *maqqef*. For example: מְלָכִים means *kings*, but מַלְכֵי means *kings of*.

מְלָכִים	kings	מַלְכֵי כָבוֹד	kings of glory
בַּיִת	house	בֵּית אֲדָמָה	house of earth
בֵּן	son	בֶּן־אָדָם	son of man[3]
רָעָה	evil	רָעַת הָעִיר	the evil of the city

The following irregular construct forms must be memorized. Other irregular forms will be noted as they occur in the vocabulary.

Absolute		Construct	
אִשָּׁה	wife	אֵשֶׁת	wife of
אָב	father	אֲבִי	father of
אָח	brother	אֲחִי	brother of
אַחִים	brothers	אֲחֵי	brothers of

---

[3] See the appendix at the end of the chapter for more types of changes.

5.3.2   Definiteness with the Construct Noun

The definite article is never attached to the construct form. Definiteness is determined by the genitive. If the genitive is definite, the construct form is also definite, but if the genitive is indefinite, the construct form is also indefinite. Examples:

בֶּן־אָדָם   son of man *or* a son of a man

בֶּן־הָאָדָם   the son of the man

With proper nouns, which are definite by nature, no article is needed. The preposition לְ is used to express a genitive relationship between a definite noun and an indefinite noun. In this case, no construct form is necessary. Examples:

בֶּן־יַעֲקֹב   the son of Jacob

בֶּן־לְיַעֲקֹב   a son of Jacob

The construct may or may not use the hyphen that we call *maqqef*. Either way, the meaning is the same. The following examples have the same meaning as those given above. The vowel points will be different, however, because the *maqqef* causes בֶּן to be unaccented, resulting in a short vowel.

בֵּן יַעֲקֹב   the son of Jacob

בֵּן לְיַעֲקֹב   a son of Jacob

5.3.3   Functions of the Construct Noun

The construct–genitive relationship may perform the following functions:

5.3.3.1. Possessive genitive – The genitive can claim the person, object, or characteristic named in the construct by relationship, by ownership, or by nature.

a. kinship   בְּנֵי יַעֲקֹב   the sons of Jacob (Gen. 34.7)

b. an object   בֵּית הַמֶּלֶךְ   the house of the king (Jer. 38.11)

c. constituent part יַד יהוה   the hand of Yahweh (Exod. 9.3)

d. characteristic   חָכְמַת שְׁלֹמֹה   the wisdom of Solomon (1 Kgs 4.34)

5.3.3.2. Subjective genitive – The genitive is the subject of the action implied by the construct.

יֵשַׁע אֱלֹהִים   the salvation of God (Ps. 50.23) *'God' is subject – the one who saves.*

אַהֲבַת נָשִׁים   the love of women (2 Sam. 1.26) *'Women' is subject – the ones who love.*

5.3.3.3. Objective genitive – The genitive is the object of the action implied by the construct.

יִרְאַת אֱלֹהִים   the fear of God (Gen. 20.11) *'God' is object – the one who is feared.*

מַצְדִּיקֵי רָשָׁע   acquitters of the wicked (Isa. 5.23) *'Wicked' is the object – the one who is acquitted.*

5.3.3.4. Partitive genitive – The construct is a part of the whole that is named in the genitive.

חֲצִי הַדָּם   half of the blood (Exod. 24.6)

טוֹב הַצֹּאן   best of the sheep (1 Sam. 15.9)

5.3.3.5. Adverbial genitive – The genitive names a means, instrument, effect, time, goal, manner, or purpose in relation to the construct.

a. instrumental	חַלְלֵי־חֶרֶב	those wounded by the sword (Lam. 4.9)
b. effect	מוּסַר שְׁלוֹמֵנוּ	punishment that effected our peace (Isa. 53.5)
c. time	בֶּן שָׁנָה	son of a year (one year old)
d. goal	יוֹרְדֵי בוֹר	those going down to the pit (Isa. 38.18)

5.3.3.6. Genitive of specification[4]– The genitive specifies the material, source, characteristic, attribute, name, topic, measure, or quality of the noun in construct.

a. material	כְּלֵי זָהָב	vessels of gold (2 Sam. 8.10)
b. source	דְּבַר מֹשֶׁה	the word of Moses (Exod. 8.13)
c. adjectival	בִּגְדֵי הַקֹּדֶשׁ	garments of holiness (=holy garments)
d. proper noun	אֶרֶץ מִצְרַיִם	land of Egypt (Gen. 13.10)
e. location	עִיר מוֹאָב	a city of Moab (Num. 22.36)

5.3.4   Adjectives in Construct: The Genitive of Limitation

In a construct–genitive relationship, the construct may be an adjective. Therefore, the construct adjective will name an attribute that applies to the domain indicated by the genitive. Thus, the genitive gives the boundary or limit to which the adjective applies. For example, Sarai is יְפַת־מַרְאֶה (*beautiful of appearance*, Gen. 12.11). The adjective 'beautiful' is applied only to her *appearance*, but it does not specify the beauty of her attitudes, morals, or mind (cf. Joüon §129i). Another example is אֶרֶךְ אַפַּיִם (slow of anger, Exod. 34.6), which means that Yahweh is slow in regard to becoming angry.

EXERCISE 5-B

Translate the following:

1. אֲבִי יַעֲקֹב
2. בְּנוֹת רָחֵל
3. אִשָּׁה לַמֶּלֶךְ
4. נְשֵׁי הַמֶּלֶךְ
5. מַלְכֵי הָאָרֶץ
6. דִּבְרֵי אֱלֹהִים

---

[4] For even more categories and examples, see Waltke and O'Connor §9.5 and Joüon §129.

5.4   The Imperative State of the Verb

The imperative expresses a command. An example would be, *Open the door.* In Hebrew, the imperative is a shortened form of the imperfect. The imperative is found only in the second person and has the same afformatives as the imperfect. The imperative, however, *does not have a preformative* (HVS 12C).

5.4.1   Afformatives of the Imperative

	Singular			Plural	
2m	-----	You	2m	‏וּ‎---	You
2f	‏י‎-----	You	2f	‏נָה‎---	You

The imperative is formed by removing the preformative from the second person of the imperfect. In the second example, below, two *sheva*s come together at the beginning of a word, causing the first *sheva* to become *chireq.*

‏תִּשְׁמֹר‎ Imperfect: You will keep   ‏שְׁמֹר‎ Imperative: Keep!

‏תִּשְׁמְרוּ‎ Imperfect: You will keep   ‏שִׁמְרוּ‎ Imperative: Keep!

Qal Imperative of ‏שָׁמַר‎: *to keep*

	Singular			Plural	
2m	‏שְׁמֹר‎	Keep	2m	‏שִׁמְרוּ‎	Keep
2f	‏שִׁמְרִי‎	Keep	2f	‏שְׁמֹרְנָה‎	Keep

Examples of the imperative:

‏זְכֹר אֶת־הַדֶּרֶךְ‎ Remember (m.s.) the way.

‏אִמְרִי אֶת־הַדָּבָר‎ Say (f.s.) the word.

‏אִמְרוּ לֵאלֹהִים‎ Speak (m.p.) to God.

‏שְׁמֹרְנָה אֶת־תּוֹרַת אֱלֹהִים‎ Keep (f.p.) the law of God.

EXERCISE 5-C

Translate the following:

1. ‏עִבְרִי עַתָּה בָאָרֶץ:‎

2. ‏עֲמֹד בַּדֶּרֶךְ כַּמֶּלֶךְ:‎

3. ‏כִּתְבוּ דָבָר טוֹב אֶל־הַכֹּהֵן:‎

4. ‏זְכֹרְנָה אֶת־רוּחַ יהוה:‎

5. ‏שִׁמְרִי הַתּוֹרָה מִן־יוֹם לְיוֹם:‎

5.5   Vocabulary

יָלַד   *v.* he begat

עָבַר   *v.* he passed over

עָמַד   *v.* he stood

כָּתַב   *v.* he wrote

מָלַךְ   *v.* he reigned

פָּקַד   *v.* he visited, he appointed

רוּחַ   *n.f.* spirit, wind (see pronunciation note above)

תּוֹרָה   *n.f.* law, instruction

עַד   *prep.* until

פָּנֶה   *n.m.* face. *construct* פְּנֵי. *With prep.,* לִפְנֵי=before, in front of

כִּי   *particle/conjunction.* because, when, that

כֹּה   *part.* thus

רָשָׁע   *adj.* wicked

מָה   *interrogative pronoun.* What?

EXERCISE 5-D

Translate the following Hebrew sentences into English.

1. וְלֹא יִשְׁמֹר הַכֹּהֵן הָרָשָׁע אֵת תּוֹרַת אֱלֹהִים׃

2. כֹּה אָמַר אֱלֹהִים שָׁמְרִי אֶת־הַמֶּלֶךְ וְאֶת־הַמַּלְכָּה׃

3. תִּכְתֹּב הָאִשָּׁה אֶת־דְּבַר רַע אֶל־הָאָח׃

4. וְלֹא יִמְלֹךְ הַמֶּלֶךְ עַד יִזְכֹּר אֶת־דִּבְרֵי הַתּוֹרָה׃

5. וְאֶת־הָאָרֶץ אֶפְקֹד אָמַר אֱלֹהִים כִּי אַתָּה הֹלֵךְ בְּדֶרֶךְ הַתּוֹרָה׃

6. מָה תִּזָּכְרוּ מִן הַדְּבָרִים הָרַבִּים אֲשֶׁר כָּתְבוּ׃

7. וּמֹשֶׁה[5] עָמַד בָּהָר הַגָּדוֹל וְלֹא שָׁמְרוּ הָאֲנָשִׁים וְאֶת־דִּבְרֵי־אֱלֹהִים [6]וְאֶת־תּוֹרַת אֱלֹהִים׃

8. וְרוּחַ אֱלֹהִים תִּפְקֹד בֶּן־יַעֲקֹב אֲשֶׁר לִפְנֵי הַכֹּהֵן׃

---

[5] Moses

[6] In Hebrew, the conjunction may be translated many different ways depending upon the context. Here, it could be translated *or*.

9. נִמְלַךְ בְּבֵית־אֱלֹהִים אָמְרוּ מַלְכֵי־הָאָרֶץ:

10. בְּנֵי יַעֲקֹב יֵשְׁבוּ בָאָרֶץ עַד עָלָה הַכֹּהֵן לְהַר אֱלֹהִים:

11. וְעַתָּה מִי יִמְלֹךְ לִפְנֵי־אֱלֹהִים כְּדָוִד:

12. אֶחָד אִישׁ יָדַע כִּי הָאֵם יָלְדָה בֵּן טוֹב:

13. מִי יִמְלֹךְ בָּאָרֶץ [7]הַיּוֹם:

14 כְּתוּבִים דִּבְרֵי־אֱלֹהִים בְּבֵית־אֱלֹהִים:

15. יִכְתֹּב הָאָדָם לַמֶּלֶךְ:

16. וְהָאֲנָשִׁים עָמְדוּ לִפְנֵי־אֱלֹהִים:

17. תִּפְקֹד רוּחַ־אֱלֹהִים אֶת־בֵּית אֱלֹהִים:

18. מָה יִכְתֹּב כִּי יִכְתֹּב לַמֶּלֶךְ:

19. וְלֹא נִפְקַד אֶת־הַמֶּלֶךְ אֲשֶׁר לֹא יָדַע אֶת־דָּבָר אֱלֹהִים:

20. וְרָחֵל אָמְרָה לֵאמֹר טוֹבִים דִּבְרֵי־אֱלֹהִים:

5.6   Appendix – Morphological Changes in Construct Nouns

5.6.1   The following list will explain the morphological changes in construct nouns.

Absolute	Construct	Absolute	Construct
ـָים or יָ֫ם	יֵ	בָּנִים	בְּנֵי
ה ָ	ת ַ	תּוֹרָה	תּוֹרַת
ה ֶ	ה ֵ	שָׂדֶה	שְׂדֵה
final ָ	-	דָּבָר	דְּבַר
initial ָ or ֱ	ְ	שֵׁמוֹת	שְׁמוֹת
monosyllable ֶ	ֵ	בֵּן	בֶּן־
וָ	וֹ	מָוֶת	מוֹת
יַ	יֵ	בַּיִת	בֵּית
זָקֵן	זְקַן	קָטֵל	קְטֵל

---

[7] This is an idiom meaning *today*.

In addition to the patterns listed above, there are the three types of *segolate* plurals and many irregular forms.

Segolate Nouns

Absolute		*Construct*	
מְלָכִים	kings	מַלְכֵי	kings of
סְפָרִים	books	סִפְרֵי	books of
חֲדָשִׁים	new moon	חָדְשֵׁי	new moons of

5.6.2   Another Name for the Imperfect: *Yiqtol*

The imperfect is also called the *yiqtol* (יקטל), based on the spelling of the third masculine singular from the root קטל.

Excerpt from Leviticus – Dead Sea Scrolls

Chapter 6

The Cohortative and Jussive

In this chapter you should learn:

- The cohortative and jussive forms of the verb
- Pronominal suffixes
- The infinitive form of the verb

6.1   The Cohortative

The cohortative is a function of the imperfect form, expressing the speaker's desire or intention to act, thus it is always in the first person, either singular or plural. Often, a volitive ה is attached to the end of the word for emphasis (HVS 13A). Because of the additional syllable, the thematic vowel (the vowel with the middle radical) is usually reduced. The cohortative expresses determination, desire, or request for permission. The following examples demonstrate the contrast between the imperfect and the cohortative. There are some instances where the cohortative lacks the volitive ה, and thus is identical to the imperfect. In these cases, the word order will determine whether the first person imperfect should be translated as future or as cohortative. If the verb is in first position in the sentence, it will be cohortative, but if it is not in first position it will usually be simple future.

Imperfect		Cohortative	
אֶשְׁמֹר	I shall keep	אֶשְׁמְרָה	Let me keep *or* I WILL keep
נִשְׁמֹר	We shall keep	נִשְׁמְרָה	Let us keep *or* We WILL keep

6.2   The Jussive

Like the cohortative, the jussive expresses the speaker's desire for an action to occur, but the action proceeds from another person. The form of the jussive is identical to the imperfect in most cases, but sometimes the jussive is shortened from the imperfect (see the second example below). Jussives are found in the second and third person. The word order will determine whether the second and third person imperfect should be translated as future or jussive. Jussives usually come first in the sentence. The jussive (and imperative) may also have the volitive ה suffix (HVS 13B).

Imperfect   Jussive

הַמֶּלֶךְ יִשְׁמֹר   The king will keep   יִשְׁמֹר הַמֶּלֶךְ   May the king keep.

Imperfect   Jussive

הַכֹּהֵן יִגְלֶה   The priest will go into exile   יִגֶל הַכֹּהֵן [1]   May the priest go into exile

6.3   Negative Commands

The imperative is used only for positive commands. It is never used to express prohibition. The negative particles, לֹא and אַל are used with the imperfect and the jussive to express negative commands. (The negative particle לֹא is also used to negate nouns, adjectives, and perfect verbs; but אַל is used only with the jussive.)

> Negative commands use the imperfect and jussive.

The second person imperfect preceded by לֹא expresses prohibition. The prohibitions found in the Ten Commandments are in this form.

לֹא תִגְנֹב   You shall not steal.

לֹא תִרְצָח   You shall not murder.

The jussive preceded by אַל expresses warning or a more immediate and urgent prohibition.

אַל תִּפְקֹד הַמֶּלֶךְ   Do not visit the king.

אַל יִכְתֹּב אֶל הַכֹּהֵן   He must not write to the priest.

EXERCISE 6-A

Translate the following from Hebrew to English:

נִזְכְּרָה אֶת־הַתּוֹרָה׃   .1

וְלֹא תִפְקֹד הַבַּיִת הָרַע׃   .2

וְאַל תִּזְכְּרוּ אֶת־דֶּרֶךְ־הָרָשָׁע׃   .3

אֶעְבְּרָה הַהַר הַגָּדוֹל׃   .4

---

[1] The final ה is dropped in the jussive.

6.4   Pronominal Suffixes

The following chart lists the possessive pronouns:

	Singular				Plural	
1c	יـ‍—	my		1c	נוּ‍—	our
2m	ךָ‍—	your[2]		2m	כֶם‍—	your
2f	ךְ‍—	your		2f	כֶן‍—	your
3m	וֹ‍—	his		3m	הֶם/ם‍—	their
3f	הּ‍—	her[3]		3f	הֶן/ן‍—	their
	הָ‍—					

In Hebrew, possession is signified by the construct-genitive relationship (see Chapter 5), for example:

סוּסֵי יַעֲקֹב = the horses of Jacob/Jacob's horses

Possessive pronouns, however, are affixed to the noun. They do not exist as separate words, for example:

> **Possessive pronouns are suffixed to the noun they modify.**

סוּסִי = the horse of me/my horse

סוּסְךָ = the horse of you/your horse

הַר־קָדְשׁוֹ = his holy mountain[4]

6.4.1   Nouns with Pronominal Suffixes

The following charts demonstrate how the pronominal suffixes function as possessive pronouns when they are attached to the noun forms.

Masculine Singular noun with suffixes

	Singular				Plural	
1c	סוּסִי	my horse		1c	סוּסֵנוּ	our horse
2m	סוּסְךָ	your horse		2m	סוּסְכֶם	your horse
2f	סוּסֵךְ	your horse		2f	סוּסְכֶן	your horse
3m	סוּסוֹ	his horse		3m	סוּסָם	their horse
3f	סוּסָהּ	her horse		3f	סוּסָן	their horse

---

[2] Sometimes ךְ‍—.

[3] Review the function of *mappiq* in Chapter 1 (§1.8.2).

[4] When a suffix comes at the end of a construct phrase, it modifies the entire phrase, not just the word to which it is attached. Thus, *mountain of his holiness* means *his holy mountain*.

The following chart illustrates that the pronominal suffixes are attached to the construct form of the noun, e.g. סוּסִים = *horses*, and the construct: סוּסֵי = *horses of*.

Masculine Plural noun with suffixes

	Singular			Plural	
1c	סוּסַי	my horses	1c	סוּסֵינוּ	our horses
2m	סוּסֶיךָ	your horses	2m	סוּסֵיכֶם	your horses
2f	סוּסַיִךְ	your horses	2f	סוּסֵיכֶן	your horses
3m	סוּסָיו	his horses	3m	סוּסֵיהֶם	their horses
3f	סוּסֶיהָ	her horses	3f	סוּסֵיהֶן	their horses

Feminine Singular noun with suffixes

	Singular			Plural	
1c	סוּסָתִי	my mare	1c	סוּסָתֵנוּ	our mare
2m	סוּסָתְךָ	your mare	2m	סוּסַתְכֶם	your mare
2f	סוּסָתֵךְ	your mare	2f	סוּסַתְכֶן	your mare
3m	סוּסָתוֹ	his mare	3m	סוּסָתָם	their mare
3f	סוּסָתָהּ	her mare	3f	סוּסָתָן	their mare

Feminine Plural noun with suffixes

	Singular			Plural	
1c	סוּסוֹתַי	my mares	1c	סוּסוֹתֵנוּ	our mares
2m	סוּסוֹתֶיךָ	your mares	2m	סוּסוֹתֵיכֶם	your mares
2f	סוּסוֹתַיִךְ	your mares	2f	סוּסוֹתֵיכֶן	your mares
3m	סוּסוֹתָיו	his mares	3m	סוּסוֹתֵיהֶם	their mares
3f	סוּסוֹתֶיהָ	her mares	3f	סוּסוֹתֵיהֶן	their mares

Note: The *yod* is inserted for phonetic purposes.

The pronominal suffix attaches to the construct form of the noun. Furthermore, the addition of a pronominal suffix may require additional changes in the pointing of the noun. For example:

אָב = father	אֲבִי = father of	אָבִי = my father
רוּחַ = spirit	רוּחַ = spirit of	רוּחִי = my spirit
בָּנִים = sons	בְּנֵי = sons of	בָּנֶיךָ = your (m.sg.) sons
בֵּן = son	בֶּן־ = son of	בְּנוֹ = his son
עֲבָדִים = servants	עַבְדֵי = servants of	עֲבָדָיו = his servants
כִּסֵּא = throne	כִּסֵּא = throne of	כִּסְאוֹ = his throne
אֱלֹהִים = God	אֱלֹהֵי = God of	אֱלֹהֶיהָ = her God
אִישׁ = husband	אִישׁ = husband of	אִישָׁהּ = her husband
עֵינַיִם = eyes	עֵינֵי = eyes of	עֵינֵינוּ = our eyes

אָבוֹת = fathers   אֲבוֹת = fathers of   אֲבוֹתֵיכֶם = your (pl) fathers
דְּבָרִים = words   דִּבְרֵי = words of   דִּבְרֵיהֶם = their words
חַטָּאָה = sin   חַטַּאת = sin of   חַטָּאתָם = their sin

6.4.2   Objective Pronouns

Not only do the pronominal suffixes function as possessives, they also function as objects. They can be affixed to the sign of the definite object, thus becoming objective pronouns.

	Singular				Plural	
1c	אֹתִי	me		1c	אֹתָנוּ	us
2m	אֹתְךָ	you		2m	אֶתְכֶם	you
2f	אֹתָךְ	you		2f	(not attested)	you
3m	אֹתוֹ	him, it		3m	אֶתְהֶם / אֹתָם	them
3f	אֹתָהּ	her, it		3f	אֶתְהֶן / אֹתָן	them

Examples:

הַמֶּלֶךְ יִזְכֹּר אֹתִי׃   The king will remember me.

פָּקְדוּ הַכֹּהֲנִים אֹתְךָ׃   The priests visited you.

> **Pronominal suffixes may be affixed to the sign of the definite object.**

6.4.3   Prepositions with Pronominal Suffixes

The pronominal suffixes may function also as objects of prepositions. The prepositions with suffixes are given below.

Inseparable preposition בְּ

	Singular				Plural	
1c	בִּי	in me		1c	בָּנוּ	in us
2m	בְּךָ/בְּכָה	in you		2m	בָּכֶם	in you
2f	בָּךְ	in you		2f	בָּכֶן	in you
3m	בּוֹ	in him		3m	בָּהֶם/בָּם	in them
3f	בָּהּ	in her		3f	בָּהֶן	in them

The preposition לְ follows the same pattern as בְּ.

	Singular			Plural	
1c	לִי	to me	1c	לָנוּ	to us
2m	לְךָ/לְכָה	to you	2m	לָכֶם	to you
2f	לָךְ	to you	2f	לָכֶן	to you
3m	לוֹ	to him	3m	לָהֶם/לָם	to them
3f	לָהּ	to her	3f	לָהֶן	to them

Inseparable Preposition כְּ

	Singular			Plural	
1c	כָּמוֹנִי	like me	1c	כָּמוֹנוּ	like us
2m	כָּמוֹךָ	like you	2m	כָּכֶם	like you
2f	כָּמוֹךְ	like you	2f	כָּכֶן	like you
3m	כָּמוֹהוּ	like him	3m	כָּהֶם	like them
3f	כָּמוֹהָ	like her	3f	כָּהֶן/כָּהֵנָה	like them

Preposition אֶל־

	Singular			Plural	
1c	אֵלַי	to me	1c	אֵלֵנוּ	to us
2m	אֵלֶיךָ	to you	2m	אֲלֵיכֶם	to you
2f	אֵלַיִךְ	to you	2f	-not attested-	
3m	אֵלָיו	to him	3m	אֲלֵיהֶם	to them
3f	אֵלֶיהָ	to her	3f	אֲלֵיהֶן	to them

EXERCISE 6-B

Translate the following sentences (Please learn the vocabulary at the end of the chapter before attempting the exercises).

1. אַנְשֵׁי־יְרוּשָׁלַם[5] יָצְאוּ מִן הַמֶּלֶךְ וְאֵלָיו הָלְכוּ:

2. וַאֲחִי־הַכֹּהֵן יָצָא עִם בְּנוֹ לַנָּהָר:

3. וְהִנֵּה אָכְלוּ אֶת־הַלֶּחֶם הֶחָדָשׁ:

4. וְלֹא עָמַד יִשְׂרָאֵל[6] וּבְנוֹתָיו לִפְנֵי הַמֶּלֶךְ:

5. אִכְלוּ הַלֶּחֶם אֲשֶׁר לְקַחְתֶּם לָכֶם:

---

[5] Jerusalem
[6] Israel

6. כֹּה אָמַר יהוה אֶפְקְדָה אֶתְכֶם:

7. לִקְחוּ דְּבַר־יהוה אֲשֶׁר לְחֶם־הַחַיִּים:

8. מִי הָלַךְ בַּהֵיכָל הַגָּדוֹל אֲשֶׁר בִּירוּשָׁלַ͏ִם:

9. כְּתֹב אֶל אָבִיךָ לֵאמֹר יֹשֵׁב אֲדוֹנִי עַל כִּסְאוֹ:

10. וּמֹשֶׁה עָלָה לָהָר לֵאמֹר יִמְלֹךְ אֱלֹהִים עַל כָּל־הָאָרֶץ:

6.5   The Infinitive Form of the Verb

There are two infinitives in Hebrew, the infinitive absolute and the infinitive construct. Although they are both called infinitives, they do not perform the same function. Both forms may function as a verbal noun (a gerund), but the infinitive construct is more consistently used in this way. The infinitive absolute, on the other hand, is most often employed to express emphasis.

6.5.1   *Qal* Infinitive Absolute

The regular form of the *qal* infinitive absolute is שָׁמֹר or שָׁמוֹר. The infinitive absolute is used most commonly to express emphasis (HVS 9B).

If the infinitive stands immediately *before* a finite verb of the same root, it represents certainty. For example:

> יִשְׁמֹר = He will keep.
>
> שָׁמוֹר יִשְׁמֹר = He will *surely* keep.
>
> זָכַרְתִּי = I remembered.
>
> זָכֹר זָכַרְתִּי = I *certainly* remembered.

> Hebrew has two
> kinds of infinitives.

If, however, the infinitive stands immediately *after* the finite verb of the same root, it signifies repetition or continuance. For example:

> יִשְׁמֹר = He will keep.
>
> יִשְׁמֹר שָׁמוֹר = He will keep *continually*.
>
> אֶזְכֹּר = I will remember.
>
> אֶזְכֹּר זָכֹר = I will *go on* remembering.

EXERCISE 6-C

Translate the following:

1. יָלֹד יָלְדָה רוּחַ־אֱלֹהִים הַתּוֹרָה:

2. עָבֹר עָבְרוּ הַנָּהָר [7] אֵלֶיךָ:

3. וְאַתָּ עָמַדְתָּ עָמֹד לִפְנֵי הַכִּסֵּא:

---

[7] See the section 6.4.3 above: Prepositions With Pronominal Suffixes.

4. וְהִנֵּה אָכַלְתִּי אֹכֶל לֶחֶם־הַחַי:

5. כָּתֹב יִכְתְּבוּ אֵלֵינוּ בַּהֵיכָל:

6. מָלֹךְ יִמְלֹךְ עַל הַכִּסֵּא הֶחָדָשׁ:

6.5.2   *Qal* Infinitive Construct

The regular form of the *qal* infinitive construct is שָׁמֹר. The infinitive construct is most commonly used with the preposition לְ, and is roughly equivalent to the infinitive in English (HVS 2). For example:

וַיֵּצֵא יוֹאָב לִשְׁמֹר הַבָּיִת׃ = Now Joab went out *to guard* the house.

אָחָז לָקַח אֶת־הַכִּסֵּא לִמְלֹךְ׃ = Ahaz seized the throne *in order to reign.*

6.5.2.1 *Infinitive Construct with Pronominal Suffixes*

The infinitive construct gets its name from its second usage, where it is bound to a pronominal suffix in a construct-genitive relationship. In these cases, the form usually changes from שָׁמֹר to שָׁמְר, but the second person suffix forms change from שָׁמֹר to שָׁמָר. This class of the infinitive construct most often functions as a gerund. For example:

מָלְכִי = my reigning   מָלְכְךָ = your reigning

שָׁמְרִי = my keeping   שָׁמָרְךָ = your keeping (HVS 14)

The pronominal suffix, however, may be an objective genitive or a subjective genitive. That is, the suffix may indicate the person doing the action, or it may indicate the person to whom the action is directed.

שָׁמְרִי = my keeping, *or* keeping me/to keep me

6.5.2.2 *Infinitive Construct with Inseparable Prepositions* בְּ *and* כְּ

The infinitive may also take the inseparable prepositions בְּ and כְּ. These prepositions indicate time. The בְּ is translated *when*, and the כְּ is translated *as soon as*.

בְּמָלְכִי = during my reigning, i.e., when I was reigning

כְּבוֹא אַבְרָם = as soon as Abram arrived

The infinitive and the participle are the only two verbal forms that take the inseparable prepositions, and the most frequent of the two is the infinitive (HVS 2).

6.5.2.3 *Negation of the Infinitive Construct*

The infinitive, unlike the perfect and imperfect, is not negated by לֹא but by בְּלִי, לְבִלְתִּי, or בִּלְתִּי.

צִוִּיתִיךָ לְבִלְתִּי אֲכָל I commanded you not to eat (Gen. 3.11)

6.6 Principal Parts of the *Qal* Stem

We have now surveyed the verb forms of the *qal* stem. It may be helpful to list the major categories of the verb. These basic forms are called the *Principal Parts* of the verb. The Principal Parts must be memorized thoroughly. You should practice until you are able to write and recite them easily.

Principal Parts of the *Qal* stem

קָטַל	Perfect (*Qatal*)	קָטוֹל	Infinitive Absolute
יִקְטֹל	Imperfect (*Yiqtol*)	קְטֹל	Infinitive Construct
קְטֹל	Imperative	קוֹטֵל	Participle

EXERCISE 6-D

Translate the following:

1. וּמֹשֶׁה יָצָא לִפְקֹד עִם הַכֹּהֵן הַטּוֹב׃

2. וּמֹשֶׁה אָמַר לַעֲמֹד בְּדֶרֶךְ יהוה׃

3. אֶזְכֹּר כְּתָבְכֶם לִי אֶת־דְּבָר־יהוה׃

4. וּמֹשֶׁה יָדַע כִּי־טוֹב מָלְכוּ עַל הָאָרֶץ׃

6.7 Vocabulary

אָכַל   *v.* he ate

יָצָא   *v.* he went out

לָקַח   *v.* he took, seized

אָדוֹן   *n.m.* lord, אֲדוֹנִי = The Lord

לֶחֶם   *n.m.* bread

חַי   life. חַיָּה *f.* living thing, beast. חַי *adj.* living. חַיִּים *m.p.* life.

כִּסֵּא   *n.m. throne*

הֵיכָל   *n.m.* temple, palace, *sometimes irreg. pl* הֵיכָלוֹת

נָהָר   *n.m.* river, *sometimes irreg. pl* נְהָרוֹת

עַל   *prep.* upon, over, against

עִם   *prep.* with

הִנֵּה   *particle.* behold!

חָדָשׁ   *adj.* new

6.8   Appendix to Chapter 8: Complete *Qal* Paradigm

Qal Active Participle

	singular		plural	
m.	שֹׁמֵר	keeping	שֹׁמְרִים	keeping
f.	שֹׁמֶרֶת	keeping	שֹׁמְרוֹת	keeping

Qal Passive Participle

	singular		plural	
m.	שָׁמוּר	being kept	שְׁמוּרִים	being kept
f.	שְׁמוּרָה	being kept	שְׁמוּרוֹת	being kept

Qal Perfect

	Singular			Plural	
1c	שָׁמַרְתִּי	I kept	1c	שָׁמַרְנוּ	We kept
2m	שָׁמַרְתָּ	You kept	2m	שְׁמַרְתֶּם	You kept
2f	שָׁמַרְתְּ	You kept	2f	שְׁמַרְתֶּן	You kept
3m	שָׁמַר	He kept	3c	שָׁמְרוּ	They kept
3f	שָׁמְרָה	She kept			

Qal Imperfect

	Singular			Plural	
1c	אֶשְׁמֹר	I shall keep	1c	נִשְׁמֹר	We shall keep
2m	תִּשְׁמֹר	You will keep	2m	תִּשְׁמְרוּ	You will keep
2f	תִּשְׁמְרִי	You will keep	2f	תִּשְׁמֹרְנָה	You will keep
3m	יִשְׁמֹר	He will keep	3m	יִשְׁמְרוּ	They will keep
3f	תִּשְׁמֹר	She will keep	3f	תִּשְׁמֹרְנָה	They will keep

Qal Imperative

	Singular			Plural	
2m	שְׁמֹר	Keep	2m	שִׁמְרוּ	Keep
2f	שִׁמְרִי	Keep	2f	שְׁמֹרְנָה	Keep

Qal Cohortatives: אֶשְׁמְרָה and נִשְׁמְרָה
Qal Infinitive Absolute: שָׁמֹר or שָׁמוֹר
Qal Infinitive Construct: שְׁמֹר (+ prep.), שָׁמְר (+ sfx), or שָׁמָר (+ 2p sfx)

Chapter 7

The *Wayyiqtol* and *Weqatal*

In this chapter you should learn:

- The *wayyiqtol* form of the imperfect
- The *weqatal* form of the perfect
- The directive ה
- The demonstrative pronoun
- How to use the Hebrew lexicon
- How to parse Hebrew verbs

7.1   The Verbs Plus the Conjunction

We have learned that the perfect often indicates completed action (past tense), and the imperfect often represents incomplete action (future tense). The perfect and imperfect states are modified, however, when they are prefixed with certain forms of the conjunction.

7.2   *Wayyiqtol* Imperfect

Wayyiqtol is the imperfect with וַ, followed by the *dagesh forte* (Before an א the pointing will be וָ). This form is often called *wayyiqtol* to distinguish it from the simple imperfect, called *yiqtol*. Some scholars call it the *vav*-consecutive or *vav*-conversive. The *wayyiqtol* is the standard verb form for narrative, and most scholars believe it to be perfective in aspect.[1] (Note: *wayyiqtol* is pronounced *vayyiqtol*.) (HVS 1A)

יִשְׁמֹר = He will keep.

וַיִּשְׁמֹר = And he kept.

7.2.1   Verb Tense within Hebrew narrative

A past tense narration is given in the *wayyiqtol*. Even though the perfect form of the verb often signifies past tense, it is not used for the narration of past events. Within a narrative, the perfect will signify background information, including

---

[1] For a recent study, see Galia Hatav, *The Semantics of Aspect and Modality: Evidence from English and Biblical Hebrew* (Philadelphia: J. Benjamins Pub., 1997).

parenthetical remarks, preliminary events, or concurrent actions. The narration may resume once again with the *wayyiqtol*

Examples of the *wayyiqtol*:

מֹשֶׁה יָצָא וַיִּפְקֹד כָּל־הַמְּלָכִים:

Moses went out and he visited all the kings.

בָּנָיו לָקְחוּ אֶת־הַכִּסֵּא וַיִּמְלְכוּ:

His sons took the throne and they reigned.

EXERCISE 7-A

Translate the following:

1. וַאֲנַחְנוּ אָכַלְנוּ אֶת־לַחְמֵנוּ וַנִּזְכֹּר דְּבַר־יהוה:

2. וְיִצְחָק[2] יָצָא מִן־הַהֵיכָל וַיִּזְכֹּר אֶת־הַדֶּרֶךְ הַטּוֹב:

7.3   *Weqatal* Perfect

The *weqatal* is the perfect with the simple conjunction (וְ) (HVS 1). Also, the stress moves toward the end of the word in the 1cs and 2ms forms. This form is called *weqatal* in order to distinguish it from a simple perfect, called *qatal*. The *weqatal* is the standard verb for discourse (direct speech), or for reporting events within a broader narrative structure. Most scholars believe the *weqatal* to be imperfective in aspect.

שָׁמַר = He kept.

וְשָׁמַר = And he will keep.

A future tense discourse is expressed by the *weqatal* (perfect with the *vav*).

וַאֲנִי אֶזְכֹּר אֶת־הַדֶּרֶךְ וְהָלַכְתִּי בּוֹ:

And I shall remember the way and I shall walk in it.

וְרָחֵל[3] תִּשְׁמֹר אֶת־הַתּוֹרָה וְזָכְרָה אֶת־אֱלֹהִים:

And Rachel will keep the law and she will remember God.

---

[2] Isaac

[3] Rachel

7.4   Hebrew Verb System[4]

The Hebrew verb system develops from only two finite verb forms: perfect and imperfect. Thus, these two forms must be usable in many tenses and moods. The following variations developed.

VERB FORM	NEGATIVE COUNTERPART
qatal (perfect in initial position)	לֹא+*qatal*
yiqtol (imperfect in initial position)	עַל+*yiqtol*
weqatal (*vav*+perfect)	לֹא+*yiqtol*
weyiqtol (*vav*+imperfect)	עַל+*yiqtol*
wayyiqtol (*vav*-consecutive)	וְלֹא+*qatal*
x-qatal (x+perfect[5])	x-לֹא+*qatal*
x-yiqtol (x+imperfect)	x-לֹא+*yiqtol* (x-עַל+*yiqtol* if volitive yiqtol)

Each of the seven variations above have particular uses. Verbal ideas are also carried by the infinitive and the participle.

FORM	USAGE
wayyiqtol	narrative, main-line events
weqatal	(a) narrative: habitual / repeated actions
	(b) direct speech: continues future tense
	(c) exhortation: continuation of exhortation
weyiqtol	(a) volitive in direct speech
	(b) indicates purpose after a cohortative, imperative, or jussive
x-qatal	(a) narrative: background in narrative
	(1) provides setting (antecedent action or condition)when coming before a *wayyiqtol*
	(2) circumstance, contrast, specification, or parenthetical when following a *wayyiqtol*
	(3) emphasis on x, when answering the question 'Who?'
	(b) direct speech: beginning of an oral report
	(c) direct speech: background if it is not the initial statement
x-yiqtol	(a) narrative: repeated action, sub-ordinate to *weqatal*
	(b) direct speech: future tense (sometimes present tense)
	(c) direct speech: continues an exhortation after a volitive, with emphasis on x
Initial *qatal*	direct speech: past tense
Initial *yiqtol*	direct speech: volitive (cohortative, jussive, injunctive)
וַיְהִי	can be either
	1) Macrosyntactic signal of new information, paragraph, or
	2) A true verb, indicating a state, *to be*, or a action, *to happen*.

[4] For further details, see (§26.1). The syntactical outline presented here is based upon Alviero Niccacci, *The Syntax of the Verb in Classical Hebrew Prose* (trans. Wilfred G. E. Watson; JSOTSup, 86; Sheffield: Sheffield Academic Press, 1990), and B.M. Rocine, *Learning Biblical Hebrew: A New Approach Using Discourse Analysis* (Macon, GA: Smyth & Helwys Publishers, 2000).

[5] Where x is any non verbal element except *vav*.

7.5   Directive ה

To indicate direction, Hebrew uses a final הָ , usually called the directive or locative ה. The directive ה is unaccented, and it may change the vocalization of the noun to which it is appended.

Examples of the directive ה:

אֶרֶץ	land	אַרְצָה	toward land/ground (Gen. 33.3)
הָהָר	the mountain	הָהָרָה	toward the mountain (Gen. 19.19)
שָׁם	there	שָׁמָּה	toward there (2 Kgs 17.27)

7.6   Demonstrative Pronoun

The most common forms of the demonstrative 'this' (pl 'these') are:

Singular	'this'	Plural	'these'
m.	זֶה	m. & f.	אֵלֶּה
f.	זֹאת		

The demonstrative takes the definite article according to the same rules as the adjective, e. g. הָאִישׁ הַזֶּה 'this man', and זֶה הָאִישׁ 'this is the man'.

Less common forms include the f.sg. זֹה or זוֹ, the pl אֵל, and זוּ, which is found mostly in the Psalms and can be used of all genders and numbers.

The personal pronouns can also function as demonstratives, e.g.:

הָאִישׁ הַהוּא	that man
בַּיָּמִים הָהֵם	in those days

7.7   The Particles יֵשׁ and אַיִן

The word יֵשׁ (translated *there is*) is known as the particle of existence, and אַיִן (translated *there is not*) is called the particle of nonexistence. These words are needed because the Hebrew word היה (*to be*) is not used in the present tense. For example, in sentences like הַמֶּלֶךְ טוֹב (*The king is good*), the present tense of *to be* is not stated, so it must be supplied in the translation (see 3.1.2.2 and 3.2). In some situations, however, the word יֵשׁ or אַיִן will be used to signify a present state of being. Therefore, יֵשׁ דֶּרֶךְ means *there is a way*, and אַיִן דֶּרֶךְ means *there is not a way*.

7.7.1   Pronominal Suffixes with יֵשׁ and אַיִן

Both יֵשׁ and אַיִן can take the pronominal suffixes: יֶשְׁךָ means *you are*, and אֵינְךָ means *you are not* (suffixes require the construct form of אַיִן which is אֵין.)

7.7.2   Negation of the Participle with אֵין

In addition to the above functions, the particle אֵין is use to negate the participle (the negative particles לֹא and אַל are used only with the perfect and imperfect). Therefore, the phrase אֲנִי שֹׁמֵעַ means *I am listening*, and אֵינֶנִּי שֹׁמֵעַ means *I am not listening* (Isa. 1.15).

7.8   Using the Hebrew Lexicon

Learning to use the Hebrew lexicon is an important skill that must be acquired. Therefore, from this point forward, many of the exercises will ask you to consult the lexicon as part of the assignment.

The words in the lexicon are listed in the order of the Hebrew alphabet. A good lexicon will normally provide the following information about each Hebrew word: part of speech, unusual spellings, word meanings, number of occurrences in the Hebrew Bible, and examples from Scripture. A list of abbreviations will be found at the beginning of the lexicon.

EXERCISE 7-B

Find the following Hebrew words in your Hebrew lexicon. List the page number and the main definitions.

	Page	Definition
נֹכַח		
עָלָה		
חָשַׁךְ		
בָּנָה		
פְּרִי		
שָׁלַח		

7.9   Vocabulary

דָּרַשׁ   *v.* he sought, inquired

כָּרַת   *v.* he cut, cut off

יָרַד   *v.* he went down

נָשָׂא   *v.* he lifted, carried

נָתַן   *v.* he gave

עָשָׂה   *v.* he did, made

שָׁלַח   *v.* he sent

אַחַר   *prep.* after, behind. *Construct* אַחֲרֵי

אִם   *particle,* if

יֵשׁ   *particle of existence.* There is . . .

אַיִן   *particle of nonexistence.* There is not . . . . *Construct* אֵין

בְּרִית   *n.f.* covenant, כָּרַת בְּרִית = He made (lit. cut) a covenant.

יָד   *n.f.* hand. *const. s.* יַד. *const. pl* יְדֵי

לֵב   *n.* heart (*also* לֵבָב). *w. suff.* לִבִּי *pl* לִבּוֹת

נֶפֶשׁ   *n.f.* soul, life. *pl* נְפָשׁוֹת

רֵאשִׁית   *n.f.* beginning.

EXERCISE 7-C

Translate the following sentences.

1.   יהוה יִדְרֹשׁ אֶת יַעֲקֹב וְנָתַן אֵלָיו לֵב חָדָשׁ:

2.   פָּקֹד אֶפְקֹד אֹתָךְ אָמַר אֱלֹהִים וְיָלַדְתְּ בֵּן:

3.   וּבְרֵאשִׁית יָשַׁב אַבְרָהָם⁷ בְּאֶרֶץ־כְּנַעַן⁶ וַיִּכְרֹת בְּרִית עִם יֹשְׁבֵי־הָאָרֶץ:

4.   וּמֹשֶׁה יָרַד מִן הַהַר וַיִּדְרֹשׁ אַחֲרֵי אָחִיו:

5.   וְהָאֲנָשִׁים הָרָעִים נָשְׂאוּ יְדֵיהֶם עַל מֹשֶׁה וַיִּזְכֹּר מֹשֶׁה דְּבַר־יהוה:

6.   יֵשׁ דֶּרֶךְ־חַי אִם תִּדְרְשׁוּ אֹתוֹ:

7.   תִּדְרֹשׁ נַפְשְׁךָ אֶת־יהוה:

8.   וְיַעֲקֹב נָשָׂא אֶת־לְבָבוֹ אֶל־יהוה וַיִּשְׁמֹר דְּבָרָיו:

---

⁶ Canaan

⁷ Abraham

9.   חַיָּה רָעָה אֲכָלָתְהוּ׃ (Gen. 37.33)

10. ⁸וְשָׁאוּל לֹא אָכַל לֶחֶם כָּל־הַיּוֹם׃ (1 Sam. 28.20)

11. וַיִּכְתֹּב מֹשֶׁה אֵת כָּל־דִּבְרֵי יְהוָה׃ (Exod. 24.4)

12. וַיִּמְלֹךְ דָּוִד עַל־כָּל־יִשְׂרָאֵל׃ (2 Sam. 8.15)

13. וַיִּמְלֹךְ שְׁלֹמֹה בִירוּשָׁלַם עַל־כָּל־יִשְׂרָאֵל׃ (2 Chron. 9.30)

14. וַיִּזְכֹּר אֱלֹהִים אֶת־⁹נֹחַ וְאֵת כָּל־הַחַיָּה׃ (Gen. 8.1)

15. וַיִּזְכֹּר אֱלֹהִים אֶת־בְּרִיתוֹ׃ (Exod. 2.24)

16. וְלֹא זָכְרוּ בְּנֵי יִשְׂרָאֵל אֶת־יְהוָה אֱלֹהֵיהֶם׃ (Judg. 8.34)

17. וַיהוָה פָּקַד אֶת־שָׂרָה כַּאֲשֶׁר אָמָר׃ (Gen. 21.1)

18. וַיִּפְקֹד ¹⁰שִׁמְשׁוֹן אֶת־אִשְׁתּוֹ׃ (Judg. 15.1)

19. וּמִן־הָאָרֶץ יָצָא ¹¹אַשּׁוּר׃ (Gen. 10.11)

20. וְהִיא הָלְכָה לִדְרֹשׁ אֶת־יְהוָה׃ (Gen. 25.22)

Torah Scroll from Spain, 400 to 500 year old

---

⁸ Saul. The following sentences come from the Scriptures. Some words will be omitted from the Hebrew text in order to make the translation easier.

⁹ Noah

¹⁰ Samson

¹¹ Asshur

7.10   Parsing Hebrew Verbs

We will use the following chart to do our parsing. Contents of each column are:

- **Hebrew Word** lists the Hebrew word to be parsed.
- **Stem** lists the verb stem, which will be *qal, nifal, hifil, hofal, piel, pual,* or *hitpael.* We have studied only the *qal* stem.
- **State** lists the state of the verb, which will be perfect, imperfect, imperative, participle, infinitive absolute, infinitive construct, cohortative, or jussive. W=*wayyiqtol,* and We=*weqatal.*
- **PGN** gives the person, gender, and number. Person will be 1, 2, or 3. Gender will be masculine or feminine. Number will be singular or plural.
- **Pfx** lists any prefixes that are attached to the verb (this does not include imperfect preformatives). So far, we have studied only the definite article, the prepositions, and the conjunction. Later we will study the interrogative prefix.
- **Sfx** lists any suffixes that are attached to the verb. Suffixes do not include any inflectional afformatives. The only suffixes that we have studied thus far are the volitive ה and the pronominal suffixes.
- **Root** gives the root, which usually consists of three radicals.
- **Translation** is a literal translation of the word in column one.

Examples:

He-brew Word	Stem	State	PGN	Pfx	Sfx	Root	Translation
יִדְרֹשׁ	Q	Imf	3ms	NA	NA	דרשׁ	He will seek
וְנָתַן	Q	Pf We	3ms	וְ	NA	נתן	And he will give
פָּקֹד	Q	IA	NA	NA	NA	פקד	visiting / to visit
אֶפְקֹד	Q	Imf	1cs	NA	NA	פקד	I shall visit
וַיִּכְרֹת	Q	Imf W	3ms	וַ	NA	כרת	And he cut
הַיֹּשְׁבִים	Q	Ptc	mp	הַ	NA	ישׁב	the inhabiting ones or inhabitants

Chapter 8

The *Nifal* Verb

In this chapter you should learn:

- The meaning of the *nifal* pattern
- The forms of the *nifal* pattern
- The preposition מִן

> The *nifal* pattern is passive/middle voice.

8.1   The meaning of the *Nifal* pattern

At one time, Hebrew had a *qal* passive form, the remnant of which is the *qal* passive participle. Biblical Hebrew, however, depends upon the *nifal* pattern to express the passive of the *qal*. If the *qal* says, *he buried*, the *nifal* would signify, *he was buried*. If the *qal* says, *he will abandon*, the *nifal* would be, *he will be abandoned*. However, the passive force of *nifal* is not always translated into the receptor language (e.g. the *nifal* of פָּתַח can mean *it opened*, rather than *it was opened*). Normally, verbs will not be found in all verb stems. For example, the verb שׁבע is found in the *nifal* (*to swear*) but not in the *qal*). The different verb patterns were used to create an expanded vocabulary, based on a limited number of verbal roots. With some verbal roots, the *nifal* is reflexive/middle voice. The meaning of *nifal* verbs must be determined on a case by case basis by consulting the Hebrew lexicon.

8.2   The forms of the *Nifal* pattern

8.2.1   The *Nifal* Perfect

The *nifal* perfect (Hebrew נִפְעַל) is characterized by a prefixed נ with the vowel *chireq* (HVS 5A).

Nifal perfect of שָׁמַר: *to keep*

	Singular			Plural	
1c	נִשְׁמַרְתִּי	I was kept	1c	נִשְׁמַרְנוּ	We were kept
2m	נִשְׁמַרְתָּ	You were kept	2m	נִשְׁמַרְתֶּם	You were kept
2f	נִשְׁמַרְתְּ	You were kept	2f	נִשְׁמַרְתֶּן	You were kept
3m	נִשְׁמַר	He was kept	3c	נִשְׁמְרוּ	They were kept
3f	נִשְׁמְרָה	She was kept			

The appendix to this chapter contains a complete paradigm chart with comparisons to the *qal* stem.

There is but a small difference between the forms of the *qal* and *nifal*. The follow-ing comparison holds true for the entire paradigm of the perfect.

Qal   שָׁמַרְתִּי   +   ָ   =   שָׁמַרְתִּי

Nifal   נִשְׁמַרְתִּי   +   נִ   =   שָׁמַרְתִּי

Examples of the *nifal* perfect in sentences:

התּוֹרוֹת נִכְתְּבוּ   The laws were written.

הַדָּבָר נִזְכַּר   The word was remembered.

EXERCISE 8-A

Translate the following: (You may need to consult the biblical context).

1. וְרַבִּים דְּבָרִים נִזְכְּרוּ ¹הַיּוֹם:

2. וְנַפְשׁוֹ נִלְקְחָה אֶל אֱלֹהִים:

3. וּבַת־הַמֶּלֶךְ נִשְׁלְחָה אֶל הַהֵיכָל:

4. תּוֹרַת אֱלֹהִים לֹא נִשְׁמְרָה בִּימֵי־אֲבוֹתֵכֶם:

5. וְנִזְכַּרְתֶּם לִפְנֵי יְהוָה אֱלֹהֵיכֶם: (Num. 10.9)

6. ²וַאֲרוֹן אֱלֹהִים נִלְקָח: (1 Sam. 4.11)

7. ³נִלְכְּדָה הָעִיר: (1 Kgs 16.18)

8.2.2   The *Nifal* Imperfect

The imperfect of the *nifal* assimilates the prefixed נ into the first root letter. This assimilation is indicated by a *dagesh forte* compensative. Thus, the *nifal* imperfect is characterized by the *dagesh forte* in the first root letter and the *qamets* underneath the same letter. Additionally, the vowel of the second letter changes from *cholem* to *tsere* (HVS 5A & 6A).

The form ינזכר becomes יזכר

---

[1] Idiom meaning *today*.

[2] The word אֲרוֹן means *ark*.

[3] Find לכד in your lexicon. The same verb will be used later in this chapter. Learning to use the Hebrew lexicon is an important skill that must be acquired. Therefore, from this point forward, many of the exercises will ask you to consult the lexicon as part of the assignment.

Compare the following examples of *qal* imperfect and *nifal* imperfect.

Qal	נִשְׁמֹר	We shall keep.
Nifal	נִשָּׁמֵר	We shall be kept

> The *nifal* imperfect will have *dagesh forte* in the first radical.

Nifal imperfect of שָׁמַר *to keep*

	Singular			Plural	
1c	אֶשָּׁמֵר	I shall be kept	1c	נִשָּׁמֵר	We shall be kept
2m	תִּשָּׁמֵר	You will be kept	2m	תִּשָּׁמְרוּ	You will be kept
2f	תִּשָּׁמְרִי	You will be kept	2f	תִּשָּׁמַרְנָה	You will be kept
3m	יִשָּׁמֵר	He will be kept	3m	יִשָּׁמְרוּ	They will be kept
3f	תִּשָּׁמֵר	She will be kept	3f	תִּשָּׁמַרְנָה	They will be kept

Examples of the *nifal* imperfect:

אֶנָּתֵן לַיהֹוָה	Let me be given to the Lord.
הַדְּבָרִים יִשָּׁמְרוּ ⁴בְּלִבָּהּ	The words will be kept in her heart.

EXERCISE 8-B

Translate the following:

1. אַתֶּן תִּזָּכַרְנָה בְּבֵית הַמֶּלֶךְ:

2. אֲנַחְנוּ נִנָּתֵן אֶת־חַיִּים מִן־רוּחַ־יהוה:

3. וְהִנֵּה רָחֵל תִּפָּקֵד בַּדֶּרֶךְ בְּאִישׁ מִן־אֱלֹהִים:

4. וּמֶלֶךְ רָע לֹא־יִזָּכֵר:

5. וּבְכֹל אֲשֶׁר־אָמַרְתִּי אֲלֵיכֶם תִּשָּׁמֵרוּ: (Exod. 23.13)

6. מִן־כֹּל אֲשֶׁר־אָמַרְתִּי אֶל־הָאִשָּׁה תִּשָּׁמֵר: (Judg. 13.13)

7. וְלֹא־יִכָּרֵת לְךָ אִישׁ מִן־לְפָנַי יֹשֵׁב עַל־כִּסֵּא יִשְׂרָאֵל: (1 Kgs 8.25)

8. וּרְשָׁעִים מִן־הָאָרֶץ יִכָּרֵתוּ: (Prov. 2.22)

9. וְאִישׁ עִם־אִשָּׁה יִלָּכֵדוּ: (Jer. 6.11)

---

⁴ Remember that the dot in the pronomial suffix is a *mappiq*, indicating that the ה is a consonant, not a vowel letter (see §1.8.2).

8.2.3   The *Nifal* Imperative

For unknown reasons, the *nifal* imperative has a הַ prefix. The form of the imperative, therefore, is identical to the imperfect, except that the הַ replaces the preformative תַ.

Nifal Imperfect		*Nifal* Imperative	
תִּשָּׁמֵר	You will be kept.	הִשָּׁמֵר	Be kept

Nifal imperative of שָׁמַר: *to keep*

	Singular			Plural	
2m	הִשָּׁמֵר	Be kept	2m	הִשָּׁמְרוּ	Be kept
2f	הִשָּׁמְרִי	Be kept	2f	הִשָּׁמַרְנָה	Be kept

Examples of the imperative:

הִנָּשֵׂא יהוה	Be lifted up Lord!
הִשָּׁמְרוּ מִן הָאִישׁ הָרָשָׁע	Beware of the wicked man. (Literally, be guarded from . . .)

The *nifal* imperative occurs about 110 times in the Hebrew Bible. Almost all of these are reflexive rather than passive. The second example above illustrates the reflexive usage that is predominant with the *nifal* imperative: *guard yourselves*.

EXERCISE 8-C

Translate the following sentences:

1. הִשָּׁמֶר לְךָ וּשְׁמֹר נַפְשְׁךָ (Deut. 4.9):

2. הִשָּׁמְרוּ לָכֶם וְזִכְרוּ אֶת־בְּרִית יְהוָה אֱלֹהֵיכֶם אֲשֶׁר כָּרַת עִמָּכֶם: (Deut. 4.23)

3. הִנָּשֵׂא שֹׁפֵט הָאָרֶץ (Ps. 94.2):

8.2.4   The *Nifal* Participle

The *nifal* participle has the prefixed נ, just as the *nifal* perfect.

Nifal Participle of שָׁמַר: *to keep*

	singular			plural	
m	נִשְׁמָר	being kept	m	נִשְׁמָרִים	being kept
f	נִשְׁמֶרֶת	being kept	F	נִשְׁמָרוֹת	being kept

The *nifal* masculine singular participle is *almost* identical to the *nifal* perfect, third masculine singular. The participle has a *qamets* in the second syllable, but the perfect has *patach*.

Perfect		Participle	
נִשְׁמַר	he was kept	נִשְׁמָר	being kept

Examples of the *nifal* participle:

הָאֲנָשִׁים נִפְקָדִים   The men are being visited.

הַדָּבָר נִשְׁמָר בַּכֹּהֵן   The word is being kept by the priest.

8.2.5   The *Nifal* Infinitive

The *nifal* infinitives alternate between the נ prefix and the ה prefix. The infinitive absolute of שמר is either נִשְׁמֹר or הִשָּׁמֵר. The infinitive construct is הִשָּׁמֵר. (Note: Remember that the *dagesh forte* is found only when the נ assimilates.)

Examples of the infinitive construct and infinitive absolute, respectively:

דָּוִד עָלָה לְהִנָּתֵן לַיהוָה: David went up to be given to Yahweh.

נִשְׁמֹר יִשָּׁמֵר דְּבַר־יהוה: The word of Yahweh will surely be kept.

8.3   Principal Parts of the *Nifal*

We have now surveyed the verb forms of the *qal* and *nifal* stems. The Principal Parts must be memorized thoroughly. You should practice until you are able to write and recite them easily.

Principle Parts of the *Qal* and *Nifal* stems

Qal	**Nifal**	
קָטַל	נִקְטַל	Perfect
יִקְטֹל	יִקָּטֵל	Imperfect
קְטֹל	הִקָּטֵל	Imperative
קָטוֹל	הִקָּטֵל	Infinitive Absolute
קְטֹל	הִקָּטֵל	Infinitive Construct
קוֹטֵל	נִקְטָל	Participle

8.4   The Preposition מִן

8.4.1   Forms of the Preposition מִן

The preposition מִן (*from*) appears in two forms:

8.4.1.1 Connected to the following noun by maqqef.

מִן־הָאֲדָמָה from the ground (Gen. 4.10)
מִן־הַשָּׁמַיִם from heaven (Gen. 8.2)

8.4.1.2 As a prefix with the ן *assimilated*

a. Before a strong radical (excluding gutturals, which normall do not accept the *dagesh*) a *dagesh forte* comes in the letter following the preposition.

מִן־יָדְךָ from your hand   מִיָּדְךָ from your hand (Gen. 4.11)
מִן־צִידֹן from Sidon   מִצִּידֹן from Sidon (Gen. 10.19)

b. Before gutturals and ר it is usually מֵ (compensatory lengthening).
מֵאֶרֶץ כְּנַעַן from the land of Canaan (Exo. 6.26)
מֵהָאָרֶץ from the land (1 Sam. 28.3)

c. Before nouns beginning with י the מִי contracts to מִי.
מִיהוּדָה from Judah (Gen. 49.10)
מִירוּשָׁלַיִם from Jerusalem (Est. 2.6)

8.4.1.3 Extended form of מִן

The preposition מִן also occurs some 30 times in the extended form מִנִּי. With the pronominal suffixes it can be מִמֶּנּ, or מִמְ, so that *from me* is מִמֶּנִּי, *from you* is מִמְּךָ, etc. See the appendix to this chapter (§8.6.1) for the complete declension of מִן with the pronominal suffixes.

8.4.2   Comparative and Superlative Degrees of the Adjective

In English, the comparative degree is formed by adding the suffix '–er' and the superlative is formed by adding the suffix '-est'. (e.g. *slow, slower, slowest*). In addition, some adjectives have developed entirely different words to indicate the degrees (e.g. *good, better, best*). The preposition מִן can be used with an adjective to express the comparative and superlative degrees. For example:

גִּבְעוֹן גְּדוֹלָה מִן־הָעַי   Gibeah was greater than Ai (Josh. 10.2).

אִיּוֹב גָּדוֹל מִכָּל־בְּנֵי־קֶדֶם   Job was the greatest of all the sons of the east (Job 1.3).

The superlative degree can also be expressed by other means, including the construct state and the definite article.[5] For example:

קֹדֶשׁ קָדָשִׁים   *holy of holies=most holy* (Lev. 2.3)

הַקָּטֹן   *the small one=the youngest* (Gen. 42.13)

8.4.3   Causal Function of the Preposition מִן

The preposition מִן can signify cause or reason. For example:

מִקּוֹל הַקֹּרֵא   because of the voice of the one crying out (Isa. 6.4)

8.5   Vocabulary

קָרָא   *v.* he called

רָאָה   *v.* he saw

שָׁמַע   *v.* he heard

שָׁפַט   *v.* he judged

הָיָה   *v.* he was

שָׁם   *particle.* there

עֶבֶד   *n.m.* servant. *pl* עֲבָדִים

עִיר   *n.f.* city, *pl* עָרִים

עַם   *n.m.* people, *pl* עַמִּים

קוֹל   *n.m.* voice

בָּשָׂר   *n.m.* flesh

נָבִיא   *n.m.* prophet

פֶּה   *n.m.* mouth. *Construct* פִּי

---

[5] See also Gesenius, *Grammar*, §133 and Waltke, *Hebrew Syntax*, §§14.4-5

שֵׁם   *n.m.* name. *pl* שֵׁמוֹת

זֶה   *prn.m.* this. *f.* זֹאת. *pl m.*, *f.* אֵלֶּה these

עוֹד   *adv.* again

כִּי־אִם   *conj. Combined, these two words mean* nevertheless, truly, except, *or* rather

EXERCISE 8-D

Part 1: Translate the following (Use an English translation to help with names and context):

1. וְלֹא־יִקָּרֵא עוֹד אֶת־שִׁמְךָ אַבְרָם וְהָיָה שִׁמְךָ אַבְרָהָם: (Gen. 17.5)

2. וַיֹּאמֶר אֱלֹהִים אֶל־אַבְרָהָם בְּיִצְחָק יִקָּרֵא לְךָ ⁶זֶרַע: (Gen. 21.12)⁷

3. וַיֹּאמֶר־לוֹ אֱלֹהִים שִׁמְךָ יַעֲקֹב לֹא־יִקָּרֵא שִׁמְךָ עוֹד יַעֲקֹב כִּי־אִם וְהָיָה שִׁמְךָ יִשְׂרָאֵל: (Gen. 35.10)

4. וַיֹּאמֶר הִנֵּה אָנֹכִי כֹּרֵת בְּרִית: (Exod. 34.10)

5. וַיִּלָּכֵד יוֹנָתָן וְשָׁאוּל וְהָעָם יָצָאוּ: (1 Sam. 14.41)

6. וַיִּקְרָא לָהּ יַד אַבְשָׁלֹם עַד הַיּוֹם הַזֶּה: (2 Sam. 18.18)

7. ⁸נִשְׁבְּרוּ לִפְנֵי־יְהוָה: (2 Chron. 14.12, Eng. is v. 13)

8. וּמִבְּנֵי הַכֹּהֲנִים בְּנֵי חֳבַיָּה בְּנֵי הַקּוֹץ בְּנֵי בַרְזִלַּי אֲשֶׁר לָקַח מִן־בְּנוֹת בַּרְזִלַּי הַגִּלְעָדִי אִשָּׁה וַיִּקָּרֵא עַל־שְׁמָם: (Ezra 2.61)

9. יִקָּרֵא שִׁמְךָ עָלֵינוּ: (Isa. 4.1)

10. אֱלֹהֵי כָל־הָאָרֶץ יִקָּרֵא: (Isa. 54.5)

11. וְאַתֶּם כֹּהֲנֵי יְהוָה תִּקָּרֵאוּ: (Isa. 61.6)

12. וַיִּקְרָא שְׁמָהּ ⁹בָּמָה עַד הַיּוֹם הַזֶּה: (Ezek. 20.29)

---

⁶ Find this word in your lexicon.

⁷ A very common verb form meaning *and he said* (parsed as *wayyiqtol* 3ms from אמר).

⁸ Find the verb שבר in your lexicon.

⁹ Proper noun, *Bamah*.

Part 2: Parse the following words (*qal* and *nifal* stems). You might want to review §7.9.

Hebrew Word	Stem	State	PGN	Pfx	Sfx	Root	Translation
הָלַכְנוּ							
נִשְׁפַּטְתָּ							
יָרַד							
תִּזָּכְרוּ							
יִכָּרֵת							

8.6   Appendix to Chapter 8

8.6.1   Preposition מִן with Pronominal Suffixes.

	Singular				Plural	
1c	מִמֶּנִּי	from me		1c	מִמֶּנּוּ	from us
2m	מִמְּךָ	from you		2m	מִכֶּם	from you
2f	מִמֵּךְ	from you		2f	מִכֶּן	from you
3m	מִמֶּנּוּ	from him		3m	מֵהֶם	from them
3f	מִמֶּנָּה	from her		3f	מֵהֶן / מֵהֵנָּה	from them

Yad Vashem Holocaust Memorial
Jerusalem

8.6.2 Comparison of *Qal* and *Nifal* Stems

		Qal	*Nifal*
Perf	1cs	קָטַלְתִּי	נִקְטַלְתִּי
	2ms	קָטַלְתָּ	נִקְטַלְתָּ
	2fs	קָטַלְתְּ	נִקְטַלְתְּ
	3ms	קָטַל	נִקְטַל
	3fs	קָטְלָה	נִקְטְלָה
	1cp	קָטַלְנוּ	נִקְטַלְנוּ
	2mp	קְטַלְתֶּם	נִקְטַלְתֶּם
	2fp	קְטַלְתֶּן	נִקְטַלְתֶּן
	3cp	קָטְלוּ	נִקְטְלוּ
Imf	1cs	אֶקְטֹל	אֶקָּטֵל
	2ms	תִּקְטֹל	תִּקָּטֵל
	2fs	תִּקְטְלִי	תִּקָּטְלִי
	3ms	יִקְטֹל	יִקָּטֵל
	3fs	תִּקְטֹל	תִּקָּטֵל
	1cp	נִקְטֹל	נִקָּטֵל
	2mp	תִּקְטְלוּ	תִּקָּטְלוּ
	2fp	תִּקְטֹלְנָה	תִּקָּטַלְנָה
	3mp	יִקְטְלוּ	יִקָּטְלוּ
	3fp	תִּקְטֹלְנָה	תִּקָּטַלְנָה
Imv	2ms	קְטֹל	הִקָּטֵל
	2fs	קִטְלִי	הִקָּטְלִי
	2mp	קִטְלוּ	הִקָּטְלוּ
	2fp	קְטֹלְנָה	הִקָּטַלְנָה
Infin	Abs	קָטוֹל	הִקָּטֵל
			נִקְטֹל
	Cs	קְטֹל	הִקָּטֵל
Ptc	Act	קוֹטֵל	
	Pass	קָטוּל	נִקְטָל
W		וַיִּקְטֹל	וַיִּקָּטֵל

Chapter 9

The *Hifil* Verb

In this chapter you should learn:

- The meaning of the *hifil* pattern
- The forms of the *hifil* pattern
- The meaning of the *hofal* pattern
- The forms of the *hofal* pattern

9.1   The Meaning of the *Hifil* Pattern

The *hifil* is usually designated as *active causative*. This category of verb form does not exist in English. Because of the causative nature of the *hifil* verb, it will often require a double object. In the sentence *God caused the people to eat manna*, the subject is *God*, and both *people* and *manna* are objects. Observe the following list of comparisons between verbs in the *qal*, *nifal*, and *hifil*:

ROOT	*Qal*	*Nifal*	*Hifil*
אָכַל	he ate	he was eaten	he caused to eat = he fed
שָׁמַר	he kept	he was kept	he caused to keep
קָטַל	he killed	he was killed	he caused to kill
אָזַב	he girded	he was girded	he caused to gird
עָזַב	he left	he was left	he caused to leave
קָבַר	he buried	he was buried	he caused to bury
יָצָא	he went out	N/A	he caused to go out = he brought out
בּוֹא	he came	N/A	he caused to come = he brought
גָּדַל	he was great	N/A	he caused to be great = he exalted

9.2   The Forms of the *Hifil* Pattern

> Only the *Hifil* has an infixed י.

9.2.1   The *Hifil* Perfect

The *hifil* perfect (Hebrew הִפְעִיל) is characterized by a prefixed ה and an infixed י in the 3rd person singular and plural. *Only hifil verbs have this infix.*

Hifil perfect of שָׁמַר: *to keep*

	Singular			Plural	
1c	הִשְׁמַרְתִּי	I caused to keep	1c	הִשְׁמַרְנוּ	We caused to keep
2m	הִשְׁמַרְתָּ	You caused to keep	2m	הִשְׁמַרְתֶּם	You caused to keep
2f	הִשְׁמַרְתְּ	You caused to keep	2f	הִשְׁמַרְתֶּן	You caused to keep
3m	הִשְׁמִיר	He caused to keep	3c	הִשְׁמִירוּ	They caused to keep
3f	הִשְׁמִירָה	She caused to keep			

There is but a small difference between the *qal* and *hifil*. The following comparison holds true for the entire paradigm of the perfect, except for the third person, which has an infixed י (HVS 5A & 9A).

$$\textit{Qal} \qquad שָׁמַרְתִּי \;=\; \fbox{$\,$} \;+\; שָׁמַרְתִּי$$

$$\textit{Hifil} \qquad הִשְׁמַרְתִּי \;=\; \fbox{$ה$} \;+\; שָׁמַרְתִּי$$

EXERCISE 9-A

Translate the following (Use your English Bible for contextual clues in translating the biblical exerpts).

1. הִמְלַכְתָּ אֶת־עַבְדְּךָ אַחַר דָּוִד אָבִי:

2. הִנֵּה הַנְּבִיאִים הִשְׁמִיעוּ אֶת־הָעָם אֶת קוֹל יהוה:

3. שְׁמוּאֵל הִכְתִּיב אָבִיו אֶת דְּבַר אֱלֹהִים:

4. הִפְקִיד[1] אֹתוֹ בְּבֵיתוֹ וְעַל כָּל־אֲשֶׁר יֶשׁ־לוֹ: (Gen. 39.5)

9.2.2   The *Hifil* Imperfect

The imperfect of the *hifil* assimilates the prefixed ה, and all forms have the infixed י except for the second and third feminine plural. The *hifil* imperfect may be identified further by the *patach* under the preformative (HVS 4C & 9A).

Compare the following examples of *qal* imperfect and *hifil* imperfect:

Qal	נִשְׁמֹר	We shall keep.
Hifil	נַשְׁמִיר	We shall cause to keep

---

[1] Consult the lexicon for the meaning of this verb in *hifil*.

Hifil Imperfect of שָׁמַר: *to keep*

	Singular			Plural	
1c	אַשְׁמִיר	I shall cause to keep	1c	נַשְׁמִיר	We shall cause to keep
2m	תַּשְׁמִיר	You will cause to keep	2m	תַּשְׁמִירוּ	You will cause to keep
2f	תַּשְׁמִירִי	You will cause to keep	2f	תַּשְׁמֵרְנָה	You will cause to keep
3m	יַשְׁמִיר	He will cause to keep	3m	יַשְׁמִירוּ	They will cause to keep
3f	תַּשְׁמִיר	She will cause to keep	3f	תַּשְׁמֵרְנָה	They will cause to keep

9.2.3   The *Hifil* Jussive and Wayyiqtol

The jussive is easy to identify in the *hifil*, because it is a shortened form of the imperfect. The *vav* consecutive also shortens the imperfect. In both the jussive and *wayyiqtol* the *chireq yod* is changed to *tsere*. For example:

Imperfect	יַשְׁמִיר	he will cause to keep	
Jussive	יַשְׁמֵר	let him cause to keep	
wayyiqtol	וַיַּשְׁמֵר	and he caused to keep	

> The *hifil* imperfect has infixed י.

EXERCISE 9-B

Translate the following (Use your English Bible for contextual clues in translating the biblical exerpts).

1. הִנֵּה שָׁמַעְתִּי אֶת קוֹלְכֶם לְכֹל אֲשֶׁר אֲמַרְתֶּם וָאַמְלִךְ עֲלֵיכֶם מֶלֶךְ:

2. הַכֹּהֲנִים יַשְׁמִיעוּ אֶתְכֶם אֶת־הַתּוֹרָה מִפִּי־יהוה:

3. מֹשֶׁה אָמַר אַדְרִישׁ אֶת־נַפְשִׁי אֶת־אֱלֹהִים:

4. אַזְכִּירָה שִׁמְךָ בְּכָל־דֹּר:[2]   (Ps. 45.18 [17 Engl.])

5. וַיַּמְלֵךְ אֶת־שְׁלֹמֹה בְנוֹ עַל־יִשְׂרָאֵל: (1Chron. 23.1)

9.2.4   The *Hifil* Imperative

The *hifil* imperative is almost identical to the *hifil* imperfect, except that the ה replaces the preformative ת. Also, the second masculine singular has a *tsere* instead of a *chireq yod*.

Hifil Imperfect	**Hifil** Imperative
תַּשְׁמִיר You will cause to keep.	הַשְׁמֵר Cause to keep!

---

[2] Find this word in your lexicon.

Hifil Imperative of שָׁמַר: *to keep*

	Singular			Plural	
2m	הַשְׁמֵר	cause to keep	2m	הַשְׁמִירוּ	cause to keep
2f	הַשְׁמִירִי	cause to keep	2f	הַשְׁמֵרְנָה	cause to keep

9.2.5   The *Hifil* Participle

The *hifil* participle has the prefixed מַ which makes it very distinctive and easy to identify (HVS 5B).

Hifil Participle of שָׁמַר: *to keep*

	singular			plural	
m	מַשְׁמִיר	causing to keep	m	מַשְׁמִירִים	causing to keep
f	מַשְׁמֶרֶת	causing to keep	f	מַשְׁמִירוֹת	causing to keep

9.2.6   The *Hifil* Infinitives

The *hifil* infinitive absolute is הַשְׁמֵר, which is identical to the imperative m.s.. The context will determine if it is the infinitive or the imperative. The infinitive construct is הַשְׁמִיר.

בָּאתָ אֵלַי לְהַזְכִּיר אֶת־עֲוֹנִי וּלְהָמִית אֶת־בְּנִי   1 Kgs 17.18

Did you come to me **to bring to remembrance** my sin and **to put to death** my son?

EXERCISE 9-C

Translate the following (Use your English Bible for contextual clues in translating the biblical excerpts).

1. הַזְכִּירִי[3] אֶת־לִבֵּךְ דִּבְרֵי־הַתּוֹרָה:

2. הַעֲבֵר[4] אֶת־הָעָם הַנָּהָר הַזֶּה:

3. הָאֲנָשִׁים מַעֲמִידִים אֶת־הַנָּבִיא הָרַע לִפְנֵי הָעָם:

4. אֲנִי מַזְכִּיר אֶת־בָּתַּי אֶת־קוֹל־יהוה:

5. אֶת־חֲטָאַי[5] אֲנִי מַזְכִּיר הַיּוֹם: (Gen. 41.9)

6. הַשֹּׁפֵט יַשְׁפִּיט אֱלֹהִים אֶת־רוּחוֹ כָּל בָּשָׂר שָׁם:

7. יַעֲקֹב יָרַד הֵיכָלָה לְהַקְרִיא אֶת־לִבּוֹ אֶל יהוה:

---

[3] Consult the lexicon for the meaning of this verb in *hifil*.

[4] Remember that a guttural letter takes a composite *sheva* instead of simple *sheva*.

[5] Find this noun in your lexicon.

9.3   The Meaning of the *Hofal* Pattern

The *hofal* is the passive counterpart to the *hifil*. The *hofal* does not occur very often. In the Bible, only .6% of verb forms are *hofal*, while the *hifil* accounts for 13.1%. Thus, only six of every thousand verb forms will be *hofal*. Using the same verbs as before, the *hofal* can be illustrated as follows:

ROOT	*Qal*	*Hifil*	*Hofal*
אָכַל	he ate	he fed	he was fed
שָׁמַר	he kept	he caused to keep	he was caused to keep
קָטַל	he killed	he caused to kill	he was caused to kill
אָזַב	he girded	he caused to gird	he was caused to gird
עָזַב	he left	he caused to leave	he was caused to leave
קָבַר	he buried	he caused to bury	he was caused to bury
יָצָא	he went out	he brought out	he was brought out
בּוֹא	he came	he brought	he was brought
גָּדֵל	he was great	he exalted	he was exalted

9.4   The Forms of the *Hofal* Pattern

9.4.1   The Hofal Perfect

The *hofal* perfect (Hebrew הֻפְעַל) is characterized by a prefixed הֻ (HVS 5A). Note that the *qamets* is *qamets chatuf* (short *o*). Observe this comparison between *qal* perfect and *hofal* perfect:

Qal	שָׁמַרְתִּי	=	ָ +	שָׁמַרְתִּי	
Hofal	הֻשְׁמַרְתִּי	=	הֻ +	שָׁמַרְתִּי	

> The *hofal* perfect is prefixed with הֻ.

The *Hofal* Perfect of שָׁמַר: *To Keep*

	Singular			Plural	
1c	הֻשְׁמַרְתִּי	I was caused to keep	1c	הֻשְׁמַרְנוּ	We were caused to keep
2m	הֻשְׁמַרְתָּ	You were caused to keep	2m	הֻשְׁמַרְתֶּם	You were caused to keep
2f	הֻשְׁמַרְתְּ	You were caused to keep	2f	הֻשְׁמַרְתֶּן	You were caused to keep
3m	הֻשְׁמַר	He was caused to keep	3c	הֻשְׁמְרוּ	They were caused to keep
3f	הֻשְׁמְרָה	She was caused to keep			

9.4.2   The Hofal Imperfect

The imperfect of the *hofal* assimilates the prefixed ה, and the *qamets* remains under the preformative. The middle radical will have *patach* (like the perfect).

Hofal Imperfect of שָׁמַר: *to keep*

	Singular			Plural	
1c	אָשְׁמַר	I shall be caused to keep	1c	נָשְׁמַר	We shall be caused to keep
2m	תָּשְׁמַר	You will be caused to keep	2m	תָּשְׁמְרוּ	You will be caused to keep
2f	תָּשְׁמְרִי	You will be caused to keep	2f	תָּשְׁמַרְנָה	You will be caused to keep
3m	יָשְׁמַר	He will be caused to keep	3m	יָשְׁמְרוּ	They will be caused to keep
3f	תָּשְׁמַר	She will be caused to keep	3f	תָּשְׁמַרְנָה	They will be caused to keep

9.4.3   The Hofal Imperative

There is no *hofal* imperative in the Hebrew Bible.

> The *hofal* imperfect has *qamets* under the preformative.

9.4.4   The Hofal Participle

The *hofal* participle is characterized by a prefixed מָ (HVS 5B).

Hofal Participle of שָׁמַר: *to keep*

	Singular			plural	
m	מָשְׁמָר	being caused to keep	m	מָשְׁמָרִים	being caused to keep
f	מָשְׁמֶרֶת	being caused to keep	f	מָשְׁמָרוֹת	being caused to keep

9.4.5   The Hofal Infinitives

The *hofal* infinitive absolute is הָשְׁמֵר, and there is no *hofal* infinitive construct.

9.5   Principal Parts of the Verb

We have now surveyed the verb forms of the *qal, nifal, hifil,* and *hofal* stems. The Principal Parts must be memorized thoroughly. You should practice until you are able to write and recite them easily.

PRINCIPAL PARTS

Qal	*Nifal*	*Hifil*	*Hofal*	
קָטַל	נִקְטַל	הִקְטִיל	הָקְטַל	Perfect
יִקְטֹל	יִקָּטֵל	יַקְטִיל	יָקְטַל	Imperfect
קְטֹל	הִקָּטֵל	הַקְטֵל		Imperative
קָטוֹל	הִקָּטֹל	הַקְטֵל	הָקְטֵל	Infinitive Absolute
קְטֹל	הִקָּטֵל	הַקְטִיל		Infinitive Construct
קוֹטֵל	נִקְטָל	מַקְטִיל	מָקְטָל	Participle

EXERCISE 9-D

Parse the following verbs in *hifil* and *hofal*:

Hebrew Word	Stem	State	PGN	Pfx	Sfx	Root	Translation
מַכְתִּיב							
יָשְׁפַּט							
וַיִּשָּׁמֶר							
הִמְלִיכוּ							
תַּשְׁמִירוּ							
הָשְׁמְרוּ							

9.6   Accent Marks and Pausal Forms

As stated earlier (§2.1.5) every word in the Hebrew text will have an accent mark that indicates which syllable should be stressed. The Hebrew Bible utilizes 48 different accent marks, which function as stress markers, punctuation signals, and cantillation signs. These accent marks are not commonly used outside the Bible text itself (For further explanation of the accent marks, see §9.6 and §28.1).

In words that carry a strong accent, a short vowel may be lengthened. Lengthened vowels are said to be *in pause*. Pausal forms are most common on the last word or middle word in a verse. Note the following examples:

מַיִם is lengthened to מָיִם in Gen. 1.2

בָּחֲרוּ is lengthened to בָּחָרוּ in Gen. 6.2

9.7   Vocabulary

נָפַל   *v.* he fell

סָפַר   *v.* he counted, wrote

קָבַץ   *v.* he gathered

שָׁכַב   *v.* he lay down

שָׁפַךְ   *v.* he poured out

חֶסֶד   *n.m.* covenant loyalty, favor

מַיִם   *n.m.* water, *const.* מֵי

יָם   *n.m.* sea, *pl* יַמִּים

עוֹלָם   *n.m.* eternity

קֶרֶב   *n.m.* inside, nearness

יֶלֶד   *n.m.* child, boy, *f.* girl = יַלְדָּה

שְׁנֵי   *adj.* two

שָׁלֹשׁ   *adj.* three

אַחֵר   *adj.* other

כֵּן   *adv.* so, thus

בֵּין   *prep.* between. Like other prep., בֵּין takes pron. suffixes. For example, בֵּינִי = between me; בֵּינְךָ = between you.

תַּחַת   *prep.* under, instead of. With suffix: תַּחְתֶּיהָ = instead of her.

EXERCISE 9-E

Translate the following sentences from the Bible (Use an English translation to help with names and context).

1. וַיֹּאמֶר מֹשֶׁה זֶה הַדָּבָר אֲשֶׁר אָמַר יְהוָה: (Exod. 16.32)

2. וּבְכֹל אֲשֶׁר־אָמַרְתִּי אֲלֵיכֶם תִּשָּׁמֵרוּ וְשֵׁם אֱלֹהִים אֲחֵרִים לֹא [6]תַזְכִּירוּ: (Exod. 23.13)

3. וְיִשְׁמְעוּ [8]הַכְּנַעֲנִי וְכֹל יֹשְׁבֵי הָאָרֶץ [7]וְהִכְרִיתוּ אֶת־שְׁמֵנוּ מִן־הָאָרֶץ: (Josh. 7.9)

4. יַד בְּנֵי־יִשְׂרָאֵל הָיָה עַל יָבִין מֶלֶךְ־כְּנָעַן עַד אֲשֶׁר הִכְרִיתוּ אֵת יָבִין מֶלֶךְ־כְּנָעַן: (Judg. 4.24)

5. וַיֹּאמֶר יְהוָה אֶל־שְׁמוּאֵל [9]שְׁמַע בְּקוֹלָם וְהִמְלַכְתָּ לָהֶם מֶלֶךְ: (1 Sam. 8.22)

6. כָּל־הָעָם הָלַךְ הַגִּלְגָּל וַיַּמְלִכוּ שָׁם אֶת־שָׁאוּל לִפְנֵי יְהוָה בַּגִּלְגָּל (1 Sam. 11.15)

7. וַיֹּאמֶר שְׁמוּאֵל אֶל־כָּל־יִשְׂרָאֵל הִנֵּה שָׁמַעְתִּי בְקֹלְכֶם לְכֹל אֲשֶׁר־אֲמַרְתֶּם לִי וָאַמְלִיךְ עֲלֵיכֶם מֶלֶךְ: (1 Sam. 12.1)

---

[6] Consult the lexicon for possible meanings of this verb in *hifil*.

[7] Consult the lexicon for the meaning of this verb in *hifil*.

[8] There are quite a few proper names in these exercises. English translations will help.

[9] שְׁמַע is *Qal* imv. The *patach* is found in verbs that end with a guttural letter. See Chapter 18.

8. וְלֹא־תַכְרִת אֶת־חַסְדְּךָ ¹⁰מֵעִם בֵּיתִי עַד־עוֹלָם (1 Sam. 20.15)

9. הִנֵּה אַתָּה יָדַעְתָּ אֵת אֲשֶׁר־עָשָׂה שָׁאוּל: (1 Sam. 28.9)

10. אֲדֹנֵינוּ הַמֶּלֶךְ־דָּוִד הִמְלִיךְ אֶת־שְׁלֹמֹה: (1 Kgs 1.43)

11. וְעַתָּה יְהוָה אֱלֹהַי אַתָּה הִמְלַכְתָּ אֶת־עַבְדְּךָ תַּחַת דָּוִד אָבִי: (1 Kgs 3.7)

12. וְהִכְרַתִּי אֶת־יִשְׂרָאֵל מֵעַל פְּנֵי הָאֲדָמָה: (1 Kgs 9.7)

13. וַיַּמְלִכוּ¹¹ אֹתוֹ תַּחַת אָבִיו אֲמַצְיָהוּ: (2 Kgs 14.21)

14. וַיַּמְלִיכוּ עַם־הָאָרֶץ אֶת־יֹאשִׁיָּהוּ בְנוֹ תַּחְתָּיו: (2 Kgs 21.24)

15. חַסְדֵי יְהוָה אַזְכִּיר: (Isa. 63.7)

16. וְהִכְרַתִּי יוֹשֵׁב מֵאַשְׁדּוֹד: (Amos 1.8)

17. וְהָיָה בַיּוֹם־הַהוּא ¹³נְאֻם־יְהוָה ¹²וְהִכְרַתִּי סוּסֶיךָ מִקִּרְבֶּךָ: (Mic. 5.9; Eng. is v. 10)

18. וְהִכְרַתִּי עָרֵי אַרְצֶךָ: (Mic. 5.10; Eng. is v. 11)

19. וְהִכְרַתִּי אֶת־הָאָדָם מֵעַל פְּנֵי הָאֲדָמָה נְאֻם־יְהוָה: (Zeph. 1.3)

20. וְהָיָה בַיּוֹם הַהוּא נְאֻם יְהוָה ¹⁵צְבָאוֹת אַכְרִית אֶת־שְׁמוֹת ¹⁴הָעֲצַבִּים מִן־הָאָרֶץ וְלֹא יִזָּכְרוּ עוֹד: (Zech. 13.2)

21. וַיַּמְלֵךְ מֶלֶךְ־מִצְרַיִם אֶת־אֶלְיָקִים אָחִיו עַל־יְהוּדָה וִירוּשָׁלָ͏ִם: (2 Chron. 36.4)

9.8   APPENDIX

9.8.1   Statistical Summary of the Uses of the Verb Stems.

Qal verbs account for 68.8% of all verbs in the Hebrew Bible: 49,180 occurrences.

Nifal verbs make up 5.8% of all verbs in the Hebrew Bible: 4,140 occurrences.

Hifil verbs make up 13.1% of all verbs in the Hebrew Bible: 9,370 occurrences.

Hofal verbs account for only 0.6% of the verbs in the Bible: 400 occurrences.

These numbers indicate that the bulk of study time should be given to *qal* and *hifil*, so that we will be able to recognize the larger portion of Hebrew verbs.

---

¹⁰ Contraction of מִן עִם

¹¹ This apocopated form occurs five time in the Hebrew Bible, while the long form (as found below in #14) occurs 11 times. The omission of a vowel letter is not unusual.

¹² Note how the final root letter assimilates in the first person.

¹³ Find this word in your lexicon.

¹⁴ *idols*

¹⁵ Find this word in your lexicon.

9.8.2 Comparison of *Qal*, *Nifal*, and *Hifil* Stems

		Qal	*Nifal*	*Hifil*	*Hofal*
Perf	1cs	קָטַלְתִּי	נִקְטַלְתִּי	הִקְטַלְתִּי	הָקְטַלְתִּי
	2ms	קָטַלְתָּ	נִקְטַלְתָּ	הִקְטַלְתָּ	הָקְטַלְתָּ
	2fs	קָטַלְתְּ	נִקְטַלְתְּ	הִקְטַלְתְּ	הָקְטַלְתְּ
	3ms	קָטַל	נִקְטַל	הִקְטִיל	הָקְטַל
	3fs	קָטְלָה	נִקְטְלָה	הִקְטִילָה	הָקְטְלָה
	1cp	קָטַלְנוּ	נִקְטַלְנוּ	הִקְטַלְנוּ	הָקְטַלְנוּ
	2mp	קְטַלְתֶּם	נִקְטַלְתֶּם	הִקְטַלְתֶּם	הָקְטַלְתֶּם
	2fp	קְטַלְתֶּן	נִקְטַלְתֶּן	הִקְטַלְתֶּן	הָקְטַלְתֶּן
	3cp	קָטְלוּ	נִקְטְלוּ	הִקְטִילוּ	הָקְטְלוּ
Imf	1cs	אֶקְטֹל	אֶקָּטֵל	אַקְטִיל	אָקְטַל
	2ms	תִּקְטֹל	תִּקָּטֵל	תַּקְטִיל	תָּקְטַל
	2fs	תִּקְטְלִי	תִּקָּטְלִי	תַּקְטִילִי	תָּקְטְלִי
	3ms	יִקְטֹל	יִקָּטֵל	יַקְטִיל	יָקְטַל
	3fs	תִּקְטֹל	תִּקָּטֵל	תַּקְטִיל	תָּקְטַל
	1cp	נִקְטֹל	נִקָּטֵל	נַקְטִיל	נָקְטַל
	2mp	תִּקְטְלוּ	תִּקָּטְלוּ	תַּקְטִילוּ	תָּקְטְלוּ
	2fp	תִּקְטֹלְנָה	תִּקָּטַלְנָה	תַּקְטֵלְנָה	תָּקְטַלְנָה
	3mp	יִקְטְלוּ	יִקָּטְלוּ	יַקְטִילוּ	יָקְטְלוּ
	3fp	תִּקְטֹלְנָה	תִּקָּטַלְנָה	תַּקְטֵלְנָה	תָּקְטַלְנָה
Imv	2ms	קְטֹל	הִקָּטֵל	הַקְטֵל	
	2fs	קִטְלִי	הִקָּטְלִי	הַקְטִילִי	
	2mp	קִטְלוּ	הִקָּטְלוּ	הַקְטִילוּ	
	2fp	קְטֹלְנָה	הִקָּטַלְנָה	הַקְטֵלְנָה	
Inf	Abs	קָטוֹל	הִקָּטֹל	הַקְטֵל	הָקְטֵל
			נִקְטֹל		
	Cs	קְטֹל	הִקָּטֵל	הַקְטִיל	
Ptc	Act	קוֹטֵל		מַקְטִיל	
	Pass	קָטוּל	נִקְטָל		מָקְטָל
W		וַיִּקְטֹל	וַיִּקָּטֵל	וַיַּקְטֵל	

Chapter 10

The *Piel* Verb

In this chapter you should learn:

- The *Qal* stative verb
- The meaning of the *piel* pattern
- The forms of the *piel* pattern

10.1   The *Qal* Stative Verb

The *qal* stative verbs have implications for the understanding of the *piel*; thus, we will look first at the statives. Up to this point, we have studied only fientive verbs (verbs of action or motion, the *qatal* pattern), for example:

אָכַל   he ate

שָׁמַר   he kept

קָטַל   he killed

יָצָא   he went out

In contrast to fientive verbs, stative verbs present a situation or event involving a state or condition. These verbs are intransitive[1] in the *qal* stem. The English language has no stative verbs except for the verb *to be*. In English, states and conditions are described through the use of predicate adjectives. See the translations in the following examples of *qal* stative verbs:

גָּדֵל   He was great.

קָטֹן   He was small.

כָּבֵד   He was heavy.

זָקֵן   He was old.

> Stative verbs describe a state of being or condition.

As you can see from the examples given above, the vocalization of *qal* stative verbs is slightly different from that of fientive verbs. The four verbs given above are illustrative of the two conjugations of the *qal* statives: the *qatol* and the *qatel*.

10.1.1   Notes on the Stative Verb Paradigm (see chart below)

In the perfect of the כָּבֵד pattern, the *tsere* replaces the *patach* of שָׁמַר, but only in the 3 ms. In the קָטֹן pattern, the *cholem* replaces the *patach* in all places. In the

---

[1] That is, they do not require a direct object.

imperfect of both stative patterns, the *cholem* of יִשְׁמֹר is replaced by a *patach* (יִקְטַן).
The chart below compares the fientive and stative verbs. While they are identical
in most points, it is important to learn the identifying marks of the *qal* stative
verbs that are circled below.

		Qal qatal Fientive	*Qal* qatel Stative	*Qal* qatol Stative
Perf	1cs	שָׁמַרְתִּי	כָּבַדְתִּי	קָטֹנְתִּי
	2ms	שָׁמַרְתָּ	כָּבַדְתָּ	קָטֹנְתָּ
	2fs	שָׁמַרְתְּ	כָּבַדְתְּ	קָטֹנְתְּ
	3ms	שָׁמַר	כָּבֵד	קָטֹן
	3fs	שָׁמְרָה	כָּבְדָה	קָטְנָה
	1cp	שָׁמַרְנוּ	כָּבַדְנוּ	קָטֹנּוּ
	2mp	שְׁמַרְתֶּם	כְּבַדְתֶּם	קְטָנְתֶּם
	2fp	שְׁמַרְתֶּן	כְּבַדְתֶּן	קְטָנְתֶּן
	3cp	שָׁמְרוּ	כָּבְדוּ	קָטְנוּ
Imf	1cs	אֶשְׁמֹר	אֶכְבַּד	אֶקְטַן
	2ms	תִּשְׁמֹר	תִּכְבַּד	תִּקְטַן
	2fs	תִּשְׁמְרִי	תִּכְבְּדִי	תִּקְטְנִי
	3ms	יִשְׁמֹר	יִכְבַּד	יִקְטַן
	3fs	תִּשְׁמֹר	תִּכְבַּד	תִּקְטַן
	1cp	נִשְׁמֹר	נִכְבַּד	נִקְטַן
	2mp	תִּשְׁמְרוּ	תִּכְבְּדוּ	תִּקְטְנוּ
	2fp	תִּשְׁמֹרְנָה	תִּכְבַּדְנָה	תִּקְטַנָּה
	3mp	יִשְׁמְרוּ	יִכְבְּדוּ	תִּקְטְנוּ
	3fp	תִּשְׁמֹרְנָה	תִּכְבַּדְנָה	תִּקְטַנָּה
Imv	2ms	שְׁמֹר	כְּבַד	קְטַן
	2fs	שִׁמְרִי	כִּבְדִי	קְטְנִי
	2mp	שִׁמְרוּ	כִּבְדוּ	קְטְנוּ
	2fp	שְׁמֹרְנָה	כְּבַדְנָה	קְטַנָּה
Inf A		שָׁמוֹר	כָּבוֹד	קָטוֹן
Inf C		לִשְׁמֹר	לִכְבַּד	לִקְטַן
Ptc	Act	שֹׁמֵר	כָּבֵד	קָטֹן
	Pass	שָׁמוּר	NA	NA
W		וַיִּשְׁמֹר	וַיִּכְבַּד	וַיִּקְטַן

Cholem rather than *patach* in
five forms of the perfect.

Tsere rather than
patach in the 3ms.

Qamets qatan

Patach rather than *cholem*
in the imperfect and in
the imperative.

Note the distinctive
pointing of the partici-
ples and *wayyiqtol*.

10.2   The Meaning of the *Piel* Pattern

10.2.1   Factitive

The study of stative verbs is a necessary backdrop to the *piel* stem. The *piel* is used often to express the bringing about of a state or condition that corresponds to a stative verb. The *qal* stative verb is intransitive, but in the *piel* it becomes transitive. This usage is called *factitive*. Observe the following list:

ROOT	*Qal*	*Piel*
גדל	he was great	he brought to a state of greatness = exalted[2]
זקן	he was old	he brought to a state of old age
כבד	he was important	he brought to a state of importance = honored
ירא	he was afraid	he brought to a state of fear

10.2.2   Resultative

If the verbal root is transitive in the *qal*, the *piel* designates the bringing about of the outcome of an action, without regard for the process of the action. The *qal* emphasizes the action, but the *piel* emphasizes the state that results from the action.

ROOT	*Qal*	*Piel*
שבר	he broke	he brought to a state of brokenness
זרה	he scattered	he brought to a state of scatteredness
חלק	he apportioned	he brought to a state of apportionedness
למד	he learned	he brought to a state of learnedness = taught
מכר	he bought	he brought to a state of boughtness = sold

The *qal* seems to emphasize the verbal action, and the *piel* emphasizes the result of the action. This difference, however, is barely discernable and does not usually have a significant impact on translation or exegetical conclusions.

10.2.3   Denominative

Most Hebrew nouns are formed from verbs, but the opposite is sometimes true. A verb formed from a noun is called a *denominative*. The *piel* may be used to form denominatives. These denominatives are usually translated like the *qal* stem.

NOUN		*PIEL* VERB	
כֹּהֵן	priest	כִּהֵן	he served as a priest
דָּבָר	Word	דִּבֶּר	he spoke
עָפָר	dust	עִפֵּר	he dusted (threw dust)

---

[2] For other meanings of these roots in *Piel*, consult your lexicon.

נָחָשׁ serpent   נִחֵשׁ he practiced sorcery
שֹׁרֶשׁ root   שֵׁרֵשׁ he uprooted

IMPORTANT NOTE:
The meaning of a verb in the *Qal* stem is not a reliable indicator of its meaning in the other stems (*Nifal, Piel,* etc.). You should always consult a lexicon in order to determine the meaning of a verb in its various stems.

10.3   The Forms of the *Piel* Pattern

10.3.1 The Piel Perfect

The *piel* perfect (Hebrew פָּעֵל) is characterized by a *chireq* under the first root letter and a *dagesh forte* in the second root letter (HVS 8A).[3] The 3 ms normally has *tsere* (דִּבֵּר and קִטֵּל), but some verbs (like גִּדַּל) have *patach*.

> **All forms of the *piel* have *dagesh forte* in the middle radical (unless, of course, the middle radical is a guttural).**

Piel Perfect of גָּדַל: *to be great* (Qal),[4] *to exalt* (Piel)

	Singular			Plural	
1c	גִּדַּלְתִּי	I exalted	1c	גִּדַּלְנוּ	We exalted
2m	גִּדַּלְתָּ	You exalted	2m	גִּדַּלְתֶּם	You exalted
2f	גִּדַּלְתְּ	You exalted	2f	גִּדַּלְתֶּן	You exalted
3m	גִּדֵּל	He exalted	3c	גִּדְּלוּ	They exalted
3f	גִּדְּלָה	She exalted			

EXERCISE 10-A

Translate the following excerpts and paraphrases from Scripture (some words are found in the vocabulary at the end of the chapter):

Gen. 6.22   כֵּן עָשָׂה נֹחַ כְּכֹל אֲשֶׁר צִוָּה אֹתוֹ אֱלֹהִים כֵּן עָשָׂה:

Gen. 12.4   אַבְרָם הָלַךְ כַּאֲשֶׁר דִּבֶּר אֵלָיו יְהוָה:

Gen. 21.1   וַיהוה עָשָׂה לְשָׂרָה כַּאֲשֶׁר דִּבֵּר:[5] וַיהוה פָּקַד אֶת־שָׂרָה

כַּאֲשֶׁר אָמַר

---

[3] If the middle letter is a guttural, it will not have the *dagesh* (see §2.1.2 and §14.2).

[4] Consult chart above (§10.1.1) and the full paradigm at the end of this chapter (§10.6) for variations on the *Piel* conjugation.

[5] Note the lengthening of the vowel *tsere* because the word is *in pause*. Pausal forms are those that occur with a strong accent, as on the last word or middle word in a verse (§§9.6 and 28.1).

אֱלֹהִים עָלָה מֵעָלָיו בַּמָּקוֹם אֲשֶׁר־דִּבֶּר ⁶אִתּוֹ:   Gen. 35.13

וַיְהִי כִּי שָׁמַע אֲדֹנָיו אֶת־דִּבְרֵי אִשְׁתּוֹ אֲשֶׁר דִּבְּרָה   Gen. 39.19

אֵלָיו לֵאמֹר כַּדְּבָרִים הָאֵלֶּה עָשָׂה לִי עַבְדֶּךָ:

⁷הוּא הַדָּבָר אֲשֶׁר דִּבַּרְתִּי אֶל־פַּרְעֹה: Gen. 41.28

10.3.2 The Piel Imperfect

In all forms, the imperfect of the *piel* has a *sheva* under the preformative, a *patach* under the first root letter, and the *dagesh forte* in the middle root letter (HVS 4C). Also, the *tsere* replaces the *cholem*.

Compare the following examples of *qal* imf and *piel* imf.

Qal	יִגְדַּל	He will be great.
Piel	יְגַדֵּל	He will exalt ...

Piel Imperfect of כָּבֵר: *to be heavy* or *important* (Qal), *to glorify* (Piel)

	Singular			Plural	
1c	אֲכַבֵּד	I shall glorify	1c	נְכַבֵּד	We shall glorify
2m	תְּכַבֵּד	You will glorify	2m	תְּכַבְּדוּ	You will glorify
2f	תְּכַבְּדִי	You will glorify	2f	תְּכַבֵּדְנָה	You will glorify
3m	יְכַבֵּד	He will glorify	3m	יְכַבְּדוּ	They will glorify
3f	תְּכַבֵּד	She will glorify	3f	תְּכַבֵּדְנָה	They will glorify

10.3.2.1 Dagesh forte *and* sheva

Sometimes the *dagesh forte* will be omitted from a letter that is pointed with a *sheva*. In the *piel* imperfect, those forms would be 2fs, 2mp, 3mp. In the *wayyiqtol*, the usual *dagesh* in the preformative may drop out (cf. Gesenius §20m). For example:

יְכַבְּדוּ They will glorify ...   וַיְכַבְּדוּ And they glorified ...

10.3.3 The *Piel* Imperative

The *piel* imperative is formed by removing the preformative from the *piel* imperfect.

Piel Imperfect	*Piel* Imperative
תְּדַבֵּר You will speak.	דַּבֵּר Speak!

---

⁶ Find this preposition in your lexicon.

⁷ In addition to *he* and *she* the pronouns הוּא and הִיא can mean *it* or *that* (see §7.6).

Piel Imperative of דַּבֵּר: *to speak* (Piel)

	Singular			Plural	
2m	דַּבֵּר	speak!	2m	דַּבְּרוּ	speak!
2f	דַּבְּרִי	speak!	2f	דַּבֵּרְנָה	speak!

EXERCISE 10-B

Translate the following:

Gen. 44.7 וַיֹּאמְרוּ אֵלָיו לָמָּה [8] יְדַבֵּר אֲדֹנִי כַּדְּבָרִים הָאֵלֶּה:

Exod. 7.2 וְאַהֲרֹן אָחִיךָ יְדַבֵּר אֶל־פַּרְעֹה וְשִׁלַּח

אֶת־בְּנֵי־יִשְׂרָאֵל מֵאַרְצוֹ:

Exod. 19.6 אֵלֶּה הַדְּבָרִים אֲשֶׁר תְּדַבֵּר אֶל־בְּנֵי יִשְׂרָאֵל:

10.3.4   The *Piel* Participle

The *piel* participle has the prefixed מְ, followed by a *patach* under the first root letter and a *dagesh forte* in the second root letter, which makes it very distinctive and easy to identify (HVS 5B).

Piel Participle of דִּבֵּר: *to speak* (Piel)

	singular			plural	
m	מְדַבֵּר	speaking	m	מְדַבְּרִים	speaking
f	מְדַבֶּרֶת	speaking	f	מְדַבְּרוֹת	speaking

EXERCISE 10-C

Translate the following:

Gen. 37.15 . . . מַה־תְּבַקֵּשׁ:

Gen. 37.16 וַיֹּאמֶר אֶת־אַחַי אָנֹכִי מְבַקֵּשׁ: [9]

Exod. 2.15 וַיִּשְׁמַע פַּרְעֹה אֶת־הַדָּבָר הַזֶּה וַיְבַקֵּשׁ אֶת־מֹשֶׁה:

---

[8] Find this word in your lexicon.

[9] This is one of the most common verb forms in the Bible (over 1800 occurrences). It is a *qal* imperfect, 3ms, from אמר, *wayyiqtol*, translated: *And he said*. Verbs beginning with guttural letters (*alef* in this case) are called *weak verbs*, and they are pointed differently from other verbs.

10.3.5   The *Piel* Infinitives

The *piel* infinitives exhibit the characteristic *dagesh forte* in the second root letter (the infinitive is identical in form to the imperative 2ms).

Piel infinitive absolute: דַּבֵּר or דַּבֹּר
Piel infinitive construct: דַּבֵּר

10.4   Principal Parts of the Verb

We have now surveyed the verb forms of the *qal, nifal, hifil, hofal,* and *piel* stems. The Principal Parts must be memorized thoroughly. You should be able to write and recite them easily.

Qal	Nifal	Hifil	Hofal	Piel	
קָטַל	נִקְטַל	הִקְטִיל	הָקְטַל	קִטֵּל	Perfect
יִקְטֹל	יִקָּטֵל	יַקְטִיל	יָקְטַל	יְקַטֵּל	Imperfect
קְטֹל	הִקָּטֵל	הַקְטֵל		קַטֵּל	Imperative
קָטוֹל	הִקָּטֹל	הַקְטֵל	הָקְטֵל	קַטֵּל	Infinitive Absolute
קְטֹל	הִקָּטֵל	הַקְטִיל		קַטֵּל	Infinitive Construct
קוֹטֵל	נִקְטָל	מַקְטִיל	מָקְטָל	מְקַטֵּל	Participle

EXERCISE 10-D

Parse the following verbs from the *qal, nifal, hifil, hofal,* and *piel* patterns.

Verb	Stem	State	PGN	Pfx	Sfx	Root	Translation
תְּדַבְּרוּ							
הִזְכַּרְתִּי							
מְדַבְּרִים							
בַּקֵּשׁ							
אֶשְׁפֹּט							
וַיִּשְׁמֹר							
דַּבְּרִי							
הִשְׁמַרְתֶּם							

Stem = Q, N, H, Ho, P   **State** = Pf, Imf, *wyyqtl*, Ptc, Imv, IA, IC, Coh, Jus
P = 1, 2, 3   **G** = M, F   **N** = S, P   **Pfx** = Def. Art., conjunction, prep.

10.5   Vocabulary

בִּקֵּשׁ	*v.* he sought (*piel*)
בָּרַךְ	*v.* he blessed (*usually piel*)
דִּבֶּר	*v.* he spoke (*piel*)
צִוָּה	*v.* he commanded (*piel*)
זָבַח	*v.* he slaughtered (*qal*); he offered (*piel*)
נִשְׁבַּע	*v.* he swore (*nifal*) > שבע[10]
הִכָּה	*v.* he struck, hit, defeated (*hifil*) > נכה
יָסַף	*v.* added, he did again
עַיִן	*n.* eye, spring
קֹדֶשׁ	*n.* holiness
רֹאשׁ	*n.* head
שָׁנָה	*n.* year
דָּם	*n.* blood
שָׂדֶה	*n.* field
חֶרֶב	*n.* sword
שָׁמַיִם	*n.* heaven
מָקוֹם	*n.* place
וַיְהִי	And it happened, *or* And he/it was. *wayyiqtol form of* הָיָה

EXERCISE 10-E

Translate the following sentences from the Bible (Use an English translation to help with names and context).

וַיְדַבֵּר מֹשֶׁה כֵּן אֶל־בְּנֵי יִשְׂרָאֵל וְלֹא שָׁמְעוּ אֶל־מֹשֶׁה׃   Exod. 6.9

וַיְדַבֵּר מֹשֶׁה לִפְנֵי יְהוָה לֵאמֹר [11]הֵן בְּנֵי־יִשְׂרָאֵל   Exod. 6.12

לֹא־שָׁמְעוּ אֵלַי׃

וַיְהִי בְּיוֹם דִּבֶּר יְהוָה אֶל־מֹשֶׁה בְּאֶרֶץ מִצְרָיִם׃   Exod. 6.28

---

[10] The symbol > means *verb root.*

[11] Find this word in your lexicon.

וַיְדַבֵּר יְהוָה אֶל־מֹשֶׁה לֵּאמֹר אֲנִי [12]יְהוָה דַּבֵּר אֶל־פַּרְעֹה   Exod. 6.29

מֶלֶךְ מִצְרַיִם אֵת כָּל־אֲשֶׁר אֲנִי דֹבֵר אֵלֶיךָ:

עוֹד הָעָם מְזַבְּחִים [14]וּמְקַטְּרִים [13]בַּבָּמוֹת: 1 Kgs 22.44 [43]

וַיְזַבֵּחַ וַיְקַטֵּר בַּבָּמוֹת: 2 Kgs 16.4

וַיִּשְׁפְּכוּ דָם־בְּנֵיהֶם וּבְנוֹתֵיהֶם אֲשֶׁר זִבְּחוּ [15]לַעֲצַבֵּי כְנָעַן: Ps. 106.38

עַל־רָאשֵׁי הֶהָרִים יְזַבֵּחוּ:   Hos. 4.13

וַיְדַבֵּר אֱלֹהִים אֶל־נֹחַ לֵאמֹר: Gen. 8.15

וַיֵּלֶךְ אַבְרָם כַּאֲשֶׁר דִּבֶּר אֵלָיו יְהוָה וַיֵּלֶךְ אִתּוֹ לוֹט   Gen. 12.4

אָמְרָה אֶל־יַעֲקֹב בְּנָהּ לֵאמֹר הִנֵּה שָׁמַעְתִּי אֶת־אָבִיךָ   Gen. 27.6
וְרִבְקָה

מְדַבֵּר אֶל־עֵשָׂו אָחִיךָ

וַיִּשְׁמַע פַּרְעֹה אֶת־הַדָּבָר הַזֶּה וַיְבַקֵּשׁ [16]לַהֲרֹג אֶת־מֹשֶׁה: Exod. 2.15

בִּקֵּשׁ יְהוָה לוֹ אִישׁ כִּלְבָבוֹ:   1 Sam. 13.14

וְלָקַחְתִּי אֶתְכֶם מִן־[17]הַגּוֹיִם וְקִבַּצְתִּי אֶתְכֶם מִכָּל־הָאֲרָצוֹת: Ezek. 36.24

וַיְסַפֵּר [18]הָעֶבֶד לְיִצְחָק אֵת כָּל־הַדְּבָרִים אֲשֶׁר עָשָׂה: Gen. 24.66

וַיְסַפֵּר יַעֲקֹב לְלָבָן אֵת כָּל־הַדְּבָרִים הָאֵלֶּה: Gen. 29.13

וַיְסַפֵּר מֹשֶׁה לְעָם אֵת כָּל־דִּבְרֵי יְהוָה: Exod. 24.3

סַפְּרָה־נָּא לִי אֵת כָּל־הַגְּדֹלוֹת אֲשֶׁר־עָשָׂה אֱלִישָׁע: 2 Kgs 8.4

הַשָּׁמַיִם מְסַפְּרִים [19]כְּבוֹד־אֵל: Ps. 19.2

אֲשֶׁר שָׁמַעְנוּ וַאֲבוֹתֵינוּ סִפְּרוּ־לָנוּ:   Ps. 78.3

לְסַפֵּר בְּצִיּוֹן שֵׁם יְהוָה: Ps. 102.22

מֹשֶׁה עָשָׂה וְאַהֲרֹן כַּאֲשֶׁר צִוָּה יְהוָה אֹתָם: Exod. 7.6

זֶה הַדָּבָר אֲשֶׁר צִוָּה יְהוָה: Exod. 16.16

---

[12] The accent mark ˰ is called *atnach*. It divides each verse into two major parts, and often suggests a period or semicolon in the translation.

[13] Find בָּמָה in your lexicon.

[14] Find קטר in your lexicon.

[15] Find עצב in your lexicon.

[16] *to kill*

[17] *the nations*

[18] Consult your lexicon for the meaning of this word in *Piel*.

[19] *glory*

10.6 Verb Paradigms with the Statives (*qatel* and *qatol*) and the *piel*.

		Qatal	Qatel	Qatol	Nifal	Hifil	Hofal	Piel
Perf	1cs	קָטַלְתִּי	כָּבֵדְתִּי	קָטֹנְתִּי	נִקְטַלְתִּי	הִקְטַלְתִּי	הָקְטַלְתִּי	קִטַּלְתִּי
	2ms	קָטַלְתָּ	כָּבֵדְתָּ	קָטֹנְתָּ	נִקְטַלְתָּ	הִקְטַלְתָּ	הָקְטַלְתָּ	קִטַּלְתָּ
	2fs	קָטַלְתְּ	כָּבֵדְתְּ	קָטֹנְתְּ	נִקְטַלְתְּ	הִקְטַלְתְּ	הָקְטַלְתְּ	קִטַּלְתְּ
	3ms	קָטַל	כָּבֵד	קָטֹן	נִקְטַל	הִקְטִיל	הָקְטַל	קִטֵּל
	3fs	קָטְלָה	כָּבְדָה	קָטְנָה	נִקְטְלָה	הִקְטִילָה	הָקְטְלָה	קִטְּלָה
	1cp	קָטַלְנוּ	כָּבֵדְנוּ	קָטֹנּוּ	נִקְטַלְנוּ	הִקְטַלְנוּ	הָקְטַלְנוּ	קִטַּלְנוּ
	2mp	קְטַלְתֶּם	כְּבֵדְתֶּם	קְטָנְתֶּם	נִקְטַלְתֶּם	הִקְטַלְתֶּם	הָקְטַלְתֶּם	קִטַּלְתֶּם
	2fp	קְטַלְתֶּן	כְּבֵדְתֶּן	קְטָנְתֶּן	נִקְטַלְתֶּן	הִקְטַלְתֶּן	הָקְטַלְתֶּן	קִטַּלְתֶּן
	3cp	קָטְלוּ	כָּבְדוּ	קָטְנוּ	נִקְטְלוּ	הִקְטִילוּ	הָקְטְלוּ	קִטְּלוּ
Imf	1cs	אֶקְטֹל	אֶכְבַּד	(Same	אֶקָּטֵל	אַקְטִיל	אָקְטַל	אֲקַטֵּל
	2ms	תִּקְטֹל	תִּכְבַּד	as כבד)	תִּקָּטֵל	תַּקְטִיל	תָּקְטַל	תְּקַטֵּל
	2fs	תִּקְטְלִי	תִּכְבְּדִי		תִּקָּטְלִי	תַּקְטִילִי	תָּקְטְלִי	תְּקַטְּלִי
	3ms	יִקְטֹל	יִכְבַּד		יִקָּטֵל	יַקְטִיל	יָקְטַל	יְקַטֵּל
	3fs	תִּקְטֹל	תִּכְבַּד		תִּקָּטֵל	תַּקְטִיל	תָּקְטַל	תְּקַטֵּל
	1cp	נִקְטֹל	נִכְבַּד		נִקָּטֵל	נַקְטִיל	נָקְטַל	נְקַטֵּל
	2mp	תִּקְטְלוּ	תִּכְבְּדוּ		תִּקָּטְלוּ	תַּקְטִילוּ	תָּקְטְלוּ	תְּקַטְּלוּ
	2fp	תִּקְטֹלְנָה	תִּכְבַּדְנָה	תִּקְטַנָּה	תִּקָּטַלְנָה	תַּקְטֵלְנָה	תָּקְטַלְנָה	תְּקַטֵּלְנָה
	3mp	יִקְטְלוּ	יִכְבְּדוּ		יִקָּטְלוּ	יַקְטִילוּ	יָקְטְלוּ	יְקַטְּלוּ
	3fp	תִּקְטֹלְנָה	תִּכְבַּדְנָה	תִּקְטַנָּה	תִּקָּטַלְנָה	תַּקְטֵלְנָה	תָּקְטַלְנָה	תְּקַטֵּלְנָה
Imv	2ms	קְטֹל	כְּבַד	(Same	הִקָּטֵל	הַקְטֵל	Not found	קַטֵּל
	2fs	קִטְלִי	כִּבְדִי	as כבד)	הִקָּטְלִי	הַקְטִילִי	in OT	קַטְּלִי
	2mp	קִטְלוּ	כִּבְדוּ		הִקָּטְלוּ	הַקְטִילוּ		קַטְּלוּ
	2fp	קְטֹלְנָה	כְּבַדְנָה		הִקָּטַלְנָה	הַקְטֵלְנָה		קַטֵּלְנָה
Inf	Abs	קָטוֹל	(regular)	(regular)	הִקָּטֹל / נִקְטֹל	הַקְטֵל	הָקְטֵל	קַטֹּל / קַטֵּל
	Cs	קְטֹל	(regular)	(regular)	הִקָּטֵל	הַקְטִיל		קַטֵּל
Ptc	Act	קֹטֵל	כָּבֵד	קָטֹן		מַקְטִיל		מְקַטֵּל
	Pass	קָטוּל			נִקְטָל		מָקְטָל	מְקֻטָּל
W		וַיִּקְטֹל	וַיִּכְבַּד	וַיִּקְטֹן	וַיִּקָּטֵל	וַיַּקְטֵל	וַיָּקְטַל	וַיְקַטֵּל

Chapter 11

The *Hitpael* Verb

In this chapter you should learn:

- The forms and meaning of the *hitpael* pattern
- The forms and meaning of the *pual* pattern
- Rare verb patterns
- Cardinal and ordinal numbers

> The *hitpael* is often reflexive.

11.1 The Meaning of the *Hitpael*

The *hitpael* is usually designated as reflexive. The reflective voice directs the action back upon the agent or the subject. Observe the following list of variations:

ROOT	*Qal*	*Nifal*	*Hifil*	*Hitpael*
קטל	he killed	he was killed	he caused to kill	he killed himself
אזב	he girded	he was girded	he caused to gird	he girded himself
גדל	he was great	N/A	he exalted	he exalted himself
קדש	he was holy	N/A	he sanctified	he sanctified himself

The reflexive force of *hitpael* is not always discernable and is not necessarily translated into the receptor language (e.g. הִתְהַלֵּךְ = he walked about). The different verb patterns were used to create an expanded vocabulary, based on a limited number of verbal roots.

11.2 The Form of the *Hitpael*

> The *hitpael* is characterized by prefixed הִת.

11.2.1 The *Hitpael* Perfect

The *hitpael* perfect (Hebrew הִתְפַּעֵל) is characterized by a prefixed הִת and a *dagesh forte* in the middle radical (HVS 5A & 8A, but see §10.3.2.1).

This pattern holds true for all forms of the perfect except for 3ms, where *tsere* replaces *patach*.

Qal שָׁמַרְתִּי = ְ + שָׁמַרְתִּי

Hitpael הִתְשַׁמַּרְתִּי = הִתְ + שָׁמַרְתִּי

11.2.2 The *Hitpael* in Parallel with the *Qal*.

		Qal	*Hitpael*
Perf	1cs	שָׁמַרְתִּי	הִתְקַטַּלְתִּי
	2ms	שָׁמַרְתָּ	הִתְקַטַּלְתָּ
	2fs	שָׁמַרְתְּ	הִתְקַטַּלְתְּ
	3ms	שָׁמַר	הִתְקַטֵּל
	3fs	שָׁמְרָה	הִתְקַטְּלָה
	1cp	שָׁמַרְנוּ	הִתְקַטַּלְנוּ
	2mp	שְׁמַרְתֶּם	הִתְקַטַּלְתֶּם
	2fp	שְׁמַרְתֶּן	הִתְקַטַּלְתֶּן
	3cp	שָׁמְרוּ	הִתְקַטְּלוּ
Imf	1cs	אֶשְׁמֹר	אֶתְקַטֵּל
	2ms	תִּשְׁמֹר	תִּתְקַטֵּל
	2fs	תִּשְׁמְרִי	תִּתְקַטְּלִי
	3ms	יִשְׁמֹר	יִתְקַטֵּל
	3fs	תִּשְׁמֹר	תִּתְקַטֵּל
	1cp	נִשְׁמֹר	נִתְקַטֵּל
	2mp	תִּשְׁמְרוּ	תִּתְקַטְּלוּ
	2fp	תִּשְׁמֹרְנָה	תִּתְקַטֵּלְנָה
	3mp	יִשְׁמְרוּ	יִתְקַטְּלוּ
	3fp	תִּשְׁמֹרְנָה	תִּתְקַטֵּלְנָה
Imv	2ms	שְׁמֹר	הִתְקַטֵּל
	2fs	שִׁמְרִי	הִתְקַטְּלִי
	2mp	שִׁמְרוּ	הִתְקַטְּלוּ
	2fp	שְׁמֹרְנָה	הִתְקַטֵּלְנָה
Inf	Abs	שָׁמוֹר	הִתְקַטֵּל
	Inf Cs	שְׁמֹר	הִתְקַטֵּל
Ptc	Act	שׁוֹמֵר	מִתְקַטֵּל
	Pass	שָׁמוּר	
W		וַיִּשְׁמֹר	וַיִּתְקַטֵּל

IMPORTANT NOTE: The form of the perfect 3ms (הִתְקַטֵּל) is identical to the imperative 2ms and to the infinitive.

EXERCISE 11-A

Translate the following:

1. שְׁלֹמֹה הִתְהַלֵּךְ אַחַר דָּוִד אָבִיו:

2. אָדָם הִתְהַלֵּךְ עִם אֱלֹהִים:

3. הִנֵּה לֹא הִתְהַלְכוּ הָעָם כְּקוֹל נְבִיאֵי־יהוה:

11.2.3   The *Hitpael* Imperfect

In the imperfect of the *hitpael*, the ה of the prefixed הת is replaced by the imperfect preformative. The characteristic ת remains, and all forms have the doubling of the middle radical (but see §10.3.2.1).

11.2.4   Transposition and Assimilation of the Preformative ת

11.2.4.1 Metathesis

When a verb begins with a sibilant (ס, ז, שׁ, שׂ, or צ), the first root letter will switch places with the ת in the *hitpael*. This transposition of letters for euphony is called metathesis. Instead of הִתְשַׁמֵּר, we find הִשְׁתַּמֵּר; and instead of הִתְסַבֵּל, we find הִסְתַּבֵּל (HVS 6D).

11.2.4.2 Assimilation

When a verb begins with a *d* or *t* sound (ד, ט, ת), the ת of the *hifil's* prefixed הת will assimilate. Instead of the expected מִתְדַבֵּר, we find מִדַּבֵּר *speaking*; and instead of הִתְטַהֵר; we find הִטַּהֵר *he purified himself* (see Gesenius §54b and c).

EXERCISE 11-B

Translate the following:

1. עַתָּה ¹שָׁאוּל יִתְנַשֵּׂא עַל שְׁמוּאֵל וְעַל אֱלֹהִים:

2. הַכֹּהֵן מִתְנַשֵּׂא עַל אֶת־תּוֹרַת־יהוה:

3. מֹשֶׁה דִּבֶּר לֵאמֹר יִתְנַשֵּׂא אֱלֹהִים:

11.3   The Meaning of the *Pual*

The *pual* is the passive counterpart to the *piel*.

> **The *pual* is passive voice.**

Piel		*Pual*	
בִּקֵּשׁ	he sought	בֻּקַּשׁ	he was sought
בִּשֵּׁל	it boiled	בֻּשַּׁל	it was boiled

---

¹ Saul

דִּבֶּר   he spoke   דֻּבַּר   it was spoken

The *pual* does not occur very often. In the Bible, only .6% of verb forms are *pual*, while the *piel* accounts for 13.1%. Thus, only six of every thousand verb forms will be *pual*.

11.4   The Form of the *Pual*

All forms of the *pual* are characterized by *qibbuts* under the first root letter. The chart on the following page lists the *qal* pattern and the three patterns that have the doubled middle radical (HVS 5B & 8A, but see §10.3.2.1).

11.5   Principal Parts of the Verb

We have now surveyed the verb forms of the *qal*, *nifal*, *hifil*, *hofal*, *piel*, *pual*, and *hitpael* stems. The Principal Parts must be memorized thoroughly. You should be able to write and recite them easily.

PRINCIPAL PARTS

Qal	*Nifal*	*Hifil*	*Hofal*	*Piel*	*Pual*	*Hitpael*	
קָטַל	נִקְטַל	הִקְטִיל	הָקְטַל	קִטֵּל	קֻטַּל	הִתְקַטֵּל	Pf
יִקְטֹל	יִקָּטֵל	יַקְטִיל	יָקְטַל	יְקַטֵּל	יְקֻטַּל	יִתְקַטֵּל	Imf
קְטֹל	הִקָּטֵל	הַקְטֵל		קַטֵּל		הִתְקַטֵּל	Imv
קָטוֹל	הִקָּטֹל	הַקְטֵל	הָקְטֵל	קַטֹּל	קֻטֹּל	הִתְקַטֵּל	Inf A
קְטֹל	הִקָּטֵל	הַקְטִיל		קַטֵּל		הִתְקַטֵּל	Inf C
קוֹטֵל	נִקְטָל	מַקְטִיל	מָקְטָל	מְקַטֵּל	מְקֻטָּל	מִתְקַטֵּל	Ptc

11.6   Verb Paradigms

		Qal	*Piel*	*Pual*	*Hitpael*
Perf	1cs	שָׁמַרְתִּי	קִטַּלְתִּי	קֻטַּלְתִּי	הִתְקַטַּלְתִּי
	2ms	שָׁמַרְתָּ	קִטַּלְתָּ	קֻטַּלְתָּ	הִתְקַטַּלְתָּ
	2fs	שָׁמַרְתְּ	קִטַּלְתְּ	קֻטַּלְתְּ	הִתְקַטַּלְתְּ
	3ms	שָׁמַר	קִטֵּל	קֻטַּל	הִתְקַטֵּל
	3fs	שָׁמְרָה	קִטְּלָה	קֻטְּלָה	הִתְקַטְּלָה
	1cp	שָׁמַרְנוּ	קִטַּלְנוּ	קֻטַּלְנוּ	הִתְקַטַּלְנוּ
	2mp	שְׁמַרְתֶּם	קִטַּלְתֶּם	קֻטַּלְתֶּם	הִתְקַטַּלְתֶּם
	2fp	שְׁמַרְתֶּן	קִטַּלְתֶּן	קֻטַּלְתֶּן	הִתְקַטַּלְתֶּן
	3cp	שָׁמְרוּ	קִטְּלוּ	קֻטְּלוּ	הִתְקַטְּלוּ
Imf	1cs	אֶשְׁמֹר	אֲקַטֵּל	אֲקֻטַּל	אֶתְקַטֵּל
	2ms	תִּשְׁמֹר	תְּקַטֵּל	תְּקֻטַּל	תִּתְקַטֵּל
	2fs	תִּשְׁמְרִי	תְּקַטְּלִי	תְּקֻטְּלִי	תִּתְקַטְּלִי
	3ms	יִשְׁמֹר	יְקַטֵּל	יְקֻטַּל	יִתְקַטֵּל
	3fs	תִּשְׁמֹר	תְּקַטֵּל	תְּקֻטַּל	תִּתְקַטֵּל
	1cp	נִשְׁמֹר	נְקַטֵּל	נְקֻטַּל	נִתְקַטֵּל
	2mp	תִּשְׁמְרוּ	תְּקַטְּלוּ	תְּקֻטְּלוּ	תִּתְקַטְּלוּ
	2fp	תִּשְׁמֹרְנָה	תְּקַטֵּלְנָה	תְּקֻטַּלְנָה	תִּתְקַטֵּלְנָה
	3mp	יִשְׁמְרוּ	יְקַטְּלוּ	יְקֻטְּלוּ	יִתְקַטְּלוּ
	3fp	תִּשְׁמֹרְנָה	תְּקַטֵּלְנָה	תְּקֻטַּלְנָה	תִּתְקַטֵּלְנָה
Imv	2ms	שְׁמֹר	קַטֵּל		הִתְקַטֵּל
	2fs	שִׁמְרִי	קַטְּלִי		הִתְקַטְּלִי
	2mp	שִׁמְרוּ	קַטְּלוּ		הִתְקַטְּלוּ
	2fp	שְׁמֹרְנָה	קַטֵּלְנָה		הִתְקַטֵּלְנָה
Inf	Abs	שָׁמוֹר	קַטֹּל / קַטֵּל	קֻטֹּל	הִתְקַטֵּל
	Cs	שְׁמֹר	קַטֵּל		הִתְקַטֵּל
Ptc	Act	שׁוֹמֵר	מְקַטֵּל		מִתְקַטֵּל
	Pass	שָׁמוּר		מְקֻטָּל	
W		וַיִּשְׁמֹר	וַיְקַטֵּל	וַיְקֻטַּל	וַיִּתְקַטֵּל

This chapter completes our study of the seven most prominent verb stems. For a summary of the significance of each pattern, see the Appendix: *Characteristics of the Verb Stems* (§25.1). For help with parsing the various stems, see *Guide to Parsing Hebrew Verbs* (§27.1).

11.7   Rare Verb Stems

In addition to the seven basic verb stems, biblical Hebrew includes several other stems that occur infrequently. The rare stems include the *Poel, Palel, Pilpel, Polpal, Hitpalpel, Palal, Nitpael, Nufal,* and *Hishtafel* (cf. Gesenius §55 and Joüon §59).

11.7.1   *Poel, Poal,* and *Hitpoel*

The most common of the rare verb stems is the *Poel*, along with its passive and reflexive counterparts *Poal* and *Hitpoel*. These stems correspond in meaning to the *Piel, Pual,* and *Hitpael*. Examples:

וְעוֹנֵן (*Poel* pf 3ms+ו pfx>ענן) *he practiced soothsaying* (2 Kgs 21.6)

לְקֹשֵׁשׁ (*Poel* inf. constr.+ל pfx>קשׁשׁ) *to gather* (Exod. 5.12)

מְהוֹלָל (*Poal* ptc ms>הלל) *maddening* (Eccl. 2.2)

וְהִתְגֹּעֲשׁוּ (*Hitpoel* pf 3m pl+ו pfx>געשׁ) *and they will stagger* (Jer. 25.16)

11.7.2   *Pilpel, Polpal,* and *Hitpalpel*

The *Pilpel*, along with its passive and reflexive counterparts *Polpal* and *Hitpalpel*, reduplicates the first and third root letters. Examples:

וְכִלְכַּלְתִּי (*Pilpel* pf 1cs+ו pfx>כול) *and I will support* (Gen. 45.11)

וְכָלְכְּלוּ (*Polpal* pf 1cs+ו pfx>כול) *and they were supported* (1 Kgs 20.27)

וַתִּתְחַלְחַל (*Hitpalpel* imf 3fs *wayyiqtol* >חיל) *and she writhed in terror* (Esther 4.4)

11.7.3   *Hishtafel*

The only verb that occurs in the *Hishtafel* stem is חוה, which means *to bow down, to worship* (found 173 times in the Hebrew Bible). Examples:

וְהִשְׁתַּחֲווּ (*Hishtafel* pf 3cp+ו pfx >חוה) *and they worshiped* (Exod. 33.10)

וַיִּשְׁתַּחֲוֶה (*Hishtafel* imf 3ms *wayyiqtol* >חוה) *and he worshiped* (1 Kgs 22.54)

לְהִשְׁתַּחֲוֺת (*Hishtafel* inf. const+ל>חוה) *to worship* (2 Kgs 5.18)

EXERCISE 11-C

Translate these verses with *pual* verbs.

שָׁמָּה ²קֻבַּר אַבְרָהָם וְשָׂרָה אִשְׁתּוֹ:	Gen. 25.10
וְהָאֲנָשִׁים שֻׁלְּחוּ:	Gen. 44.3
כִּי גָדוֹל יְהוָה ³וּמְהֻלָּל מְאֹד:	1 Chr. 16.25
וַיְבֻקַּשׁ הַדָּבָר ⁴וַיִּמָּצֵא:	Est. 2.23
מְהֻלָּל שֵׁם יְהוָה:	Psa. 113.3

11.8   Hebrew Numerals

11.8.1   Cardinal Numbers

11.8.1.1   *Numbers one to ten*

	With Masculine Nouns		With Feminine Nouns	
	Absolute	Construct	Absolute	Construct
1	אֶחָד	אַחַד	אַחַת	אַחַת
2	שְׁנַיִם	שְׁנֵי	שְׁתַּיִם	שְׁתֵּי
3	שְׁלֹשָׁה	שְׁלֹשֶׁת	שָׁלֹשׁ	שְׁלֹשׁ
4	אַרְבָּעָה	אַרְבַּעַת	אַרְבַּע	אַרְבַּע
5	חֲמִשָּׁה	חֲמֵשֶׁת	חָמֵשׁ	חֲמֵשׁ
6	שִׁשָּׁה	שֵׁשֶׁת	שֵׁשׁ	שֵׁשׁ
7	שִׁבְעָה	שִׁבְעַת	שֶׁבַע	שֶׁבַע
8	שְׁמֹנָה	שְׁמֹנַת	שְׁמֹנֶה	שְׁמֹנֶה
9	תִּשְׁעָה	תִּשְׁעַת	תֵּשַׁע	תֵּשַׁע
10	עֲשָׂרָה	עֲשֶׂרֶת	עֶשֶׂר	עֶשֶׂר

1- The numeral *one* is considered an attributive adjective. It follows the noun and agrees with it in gender and definiteness, e.g.:

אִישׁ אֶחָד one man   אִשָּׁה אַחַת one woman

2- It may also be used in the construct state before a plural noun, e.g.:

אַחַד הַשִּׂיחִים one of the bushes (Gen. 21.15)

3- The numeral *two* may stand in construct before the noun it modifies, or it may stand as an absolute in apposition to the noun, e.g.:

---

² This verb in the *qal* means *to bury.*

³ This verb in the *Piel* means *to praise.*

⁴ This verb in the *qal* means *to find.*

two men	שְׁנֵי אֲנָשִׁים (Exod. 2.13)	שְׁנַיִם־אֲנָשִׁים (Josh 2.1)	
two women	שְׁתֵּי נָשִׁים (Gen. 4.19)	שְׁתַּיִם נָשִׁים (1 Kgs 3.16)	

4- Pronominal suffixes may be attached to the numeral "2", e.g.

two of them	שְׁנֵיהֶם (Gen. 22.6)	
two of us	שְׁנֵינוּ (1 Sam. 20.42)	

5- The numerals *three* through *ten* most often occur in the construct, preceding the noun that they modify; but they can be found in apposition as well.

שְׁלֹשֶׁת הָאֲנָשִׁים הָאֵלֶּה	these three men	Construct (Job 32.1)
שְׁלֹשׁ נָשִׁים	three women	Construct
שְׁלֹשָׁה אֲנָשִׁים	three men	Appositional (Gen. 18.2)

11.8.1.2   *Numbers eleven through nineteen*

	With Masculine	With Feminine
11	אַחַד עָשָׂר	אַחַת עֶשְׂרֵה
	עַשְׁתֵּי עָשָׂר	עַשְׁתֵּי עֶשְׂרֵה
12	שְׁנֵי עָשָׂר	שְׁתֵּים עֶשְׂרֵה
	שְׁנֵי עָשָׂר	שְׁתֵּי עֶשְׂרֵה
13	שְׁלֹשָׁה עָשָׂר	שְׁלֹשׁ עֶשְׂרֵה
14	אַרְבָּעָה עָשָׂר	אַרְבַּע עֶשְׂרֵה
15	חֲמִשָּׁה עָשָׂר	חֲמֵשׁ עֶשְׂרֵה
16	שִׁשָּׁה עָשָׂר	שֵׁשׁ עֶשְׂרֵה
17	שִׁבְעָה עָשָׂר	שְׁבַע עֶשְׂרֵה
18	שְׁמֹנָה עָשָׂר	שְׁמֹנֶה עֶשְׂרֵה
19	תִּשְׁעָה עָשָׂר	תְּשַׁע עֶשְׂרֵה

The plural noun is generally used with the numbers *eleven* through *nineteen*, but the singular form is preferred with certain nouns (e.g. אִישׁ, יוֹם, שָׁנָה, נֶפֶשׁ, and a few others.)

eleven stars	אַחַד עָשָׂר כּוֹכָבִים (Gen. 37.9)	
twelve years	שְׁתֵּים עֶשְׂרֵה שָׁנָה (Gen. 14.4)	

11.8.1.3   *Numbers twenty through ninety*

20	עֶשְׂרִים	60	שִׁשִּׁים
30	שְׁלֹשִׁים	70	שִׁבְעִים
40	אַרְבָּעִים	80	שְׁמֹנִים
50	חֲמִשִּׁים	90	תִּשְׁעִים

twenty years   עֶשְׂרִים שָׁנָה   (Gen. 31.38)
thirty men   שְׁלֹשִׁים אִישׁ   (Judg. 14.19)

11.8.1.4   *The hundreds and thousands*

100	מֵאָה (cs. מְאַת)	1000	אֶלֶף
200	מָאתַיִם	2000	אַלְפַּיִם
300	שְׁלֹשׁ מֵאוֹת	3000	שְׁלֹשֶׁת אֲלָפִים
400	אַרְבַּע מֵאוֹת	4000	אַרְבַּעַת אֲלָפִים
500	חֲמֵשׁ מֵאוֹת	5000	חֲמֵשֶׁת אֲלָפִים
	... etc.	10,000	רִבּוֹת / רְבָבָה
		20,000	רִבּוֹתַיִם
		30,000	שְׁלֹשׁ רִבּוֹת
		40,000	אַרְבַּע רִבּוֹת
			... etc.

11.8.2 Ordinal Numbers

	Masculine	Feminine	
first	רִאשׁוֹן	רִאשׁוֹנָה	
second	שֵׁנִי	שֵׁנִית	
third	שְׁלִישִׁי	שְׁלִישִׁית	or שְׁלִישִׁיָּה
fourth	רְבִיעִי	רְבִיעִית	
fifth	חֲמִישִׁי	חֲמִישִׁית	
sixth	שִׁשִּׁי	שִׁשִּׁית	
seventh	שְׁבִיעִי	שְׁבִיעִית	
eighth	שְׁמִינִי	שְׁמִינִית	
ninth	תְּשִׁיעִי	תְּשִׁיעִית	
tenth	עֲשִׂירִי	עֲשִׂירִית	or עֲשִׂירִיָּה

The ordinal numbers are attributive adjectives, standing after the noun and agree-
ing with it in gender. Beyond *eleven*, the cardinal numbers serve as ordinals.

in the second month   בַּחֹדֶשׁ הַשֵּׁנִי (Gen. 7.11)
a second son   בֵּן שֵׁנִי (Gen. 30.7)
in the second year   בַּשָּׁנָה הַשֵּׁנִית (Gen. 47.18)

11.9   Idiomatic Use of אִישׁ

The idiomatic use of אִישׁ is a topic closely related to the Hebrew numbers. The word אִישׁ can mean *each*, and can be applied not only to men but also to women and inanimate objects. In combination with other words, it can mean *each other*.

אִישׁ חַרְבּוֹ	each his own sword (Gen. 34.25)
אִישׁ־אֶחָד	each one (Num. 1.44)
אִישׁ־בִּתְרוֹ	each of its pieces (Gen. 15.10)

11.10   Vocabulary for Genesis 1

נוּחַ	*v.* he rested, settled down
רָחַף	*v. qal* he grew soft, *piel* he hovered
הִבְדִּיל	*v. hifil* he divided, separated > בָּדַל
מוּת	*v.* he died
בָּרָא	*v.* he created
בָּנָה	*v.* he built
הִתְיַצֵּב	*v. hitpael* he stood, he stationed himself
הִתְפַּלֵל	*v. hitpael* he prayed
קָדַשׁ	*v. qal* he was holy, *hitpael* he sanctified himself
נֶגֶד	*prep.* over against, opposite
לַיְלָה	*n.m.* night
בֹּקֶר	*n.m.* morning
אוֹר	*n.m.* light
עֶרֶב	*n.m.* evening
חֹשֶׁךְ	*n.m.* darkness
עָבַד	*v.* to serve, to work
נָגַע	*v.* to touch
אָהַב	*v.* to love
יָכֹל	*v.* to be able
יָרֵא	*v.* to fear
פֶּן	*particle.* lest, so that not
גּוֹי	*n.* nation
אֵת	*prep.* with, *construct* אֶת־

EXERCISE 11-D

Part 1: Parse the following verbs from the *qal*, *nifal*, *hifil*, *hofal*, *piel*, *pual*, and *hitpael* patterns.

Verb	Stem	State	PGN	Root	Translation
תִּשְׁמְרוּ					
אַקְטִיל					
קָטְלָה					
קַטְּלוּ					
הִתְקַטַּלְנוּ					
מְקַקְטָל					
יִתְקַטְּלוּ					
שָׁמוּר					
מִתְקַטֵּל					

Stem = Q, N, H, Ho, P, Pu, Ht   **State** = Pf, Imf, Ptc, Imv, IA, IC, Coh, Jus
P = 1, 2, 3   **G** = M, F   **N** = S, P

Part 2: Translate the following excerpts from Scripture (Use an English translation to help with names and context).

וַיִּשְׁמְעוּ אֶת־קוֹל יְהוָה אֱלֹהִים מִתְהַלֵּךְ בַּגָּן: [5]   Gen. 3.8

וַיִּתְהַלֵּךְ חֲנוֹךְ אֶת־הָאֱלֹהִים וְאֵינֶנּוּ כִּי־לָקַח אֹתוֹ אֱלֹהִים: Gen. 5.24

אֶת־הָאֱלֹהִים הִתְהַלֶּךְ־נֹחַ:   Gen. 6.9

וַיִּתְפַּלֵּל אַבְרָהָם אֶל־הָאֱלֹהִים: Gen. 20.17

וְהִתְבָּרֲכוּ בְזַרְעֲךָ כֹּל גּוֹיֵי הָאָרֶץ: Gen. 26.4

וַיֹּאמֶר מֹשֶׁה זֶה הַדָּבָר אֲשֶׁר אָמַר יְהוָה: Exod. 16.32

וַיֹּאמְרוּ אֵלֶּה אֱלֹהֶיךָ יִשְׂרָאֵל: Exod. 32.4

כִּי אֲנִי יְהוָה אֱלֹהֵיכֶם וְהִתְקַדִּשְׁתֶּם: Lev. 11.44

וַיִּתְפַּלֵּל מֹשֶׁה אֶל־יְהוָה: Num. 11.2

וָאֶתְפַּלֵּל אֶל־יְהוָה: Deut 9.26

---

[5] Consult the lexicon for the meaning of גָּן.

וַיִּשְׁמְעוּ פְלִשְׁתִּים כִּי־הִתְקַבְּצוּ בְנֵי־יִשְׂרָאֵל הַמִּצְפָּתָה׃ 1 Sam. 7.7

וַיִּתְקַבְּצוּ כֹּל ⁶זִקְנֵי יִשְׂרָאֵל אֶל־שְׁמוּאֵל הָרָמָתָה׃ 1 Sam. 8.4

וַיִּתְפַּלֵּל שְׁמוּאֵל אֶל־יְהוָה׃ 1 Sam. 8.6

וְעַתָּה הִתְיַצְּבוּ לִפְנֵי יְהוָה׃ 1 Sam. 10.19

וְעַתָּה הִנֵּה הַמֶּלֶךְ מִתְהַלֵּךְ לִפְנֵיכֶם וַאֲנִי זָקַנְתִּי 1 Sam. 12.2

וַיֹּאמְרוּ כָל־הָעָם אֶל־שְׁמוּאֵל הִתְפַּלֵּל בְּעַד־עֲבָדֶיךָ 1 Sam. 12.19
אֶל־יְהוָה אֱלֹהֶיךָ׃

וַיִּתְקַבְּצוּ בְנֵי־בִנְיָמִן אַחֲרֵי אַבְנֵר׃ 2 Sam. 2.25

וּמֶלֶךְ יִשְׂרָאֵל וִיהוֹשָׁפָט מֶלֶךְ־יְהוּדָה יֹשְׁבִים אִישׁ עַל־כִּסְאוֹ׃ 1 Kgs 22.10

לוֹא־⁸יִתְנַבֵּא עָלַי טוֹב ⁷כִּי אִם־רָע׃ 1 Kgs 22.18

וַיִּתְפַּלֵּל חִזְקִיָּהוּ לִפְנֵי יְהוָה וַיֹּאמַר יְהוָה אֱלֹהֵי יִשְׂרָאֵל׃ 2 Kgs 19.15

לָהֶם אַתֶּם רָאשֵׁי הָאָבוֹת לַלְוִיִּם הִתְקַדְּשׁוּ אַתֶּם וַאֲחֵיכֶם׃ 1 Chron.
וַיֹּאמֶר 15.12

With this lesson, we have completed the paradigm for the strong verb. The complete paradigm is found on the following page. In the next chapter, we will begin to study the weak verbs.

⁶ Consult the lexicon for the meaning of this word.

⁷ Used in combination after a negative clause, כִּי אִם expresses exception or contrast, and may be translated, *except*, *rather*, or *but*.

⁸ If נָבִיא means *prophet*, then what might this verb mean?

11.11   Paradigm of the Strong Verb

	Qatal	*Qatel*	*Qatol*	Nifal	Hifil	Hofal	Piel	Pual	Hitpael
Pf	*kill*	*be heavy*	*be small*						
1cs	קָטַלְתִּי	כָּבַדְתִּי	קָטֹנְתִּי	נִקְטַלְתִּי	הִקְטַלְתִּי	הָקְטַלְתִּי	קִטַּלְתִּי	קֻטַּלְתִּי	הִתְקַטַּלְתִּי
2ms	קָטַלְתָּ	כָּבַדְתָּ	קָטֹנְתָּ	נִקְטַלְתָּ	הִקְטַלְתָּ	הָקְטַלְתָּ	קִטַּלְתָּ	קֻטַּלְתָּ	הִתְקַטַּלְתָּ
2fs	קָטַלְתְּ	כָּבַדְתְּ	קָטֹנְתְּ	נִקְטַלְתְּ	הִקְטַלְתְּ	הָקְטַלְתְּ	קִטַּלְתְּ	קֻטַּלְתְּ	הִתְקַטַּלְתְּ
3ms	קָטַל	כָּבֵד	קָטֹן	נִקְטַל	הִקְטִיל	הָקְטַל	קִטֵּל	קֻטַּל	הִתְקַטֵּל
3fs	קָטְלָה	כָּבְדָה	קָטְנָה	נִקְטְלָה	הִקְטִילָה	הָקְטְלָה	קִטְּלָה	קֻטְּלָה	הִתְקַטְּלָה
1cp	קָטַלְנוּ	כָּבַדְנוּ	קָטֹנּוּ	נִקְטַלְנוּ	הִקְטַלְנוּ	הָקְטַלְנוּ	קִטַּלְנוּ	קֻטַּלְנוּ	הִתְקַטַּלְנוּ
2mp	קְטַלְתֶּם	כְּבַדְתֶּם	קְטָנְתֶּם	נִקְטַלְתֶּם	הִקְטַלְתֶּם	הָקְטַלְתֶּם	קִטַּלְתֶּם	קֻטַּלְתֶּם	הִתְקַטַּלְתֶּם
2fp	קְטַלְתֶּן	כְּבַדְתֶּן	קְטָנְתֶּן	נִקְטַלְתֶּן	הִקְטַלְתֶּן	הָקְטַלְתֶּן	קִטַּלְתֶּן	קֻטַּלְתֶּן	הִתְקַטַּלְתֶּן
3cp	קָטְלוּ	כָּבְדוּ	קָטְנוּ	נִקְטְלוּ	הִקְטִילוּ	הָקְטְלוּ	קִטְּלוּ	קֻטְּלוּ	הִתְקַטְּלוּ
Imf									
1cs	אֶקְטֹל	אֶכְבַּד	(Same	אֶקָּטֵל	אַקְטִיל	אָקְטַל	אֲקַטֵּל	אֲקֻטַּל	אֶתְקַטֵּל
2ms	תִּקְטֹל	תִּכְבַּד	as כבד)	תִּקָּטֵל	תַּקְטִיל	תָּקְטַל	תְּקַטֵּל	תְּקֻטַּל	תִּתְקַטֵּל
2fs	תִּקְטְלִי	תִּכְבְּדִי		תִּקָּטְלִי	תַּקְטִילִי	תָּקְטְלִי	תְּקַטְּלִי	תְּקֻטְּלִי	תִּתְקַטְּלִי
3ms	יִקְטֹל	יִכְבַּד		יִקָּטֵל	יַקְטִיל	יָקְטַל	יְקַטֵּל	יְקֻטַּל	יִתְקַטֵּל
3fs	תִּקְטֹל	תִּכְבַּד		תִּקָּטֵל	תַּקְטִיל	תָּקְטַל	תְּקַטֵּל	תְּקֻטַּל	תִּתְקַטֵּל
1cp	נִקְטֹל	נִכְבַּד		נִקָּטֵל	נַקְטִיל	נָקְטַל	נְקַטֵּל	נְקֻטַּל	נִתְקַטֵּל
2mp	תִּקְטְלוּ	תִּכְבְּדוּ		תִּקָּטְלוּ	תַּקְטִילוּ	תָּקְטְלוּ	תְּקַטְּלוּ	תְּקֻטְּלוּ	תִּתְקַטְּלוּ
2fp	תִּקְטֹלְנָה	תִּכְבַּדְנָה		תִּקָּטַלְנָה	תַּקְטֵלְנָה	תָּקְטַלְנָה	תְּקַטֵּלְנָה	תְּקֻטַּלְנָה	תִּתְקַטֵּלְנָה
3mp	יִקְטְלוּ	יִכְבְּדוּ		יִקָּטְלוּ	יַקְטִילוּ	יָקְטְלוּ	יְקַטְּלוּ	יְקֻטְּלוּ	יִתְקַטְּלוּ
3fp	תִּקְטֹלְנָה	תִּכְבַּדְנָה		תִּקָּטַלְנָה	תַּקְטֵלְנָה	תָּקְטַלְנָה	תְּקַטֵּלְנָה	תְּקֻטַּלְנָה	תִּתְקַטֵּלְנָה
Imv									
2ms	קְטֹל	כְּבַד	(Same	הִקָּטֵל	הַקְטֵל		קַטֵּל		הִתְקַטֵּל
2fs	קִטְלִי	כִּבְדִי	as כבד)	הִקָּטְלִי	הַקְטִילִי		קַטְּלִי		הִתְקַטְּלִי
2mp	קִטְלוּ	כִּבְדוּ		הִקָּטְלוּ	הַקְטִילוּ		קַטְּלוּ		הִתְקַטְּלוּ
2fp	קְטֹלְנָה	כְּבַדְנָה		הִקָּטַלְנָה	הַקְטֵלְנָה		קַטֵּלְנָה		הִתְקַטֵּלְנָה
IA	קָטוֹל	(reg.)	(reg.)	הִקָּטֹל נִקְטֹל	הַקְטֵל	הָקְטֵל	קַטֹּל קַטֵּל	קֻטֹּל	הִתְקַטֵּל
ICs	קְטֹל	(reg.)	(reg.)	הִקָּטֵל	הַקְטִיל	הָקְטֵל	קַטֵּל		הִתְקַטֵּל
APtc	קוֹטֵל	כָּבֵד	קָטֹן		מַקְטִיל		מְקַטֵּל		מִתְקַטֵּל
PPtc	קָטוּל			נִקְטָל		מָקְטָל		מְקֻטָּל	
W	וַיִּקְטֹל	וַיִּכְבַּד	וַיִּקְטַן	וַיִּקָּטֵל	וַיַּקְטֵל	וַיָּקְטַל	וַיְקַטֵּל	וַיְקֻטַּל	וַיִּתְקַטֵּל

Chapter 12

Verbal Suffixes and Reading Genesis 1.1-5

In this chapter you should learn:

- The pronominal suffixes that are attached to verbs
- Forms of weak verbs ending with the letter ה
- Interrogative הַ

12.1 Pronominal Suffixes for the Verb

Sometimes the direct object of the verb is attached to the verb. Compare the following examples. In the first sentence, the pronominal suffix (וֹ) is attached to the sign of the definite object (את). In the second sentence, the same pronominal suffix is attached to the verb itself.

Observe, however, that when a suffix is added to the verb, the vowel letters will change because the accent moves forward one syllable. The initial *qamets* becomes *sheva*, according to the rules that we learned earlier (§2.2.3). Furthermore, the *patach* changes to a *qamets* because it is now in an open syllable (HVS 14).

The following chart lists the most common forms of the pronominal suffixes. A full chart of the pronominal suffixes attached to verbs is included as an appendix to this chapter.

	Singular			Plural	
1c	נִי֚	me	1c	נוּ֚	us
2m	ךָ֚	you	2m	כֶם֚	you
	ךְ֚				
2f	ךְ֚	you	2f	כֶן֚	*Does not occur in the* Bible
3m	וֹ֚	him	3m	הֶם֚	them
	הוּ֚			ם֚	
3f	הּ֚	her	3f	הֶן֚	them
	הָ֚			ן֚	

12.1.1 Pronominal Suffixes with energic נ

Verbs with suffixes are given extra strength and emphasis when the letter נ is inserted between the verb and the suffix, e.g. יְכַבְּדָנְנִי *he will honour me* (Ps. 50.23). (§22.12.2). This is called energic נ, and it is most often assimilated, which results in a *dagesh forte* in the suffix: 1st person sg. ־ֵּנִי (for ־ֵנְנִי), 2nd person sg. ־ֶּךָ or ־ֶּכָה (for ־ֶנְךָ), 3rd person sg. ־ֶּנּוּ (for ־ֶנְהוּ), 1st person pl ־ֶּנּוּ (for ־ֶנְנוּ) (HVS 13E).

12.2   Pronominal Suffixes and the Perfect

Perf 3ms

קְטָלַנִי	He killed me.
קְטָלְךָ	He killed you (m).
קְטָלֵךְ	He killed you (f).
קְטָלוֹ	He killed him.
or קְטָלָהוּ	
קְטָלָהּ	He killed her.
קְטָלָנוּ	He killed us.
קְטַלְכֶם	He killed you (m).
קְטַלְכֶן	He killed you (f). (*This form is not found in the Bible.*)
קְטָלָם	He killed them (m).
קְטָלָן	He killed them (f).
or קְטָלֵן	

Examples:

Gen. 30.29 אַתָּה יָדַעְתָּ אֵת אֲשֶׁר עֲבַדְתִּיךָ
You yourself know I have served you

Gen. 17.20 וּלְיִשְׁמָעֵאל שְׁמַעְתִּיךָ
And for Ishmael I have heard you.

Gen. 1.27 זָכָר וּנְקֵבָה בְּרָאָם
Male and female he created them.

Gen. 27.45 וְשָׁלַחְתִּי וּלְקַחְתִּיךָ מִשָּׁם
...and I will send, and fetch you from there...

12.3   Pronominal Suffixes and the Infinitive

The pronominal suffix may be translated either of two ways when it is attached to the infinitive. The suffix may be the object of the verb, or it may be the subject of the verb.

Infinitive Construct

קָטְלִי	killing me or my killing
קָטְלְךָ	killing you or your killing
קָטְלֵךְ	killing you or your killing
קָטְלוֹ	killing him or his killing
קָטְלָהּ	killing her or her killing
קָטְלֵנוּ	killing us or our killing
קָטְלְכֶם	killing you or your killing
קָטְלָם	killing them or their killing
קָטְלָן	killing them or their killing

> The suffix on an infinitive may be either the subject or the object.

Examples:

וַיִּשְׂנְאוּ אֹתוֹ וְלֹא יָכְלוּ דַּבְּרוֹ לְשָׁלֹם׃   Gen. 37.4

And they hated him, and were not able to speak peaceably to him.

אֵלֶּה תוֹלְדוֹת הַשָּׁמַיִם וְהָאָרֶץ בְּהִבָּרְאָם   Gen. 2.4

These are the generations of the heaven and the earth when they were created.

יְהוָה אֱלֹהִים לָקַח אֶת־הָאָדָם וַיַּנִּחֵהוּ   Gen. 2.15

Yahweh God took the man and he planted him

בְגַן־עֵדֶן לְעָבְדָהּ וּלְשָׁמְרָהּ׃

in the Garden of Eden to work it and to keep it.

12.4   Pronominal Suffixes and the Imperfect

In the imperfect, the *cholem* is reduced to a *sheva* or to a short *qamets*.

Imf 3ms

יִקְטְלֵנִי	He will kill me.	יִקְטְלֵנוּ	He will kill us.
יִקְטָלְךָ	He will kill you (m).	יִקְטָלְכֶם	He will kill you (m).
יִקְטְלֵךְ	He will kill you (f).	יִקְטְלֵם	He will kill them (m).
יִקְטְלֵהוּ	He will kill him.	יִקְטְלֵן	He will kill them (f).

Examples:

וַיְשַׁלְּחֵנוּ יְהוָה לְשַׁחֲתָהּ׃ Gen. 19.13
And Yahweh has sent us to destroy it.

אֱלֹהִים עָשָׂה לְאָדָם וּלְאִשְׁתּוֹ כָּתְנוֹת עוֹר וַיַּלְבִּשֵׁם׃ Gen. 3.21
God made for Adam and his wife garments of skin and he clothed them.

וַיִּמְצָאָהּ מַלְאַךְ יְהוָה עַל־עֵין הַמַּיִם בַּמִּדְבָּר Gen. 16.7
The Angel of Yahweh found her beside the spring of water in the wilderness.

מִשָּׁם יְקַבֶּצְךָ יְהוָה אֱלֹהֶיךָ וּמִשָּׁם יִקָּחֶךָ׃ Deut. 30.4
…from there the LORD your God will gather you, and from there he will fetch you.

12.5   Pronominal Suffixes and the Imperative

Neither the feminine object suffixes nor second person suffixes are used with the imperative.

Imv 2ms	with sg.		Imv 2ms	with pl
קָטְלֵנִי	Kill me!		קָטְלֵנוּ	Kill us!
----			----	
----			----	
קָטְלֵהוּ	Kill him!		קָטְלֵם	Kill them!

Examples:

שִׁמְעֵנוּ אֲדֹנִי   *Hear us, Lord.*   Gen. 23.6
וַיֹּאמֶר שַׁלְּחֻנִי לַאדֹנִי׃   *And he said, 'Send me to my master'.*   Gen. 24.54

EXERCISE 12A

Translate the following:

וּכְשָׁמְעוֹ אֶת־דִּבְרֵי רִבְקָה אֲחֹתוֹ . . .   Gen. 24.30

וְאַבְרָהָם הֹלֵךְ עִמָּם לְשַׁלְּחָם׃   Gen. 18.16

נֹחַ עָשָׂה כְּכֹל אֲשֶׁר־צִוָּהוּ יְהוָה׃   Gen. 7.5

יְהוָה אֱלֹהֵי הַשָּׁמַיִם אֲשֶׁר לְקָחַנִי מִבֵּית אָבִי . . .   Gen. 24.7

יִהְיֶה אֱלֹהִים עִמָּדִי וּשְׁמָרַנִי בַּדֶּרֶךְ הַזֶּה   Gen. 28.20

אֲשֶׁר אָנֹכִי הוֹלֵךְ

12.6   Final ה Verbs

Weak verbs are those that contain either a guttural letter, a נ , a ו , or a י as one of the three root letters. In addition, there are several weak verbs that are unique, e.g. לָקַח. The verb radicals (root letters) are identified by the three letters of the Hebrew word פָּעַל. Thus, a word that begins with the letter נ is called a פ"נ verb. The chart on the following page describes ל"ה verbs, those verbs that end with the letter ה. Some scholars prefer to designate the radicals by the Roman numerals I, II, and III. In that case, we would be studying III-ה verbs (HVS 10A, B, & C).

The most notable characteristic of these verbs is the changes that occur in relation to the final ה (See the Appendix, *Guide to Parsing Hebrew Verbs*).

1.   **ה Changed to י**. In the perfect first and second person forms, the ה reverts back to its original י. This occurs also in the imperfect 2fp, 3fp and in the imperative 2fp.

   Q Pf 1cs is not גָּלַהְתִּי but is גָּלִיתִי

2.   **ה Dropped**. The ה is lost altogether in the perfect 3cp, imperfect 2fs, 2mp, 3mp, imperative 2fs, 2mp, jussive and *wayyiqtol*.

   Example: Q Pf 3cp is not גָּלְהוּ but is גָּלוּ

3.   **Infinitive Construct**. Note the peculiar form of the infinitive construct, ending with ־וֹת.

   Q I C is not גְּלוֹה but is גְּלוֹת

4.   ***Segol.*** Another item of note is the pointing under the second root letter. When the final ה is retained, it prefers the *segol*.

   Q Imf 3ms is not יִגְלָה but is יִגְלֶה

12.6.1   Examples of ל"ה Verbs

עָשָׂה	*to do, to make*	רָאָה	*to see*	הָיָה	*to be*

   וַיַּעַשׂ אֱלֹהִים אֶת־הָרָקִיעַ Gen. 1.7
   And God **made** (Q imf W 3m s) the firmament

   לֹא־יִבָּצֵר מֵהֶם כֹּל אֲשֶׁר יָזְמוּ לַעֲשׂוֹת Gen. 11.6
   nothing will be restrained from them which they have imagined **to do** (Q inf cs.)

   וַיַּרְא אֱלֹהִים אֶת־הָאוֹר כִּי־טוֹב Gen. 1.4
   And God saw (Q imf W 3m s) the light that it was good.

   כִּי־אֹתְךָ רָאִיתִי צַדִּיק לְפָנַי Gen. 7.1
   Because you **I have seen** (Q pf 1c s) righteous before me.

   וַיְהִי רָעָב בָּאָרֶץ Gen. 12.10
   And there was (Q imf W 3m s) a famine in the land.

12.6.2 ל"ה Verb Paradigm

		Qal	Nifal	Hifil	Hofal	Piel	Pual	Hitpael
Pf	1cs	גָּלִיתִי	נִגְלֵיתִי	הִגְלֵיתִי	הָגְלֵיתִי	גִּלִּיתִי	גֻּלֵּיתִי	הִתְגַּלֵּיתִי
	2ms	גָּלִיתָ	נִגְלֵיתָ	הִגְלֵיתָ	הָגְלֵיתָ	גִּלִּיתָ	גֻּלֵּיתָ	הִתְגַּלֵּיתָ
	2fs	גָּלִית	נִגְלֵית	הִגְלֵית	הָגְלֵית	גִּלִּית	גֻּלֵּית	הִתְגַּלֵּית
	3ms	גָּלָה	נִגְלָה	הִגְלָה	הָגְלָה	גִּלָּה	גֻּלָּה	הִתְגַּלָּה
	3fs	גָּלְתָה	נִגְלְתָה	הִגְלְתָה	הָגְלְתָה	גִּלְּתָה	גֻּלְּתָה	הִתְגַּלְּתָה
	1cp	גָּלִינוּ	נִגְלֵינוּ	הִגְלֵינוּ	הָגְלֵינוּ	גִּלִּינוּ	גֻּלֵּינוּ	הִתְגַּלֵּינוּ
	2mp	גְּלִיתֶם	נִגְלֵיתֶם	הִגְלֵיתֶם	הָגְלֵיתֶם	גִּלִּיתֶם	גֻּלֵּיתֶם	הִתְגַּלֵּיתֶם
	2fp	גְּלִיתֶן	נִגְלֵיתֶן	הִגְלֵיתֶן	הָגְלֵיתֶן	גִּלִּיתֶן	גֻּלֵּיתֶן	הִתְגַּלֵּיתֶן
	3cp	גָּלוּ	נִגְלוּ	הִגְלוּ	הָגְלוּ	גִּלּוּ	גֻּלּוּ	הִתְגַּלּוּ
Imf	1cs	אֶגְלֶה	אֶגָּלֶה	אַגְלֶה	אָגְלֶה	אֲגַלֶּה	אֲגֻלֶּה	אֶתְגַּלֶּה
	2ms	תִּגְלֶה	תִּגָּלֶה	תַּגְלֶה	תָּגְלֶה	תְּגַלֶּה	תְּגֻלֶּה	תִּתְגַּלֶּה
	2fs	תִּגְלִי	תִּגָּלִי	תַּגְלִי	תָּגְלִי	תְּגַלִּי	תְּגֻלִּי	תִּתְגַּלִּי
	3ms	יִגְלֶה	יִגָּלֶה	יַגְלֶה	יָגְלֶה	יְגַלֶּה	יְגֻלֶּה	יִתְגַּלֶּה
	3fs	תִּגְלֶה	תִּגָּלֶה	תַּגְלֶה	תָּגְלֶה	תְּגַלֶּה	תְּגֻלֶּה	תִּתְגַּלֶּה
	1cp	נִגְלֶה	נִגָּלֶה	נַגְלֶה	נָגְלֶה	נְגַלֶּה	נְגֻלֶּה	נִתְגַּלֶּה
	2mp	תִּגְלוּ	תִּגָּלוּ	תַּגְלוּ	תָּגְלוּ	תְּגַלּוּ	תְּגֻלּוּ	תִּתְגַּלּוּ
	2fp	תִּגְלֶינָה	תִּגָּלֶינָה	תַּגְלֶינָה	תָּגְלֶינָה	תְּגַלֶּינָה	תְּגֻלֶּינָה	תִּתְגַּלֶּינָה
	3mp	יִגְלוּ	יִגָּלוּ	יַגְלוּ	יָגְלוּ	יְגַלּוּ	יְגֻלּוּ	יִתְגַּלּוּ
	3fp	תִּגְלֶינָה	תִּגָּלֶינָה	תַּגְלֶינָה	תָּגְלֶינָה	תְּגַלֶּינָה	תְּגֻלֶּינָה	תִּתְגַּלֶּינָה
Imv	2ms	גְּלֵה	הִגָּלֵה	הַגְלֵה		גַּלֵּה		הִתְגַּלֵּה
	2fs	גְּלִי	הִגָּלִי	הַגְלִי		גַּלִּי		הִתְגַּלִּי
	2mp	גְּלוּ	הִגָּלוּ	הַגְלוּ		גַּלּוּ		הִתְגַּלּוּ
	2fp	גְּלֶינָה	הִגָּלֶינָה	הַגְלֶינָה		גַּלֶּינָה		הִתְגַּלֶּינָה
Inf	Abs	גָּלֹה	נִגְלֹה	הַגְלֵה	הָגְלֵה	גַּלֵּה		
			הִגָּלֵה			גַּלֹּה		
	Cs	לִגְלוֹת	לְהִגָּלוֹת	לְהַגְלוֹת		לְגַלּוֹת	גֻּלּוֹת	הִתְגַּלּוֹת
Ptc	Act	גֹּלֶה		מַגְלֶה		מְגַלֶּה		מִתְגַּלֶּה
	Pass	גָּלוּי	נִגְלֶה		מֻגְלֶה		מְגֻלֶּה	
W		וַיִּגֶל	וַיִּגָּל	וַיַּגֶל		וַיְגַל	וַיְגֻל	וַיִּתְגַּל
Juss		יִגֶל	יִגָּל	יֶגֶל		יְגַל	יְגֻל	יִתְגַּל

12.7   Interrogative הֲ

The most common way to introduce a question is with the prefix הֲ (HVS 1B).

שָׁמַרְתָּ You have kept.   But . . .   הֲשָׁמַרְתָּ Have you kept?

לֹא שָׁמַרְתָּ You have not kept.   But . . .   הֲלֹא שָׁמַרְתָּ Have you not kept?

יֵשׁ There is.   But . . .   הֲיֵשׁ Is there?

Before a simple *sheva* and before gutturals the pointing is הַ; unless the guttural has *qamets*, in which case it will be הֶ. For example:

הַיְדַעְתֶּם   Do you know?   הַאַתָּה   Are you?

הַאֵן   Is there not?   הֶעָצוּם הוּא   Is he mighty?

The interrogative הֲ looks very much like the definite article הַ.

12.8   Vocabulary for Genesis 3

בּוֹא	*v.* he came	צֶדֶק	*n.* righteousness
גַּן	*n.m.* garden	שַׂר	*n.* leader, official
לְבַד	*n.m.* solitude, alone	לָמָּה	*interr.* why?
דַּעַת	*n.f.* knowledge	מְאֹד	*adv.* very
בְּהֵמָה	*n.f.* cattle	גַּם	*adv.* also, even
נָחָשׁ	*n.* serpent	מִזְבֵּחַ	*n.* altar
עָרוּם	*adj.* 1. cunning; 2. naked	מִלְחָמָה	*n.* war
אַף	*particle.* indeed	מִשְׁפָּט	*n.* justice
פְּרִי	*n.* fruit	זָהָב	*n.* gold
תָּוֶךְ	*n.* midst. *cs* תּוֹךְ midst of	כֶּסֶף	*n.* silver
צֹאן	*n.m.* flock, sheep	קֵץ	*n.m.* end, boundary

EXERCISE 12B

12.9 Reading Genesis 1.1-5

Translate the following verses; parse the verbs that are indicated; and answer all questions. The questions are intended to be reminders of grammatical rules that you have learned in previous lessons. In this exercise, the Hebrew words and phrases are listed, followed by discussion or questions.

Throughout the remaining chapters, reference will be made to the following resources:

Gesenius, Wilhelm, E. Kautzsch, and A.E. Cowley, *Gesenius' Hebrew Grammar* (Oxford: The Clarendon Press, 2nd English edn, 1910).

Joüon, Paul, and T. Muraoka, *A Grammar of Biblical Hebrew* (Subsidia Biblica, 14; 2 vols.; Roma: Editrice Pontificio Instituto Biblico, 1991).

Kelley, Page H., Daniel S. Mynatt, and Timothy G. Crawford, *The Masorah of Biblia Hebraica Stuttgartensia: Introduction and Annotated Glossary* (Grand Rapids: W.B. Eerdmans, 1998).

Niccacci, Alviero, *The Syntax of the Verb in Classical Hebrew Prose* (trans. Wilfred G.E. Watson; JSOTSup, 86; Sheffield: Sheffield Academic Press, 1990).

Seow, C.L., *A Grammar for Biblical Hebrew* (Nashville: Abingdon Press, 1987).

Waltke, Bruce K., and Michael Patrick O'Connor, *An Introduction to Biblical Hebrew Syntax* (Winona Lake, IN: Eisenbrauns, 1990).

Williams, Ronald J., *Hebrew Syntax: An Outline* (Toronto: University of Toronto Press, 2nd edn, 1976).

Although I have given you the complete Hebrew text, you should use your Hebrew Bible (*Biblia Hebraica Stuttgartensia*) as you complete your assignments. By using the Hebrew Bible each week, you will grow accustomed to the appearance of the text.

One of your first obstacles will be the look of clutter on the page. The accent marks on every word, the Masorah in the side margin, and the textual notes at the bottom are distracting to the beginning student (See §28.1).

¹ בְּרֵאשִׁית בָּרָא אֱלֹהִים אֵת הַשָּׁמַיִם וְאֵת הָאָרֶץ

² וְהָאָרֶץ הָיְתָה תֹהוּ וָבֹהוּ וְחֹשֶׁךְ עַל־פְּנֵי תְהוֹם

וְרוּחַ אֱלֹהִים מְרַחֶפֶת עַל־פְּנֵי הַמָּיִם ³ וַיֹּאמֶר אֱלֹהִים יְהִי

אוֹר וַיְהִי־אוֹר ⁴ וַיַּרְא אֱלֹהִים אֶת־הָאוֹר כִּי־טוֹב וַיַּבְדֵּל

אֱלֹהִים בֵּין הָאוֹר וּבֵין הַחֹשֶׁךְ ⁵ וַיִּקְרָא אֱלֹהִים לָאוֹר יוֹם

וְלַחֹשֶׁךְ קָרָא לָיְלָה וַיְהִי־עֶרֶב וַיְהִי־בֹקֶר יוֹם אֶחָד פ

Genesis 1.1

[א]

An abbreviation for א סְדָרָה, meaning '*division one*', dividing the Hebrew Bible into 452 lessons (סְדָרוֹת) according to the Palestinian tradition. They predate the chapter divisions, which were made in the 14th century. *Sidrah,* סְדָרָה, means 'order, division'. *Sidrah two*, [ב], begins at Gen. 2.4. The numbering begins anew with each book. The Torah has 54 lessons (Kelley, p. 155).

בְּרֵאשִׁית

Occurs 51 times (See Waltke §9.6e, Gesenius §130d, and Joüon §129p). Notice that this word is in construct, 'In the beginning of....'

Other constructs followed by finite verbs are: Exod. 6.28; Lev. 25.48; Num. 3.1; Deut. 4.15; 1 Sam. 25.15; 2 Sam. 22.1; Ps. 18.1; 56.10; 102.3; 116.2; Hos. 1.2, and Zech. 8.9. The force of the construct is to present the entire phrase as a noun. The sentence reads: *In the beginning of God's creating the heaven and the earth, the earth was uninhabited and empty, and darkness was upon the face of the deep, and the Spirit of God was hovering over the face of the waters.*

בָּרָא אֱלֹהִים

בָּרָא is *qal* perf 3ms. The second vowel is a *qamets* instead of *patach* because the verb ends in *alef*. We will study this weak pattern in lesson 13. Since this verb is in a construct phrase, it does not stand alone. The entire phrase provides setting for the upcoming narrative. The perfect verb בָּרָא preceded by the temporal phrase בְּרֵאשִׁית is called an x-*qatal*. See §26.1.1 # 1 (section numbers without an author name refer to sections in this book).

אֵת הַשָּׁמַיִם

Q1: What part of speech is אֵת? (§4.5)

Q2: Is the Hebrew word הַשָּׁמַיִם singular?   (§2.1.1)

Q3: Why is there a *dagesh* in the letter *sheen*?   (§2.3)

וְאֵת הָאָרֶץ:

Q4: Why does the article take *qamets* instead of *patach*? (§2.3)

Q5: *Dagesh* follows the article; why is there no *dagesh* in the *alef*? (§2.3 and §2.1.2)

Genesis 1.2

וְהָאָרֶץ

Q6: *Dagesh* follows the article; why is there no *dagesh* in the *alef*? (§2.3 and §2.1.2)

הָיְתָה *was*

The root is הָיָה. In verbs ending with ה the ה changes to ת in the 3fs. (See the paradigms earlier in this chapter, §12.6.2). The verb הָיָה here does not mean 'became'. It means 'became' ONLY when followed by the prep. ל (Cf. Gen. 2.7).

Q7: Why is the verb feminine?

The verb הָיָה preceded by וְהָאָרֶץ is an x-*qatal* and continues to provide setting or background (See §26.1.1 #1).

תֹּהוּ וָבֹהוּ   *uninhabited and empty*

> **Q8:** Are these two words nouns or adjectives?
>
> **Q9:** Why is there a *qamets* under the *vav* instead of *sheva*? (§3.3)

וְחֹשֶׁךְ עַל־פְּנֵי

> Is there a verb in this clause? What is the syntactical function of this clause? (See §26.1.1 #3)

תְהוֹם   *the deep*

וְרוּחַ אֱלֹהִים

> **Q10:** What type of construct–genitive phrase is וְרוּחַ אֱלֹהִים. See §5.3.3.

מְרַחֶפֶת   *(was) hovering* (PARSE this form). See §10.3.4.

> The root is רחף, and we have studied the form. The middle letter should have a *dagesh*, but gutturals do not take the *dagesh* (§2.1.2 and §14.2).
>
> **Q11:** What do the תֶ ֶ ֶ vowels and ending indicate? (§3.4)
>
> **Q12:** Does this ptc. function as a substantive, adjective, or verb? (§3.4.1)
>
> **Q13:** Why is the ptc. feminine?
>
> The ptc. presents action that is contemporary with the previous verb. We still have not begun the narrative (See §26.1.1 #2).

עַל־פְּנֵי הַמָּיִם:

> **Q14:** Why is there a *dagesh* in the *mem*? (§2.3)
>
> **Note:** The vowel in הַמַּיִם is lengthened to הַמָּיִם because it is in pause (§9.6).

Genesis 1.3

וַיֹּאמֶר אֱלֹהִים   *and God said,*

> There are five verbs that begin with *alef* and follow this irregular form of the imperfect (§13.1.2).
>
> **Q15:** What do we call the וַ followed by a *dagesh*? (§7.2)
>
> **Q16:** What is the י in וַיֹּאמֶר ? (§5.1.1)
>
> This *wayyiqtol* verb signals the beginning of the narrative proper (See §26.1.1 #6).

יְהִי אוֹר   *let there be light*

> יְהִי is a jussive (See §26.1.1 #59), shortened from the imf. 3ms: יִהְיֶה. Verbs ending with ה will drop the ה in the jussive (see the paradigms earlier in this chapter, §12.6.2). See also §5.1.2.
>
> **Q17:** What is the י in יְהִי.

וַיְהִי־אוֹר׃ *and light was.*

וַיְהִי is the *wayyiqtol*, shortened from the imf. 3ms: יִהְיֶה. Verbs ending with ה will drop the ה in the *wayyiqtol* (§12.6.2).

Genesis 1.4

וַיַּרְא *and he saw* (וַ יַ רְא)

Qal imf 3ms from רָאָה.

Q18: Is this a *wayyiqtol*?

Verbs ending with ה will drop the ה in the *wayyiqtol*. (§12.6)

Q19: What is the י in וַיַּרְא?

אֱלֹהִים אֶת־הָאוֹר

כִּי־טוֹב

וַיַּבְדֵּל אֱלֹהִים *and God divided* (PARSE וַיַּבְדֵּל)

Q20: Is this verb a *wayyiqtol*?

Q21: Why is there a *patach* under the *yod*? (§9.2.2)

בֵּין הָאוֹר וּבֵין

Q22: Why is there a *qamets* under the ה instead of *patach*? (§2.3)

Q23: In וּבֵין, why is the conjunction וּ instead of וְ? (§3.3)

הַחֹשֶׁךְ׃ *the darkness*

Q24: The definite article is usually followed by a *dagesh* in the next letter. Why is there no *dagesh* here? (§2.3 and §2.1.2)

Genesis 1.5

וַיִּקְרָא אֱלֹהִים (וַ יִ קְרָא)

Q25: Is וַיִּקְרָא an imperfect?

Q26: Is it a *wayyiqtol*?

The final *alef* causes the preceding vowel to be *qamets* instead of *cholem* (§13.2).

לָאוֹר יוֹם

The verb קָרָא is followed by various prepositions, in this case it is followed by the ל. See your Hebrew lexicon for the different meanings.

Q27: Should לָאוֹר be translated *light* or *the light*? (§4.4.2 and §2.3)

לַחֹשֶׁךְ קָרָא לָיְלָה

Q28: Should לַחֹשֶׁךְ be translated *darkness* or *the darkness*? (§4.4.2 and §2.3)

וַיְהִי־עֶרֶב   *and it was evening*

וַיְהִי is the *wayyiqtol*, shortened from the imf. 3ms: יִהְיֶה. Verbs ending with ה will drop the ה in the *wayyiqtol*.

וַיְהִי־בֹקֶר   *and it was morning*

יוֹם אֶחָד:

The most natural translation of יוֹם אֶחָד would be *one day* because אֶחָד means *first* only rarely. However, the fact that it can mean *first*, coupled with the fact that the following verses use the ordinals *second, third*, etc., suggests that יוֹם אֶחָד should be translated *the first day*.

פ Abbreviation for the word פְּתוּחָה (*petucha*), meaning 'open'. It signifies the end of a paragraph that also ends a line. A paragraph that does not end the line is closed with the abbreviation ס, for פְּתוּמָה, *setuma*, meaning 'closed' (see Gen. 3.15). As you can see, this convention is ignored in the *BHS* (Kelley, p. 167).

Qumran Caves near the Dead Sea
where manuscripts of the Hebrew Bible were found.

12.10   Appendix to Chapter 12

12.10.1 Perfect Verb with Pronominal Suffixes

Qal	1cs	2ms	2fs	3ms	3fs	1cp	2m/fp	3cp	Piel 3ms
Suff	קָטַלְתִּי	קָטַלְתָּ	קָטַלְתְּ	קָטַל	קָטְלָה	קָטַלְנוּ	קְטַלְתֶּם/ן	קָטְלוּ	קִטֵּל
1cs		קְטַלְתַּנִי	קְטַלְתִּינִי	קְטָלַנִי	קְטָלַתְנִי		קְטַלְתּוּנִי	קְטָלוּנִי	קִטְּלַנִי
2ms	קְטַלְתִּיךָ			קְטָלְךָ	קְטָלַתְךָ	קְטַלְנוּךָ		קְטָלוּךָ	קִטֶּלְךָ
2fs	קְטַלְתִּיךְ			קְטָלֵךְ	קְטָלַתֶךְ	קְטַלְנוּךְ		קְטָלוּךְ	קִטְּלֵךְ
3ms	קְטַלְתִּיהוּ קְטַלְתִּיו	קְטַלְתָּהוּ קְטַלְתּוֹ	קְטַלְתִּיהוּ	קְטָלוֹ קְטָלָהוּ	קְטָלַתְהוּ	קְטַלְנוּהוּ	קְטַלְתּוּהוּ	קְטָלוּהוּ	קִטְּלוֹ
3fs	קְטַלְתִּיהָ	קְטַלְתָּהּ	קְטַלְתִּיהָ	קְטָלָהּ	קְטָלַתָּהּ	קְטַלְנוּהָ		קְטָלוּהָ	קִטְּלָהּ
1cp		קְטַלְתָּנוּ	קְטַלְתִּינוּ	קְטָלָנוּ	קְטָלַתְנוּ		קְטַלְתּוּנוּ	קְטָלוּנוּ	קִטְּלָנוּ
2mp	קְטַלְתִּיכֶם				קְטָלַנוּכֶם				
2fp	קְטַלְתִּיכֶן								
3mp	קְטַלְתִּים	קְטַלְתָּם	קְטַלְתִּים	קְטָלָם	קְטָלַתַם	קְטַלְנוּם		קְטָלוּם	קִטְּלָם
3fp	קְטַלְתִּין	קְטַלְתָּן	קְטַלְתִּין	קְטָלָן	קְטָלַתַן			קְטָלוּן	קִטְּלָן

12.10.2 Imperfect Verb with Pronominal Suffixes

	Qal Imf 3ms		3mp	Qal Imv Sing.	Plur.	Qal Infin Const	Piel Imf 3ms	Hifil Imf 3ms
Suff	יִקְטֹל	energic נ §12.1.1	יִקְטְלוּ	קְטֹל	קִטְלוּ	קְטֹל	יְקַטֵּל	יַקְטִיל
1cs	יִקְטְלֵנִי	יִקְטְלֵנִּי	יִקְטְלוּנִי	קְטְלֵנִי	קִטְלוּנִי	קָטְלֵנִי	יְקַטְּלֵנִי	יַקְטִילֵנִי
2ms	יִקְטָלְךָ		יִקְטְלוּךָ			קָטְלְךָ קָטְלֶךָ	יְקַטֶּלְךָ	יַקְטִילְךָ
2fs	יִקְטְלֵךְ		יִקְטְלוּךְ			קָטְלֵךְ	יְקַטְּלֵךְ	יַקְטִילֵךְ
3ms	יִקְטְלֵהוּ	יִקְטְלֶנּוּ	יִקְטְלוּהוּ	קָטְלֵהוּ	קִטְלוּהוּ	קָטְלוֹ	יְקַטְּלֵהוּ	etc.
3fs	יִקְטְלֶהָ	יִקְטְלֶנָּה	יִקְטְלוּהָ	קָטְלֶהָ	קִטְלוּהָ	קָטְלָהּ	etc.	
1cp	יִקְטְלֵנוּ		יִקְטְלוּנוּ	קָטְלֵנוּ	קִטְלוּנוּ	קָטְלֵנוּ		
2mp	יִקְטָלְכֶם		יִקְטְלוּכֶם		קִטְלוּכֶם	קָטְלְכֶם		
2fp	יִקְטָלְכֶן		יִקְטְלוּכֶן		קִטְלוּכֶן	קָטְלְכֶן		
3mp	יִקְטְלֵם		יִקְטְלוּם	קָטְלֵם	קִטְלוּם	קָטְלָם		
3fp	יִקְטְלֵן		יִקְטְלוּן		קִטְלוּן	קָטְלָן		

Chapter 13

Initial Guttural Verbs and Reading Genesis 3.1-6

In this chapter you should:

- Learn the characteristics of weak verbs beginning with a guttural letter
- Learn the characteristics of weak verbs ending in the letter א
- Translate Gen. 3.1-6

13.1 Initial Guttural Verbs

Verbs that begin with a guttural letter are called *Initial Guttural* verbs, *I-Guttural* verbs, or the traditional designation the פּ-*Guttural* verbs. There are very few differences between the strong verb and the פּ-Guttural verb:

1. **Sheva.** The simple *sheva* is changed to a composite whenever it is under the guttural.

   Q Imv 2ms is not עְמֹד but is עֲמֹד

2. **Patach for Chireq.** In the *qal* imperfect, the *chireq* becomes *patach* under the influence of the composite.

   Q Imf 3ms is not יְעְמֹד but is יַעֲמֹד

3. **Segol for Chireq.** In the *nifal* perfect and the *hifil* perfect, the *chireq* becomes *segol* under the influence of the composite.

   N Pf 1cs is not נְעֲמַדְתִּי but is נֶעֱמַדְתִּי

4. **Tsere for Chireq.** In the *nifal* imperfect, the *chireq* becomes *tsere* because the guttural cannot take the *dagesh*.

   N Imf 3ms is not יְעָמֵד but is יֵעָמֵד

13.1.1 Examples of Initial Guttural Verbs

Gen. 43.15 וַיַּעַמְדוּ לִפְנֵי יוֹסֵף

And they stood (*Q* imf W 3m pl) before Joseph.

Lev. 16.7 וְהֶעֱמִיד אֹתָם לִפְנֵי יְהֹוָה

And **he will present** (*H* pf We 3m s) them before Yahweh.

Isa. 18.6 יֵעָזְבוּ יַחְדָּו לְעֵיט הָרִים וּלְבֶהֱמַת הָאָרֶץ

They will be forsaken (*N* imf 3m pl) together to the birds of the mountains and to the beasts of the earth.

13.1.2 פ-Guttural Verb Paradigm

		*Qal-*ע	*Qal-*ח	*Qal-*א	*Nifal*	*Hifil*	*Hofal*
Pf	1cs	עָמַדְתִּי	חָזַקְתִּי	אָכַלְתִּי	נֶעֱזַבְתִּי¹	הֶעֱמַדְתִּי	הָעֳמַדְתִּי
	2ms	עָמַדְתָּ	חָזַקְתָּ	אָכַלְתָּ	נֶעֱזַבְתָּ	הֶעֱמַדְתָּ	הָעֳמַדְתָּ
	2fs	עָמַדְתְּ	חָזַקְתְּ	אָכַלְתְּ	נֶעֱזַבְתְּ	הֶעֱמַדְתְּ	הָעֳמַדְתְּ
	3ms	עָמַד	חָזַק	אָכַל	נֶעֱזַב	הֶעֱמִיד	הָעֳמַד
	3fs	עָמְדָה	חָזְקָה	אָכְלָה	נֶעֶזְבָה	הֶעֱמִידָה	הָעֳמְדָה
	1cp	עָמַדְנוּ	חָזַקְנוּ	אָכַלְנוּ²	נֶעֱזַבְנוּ	הֶעֱמַדְנוּ	הָעֳמַדְנוּ
	2mp	עֲמַדְתֶּם	חֲזַקְתֶּם	אֲכַלְתֶּם	נֶעֱזַבְתֶּם	הֶעֱמַדְתֶּם	הָעֳמַדְתֶּם
	2fp	עֲמַדְתֶּן	חֲזַקְתֶּן	אֲכַלְתֶּן	נֶעֱזַבְתֶּן	הֶעֱמַדְתֶּן	הָעֳמַדְתֶּן
	3cp	עָמְדוּ	חָזְקוּ	אָכְלוּ	נֶעֶזְבוּ	הֶעֱמִידוּ	הָעֳמְדוּ
Imf	1cs	אֶעֱמֹד	אֶחֱזַק³	אֹכַל⁴	אֵעָזֵב	אַעֲמִיד	אָעֳמַד
	2ms	תַּעֲמֹד	תֶּחֱזַק	תֹּאכַל	תֵּעָזֵב	תַּעֲמִיד	תָּעֳמַד
	2fs	תַּעַמְדִי	תֶּחֱזְקִי	תֹּאכְלִי	תֵּעָזְבִי	תַּעֲמִידִי	תָּעֳמְדִי
	3ms	יַעֲמֹד	יֶחֱזַק	יֹאכַל	יֵעָזֵב	יַעֲמִיד	יָעֳמַד
	3fs	תַּעֲמֹד	תֶּחֱזַק	תֹּאכַל	תֵּעָזֵב	תַּעֲמִיד	תָּעֳמַד
	1cp	נַעֲמֹד	נֶחֱזַק	נֹאכַל	נֵעָזֵב	נַעֲמִיד	נָעֳמַד
	2mp	תַּעַמְדוּ	תֶּחֱזְקוּ	תֹּאכְלוּ	תֵּעָזְבוּ	תַּעֲמִידוּ	תָּעֳמְדוּ
	2fp	תַּעֲמֹדְנָה	תֶּחֱזַקְנָה	תֹּאכַלְנָה	תֵּעָזַבְנָה	תַּעֲמֵדְנָה	תָּעֳמַדְנָה
	3mp	יַעַמְדוּ	יֶחֱזְקוּ	יֹאכְלוּ	יֵעָזְבוּ	יַעֲמִידוּ	יָעֳמְדוּ
	3fp	תַּעֲמֹדְנָה	תֶּחֱזַקְנָה	תֹּאכַלְנָה	תֵּעָזַבְנָה	תַּעֲמֵדְנָה	תָּעֳמַדְנָה
Imv	2ms	עֲמֹד	חֲזַק	אֱכֹל	הֵעָזֵב	הַעֲמֵד	
	2fs	עִמְדִי	חִזְקִי	אִכְלִי	הֵעָזְבִי	הַעֲמִידִי	
	2mp	עִמְדוּ	חִזְקוּ	אִכְלוּ	הֵעָזְבוּ	הַעֲמִידוּ	
	2fp	עֲמֹדְנָה	חֲזַקְנָה	אֱכֹלְנָה	הֵעָזַבְנָה	הַעֲמֵידְנָה	
Inf A		עָמוֹד		אָכוֹל הֵאָכֹל	נַעֲזוֹב	הַעֲמֵד	הָעֳמֵד
Inf C		עֲמֹד		אֱכֹל⁵	הֵעָזֵב	הַעֲמִיד	
Ptc A		עֹמֵד		אֹכֵל		מַעֲמִיד	
Pass		עָמוּד		אָכוּל	נֶעֱזָב		מָעֳמָד

---

¹ Sometimes you will find *patach* instead of *segol*.

² There are variations on this that you must learn from the lexicon.

³ Sometimes the letter ח takes a simple *sheva*.

⁴ Note that because of the *alef* the *cholem* rests further to the left than would be expected.

⁵ Also found in this form: אֹכַל

13.2   Final א Verbs

The most notable characteristics of ל"א verbs are the changes that occur in relation to the final א.

1. **Quiescent א.** In all forms of the perfect except 3fs, the א is quiescent–it does not take a vowel. To compensate, *patach* is lengthened to *qamets*.

    Q **Pf 1cs is not** מָצַאְתִי **but is** מָצָאתִי

2. *Qamets* **for** *Cholem.* In the *qal* imperfect and imperative, *qamets* replaces the *cholem.*

    Q **Imf 3ms is not** יִמְצֹא **but is** יִמְצָא

13.2.1   Examples of Final א verbs

וְלֹא־מָצְאָה הַיּוֹנָה מָנוֹחַ לְכַף־רַגְלָהּ   Gen. 8.9
But the dove did not **find** (*Q* pf 3f s) a resting place for the sole of her foot.

וַיִּמְצְאוּ בִקְעָה בְּאֶרֶץ שִׁנְעָר   Gen. 11.2
And they found (*Q* imf W 3m pl) a plain in the land of shinar.

וַיִּמְצָאָהּ מַלְאַךְ יְהוָה עַל־עֵין הַמַּיִם   Gen. 16.7
And the angel of Yahweh **found her** (*Q* imf W 3m s+3fs sfx) by the spring of water.

וַיִּלְאוּ לִמְצֹא הַפָּתַח   Gen. 19.11
And they wearied themselves **to find** (*Q* inf cs) the door.

וַיִּמְצָאֵהוּ אִישׁ וְהִנֵּה תֹעֶה בַשָּׂדֶה   Gen. 37.15
And a man **found him** (*Q* imf W 3m s+3ms sfx) and behold,
he was wandering in the field.

Tile Mosaic from the Floor of the
Hamat Gader Synagogue

13.2.2 Final א Verb Paradigm

	Qal	Qal	Nifal	Hifil	Hofal	Piel	Pual	Hitpael
Pf								
1cs	מָצָאתִי	שָׂנֵאתִי	נִמְצֵאתִי	הִמְצֵאתִי	הֻמְצֵאתִי	מִצֵּאתִי	מֻצֵּאתִי	הִתְמַצֵּאתִי
2ms	מָצָאתָ	שָׂנֵאתָ	נִמְצֵאתָ	הִמְצֵאתָ	הֻמְצֵאתָ	מִצֵּאתָ	מֻצֵּאתָ	הִתְמַצֵּאתָ
2fs	מָצָאת	שָׂנֵאת	נִמְצֵאת	הִמְצֵאת	הֻמְצֵאת	מִצֵּאת	מֻצֵּאת	הִתְמַצֵּאת
3ms	מָצָא	שָׂנֵא	נִמְצָא	הִמְצִיא	הֻמְצָא	מִצֵּא	מֻצָּא	הִתְמַצֵּא
3fs	מָצְאָה	שָׂנְאָה	נִמְצְאָה	הִמְצִיאָה	הֻמְצְאָה	מִצְּאָה	מֻצְּאָה	הִתְמַצְּאָה
1cp	מָצָאנוּ	שָׂנֵאנוּ	נִמְצֵאנוּ	הִמְצֵאנוּ	הֻמְצֵאנוּ	מִצֵּאנוּ	מֻצֵּאנוּ	הִתְמַצֵּאנוּ
2mp	מְצָאתֶם	שְׂנֵאתֶם	נִמְצֵאתֶם	הִמְצֵאתֶם	הֻמְצֵאתֶם	מִצֵּאתֶם	מֻצֵּאתֶם	הִתְמַצֵּאתֶם
2fp	מְצָאתֶן	שְׂנֵאתֶן	נִמְצֵאתֶן	הִמְצֵאתֶן	הֻמְצֵאתֶן	מִצֵּאתֶן	מֻצֵּאתֶן	הִתְמַצֵּאתֶן
3cp	מָצְאוּ	שָׂנְאוּ	נִמְצְאוּ	הִמְצִיאוּ	הֻמְצְאוּ	מִצְּאוּ	מֻצְּאוּ	הִתְמַצְּאוּ
Imf								
1cs	אֶמְצָא	אֶשְׂנָא	אֶמָּצֵא	אַמְצִיא	אָמְצָא	אֲמַצֵּא	אֲמֻצָּא	אֶתְמַצֵּא
2ms	תִּמְצָא	תִּשְׂנָא	תִּמָּצֵא	תַּמְצִיא	תָּמְצָא	תְּמַצֵּא	תְּמֻצָּא	תִּתְמַצֵּא
2fs	תִּמְצְאִי	תִּשְׂנְאִי	תִּמָּצְאִי	תַּמְצִיאִי	תָּמְצְאִי	תְּמַצְּאִי	תְּמֻצְּאִי	תִּתְמַצְּאִי
3ms	יִמְצָא	יִשְׂנָא	יִמָּצֵא	יַמְצִיא	יָמְצָא	יְמַצֵּא	יְמֻצָּא	יִתְמַצֵּא
3fs	תִּמְצָא	תִּשְׂנָא	תִּמָּצֵא	תַּמְצִיא	תָּמְצָא	תְּמַצֵּא	תְּמֻצָּא	תִּתְמַצֵּא
1cp	נִמְצָא	נִשְׂנָא	נִמָּצֵא	נַמְצִיא	נָמְצָא	נְמַצֵּא	נְמֻצָּא	נִתְמַצֵּא
2mp	תִּמְצְאוּ	תִּשְׂנְאוּ	תִּמָּצְאוּ	תַּמְצִיאוּ	תָּמְצְאוּ	תְּמַצְּאוּ	תְּמֻצְּאוּ	תִּתְמַצְּאוּ
2fp	תִּמְצֶאנָה	תִּשְׂנֶאנָה	תִּמָּצֶאנָה	תַּמְצֶאנָה	תָּמְצֶאנָה	תְּמַצֶּאנָה	תְּמֻצֶּאנָה	תִּתְמַצֶּאנָה
3mp	יִמְצְאוּ	יִשְׂנְאוּ	יִמָּצְאוּ	יַמְצִיאוּ	יָמְצְאוּ	יְמַצְּאוּ	יְמֻצְּאוּ	יִתְמַצְּאוּ
3fp	תִּמְצֶאנָה	תִּשְׂנֶאנָה	תִּמָּצֶאנָה	תַּמְצֶאנָה	תָּמְצֶאנָה	תְּמַצֶּאנָה	תְּמֻצֶּאנָה	תִּתְמַצֶּאנָה
Imv								
2ms	מְצָא	שְׂנָא	הִמָּצֵא	הַמְצֵא		מַצֵּא		הִתְמַצֵּא
2fs	מִצְאִי	שִׂנְאִי	הִמָּצְאִי	הַמְצִיאִי		מַצְּאִי		הִתְמַצְּאִי
2mp	מִצְאוּ	שִׂנְאוּ	הִמָּצְאוּ	הַמְצִיאוּ		מַצְּאוּ		הִתְמַצְּאוּ
2fp	מְצֶאנָה	שְׂנֶאנָה	הִמָּצֶאנָה	הַמְצֶאנָה		מַצֶּאנָה		הִתְמַצֶּאנָה
IA	מָצוֹא	שָׂנוֹא	נִמְצֹא	הַמְצֵא		מַצֵּא		הִתְמַצֵּא
IC	מְצֹא	שְׂנֹא	הִמָּצֵא	הַמְצִיא		מַצֵּא		הִתְמַצֵּא
APtc	מֹצֵא	שֹׂנֵא		מַמְצִיא		מְמַצֵּא		מִתְמַצֵּא
PPtc	מָצוּא		נִמְצָא		מֻמְצָא		מְמֻצָּא	
W	וַיִּמְצָא		וַיִּמָּצֵא	וַיַּמְצֵא	וַיָּמְצָא	וַיְמַצֵּא	וַיְמֻצָּא	וַיִּתְמַצֵּא

13.3   Vocabulary for Genesis 6

יָטַב	*v.* to be well[6]	תָּמִים	*n.m.p.* blameless
רָעָה	*v.* to shepherd	יֵצֶר	*n.m.* shape, form
מִנְחָה	*n.m.* offering	חֵן	*n.m.* grace, favor
רָבָה	*v.* to become many	רֶמֶשׂ	*n.m.* creeping thing, insect
רָבַב	by-form of רָבָה above	דּוֹר	*n.m.* generation
דּוּן	*v.* to be remain, to stay	תּוֹלְדֹת	*n.f.pl* descendents
עָצֵב	*v.* to grieve	שְׁלֹשָׁה	*adj. f.* three
בָּחַר	*v.* to choose	עֶשְׂרִים	*adj.* twenty
מָחָה	*v.* to blot out	מֵאָה	*adj.* one hundred
חָלַל	*v.* to begin	נְפִילִים	*n.* giants or *pr.n.* Nephilim
נָחַם	*v. nifal* to be sorry	עוֹלָם	*n.* forever, a long time
יֶפֶת	*p.n.* Japheth	מַחֲשָׁבָה	*n. f.* thought
חָם	*p.n.* Ham	שֶׁ	*rel. prn.* who, which
נֹחַ	*p.n.* Noah	צַדִּיק	*adj.* righteous
רַק	*adv.* only	גִּבּוֹר	*adj.* mighty, strong

EXERCISE 13

13.4 Reading Genesis 3.1-6

Translate the following verses; parse the verbs that are indicated; and answer all questions. The questions are intended to be reminders of grammatical rules that you have learned in previous lessons. In this exercise, the Hebrew words and phrases are listed, followed by discussion or questions.

Although I have given you the complete Hebrew text, you should use your Hebrew Bible (*Biblia Hebraica Stuttgartensia*) as you complete this assignment. By using the Hebrew Bible each week, you will grow accustomed to the appearance of the text.

You may use any reference works that you find helpful. One of your first obstacles will be the look of clutter on the page. The accent marks on every word, the Masorah in the side margin, and the textual notes at the bottom are distracting to the beginning student. You will soon grow accustomed to them.

---

[6] From this point forward, the definition of verbs will be given in the English infinitive form, just as they would be defined in the lexicon. Keep in mind that the lexical form of the verb is the masc. singular, third person, *he* . . . .

וְהַנָּחָשׁ הָיָה עָרוּם מִכֹּל חַיַּת הַשָּׂדֶה אֲשֶׁר ¹
עָשָׂה יְהוָה אֱלֹהִים וַיֹּאמֶר אֶל־הָאִשָּׁה אַף כִּי־אָמַר אֱלֹהִים
לֹא תֹאכְלוּ מִכֹּל עֵץ הַגָּן ²וַתֹּאמֶר הָאִשָּׁה אֶל־הַנָּחָשׁ
מִפְּרִי עֵץ־הַגָּן נֹאכֵל ³וּמִפְּרִי הָעֵץ אֲשֶׁר בְּתוֹךְ־הַגָּן אָמַר
אֱלֹהִים לֹא תֹאכְלוּ מִמֶּנּוּ וְלֹא תִגְּעוּ בּוֹ פֶּן־תְּמֻתוּן
⁴וַיֹּאמֶר הַנָּחָשׁ אֶל־הָאִשָּׁה לֹא־מוֹת תְּמֻתוּן ⁵כִּי יֹדֵעַ אֱלֹהִים
כִּי בְּיוֹם אֲכָלְכֶם מִמֶּנּוּ וְנִפְקְחוּ עֵינֵיכֶם וִהְיִיתֶם כֵּאלֹהִים
יֹדְעֵי טוֹב וָרָע ⁶וַתֵּרֶא הָאִשָּׁה כִּי טוֹב הָעֵץ לְמַאֲכָל וְכִי
תַאֲוָה־הוּא לָעֵינַיִם וְנֶחְמָד הָעֵץ לְהַשְׂכִּיל וַתִּקַּח מִפִּרְיוֹ
וַתֹּאכַל וַתִּתֵּן גַּם־לְאִישָׁהּ עִמָּהּ וַיֹּאכַל

Genesis 3.1

וְהַנָּחָשׁ

וְ הַ נָּחָשׁ

Q1: What is the הַ?

Q2: Why is there a *dagesh* in the נָ? (§2.3)

This clause is an x-*qatal*, indicating antecedent information (See §26.1.1 #1). It gives background information that precedes the account that is to follow.

הָיָה עָרוּם

Q3: Parse הָיָה

מִכֹּל חַיַּת הַשָּׂדֶה

מִ כֹּל

The preposition is used for the comparative *more than* (§8.4.2). See Williams §317.

Q4: Is there any difference in meaning between כֹּל and כּוֹל? (§1.8.2)

Q5: The word חַיַּת is from חַיָּה, so why does it end with a ת?

הַ שָּׂדֶה

Q6: What is the הַ?

Q7: Why is there a *dagesh* in the שׂ? (§2.3)

אֲשֶׁר עָשָׂה יְהוָה אֱלֹהִים

Q8: Parse עָשָׂה

Q9: Why is עָשָׂה not spelled עָשַׂה? (§12.6.2)

Note: The action of this verb preceded the previous clause, therefore עָשָׂה should be translated as a pluperfect *had made*.

וַיֹּאמֶר אֶל־הָאִשָּׁה

וַ יֹּ אמֶר

Q10: What part of speech is the יֹּ? (§5.1.1)

Q11: Is וַיֹּאמֶר a *wayyiqtol*? (§13.1.2)

Q12: Parse וַיֹּאמֶר

Important Syntax Note: The *wayyiqtol* following a stative verb does not indicate succession, Joüon §118c. The main verb in this sentence is *was*, so וַיֹּאמֶר is not successive. As mentioned above, the first part of this verse is antecedent information and וַיֹּאמֶר is the first action in the narrative.

Q13: What is the הָ in הָאִשָּׁה?

Q14: Why is there no *dagesh* in the א? (§2.1.2 and §2.3)

אַף כִּי־אָמַר אֱלֹהִים   Williams §383-87

The combination אַף כִּי is found 19 times in the Bible, and usually indicates a question.

Q15: Parse אָמַר

לֹא תֹאכְלוּ

Remember, the imperfect with לֹא is used as a negative command (§6.3).

תֹ אכל וּ

Q16: What part of speech is the וּ? (§5.1.1)

Q17: Parse תֹאכְלוּ   (§13.1.2)

מִכֹּל עֵץ הַגָּן׃

מִ כֹּל   (See §8.4)

Remember that כֹּל can be translated as *all* or *every*.

Q18: Is עֵץ singular or plural?

הַ גָּן

Q19: What is the הַ? (§2.3)

Q20: Why is there a *dagesh* in the גּ? (§2.3)

Genesis 3.2

וַתֹּאמֶר הָאִשָּׁה

וַ ‍תֹ אמֶר

Q21: Why is וַתֹּאמֶר not spelled וַתְּאמֹר? (§13.1.2)

Q22: What part of speech is the תֹ in וַתֹּאמֶר? (§5.1.1)

Q23: Parse וַתֹּאמֶר

Note the naming of the subject, showing the move to a new speaker.

מִפְּרִי עֵץ־הַגָּן

Q24: This phrase contains two construct forms. Classify them, §5.3.3.

נאכֵל:

נ אכֵל:

Q25: Parse נאכֵל   (§5.1.1)

Q26: Why isn't נאכֵל spelled נֹאכֹל? (§13.1.2)

Genesis 3.3

וּמִפְּרִי הָעֵץ

וּ מִ פְּרִי

Q27: What part of speech is the מִ? (§8.4)

הָ עֵץ

Q28: What part of speech is the הָ? (§2.3)

Q29: Why is the pointing הָ instead of הַ? (§2.3)

אֲשֶׁר בְּתוֹך־הַגָּן

Q30: Where is the verb in this clause?

תוֹך is the construct form of תָּוֶך

אָמַר אֱלֹהִים

Q31: Parse אָמַר

לֹא תֹאכְלוּ מִמֶּנּוּ

Q32: Analyze and describe מִמֶּנּוּ. (See §8.6.1)

Q33: Parse תֹאכְלוּ (§13.1.2)

וְלֹא תִגְּעוּ בּוֹ

תִ גְּע וּ

תִּגְּעוּ is *qal* imf, 2d masc. plural, from נָגַע. When the letter *nun* begins a word, it will assimilate in the imperfect (§14.1.2).

Q34: Analyze and describe בּוֹ. (§6.4.3)

פֶּן־תְּמֻתוּן: Williams §461, §175

תְּ מֻת וּ ן

This usage of the letter וּ is called *paragogic nun*, and it appears at the end of certain imperfects that end in open syllables. Hebrew scholars do not agree on the significance of the *paragogic nun*, and most would contend that the letter is added for euphony and adds no meaning to the text.

Remember, there is no difference in meaning between מֵת and מוּת. Verbs that have *vav* or *yod* as the middle radical are called hollow verbs. They form a class of weak verbs that we will study in a later chapter.

תְּמֻתוּן is *qal* imf, 2nd masc. plural, from מוּת.

Grammatical note: The uncertainty implied by the word פֶּן will cause any imperfect that follows it to be understood as subjunctive.

Genesis 3.4

וַיֹּאמֶר הַנָּחָשׁ אֶל־הָאִשָּׁה

לֹא־מוֹת תְּמֻתוּן:

מוֹת is the *qal* infinitive absolute (§6.5.1) and תְּמֻתוּן is parsed above.

See also Williams §205

Genesis 3.5

כִּי יֹדֵעַ אֱלֹהִים

יֹדֵעַ is the *qal* active participle of יָדַע. Verbs ending with a guttural often have a *furtive patach*. Williams §213

כִּי בְּיוֹם אֲכָלְכֶם מִמֶּנּוּ

אֲכָל כֶם

Q35: Define/explain כֶם. (§12.3) Williams §109

וְנִפְקְחוּ עֵינֵיכֶם   Williams §440

וְ נִ פְקַח וּ

Q36: What part of speech is the וְ? (§3.3)

Q37: What part of speech is the נִ? (§8.2.1)

Q38: Parse וְנִפְקְחוּ

Q39: Should וְנִפְקְחוּ be translated as past, present, or future? Why? (§7.3)

וִהְיִיתֶם כֵּאלֹהִים

וְ הְיִי תֶם

This form is on the chart for ל"ה verbs (§12.6.2). The chart, of course, will not have the form with the conjunction attached.

Q40: Parse וִהְיִיתֶם

Q41: Should וִהְיִיתֶם be translated as past, present, or future? Why? (§7.3 and Williams §179)

יֹדְעֵי טוֹב וָרָע:

Note that יֹדְעֵי is in construct; therefore, the phrase is translated literally, *knowers of good and evil* (§5.3).

Genesis 3.6

וַתֵּרֶא הָאִשָּׁה

Q42: Parse וַתֵּרֶא (§12.6.2)

כִּי טוֹב הָעֵץ לְמַאֲכָל

Q43: Is there a verb in this clause? (§3.2)

וְכִי תַאֲוָה־הוּא לָעֵינַיִם

Find תַאֲוָה in your Hebrew lexicon.

וְנֶחְמָד הָעֵץ לְהַשְׂכִּיל

וְ נֶ חְמָד

Find חָמַד in your lexicon.

Q44: What is the significance of the וְ?

Q45: Parse וְנֶחְמָד (see the chart of פ-Guttural verbs, (§13.1 and §13.1.2)

לְ הַ שְׂכִּיל

Q46: What does the infixed י indicate? (§9.2.2)

Q47: What verb form usually has the prefixed preposition? (§6.5.2)

וַתִּקַּח מִפִּרְיוֹ

וַ תִּ קַּח   *and she took*

Note the *dagesh* in the *qof*, indicating the assimilation of the first root letter. This irregular verb is *qal* imperfect, 3d fem. sing. from לָקַח. We will look at this verb in Chapter 14.

מִ פְּרִי וֹ

Q48: What part of speech is the וֹ? (§6.4.1)

וַתֹּאכַל

Q49: Parse וַתֹּאכַל

וַתִּתֵּן גַּם־לְאִישָׁהּ

וַ תּ תֵּן   *and she gave*

Note the *dagesh* in the *tav*, indicating the assimilation of the first root letter, נ. This verb is *Qal* imperfect W, 3rd fem. sing. from נָתַן (Williams §378). We will look at this verb in Chapter 14.

עִמָּהּ וַיֹּאכַל:

עִמָּ הּ

Q50: What part of speech is הּ? (§6.4.3)

וַיֹּאכַל   may be divided into the following parts: וַ יֹּ אכַל

וַיֹּאכַל   is *qal* imperfect (*wayyiqtol*) 3ms, from אכל.

Leningrad Codex (Mic. 7.18-Jon. 2.7)—1010 CE

Initial *Nun* Verbs and Reading Genesis 6.1-8

In this chapter you should:

- Learn the forms of weak verbs beginning with the letter נ (called פ"נ verbs)
- Learn the forms of weak verbs with a guttural as the middle radical
- Translate Gen. 6.1-8

14.1   Weak Verbs Beginning with נ

When a verb begins with the letter נ, that נ will often be assimilated in the *qal* imperfect, the *nifal*, the *hifil*, and the *hofal*. For example, the *qal* Imperfect 3ms of נסך is not יִנְסֹךְ , but is יִסֹּךְ (HVS 6B).

$$יִסֹּךְ \rightarrow יִנְסֹךְ$$

The *dagesh forte* in the ס compensates for the assimilation of the נ. However, some verbs that begin with נ do not assimilate the נ. These verbs have been separated in the following lists.

Common Verbs that Assimilate the נ in the Imperfect:

נָבַט	look at	נָפַל	fall (very common verb)
נָגַע	touch	נָתַר	fall
נָגַשׁ	approach	נָקַם	take revenge
נָזָה	be sprinkled, spatter	נָשָׂא	lift up, bear up (very common)
נָחַת	march	נָשַׁךְ	bite
נָטָה	extend, stretch out	נָתַן	give (very common)
נָטַע	plant	נָתַץ	tear down
נָטַר	keep, guard	נָתַק	tear away
נָטַשׁ	abandon	נָתַשׁ	uproot
נָסַךְ	pour out	נָצַר	keep, guard
נָסַע	tear out		

There are numerous less common examples. Also, many other common פ"נ verbs do not occur in the *qal* imperfect, e.g. נגד, נחם, נבט, נכה, נסה, נצב, and נצל.

Some פ"נ Verbs that Assimilate the נ only in the *Nifal*:

נָאַף	commit adultery	נָהַק	shriek
נָאַץ	distain	נָהַר	flow
נָאַק	groan	נוא	hinder
נָבָא	prophesy	נוב	prosper
נָדַף	blow away, scatter	נוד	sway
נָהַג	lead, urge	נוה	succeed
נָהַם	growl	נָחַל	possess
נוט	quake	נָעַל	tie, bind
נום	fall asleep	נָעַם	be pleasant
נוס	flee, escape	נָקַב	pierce
נוע	shake, tremble	נָקַף	go around a circuit
נוף	swing, wave	נחה	lead

14.1.1   Notes on the פ"נ Paradigm

The following chart gives the paradigm for the פ"נ verbs Note these distinguishing marks:

1. **Assimilation**

   a. In the *qal* imperfect, the letter נ is assimilated, resulting in a *dagesh forte* in the middle radical. Assimilation also occurs in the imperative.

   Q Imf 3ms of נסך is not יִנְסֹךְ , but is יִסֹּךְ

   b. In the *nifal*, *hifil*, and *hofal*, assimilation occurs in all forms.

   H Pf 3ms of נצל is not הִנְצִיל , but is הִצִּיל

2. **Doubly Weak Verbs.** The verb נגע is doubly weak; it begins with נ and ends with a guttural. Therefore, in addition to the assimilation of נ, the furtive *patach* is evident in 5 forms, and the imperfect has *patach*. Note also the loss of נ in the imperative.

   Q Imf 3ms of נגע is not יִנְגַּע , but is יִגַּע

3. The verb נתן is unique and must be learned separately. In some forms of the verb, the middle ת is the only one of the three radicals that remains. The verb נָתַן is very common. It must be mastered (see §22.13).

   Q Imf 2fp is תִּתֵּנָה, and Q infinitive construct is תֵּת

   Q Imf 3ms of נתן is not יִנְתֹּן , but is יִתֵּן

   Q Imv 2ms of נתן is not נְתֹן , but is תֵּן

4.   The verb לָקַח, *to take,* is irregular and behaves as if the ל were a נ. Therefore, whenever you see a verb whose root appears to be קח, it will always be לָקַח.[1] The verb לָקַח is very common, occurring 966 times.

Q Imf 3ms of לָקַח **is not** יִלְקַח **, but is** יִקַּח[2]

Q Imv 2ms of לָקַח **is not** לְקַח **, but is** קַח

The infinitive is לָקַחַת

14.1.1.1 Examples of פ"נ verbs

נָשָׂא to bear, to carry, to lift   נָתַן to give   לָקַח to take

וַיִּשָּׂא עֵינָיו וַיַּרְא Gen. 18.2
And he lifted up (*Q* imf 3m s) his eyes and he saw . . .

וַתִּשָּׂא אֶת־קֹלָהּ וַתֵּבְךְּ Gen. 21.16
And she lifted up (*Q* imf 3f s) her voice and she wept.

וּמַדּוּעַ תִּתְנַשְּׂאוּ עַל־קְהַל יְהוָה Num. 16.3
And why do **you lift up yourselves** (*Ht* imf 2m pl) over the congregation of Yahweh?

וְשָׂא עֵינֶיךָ יָמָּה Deut. 3.27
And lift up (*Q* imv 2m s) your eyes seaward.

וַתִּתֵּן גַּם־לְאִישָׁהּ עִמָּהּ וַיֹּאכַל Gen. 3.6
And she gave (*Q* imf 3f s) also to her husband with her, and he ate.

וַיִּתֵּן אַבְרָהָם אֶת־כָּל־אֲשֶׁר־לוֹ לְיִצְחָק Gen. 25.5
And Abraham **gave** (Q imf 3m s) all that was his to Isaac.

וְאֶת־הָאָרֶץ אֲשֶׁר נָתַתִּי לְאַבְרָהָם וּלְיִצְחָק לְךָ אֶתְּנֶנָּה Gen. 35.12
The land that **I gave** (*Q* pf 1c s) to Abraham and to Isaac—to you **I give it** (*Q* imf 1c s+3fs sfx).

מִשָּׁם יְקַבֶּצְךָ יְהוָה אֱלֹהֶיךָ וּמִשָּׁם יִקָּחֶךָ׃ Deut. 30.4
From there Yahweh your God will gather you and from there **he will take you** (*Q* imf 3m s+2ms sfx).

קַח־נָא אֶת־בִּנְךָ אֶת־יְחִידְךָ אֲשֶׁר־אָהַבְתָּ אֶת־יִצְחָק Gen. 22.2
Take (*Q* imv 2m s) now your son, your only one, whom you love, Isaac.

---

[1] The only exception is Num. 16.1, where the form וַיִּקַּח appears, possibly derived from the root יקח, meaning *act shamelessly.*

[2] The *qal* imperative 2ms occurs 81 times, and only twice does it retain the ל. Note the *dagesh forte* compensative that occurs because of the assimilation.

14.1.2 פ"נ Verb Pattern (When Assimilation Occurs)

		Qal	Qal	Qal	Nifal	Hifil	Hofal
		fall	*touch*	*give*	*delivered*	*deliver*	*deliver*
Pf	1cs	נָפַלְתִּי	נָגַעְתִּי	נָתַתִּי	נִצַּלְתִּי	הִצַּלְתִּי	הֻצַּלְתִּי
	2ms	נָפַלְתָּ	נָגַעְתָּ	נָתַתָּ	נִצַּלְתָּ	הִצַּלְתָּ	הֻצַּלְתָּ
	2fs	נָפַלְתְּ	נָגַעְתְּ	נָתַתְּ	נִצַּלְתְּ	הִצַּלְתְּ	הֻצַּלְתְּ
	3ms	נָפַל	נָגַע	נָתַן	נִצַּל	הִצִּיל	הֻצַּל
	3fs	נָפְלָה	נָגְעָה	נָתְנָה	נִצְּלָה	הִצִּילָה	הֻצְּלָה
	1cp	נָפַלְנוּ	נָגַעְנוּ	נָתַנּוּ	נִצַּלְנוּ	הִצַּלְנוּ	הֻצַּלְנוּ
	2mp	נְפַלְתֶּם	נְגַעְתֶּם	נְתַתֶּם	נִצַּלְתֶּם	הִצַּלְתֶּם	הֻצַּלְתֶּם
	2fp	נְפַלְתֶּן	נְגַעְתֶּן	נְתַתֶּן	נִצַּלְתֶּן	הִצַּלְתֶּן	הֻצַּלְתֶּן
	3cp	נָפְלוּ	נָגְעוּ	נָתְנוּ	נִצְּלוּ	הִצִּילוּ	הֻצְּלוּ
Imf	1cs	אֶפֹּל	אֶגַּע	אֶתֵּן	אֶנָּצֵל	אַצִּיל	אֻצַּל
	2ms	תִּפֹּל	תִּגַּע	תִּתֵּן	תִּנָּצֵל	תַּצִּיל	תֻּצַּל
	2fs	תִּפְּלִי	תִּגְּעִי	תִּתְּנִי	תִּנָּצְלִי	תַּצִּילִי	תֻּצְּלִי
	3ms	יִפֹּל	יִגַּע	יִתֵּן	יִנָּצֵל	יַצִּיל	יֻצַּל
	3fs	תִּפֹּל	תִּגַּע	תִּתֵּן	תִּנָּצֵל	תַּצִּיל	תֻּצַּל
	1cp	נִפֹּל	נִגַּע	נִתֵּן	נִנָּצֵל	נַצִּיל	נֻצַּל
	2mp	תִּפְּלוּ	תִּגְּעוּ	תִּתְּנוּ	תִּנָּצְלוּ	תַּצִּילוּ	תֻּצְּלוּ
	2fp	תִּפֹּלְנָה	תִּגַּעְנָה	תִּתֵּנָּה	תִּנָּצַלְנָה	תַּצֵּלְנָה	תֻּצַּלְנָה
	3mp	יִפְּלוּ	יִגְּעוּ	יִתְּנוּ	יִנָּצְלוּ	יַצִּילוּ	יֻצְּלוּ
	3fp	תִּפֹּלְנָה	תִּגַּעְנָה	תִּתֵּנָּה	תִּנָּצַלְנָה	תַּצֵּלְנָה	תֻּצַּלְנָה
Imv	2ms	נְפֹל	גַּע³	תֵּן	הִנָּצֵל	הַצֵּל	
	2fs	נִפְלִי	גְּעִי	תְּנִי	הִנָּצְלִי	הַצִּילִי	
	2mp	נִפְלוּ	גְּעוּ	תְּנוּ	הִנָּצְלוּ	הַצִּילוּ	
	2fp	נְפֹלְנָה	גַּעְנָה	תֵּנָּה	הִנָּצַלְנָה	הַצֵּלְנָה	
Inf	Abs	נָפוֹל	נָגוֹעַ	נָתוֹן	הִנָּצֵל	הַצֵּל	הֻצֵּל
	Cs	נְפֹל	גַּעַת	תֵּת	הִנָּצֵל	הַצִּיל	הֻצַּל
	Alt		נְגֹעַ	נָתֹן			
Ptc	Act	נֹפֵל	נֹגֵעַ	נֹתֵן		מַצִּיל	
	Pass	נָפוּל	נָגוּעַ	נָתוּן	נִצָּל		מֻצָּל
W		וַיִּפֹּל	וַיִּגַּע	וַיִּתֵּן	וַיִּנָּצֵל	וַיַּצֵּל	וַיֻּצַּל

---

3 Note the *dagesh lene* (not *dagesh forte*) in the imperative conjugations beginning with גַּע and תֵּן.

14.2   Medial Guttural Verbs

The ע-guttural verbs have a guttural letter as their middle radical. Because of few changes, the ע-guttural verbs are very easy to recognize. The ע-guttural verbs are pointed differently from the strong verbs in only three ways.

1.   *Sheva.* The simple *sheva*s under the guttural letter will become composite *sheva*s.

     Q Pf 3mp of בָּחַר is not בָּחְרוּ , but is בָּחֲרוּ

2.   *Patach* for *Cholem.* The second vowel of the *qal* imperfect will be *patach* instead of *cholem.*

     Q Imf 3ms of בָּחַר is not יִבְחֹר , but is יִבְחַר

3.   **Compensatory Lengthening.** Guttural letters do not accept the *dagesh*; therefore, the vowel preceding the guttural will be lengthened in any verb form where a *dagesh* would have been expected to occur in the guttural. In the *piel*, *chireq* is lengthened to *tsere*; in the *pual*, *qibbuts* is lengthened to *cholem*; and in the *hitpael*, *patach* is lengthened to *qamets*.

     Hitpael Pf 3ms of בָּחַר is not הִתְבַּחֵר , but is הִתְבָּחֵר

Notice, however, that a few verbs (like the *piel* of מהר) do not fit the standard paradigm. They do not have the *dagesh*, but they do not lengthen the preceding vowel.

Stones from the Capernaum Synagogue
Decorated with the Star of David

14.2.1 Medial Guttural Verb Paradigm

		Qal choose	*Nifal* be chosen	*Piel* refuse	*Piel* hasten	*Pual* blessed	*Hitpael* bless oneself
Pf	1cs	בָּחַרְתִּי	נִבְחַרְתִּי	מֵאַנְתִּי	מִהַרְתִּי	בֹּרַכְתִּי	הִתְבָּרַכְתִּי
	2ms	בָּחַרְתָּ	נִבְחַרְתָּ	מֵאַנְתָּ	מִהַרְתָּ	בֹּרַכְתָּ	הִתְבָּרַכְתָּ
	2fs	בָּחַרְתְּ	נִבְחַרְתְּ	מֵאַנְתְּ	מִהַרְתְּ	בֹּרַכְתְּ	הִתְבָּרַכְתְּ
	3ms	בָּחַר	נִבְחַר	מֵאֵן	מִהַר	בֹּרַךְ	הִתְבָּרֵךְ
	3fs	בָּחֲרָה	נִבְחֲרָה	מֵאֲנָה	מִהֲרָה	בֹּרְכָה	הִתְבָּרְכָה
	1cp	בָּחַרְנוּ	נִבְחַרְנוּ	מֵאַנּוּ	מִהַרְנוּ	בֹּרַכְנוּ	הִתְבָּרַכְנוּ
	2mp	בְּחַרְתֶּם	נִבְחַרְתֶּם	מֵאַנְתֶּם	מִהַרְתֶּם	בֹּרַכְתֶּם	הִתְבָּרַכְתֶּם
	2fp	בְּחַרְתֶּן	נִבְחַרְתֶּן	מֵאַנְתֶּן	מִהַרְתֶּן	בֹּרַכְתֶּן	הִתְבָּרַכְתֶּן
	3cp	בָּחֲרוּ	נִבְחֲרוּ	מֵאֲנוּ	מִהֲרוּ	בֹּרְכוּ	הִתְבָּרְכוּ
Imf	1cs	אֶבְחַר	אֶבָּחֵר	אֲמָאֵן	אֲמַהֵר	אֲבֹרַךְ	אֶתְבָּרֵךְ
	2ms	תִּבְחַר	תִּבָּחֵר	תְּמָאֵן	תְּמַהֵר	תְּבֹרַךְ	תִּתְבָּרֵךְ
	2fs	תִּבְחֲרִי	תִּבָּחֲרִי	תְּמָאֲנִי	תְּמַהֲרִי	תְּבֹרְכִי	תִּתְבָּרְכִי
	3ms	יִבְחַר	יִבָּחֵר	יְמָאֵן	יְמַהֵר	יְבֹרַךְ	יִתְבָּרֵךְ
	3fs	תִּבְחַר	תִּבָּחֵר	תְּמָאֵן	תְּמַהֵר	תְּבֹרַךְ	תִּתְבָּרֵךְ
	1cp	נִבְחַר	נִבָּחֵר	נְמָאֵן	נְמַהֵר	נְבֹרַךְ	נִתְבָּרֵךְ
	2mp	תִּבְחֲרוּ	תִּבָּחֲרוּ	תְּמָאֲנוּ	תְּמַהֲרוּ	תְּבֹרְכוּ	תִּתְבָּרְכוּ
	2fp	תִּבְחַרְנָה	תִּבָּחַרְנָה	תְּמָאֵנָּה	תְּמַהֵרְנָה	תְּבֹרַכְנָה	תִּתְבָּרַכְנָה
	3mp	יִבְחֲרוּ	יִבָּחֲרוּ	יְמָאֲנוּ	יְמַהֲרוּ	יְבֹרְכוּ	יִתְבָּרְכוּ
	3fp	תִּבְחַרְנָה	תִּבָּחַרְנָה	תְּמָאֵנָּה	תְּמַהֵרְנָה	תְּבֹרַכְנָה	תִּתְבָּרַכְנָה
Imv	2ms	בְּחַר	הִבָּחֵר	מָאֵן	מַהֵר		הִתְבָּרֵךְ
	2fs	בַּחֲרִי	הִבָּחֲרִי	מָאֲנִי	מַהֲרִי		הִתְבָּרְכִי
Inf	2mp	בַּחֲרוּ	הִבָּחֲרוּ	מָאֲנוּ	מַהֲרוּ		הִתְבָּרְכוּ
	2fp	בְּחַרְנָה	הִבָּחַרְנָה	מָאֵנָה	מַהֵרְנָה		הִתְבָּרַכְנָה
	Abs	בָּחוֹר	נִבְחוֹר	מָאֵן	מַהֵר		הִתְבָּרֵךְ
	Cs	בְּחֹר	הִבָּחֵר	מָאֵן	מַהֵר		הִתְבָּרֵךְ
Ptc	Act	בֹּחֵר	נִבְחָר	מְמָאֵן	מְמַהֵר		מִתְבָּרֵךְ
	Pass	בָּחוּר				מְבֹרָךְ	
W		וַיִּבְחַר	וַיִּבָּחֵר	וַיְמָאֵן	וַיְמַהֵר		וַיִּתְבָּרֵךְ

14.3   Vocabulary for Genesis 9

אָסַף   *v.* to gather[4]

חָזַק   *v.* to be strong

חָטָא   *v.* to sin

חָיָה   *v.* to live, be alive

יָשַׁע[5]   *v.* to save; *nifal*, נוֹשַׁע he was saved; *hifil*, הוֹשִׁעַ, he saved

כּוּן   *v.* to stand fast, stand firm

מָלֵא   *v.* to be full

הִגִּיד   *v. hifil*, he told, > נָגַד to report, to tell

נָטָה   *v.* to stretch out, extend

עָנַן   *v.* to make clouds (*piel*)

פָּרָה   *v.* to bear fruit

שִׂים   *v.* to put, place

שׁוּב   *v.* to turn, return

שָׁרַץ   *v.* to teem, swarm

מַאֲכָל   *n.* food

רָבָה   *v.* to multiply, become many

קוּם   *v. qal:* to arise, stand; *hifil*, הֵקִים, establish

מַבּוּל   *n.* flood

עָנָן   *n.* cloud

קֶשֶׁת   *n.* bow

תֵּבָה   *n.* ark, box

---

[4] Beginning with Chapter 13, the definition of verbs are given in the English infinitive form, just as they would be defined in the lexicon. Keep in mind that the lexical form of the verb is the masc. singular, third person, *he gathered*, etc.

[5] When a word does not occur in the *Qal*, we often omit the vowel letters from the lexical form, cf. Holladay, p. 147.

EXERCISE 14

14.4   Genesis 6.1-8

Translate the following verses; parse the verbs that are indicated; and answer all questions.

¹ וַיְהִי כִּי־הֵחֵל הָאָדָם לָרֹב עַל־פְּנֵי הָאֲדָמָה

וּבָנוֹת יֻלְּדוּ לָהֶם ² וַיִּרְאוּ בְנֵי־הָאֱלֹהִים אֶת־בְּנוֹת הָאָדָם

כִּי טֹבֹת הֵנָּה וַיִּקְחוּ לָהֶם נָשִׁים מִכֹּל אֲשֶׁר בָּחָרוּ ³ וַיֹּאמֶר

יְהוָה לֹא־יָדוֹן רוּחִי בָאָדָם לְעֹלָם בְּשַׁגַּם הוּא בָשָׂר וְהָיוּ

יָמָיו מֵאָה וְעֶשְׂרִים שָׁנָה ⁴ הַנְּפִלִים הָיוּ בָאָרֶץ בַּיָּמִים הָהֵם

וְגַם אַחֲרֵי־כֵן אֲשֶׁר יָבֹאוּ בְּנֵי הָאֱלֹהִים אֶל־בְּנוֹת הָאָדָם

וְיָלְדוּ לָהֶם הֵמָּה הַגִּבֹּרִים אֲשֶׁר מֵעוֹלָם אַנְשֵׁי הַשֵּׁם פ

⁵ וַיַּרְא יְהוָה כִּי רַבָּה רָעַת הָאָדָם בָּאָרֶץ וְכָל־יֵצֶר מַחְשְׁבֹת

לִבּוֹ רַק רַע כָּל־הַיּוֹם ⁶ וַיִּנָּחֶם יְהוָה כִּי־עָשָׂה אֶת־הָאָדָם

בָּאָרֶץ וַיִּתְעַצֵּב אֶל־לִבּוֹ ⁷ וַיֹּאמֶר יְהוָה אֶמְחֶה אֶת־הָאָדָם

אֲשֶׁר־בָּרָאתִי מֵעַל פְּנֵי הָאֲדָמָה מֵאָדָם עַד־בְּהֵמָה

עַד־רֶמֶשׂ וְעַד־עוֹף הַשָּׁמָיִם כִּי נִחַמְתִּי כִּי עֲשִׂיתִם ⁸ וְנֹחַ

מָצָא חֵן בְּעֵינֵי יְהוָה פ

Genesis 6.1

וַיְהִי כִּי־הֵחֵל הָאָדָם

Q1: PARSE וַיְהִי. For loss of the third radical see ל"ה Paradigm (§12.6.2).

There are two ways to translate וַיְהִי. It can be simply a paragraph marker, or it can function as a real verb. Thus, it can be translated two ways:

1) *And it came to pass . . .*, or

2) *And he/it was . . .*

If a subject is named, וַיְהִי is translated as a full verb. In this case, there is no subject; therefore, וַיְהִי here is a macrosyntactic marker that should be translated *And it came to pass . . .*, or *And it happened . . .* (§26.1.1 #4).

Regarding כִּי, see Williams §445 & Gesenius §164d

The only word in this line that should cause you difficulty is הֵחֵל. It is *hifil* perf. 3ms, from חָלַל, meaning: 1) to defile, 2) to begin. Could this be *double entendre*? How can you determine which meaning applies here?

Note the singular הָאָדָם, which signifies *humankind*.

לָרֹב עַל־פְּנֵי הָאֲדָמָה

לָרֹב is *qal* infin. construct from רָבַב, meaning *to multiply*. We will study this type of verb in Chapter 17.

וּבָנוֹת יֻלְּדוּ לָהֶם:

You should have no problem with these words.

Morphemes of וּבָנוֹת: ו בָּנ וֹת

Q2: What is the וֹת ending? (§2.2.2)

Q3: PARSE יֻלְּדוּ

In יֻלְּדוּ the *qibbuts* and *dagesh* in the ל should clearly define the stem for you. (§11.5)

This clause is x-*qatal*; therefore, v. 1 provides background information for the story (§26.1.1 #1).

Genesis 6.2

וַיִּרְאוּ בְנֵי־הָאֱלֹהִים

Morphemes of וַיִּרְאוּ: וַ יִּ רְא וּ

Q4: What letter always drops out in the *wayyiqtol*? For loss of the third radical see ל"ה Paradigm (§12.6.2).

Q5: PARSE וַיִּרְאוּ

See Gesenius §128v 'guild members of the gods'.

אֶת־בְּנוֹת הָאָדָם כִּי טֹבֹת הֵנָּה

Q6: Does טֹבֹת have the same meaning as טוֹבוֹת? (§1.8)

Q7: Is there a verb in this clause (כִּי טֹבֹת הֵנָּה)? §3.2 and Gesenius §117h

וַיִּקְחוּ לָהֶם נָשִׁים

Morphemes of וַיִּקְחוּ: וַ יִּ קְח וּ (§14.1.1)

Remember that קַח is always short for לָקַח, and that לָקַח follows the form of פ"נ verbs. *Dagesh* is often omitted above *sheva*.

Regarding לָהֶם see §6.4

מִכֹּל אֲשֶׁר בָּחָרוּ׃   See Williams §326 and Gesenius §119w, note 2.

מִ כֹּל

בָּחָר וּ

Q8: PARSE בָּחָרוּ

בָּחָרוּ is lengthened from בָּחֲרוּ because it is pausal (last word in the verse. See §9.6 and §28.1).

Genesis 6.3

וַיֹּאמֶר יְהוָה

וַ יֹ אמֶר

Q9: PARSE וַיֹּאמֶר

לֹא־יָדוֹן רוּחִי בָאָדָם לְעֹלָם

יָדוֹן is *qal* imf 3ms but the root is disputed. Some scholars believe it comes from דִּין, *to judge, to strive.* The imf. of דִּין, however, should be יָדִין. Furthermore, although the verb דִּין is found 45 times in the Hebrew Bible, only twice is it followed by the prep. בְּ (2 Sam. 19.10 and Psa. 110.6). In both of those cases judgment of a group is not in focus, rather the judgment is being made between members of a group.

Speiser (*JBL,* 75, pp. 126-29) suggests that the root is *dnn,* which he traces to Akkadian, meaning *be strong, protect, shield.* Speiser, therefore, translates Gen. 6.3 as *My Spirit will not always protect man* (that is, from the consequences of his sinful actions). Speiser, however, fails to address the presence of the preposition בְּ on the dir. obj. His translation does not account for the prep. at all. Joüon, on the other hand, (§80k) takes the same Akkadian and translates it as *be strong,* which could accomodate the preposition: *My Spirit will not always be strong in man. . . .*

The morphology of יָדוֹן suggests that it is derived from the root דּוּן, and if so, it would be a *hapax legomenon.* This view is adopted by Köhler, who gives the root as דּוּן, and takes the verb to mean *to stay* or something similar on account of the context.[6] The LXX and the Vulgate agree, translating יָדוֹן as καταμείνῃ and *permanebit* respectively, both of which could be translated as *remain, stay,* or *continue.*

The gender of the verb is also problematic. We would expect the verb to be feminine, because רוּחַ is feminine, but the addition of the masculine pronominal suffix transfers to the verb. Thus, on several occasions, רוּחִי takes the masculine verb.

---

[6] Ludwig Köhler, *The Hebrew and Aramaic Lexicon of the Old Testament* (2 vols.; Leiden: E. J. Brill, Study edn, 2001), s.v. דּוּן.

בְּשַׁגַּם הוּא בָשָׂר

Morphemes : of בְּשַׁגַּם : בְּ שַׁ גַּם

שַׁ is short for אֲשֶׁר

Q10: Does this clause have a verb? §3.2

וְהָיוּ יָמָיו מֵאָה וְעֶשְׂרִים שָׁנָה:

וְ הָיִ וּ

Q11: PARSE וְהָיוּ

Q12: What happened to the last radical in וְהָיוּ? For loss of the third radical see ל"ה Paradigm.

Weqatal (*vav*+perfect) = future, a continuation of לֹא־יָדוֹן

Morphemes of יָמָיו: יָמֳ יְ וּ

Q13: What part of speech is וּ? §6.4.1

שָׁנָה is often found in the singular even when it refers to more than one. §11.18.1

Genesis 6.4

הַנְּפִלִים הָיוּ בָאָרֶץ בַּיָּמִים הָהֵם

הָיִ וּ

Q14: PARSE הָיוּ

Q15: Does בָאָרֶץ have the definite article? How do you know? (§4.4.2)

This clause is an x-*qatal*; therefore, it provides parenthetical background information (§26.1.1 #12). Note: the בּ has no *dagesh lene* because it is preceded by the vowel sound וּ. See §1.6.1.

וְגַם אַחֲרֵי־כֵן

אֲשֶׁר יָבֹאוּ בְּנֵי הָאֱלֹהִים אֶל־בְּנוֹת הָאָדָם

אֲשֶׁר means *when* because it follows the word אַחַר, *after*.

Morphemes of יָבֹאוּ: יְ בֹא וּ   *they would come*

יָבֹאוּ is *qal* imperfect 3mp from בּוֹא. We will discuss middle וּ/יְ verbs in Chapter 15.

Does יָבֹאוּ refer to an event in the past? Why is the imperfect used for the past tense? See §26.1.1 #15, Williams §168 & Gesenius §107e

וַיֵּלְדוּ לָהֶם   Gesenius §112e

וְ יָלַד וּ

Q16: PARSE וַיֵּלְדוּ

This *weqatal* (*vav*+perfect) continues the past time, habitual action of יָבֹאוּ. (§26.1.1 #14)

The accent mark (*athnach*) indicates the middle of the verse.

הֵמָּה הַגִּבֹּרִים אֲשֶׁר מֵעוֹלָם אַנְשֵׁי הַשֵּׁם:

The verbs are unexpressed, thus the phrase is parenthetical or explanatory (§26.1.1 #19 and Williams §578).

הַ גִּבֹּר ים

In this context, מֵעוֹלָם means *long ago*.

אַנְשֵׁי הַשֵּׁם

הַשֵּׁם is an idiom, meaning *fame*. See Gesenius §128t.

Q17: Classify the construct–genitive אַנְשֵׁי הַשֵּׁם by referring to §5.3.3.

Genesis 6.5

וַיַּרְא יְהוָה   *and Yahweh saw*

וַ יְ רְא

Q18: PARSE וַיַּרְא

Q19: What happened to the third radical in וַיַּרְא?

כִּי רַבָּה רָעַת הָאָדָם בָּאָרֶץ   Williams §75, 490, 563, & Gesenius §157b

Q20: Where do we place the unexpressed verb?

Q21: Is רָעַת construct form or absolute form? (§5.6.1)

Q22: Classify the construct–genitive phrase רָעַת הָאָדָם according to §5.3.3.

וְכָל־יֵצֶר מַחְשְׁבֹת לִבּוֹ רַק רַע כָּל־הַיּוֹם:

Again, no verbs are expressed (§26.1.1 #19).

For רַק, see Williams §391 & Gesenius §153

Q23: What part of speech is וֹ in לִבּוֹ? (§6.4.3)

Q24: Classify the construct–genitive phrase מַחְשְׁבֹת לִבּוֹ according to §5.3.3.

Genesis 6.6

וַיִּנָּ֣חֶם יְהוָ֔ה כִּֽי־עָשָׂ֥ה אֶת־הָֽאָדָ֖ם בָּאָ֑רֶץ

Morphemes of וַיִּנָּחֶם: וַ יִ נָחֶם

The *dagesh* in the נ should alert you that this is not a *qal.* (§8.2.1)

וַיִּתְעַצֵּ֖ב אֶל־לִבּֽוֹ:

Morphemes of וַיִּתְעַצֵּב: וַ יִ ת עַצֵּב

Q25: What stem is clearly indicated by the infixed ת ? (§11.2.1)

Genesis 6.7

וַיֹּ֣אמֶר יְהוָ֗ה אֶמְחֶ֨ה אֶת־הָאָדָ֤ם

אֶ מְחֶה

Q26: PARSE אֶמְחֶה

The final ה causes the *segol* (See ל"ה Paradigm, §22.2).

This verb is in first place. What does its position in the clause tell you about its meaning? (§5.1.2 and §26.1.1 #24)

אֲשֶׁר־בָּרָ֨אתִי֙ מֵעַל֙ פְּנֵ֣י הָֽאֲדָמָ֔ה

בָּרָא תִי

Q27: PARSE בָּרָאתִי   (See ל"א Paradigm, §22.4)

מֵֽאָדָם֙ עַד־בְּהֵמָ֔ה עַד־רֶ֖מֶשׂ וְעַד־ע֣וֹף הַשָּׁמָ֑יִם

כִּ֥י נִחַ֖מְתִּי כִּ֥י עֲשִׂיתִֽם:

Morphemes of נִחַמְתִּי: נִ חַמְ תִּי

נִחַמְתִּי must be a perfect because of the sufformative. The only perfect that can begin with נ is *nifal.* Thus, this is a *nifal* pf 1cs from נחם. There should be a compensatory *dagesh* in the ח, but you cannot put a *dagesh* in a guttural. We would expect the *chireq* to be lengthened to *tsere*, but sometimes the lengthening does not occur.

As to the meaning of the perfect here, see Williams §163.

Morphemes of עֲשִׂיתִם: עֲשִׂי ת ם

Q28: PARSE עֲשִׂיתִם

Genesis 6.8

וְנֹחַ מָצָא חֵן בְּעֵינֵי יְהוָה׃

Q29: Parse מָצָא   (See ל״א   Paradigm, §22.4)

This clause is x-qatal and indicates contrast, *but Noah* … (§26.1.1 #10)

Williams §432, 573(2), and Gesenius §142b=pluperfect

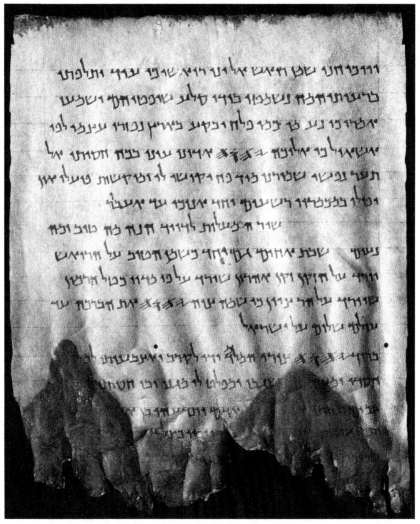

Psalm 133 – Dead Sea Scrolls

Chapter 15

Hollow Verbs and Reading
Genesis 9.8-17

In this chapter you will learn:

- Forms of weak verbs with ו or י as the middle letter.
- Read and analyze Gen. 9.8-17

15.1   Hollow Verbs

Verbs that have ו or י as their middle letter are sometimes called Hollow Verbs. When ו is the middle letter, the verb may be called a ע"ו verb, and when י is the middle letter the verb is a ע"י verb.

15.1.1   Common Hollow Verbs

These verbs are very common; therefore, you must give much attention to learning the paradigm. Failure to master this lesson will greatly hinder your reading of the Hebrew Old Testament. Some of the most common hollow verbs are:

בּוֹא	to come (2565)[1]	כּוּן	to be firm (*nifal*) (217)
שׁוּב	to return (1059)	בִּין	to perceive (171)
מוּת	to die (780)	רוּם	to be high (166)
קוּם	to rise (629)	נוּס	to flee (157)
שִׂים	to put, place (586)	בּוֹשׁ	to be ashamed (109)
סוּר	to turn aside (300)	גּוּר	to sojourn (81)

15.1.2   Characteristics of Hollow verbs

1.   In the *qal* **perfect**, the middle vowel is lost, the 3d person uses *qamets* and the other forms use *patach*.

    ***Q* Pf 3ms of שׁוּב is not שָׁוַב , but is שָׁב**

2.   In the *qal* **imperfect**, the middle vowel is retained, and the vowel under the preformative is *qamets*, e.g. the root שׁוּב gives יָשׁוּב , שִׂים gives יָשִׂים etc. (Remember, however, that the vowel will not always be the full form, so that יָשׁוּב can also be יָשֶׁב , and יָשִׂים can be יָשֵׂם etc.)

    ***Q* Imf 3ms of שׁוּב is not יְשׁוֹב , but is יָשׁוּב**

---

[1] Number of occurrences in the Hebrew Bible according to Avraham Even-Shoshan, *A New Concordance of the Old Testament* (Grand Rapids, MI: Kiryat Sefer, Baker/Ridgefield edn, 1989).

3. The *qal* **active ptc.** ms is identical to the perfect, 3ms. The appropriate inflections are attached to the other forms of the ptc. In the **wayyiqtol,** the middle vowel is shortened. יָשׁוּב becomes וַיָּשָׁב. The verb מוּת *to die,* varies in two ways from the usual paradigm of שׁוּב:

    1) The final ת may assimilate into the sufformative ת.

    2) In four forms the *patach* is replaced by a *tsere:*

    Remember: The Hollow Verbs often show only TWO root letters.

    Perfect, 3ms, *He died* is מֵת.

    Perfect, 3fs, *She died* is מֵתָה.

    Perfect, 3cp, *They died* is מֵתוּ.

    Qal active ptc., *dying* is מֵת.

    Other verbs also exhibit slight variations. These must be learned from the lexicon on a case-by-case basis.

4. The **Nifal** and **Hifil** have a connecting vowel (*cholem*) between the last root letter and the perfect consonantal afformatives.

    N Pf 1cs of כוּן is not נְכֻנְתִּי , but is נְכוּנוֹתִי

5. The **Hofal** has *shureq* throughout.

    Hp Imf 1cs of קוּם is not אָקֻם, but is אוּקַם

6. In this class of verbs, the **Polel, Polal,** and **Hitpolel** carry the same significance as the *piel, pual,* and *hitpael* of other paradigms. The *polel, polal,* and *hitpolel* have long *cholem* after the first root letter and duplication of the third root letter. Note also that ten of the *polel* forms are identical to the *polal.* The context will determine if the verb is active or passive.

    Polel Imf 1cs of קוּם is אֲקוֹמֵם

7. The hollow verbs are probably the most difficult to learn of all weak verbs. The most common forms, however, will soon be easy to recognize. Make note of identical forms, such as the *Q* pf. 3ms and the ptc. and *Hit.* pf. 3p and the imv.

15.1.3 Paradigm for ע"ו/י (Hollow) Verbs

	Qal	Qal	Nifal	Hifil	Hofal	Polel[2]	Polal	Hitpolel
Pf	*return*	*die*	*be firm*	*raise*				
1cs	שַׁבְתִּי	מַתִּי	נְכוּנוֹתִי	הֲקִימוֹתִי	הוּקַמְתִּי	קוֹמַמְתִּי	קוֹמַמְתִּי	הִתְקוֹמַמְתִּי
2ms	שַׁבְתָּ	מַתָּה	נְכוּנוֹתָ	הֲקִימוֹתָ	הוּקַמְתָּ	קוֹמַמְתָּ	קוֹמַמְתָּ	הִתְקוֹמַמְתָּ
2fs	שַׁבְתְּ	מַתְּ	נְכוּנוֹת	הֲקִימוֹת	הוּקַמְתְּ	קוֹמַמְתְּ	קוֹמַמְתְּ	הִתְקוֹמַמְתְּ
3ms	שָׁב	מֵת	נָכוֹן	הֵקִים	הוּקַם	קוֹמֵם	קוֹמַם	הִתְקוֹמֵם
3fs	שָׁבָה	מֵתָה	נָכוֹנָה	הֵקִימָה	הוּקְמָה	קוֹמְמָה	קוֹמְמָה	הִתְקוֹמְמָה
1cp	שַׁבְנוּ	מַתְנוּ	נְכוּנוֹנוּ	הֲקִימוֹנוּ	הוּקַמְנוּ	קוֹמַמְנוּ	קוֹמַמְנוּ	הִתְקוֹמַמְנוּ
2mp	שַׁבְתֶּם	מַתֶּם	נְכוּנוֹתֶם	הֲקִימוֹתֶם	הוּקַמְתֶּם	קוֹמַמְתֶּם	קוֹמַמְתֶּם	הִתְקוֹמַמְתֶּם
2fp	שַׁבְתֶּן	מַתֶּן	נְכוּנוֹתֶן	הֲקִימוֹתֶן	הוּקַמְתֶּן	קוֹמַמְתֶּן	קוֹמַמְתֶּן	הִתְקוֹמַמְתֶּן
3cp	שָׁבוּ	מֵתוּ	נָכוֹנוּ	הֵקִימוּ	הוּקְמוּ	קוֹמְמוּ	קוֹמְמוּ	הִתְקוֹמְמוּ
Imf								
1cs	אָשׁוּב	אָמוּת	אֶכּוֹן	אָקִים	אוּקַם	אֲקוֹמֵם	אֲקוֹמַם	אֶתְקוֹמֵם
2ms	תָּשׁוּב	etc.	תִּכּוֹן	תָּקִים	תּוּקַם	תְּקוֹמֵם	תְּקוֹמַם	תִּתְקוֹמֵם
2fs	תָּשׁוּבִי		תִּכּוֹנִי	תָּקִימִי	תּוּקְמִי	תְּקוֹמְמִי	תְּקוֹמְמִי	תִּתְקוֹמְמִי
3ms	יָשׁוּב		יִכּוֹן	יָקִים	יוּקַם	יְקוֹמֵם	יְקוֹמַם	יִתְקוֹמֵם
3fs	תָּשׁוּב		תִּכּוֹן	תָּקִים	תּוּקַם	תְּקוֹמֵם	תְּקוֹמַם	תִּתְקוֹמֵם
1cp	נָשׁוּב		נִכּוֹן	נָקִים	נוּקַם	נְקוֹמֵם	נְקוֹמַם	נִתְקוֹמֵם
2mp	תָּשׁוּבוּ		תִּכּוֹנוּ	תָּקִימוּ	תּוּקְמוּ	תְּקוֹמְמוּ	תְּקוֹמְמוּ	תִּתְקוֹמְמוּ
2fp	תְּשׁוּבֶינָה		תִּכּוֹנָה	תְּקִמֶינָה	תּוּקַמְנָה	תְּקוֹמֵמְנָה	תְּקוֹמַמְנָה	תִּתְקוֹמֵמְנָה
3mp	יָשׁוּבוּ		יִכּוֹנוּ	יָקִימוּ	יוּקְמוּ	יְקוֹמְמוּ	יְקוֹמְמוּ	יִתְקוֹמְמוּ
3fp	תְּשׁוּבֶינָה		תִּכּוֹנָה	תְּקִמֶינָה	תּוּקַמְנָה	תְּקוֹמֵמְנָה	תְּקוֹמַמְנָה	תִּתְקוֹמֵמְנָה
Imv								
2ms	שׁוּב		הִכּוֹן	הָקֵם		קוֹמֵם		הִתְקוֹמֵם
2fs	שׁוּבִי		הִכּוֹנִי	הָקִימִי		קוֹמְמִי		הִתְקוֹמְמִי
2mp	שׁוּבוּ		הִכּוֹנוּ	הָקִימוּ		קוֹמְמוּ		הִתְקוֹמְמוּ
2fp	שֹׁבְנָה		הִכּוֹנָה	הָקֵמְנָה		קוֹמֵמְנָה		הִתְקוֹמֵמְנָה
IA	שׁוֹב		הִכּוֹן	הָקֵם				הִתְקוֹמֵם
IC	שׁוּב		הִכּוֹן	הָקִים	הוּקַם	קוֹמֵם		הִתְקוֹמֵם
APtc	שָׁב	מֵת	נָכוֹן	מֵקִים		מְקוֹמֵם		מִתְקוֹמֵם
PPtc					מוּקָם		מְקוֹמָם	
W	וַיָּשָׁב		וַיִּכּוֹן	וַיָּקֶם	וַיּוּקַם	וַיְקוֹמֵם	וַיְקוֹמַם	
Juss	יָשֹׁב		יִכּוֹן	יָקֵם	יוּקַם	יְקוֹמֵם	יְקוֹמַם	

---

[2] The *polel*, *polal*, and *hitpolel* are equivalent in meaning to the *piel*, *pual*, and *hitpael*.

15.1.4   Examples of Hollow Verbs:

Gen. 3.19 כִּי־עָפָר אַתָּה וְאֶל־עָפָר תָּשׁוּב:
Because dust you are, and unto dust **you shall return** (*Q* imf 2m sg.).

Gen. 14.7 וַיָּשֻׁבוּ וַיָּבֹאוּ אֶל־עֵין מִשְׁפָּט
And they returned (*Q* imf *W* 3m pl), **and came** (*Q* imf *W* 3m pl) to Ein-mishpat.

Gen. 18.16 וַיָּקֻמוּ מִשָּׁם הָאֲנָשִׁים
And the men **rose up** (*Q* imf *W* 3m pl) from there.

Gen. 31.17 וַיָּקָם יַעֲקֹב וַיִּשָּׂא אֶת־בָּנָיו וְאֶת־נָשָׁיו עַל־הַגְּמַלִּים:
And Jacob **rose up** (*Q* imf *W* 3m s), and set his sons and his wives upon camels.

Gen. 2.19 וַיָּבֵא אֶל־הָאָדָם לִרְאוֹת מַה־יִּקְרָא־לוֹ
And he brought (*H* imf *W* 3m s) them unto Adam to see what he would call them.

Gen. 12.5 וַיָּבֹאוּ אַרְצָה כְּנָעַן:
And they came (*Q* imf *W* 3m pl) to the land of Canaan.

15.2   Vocabulary

שָׂפָה	*n.f.* lip		מִגְדָּל	*n.m.* tower
נָסַע	*v.* to journey, to set out on a journey		בָּצַר	*v.* to gather together, to restrain
קֶדֶם	*n.m.* east		פּוּץ	*v.* to scatter
בִּקְעָה	*n.f.* plain, valley		חָלַל	*v. Hiph.* to begin
שִׁנְעָר	*n.* Shinar		זָמַם	*v.* to plot, devise, plan
שָׁם	*part.* there		בָּלַל	*v.* to mix, confuse
רֵעַ	*n.m.* friend		חָדַל	*v.* to stop, cease
יָהַב	*v.* to give, see הַב in the lexicon		חֵמָר	*n.m.* slime, pitch, bitumen
לָבַן	*v.* I-to become white, II-to make brick		חֹמֶר	*n.m.* cement, mortar
לְבֵנָה	*n.f.* brick		נָא	*interj.* please
שָׂרַף	*v.* to burn		אָז	*adv.* then
שְׂרֵפָה	*n.f.* a burning, conflagration		בְּרָכָה	*n. f.* blessing
אֶבֶן	*n.f.* stone		בָּבֶל	*n.* Babel

EXERCISE 15

15.3 Reading Genesis 9.8-17

Translate the following verses; parse the verbs that are indicated; and answer all numbered questions. You are not required to answer the questions that are not numbered. They are intended to direct your analysis in certain directions. You will notice that, beginning with this chapter, the Hebrew accent marks are included in the text. Although the Hebrew text is included here for your convenience, please continue to use the *Biblia Hebraica Stuttgartensia* as you complete your assignments.

⁸ וַיֹּ֤אמֶר אֱלֹהִים֙ אֶל־נֹ֔חַ וְאֶל־בָּנָ֥יו אִתּ֖וֹ לֵאמֹֽר׃ ⁹ וַאֲנִ֕י הִנְנִ֥י מֵקִ֛ים אֶת־בְּרִיתִ֖י אִתְּכֶ֑ם וְאֶֽת־זַרְעֲכֶ֖ם אַחֲרֵיכֶֽם׃ ¹⁰ וְאֵ֣ת כָּל־נֶ֣פֶשׁ הַֽחַיָּה֩ אֲשֶׁ֨ר אִתְּכֶ֜ם בָּע֧וֹף בַּבְּהֵמָ֛ה וּֽבְכָל־חַיַּ֥ת הָאָ֖רֶץ אִתְּכֶ֑ם מִכֹּל֙ יֹצְאֵ֣י הַתֵּבָ֔ה לְכֹ֖ל חַיַּ֥ת הָאָֽרֶץ׃ ¹¹ וַהֲקִמֹתִ֤י אֶת־בְּרִיתִי֙ אִתְּכֶ֔ם וְלֹֽא־יִכָּרֵ֧ת כָּל־בָּשָׂ֛ר ע֖וֹד מִמֵּ֣י הַמַּבּ֑וּל וְלֹֽא־יִהְיֶ֥ה ע֛וֹד מַבּ֖וּל לְשַׁחֵ֥ת הָאָֽרֶץ׃ ¹² וַיֹּ֣אמֶר אֱלֹהִ֗ים זֹ֤את אֽוֹת־הַבְּרִית֙ אֲשֶׁר־אֲנִ֣י נֹתֵ֗ן בֵּינִי֙ וּבֵ֣ינֵיכֶ֔ם וּבֵ֛ין כָּל־נֶ֥פֶשׁ חַיָּ֖ה אֲשֶׁ֣ר אִתְּכֶ֑ם לְדֹרֹ֖ת עוֹלָֽם׃ ¹³ אֶת־קַשְׁתִּ֕י נָתַ֖תִּי בֶּֽעָנָ֑ן וְהָֽיְתָה֙ לְא֣וֹת בְּרִ֔ית בֵּינִ֖י וּבֵ֥ין הָאָֽרֶץ׃ ¹⁴ וְהָיָ֕ה בְּעַֽנְנִ֥י עָנָ֖ן עַל־הָאָ֑רֶץ וְנִרְאֲתָ֥ה הַקֶּ֖שֶׁת בֶּעָנָֽן׃ ¹⁵ וְזָכַרְתִּ֣י אֶת־בְּרִיתִ֗י אֲשֶׁ֤ר בֵּינִי֙ וּבֵ֣ינֵיכֶ֔ם וּבֵ֛ין כָּל־נֶ֥פֶשׁ חַיָּ֖ה בְּכָל־בָּשָׂ֑ר וְלֹֽא־יִֽהְיֶ֨ה ע֤וֹד הַמַּ֙יִם֙ לְמַבּ֔וּל לְשַׁחֵ֖ת כָּל־בָּשָֽׂר׃ ¹⁶ וְהָיְתָ֥ה הַקֶּ֖שֶׁת בֶּֽעָנָ֑ן וּרְאִיתִ֗יהָ לִזְכֹּר֙ בְּרִ֣ית עוֹלָ֔ם בֵּ֣ין אֱלֹהִ֔ים וּבֵין֙ כָּל־נֶ֣פֶשׁ חַיָּ֔ה בְּכָל־בָּשָׂ֖ר אֲשֶׁ֥ר עַל־הָאָֽרֶץ׃ ¹⁷ וַיֹּ֥אמֶר אֱלֹהִ֖ים אֶל־נֹ֑חַ זֹ֤את אֽוֹת־הַבְּרִית֙ אֲשֶׁ֣ר הֲקִמֹ֔תִי בֵּינִ֕י וּבֵ֥ין כָּל־בָּשָׂ֖ר אֲשֶׁ֥ר עַל־הָאָֽרֶץ׃ פ

Genesis 9.8

וַיֹּ֤אמֶר אֱלֹהִים֙ אֶל־נֹ֔חַ

וְאֶל־בָּנָ֥יו אִתּ֖וֹ לֵאמֹֽר׃

Q1: What part of speech is the ו on בָּנָיו? (§6.4.1)

Q2: What part of speech is the ו on אִתּוֹ? (§6.4.3)

Q3: What is the difference between אֹתוֹ and אִתּוֹ? (§6.4.2)

Q4: PARSE לֵאמֹר

Genesis 9.9

וַאֲנִי הִנְנִי מֵקִים אֶת־בְּרִיתִי אִתְּכֶם

The repetition of 'I' (וַאֲנִי) is emphatic.

Q5: PARSE מֵקִים (See §15.1.3)

Q6: What is the difference in meaning between the *qal* and *Hifil* of this verb? Consult the lexicon.

Q7: Does this ptc. function as a substantive, adj. or verb?

The participle suggests durative or ongoing action that is concurrent in time with the speech (§26.1.1 #21).

וְאֶת־זַרְעֲכֶם אַחֲרֵיכֶם: (§6.4.1)

Genesis 9.10

וְאֵת כָּל־נֶפֶשׁ הַחַיָּה

Q8: The phrase כָּל־נֶפֶשׁ הַחַיָּה is found only four times in Scripture: (Gen. 1.21; 9.10; Lev. 11.10, 46). What does it seem to mean?

אֲשֶׁר אִתְּכֶם בָּעוֹף בַּבְּהֵמָה

Q9: Where is the verb in this clause? (§3.2)

The use of בְּ is unusual. See Williams §250.

Q10: Why is there a *zaqqef* accent over אִתְּכֶם? (See §28.1)

וּבְכָל־חַיַּת הָאָרֶץ אִתְּכֶם

Q11: Why does חַיַּת end with ת instead of ה?

מִכֹּל יֹצְאֵי הַתֵּבָה

Q12: PARSE יֹצְאֵי

Q13: Is יֹצְאֵי a substantive, adjective, or verb?

Q14: Is it past, present, or future time?

לְכֹל חַיַּת הָאָרֶץ:

Genesis 9.11

וַהֲקִמֹתִי אֶת־בְּרִיתִי אִתְּכֶם

Morphemes of וַהֲקִמֹתִי : וַ הֲ קִמֹ תִי

Q15: PARSE וַהֲקִמֹתִי (See §15.1.3.)

Q16: Does וַהֲקִמֹתִי have an imf preformative?

Q17: What is the הֲ? (§15.1.3)

Q18: In what tense should we translate this verb? (§7.3 and §26.1.1 #47)

וְלֹא־יִכָּרֵת כָּל־בָּשָׂר עוֹד מִמֵּי הַמַּבּוּל

Q19: PARSE יִכָּרֵת

Q20: What stem has *dagesh* in the first root letter of the imf, and *qamets* underneath.

Q21: What voice is יִכָּרֵת: active, passive, reflexive, etc.?

The Hebrew listener/reader would recognize a word-play with the use of כָּרַת, which is the most common word used to designate the making of a covenant.

מִמֵּי is the prep. מִן attached to מֵי (construct of מַיִם).

The prep. !mi is causal here (§8.4.3 and Williams §319).

וְלֹא־יִהְיֶה עוֹד מַבּוּל לְשַׁחֵת הָאָרֶץ:

Morphemes of לְשַׁחֵת: לְ שַׁחֵת

Q22: What verb form is most often found with the preposition לְ? (§6.5.2)

Q23: What is the only stem that uses *patach* under the first root letter of the infinitive? (§10.3.5)

Q24: Why is there no *dagesh* in the middle radical? (§2.1.2 and §14.2)

Q25: PARSE לְשַׁחֵת (See §14.2.2)

Genesis 9.12

וַיֹּאמֶר אֱלֹהִים זֹאת אוֹת־הַבְּרִית

Q26: What part of speech is זֹאת? (§7.6)

Q27: How does it function in the clause? (§7.6)

אֲשֶׁר־אֲנִי נֹתֵן בֵּינִי וּבֵינֵיכֶם

Q28: PARSE נֹתֵן

Q29: What kind of action is signified by the ptc.: complete, incomplete, or durative? (§26.1.1 #21)

Q30: What is the tense of נֹתֵן?

Q31: How many different words have been used to designate the making of this covenant?

וּבֵין כָּל־נֶפֶשׁ חַיָּה

Unlike v. 10, there is no article on חַיָּה.

אֲשֶׁר אִתְּכֶם לְדֹרֹת עוֹלָם:

The ל on דֹרֹת is temporal (see Williams §266).

Genesis 9.13

אֶת־קַשְׁתִּי נָתַתִּי בֶּעָנָן

קַשְׁתִּי has the ending of a perfect verb, but no pf. has this vowel pattern. Thus, קַשְׁתִּי is a noun, not a verb, and י is the pronominal suffix, 1cs, *my*. Note that this clause begins with the direct object, suggesting that the object is emphatic. (§26.1.1 #23)

Q32: PARSE נָתַתִּי   (See §14.1.2)

Q33: In what tense should we translate yTit;n"? See Williams §165.

וְהָיְתָה לְאוֹת בְּרִית בֵּינִי וּבֵין הָאָרֶץ:

Q34: PARSE וְהָיְתָה   (See §12.6.2)

Q35: In what tense should we translate וְהָיְתָה? (§7.3)

Q36: Explain the presence of ה in this verb. (§22.13)

For the ל in לְאוֹת, see Williams §273.

Genesis 9.14

וְהָיָה בְּעַנְנִי עָנָן עַל־הָאָרֶץ

Morphemes of בְּעַנְנִי: בְּ עַנְנ י

Q37: What verb forms are found with prepositions? (§6.5.2)

Q38: What is the only stem that uses *patach* under the first root letter of the infinitive? (§10.3.5)

Q39: Why is there no *dagesh* in the middle radical? (§10.3.2.1)

Q40: PARSE בְּעַנְנִי

Q41: Is י the subject or object of the infinitive?

The infinitive + בְּ indicates a temporal clause, *when I make clouds* (§6.5.2.2).

Since the verb means *to make a cloud*, and the object of the verb is *a cloud*, a literal translation would be redundant in English. English, however, does have a few verbs whose objects can be a cognate noun, e.g., *to dance a dance*.

וְנִרְאֲתָה הַקֶּשֶׁת בֶּעָנָן:

Morphemes of וְנִרְאֲתָה: וְ נ רְאֲ תָ ה

The ending is pf 3fs, and only one stem of the perfect begins with נ.

Q42: PARSE וְנִרְאֲתָה (See §12.6.2)

Q43: How should we translate this verb? (1) *And it shall be seen,* or (2) *And it shall appear?* See (§25.1). This is a *nifal*, middle voice. See also §7.3, §26.1.1 #47.

Q44: Why is the *segol* under the preposition in בֶּעָנָן?

Genesis 9.15

וְזָכַרְתִּי אֶת־בְּרִיתִי

Morphemes of וְזָכַרְתִּי: וְ זָכַר תִּי

Q45: PARSE וְזָכַרְתִּי

Q46: Should this verb be translated in future time? (§7.3, §26.1.1 #47)

אֲשֶׁר בֵּינִי וּבֵינֵיכֶם וּבֵין כָּל־נֶפֶשׁ חַיָּה בְּכָל־בָּשָׂר

בְּכָל־בָּשָׂר is appositional to כָּל־נֶפֶשׁ חַיָּה, and should be translated: *every living creature, that is, all flesh.* An appositional noun may take a preposition (Gesenius §131t).

וְלֹא־יִהְיֶה עוֹד הַמַּיִם לְמַבּוּל לְשַׁחֵת כָּל־בָּשָׂר:

Q47: PARSE לְשַׁחֵת   (See §14.2.2).

לְמַבּוּל means *with respect to a flood* (Williams §273)

Genesis 9.16

וְהָיְתָה הַקֶּשֶׁת בֶּעָנָן

Q48: PARSE וְהָיְתָה (See §12.6.2)

Q49: What is the tense: past, present, or future? §7.3

וּרְאִיתִיהָ לִזְכֹּר בְּרִית עוֹלָם

Morphemes of וּרְאִיתִיהָ:   וּ רְאִי תִי הָ

Q50: PARSE וּרְאִיתִיהָ (See §12.6.2)

Q51: PARSE לִזְכֹּר

This is an infinitive of result.

The phrase בְּרִית עוֹלָם is found twelve times, and is a construct phrase, *covenant of eternity* (see §5.3.3.6 – adjectival – *eternal covenant*). It never occurs with a definite article.

בֵּין אֱלֹהִים וּבֵין כָּל־נֶפֶשׁ חַיָּה (See verse 15 above.)

בְּכָל־בָּשָׂר אֲשֶׁר עַל־הָאָרֶץ: (See verse 15 above.)

Genesis 9.17

וַיֹּאמֶר אֱלֹהִים אֶל־נֹחַ

(§3.2, §7.6) זֹאת אוֹת־הַבְּרִית אֲשֶׁר הֲקִמֹתִי

Morphemes of הֲקִמֹתִי: הֲ קִם תִי

Q52: PARSE הֲקִמֹתִי (See §15.1.3)

Q53: Why does the writer use the perfect? §26.1.1 #38 and Williams §164

בֵּינִי וּבֵין כָּל־בָּשָׂר אֲשֶׁר עַל־הָאָרֶץ:

Great Isaiah Scroll (34.1-36.2)—c. 200 BCE

Chapter 16

Geminate Verbs and Reading Genesis 11.1-9

In this chapter you will:

- Learn the paradigm for geminate verbs (weak verbs whose last two radicals are the same).
- Translate Genesis 11.1-9

16.1 The Geminate Verbs

A geminate verb is one whose last two root letters are the same. Geminates may also be called Double **ע** verbs.

16.1.1 Common Geminate Verbs

Some of the most common geminate verbs are:

סָבַב	to turn, to surround (162)
הָלַל	to praise (150)
פָּלַל	to pray (Hitpael only) (84)
חָנַן	to pity (78)
קָלַל	to be small (79)
תָּמַם	to finish (64)
חָלַל	to pierce (54)
בָּזַז	to take as spoil (42)
צָרַר	to oppress (36)
רָבַב	to multiply (24)
מָסַס	to melt (20)
גָּלַל	to roll (16)
חָנַג	to make pilgrimage, to celebrate (16)

> In Geminate verbs the last two letters are

16.1.2 Characteristics of Geminate Verbs:

1. In the **perfect** of the *qal*, *nifal*, *Hifil*, and *hofal*, all first and second person have *dagesh forte* in the middle radical, followed by a connective vowel (*cholem*). The third person may or may not use the *dagesh forte*.

   Q pf 3ms of סבב is סָבַב (like the strong verb), but

   Q pf 3ms of תמם is תַּמּוּ and

Q pf 1cs is סַבּוֹתִי and תַּמּוֹתִי

2. In the *qal* **imperfect and imperative**, the last root letter does not appear, except in the form of the *dagesh forte* that precedes the sufformatives.

Q imf 3mp of סבב סבב is יָסֹבּוּ

3. The *qal* **active ptc**. is regular.

4. In **wayyiqtol** looks like the hollow verbs.

Q imf 3ms *Wayyiqtol* of סבב סבב is וַיָּסָב

5. The **Nifal** and **Hifil** and **Hofal** have the characteristic נ and ה, and הו stem indicators in the perfect. The *Nifal* imperfect has the usual *chireq* under the preformative with *dagesh forte* in the first root letter. *Hifil* imperfect has *qamats* under the preformative, like a hollow verb, and the i-class vowel under the first root letter.

Q Imf 3ms = יָסֹב   *Nifal* = יִסַּב & *Hifil* = יָסֵב

6. In this class of verbs, the **Polel, Polal,** and **Hitpolel** carry the same significance as the *piel, pual,* and *hitpael* of other paradigms. The *polel, polal,* and *hitpolel* have long *cholem* after the first root letter. In some geminate verbs, however, we find the strong form of the *piel, pual,* and *hitpael*.

Hitpael Imf 3ms = יִתְסוֹבֵב

Aleppo Codex—c. 930 CE

16.1.3 Geminate Verb Paradigm

	Qal surround	*Qal* finished	*Nifal*	*Hifil*	*Hofal*	*Polel* to roll	*Polal*	*Hitpolel*
Pf								
1cs	סַבּוֹתִי	תַּמּוֹתִי	נְסַבּוֹתִי	הֲסִבּוֹתִי	הוּסַבּוֹתִי	גּוֹלַלְתִּי	גּוֹלַלְתִּי	הִתְגּוֹלַלְתִּי
2ms	סַבּוֹתָ	תַּמּוֹתָ	נְסַבּוֹתָ	הֲסִבּוֹתָ	הוּסַבּוֹתָ	גּוֹלַלְתָּ	גּוֹלַלְתָּ	הִתְגּוֹלַלְתָּ
2fs	סַבּוֹת	תַּמּוֹת	נְסַבּוֹת	הֲסִבּוֹת	הוּסַבּוֹת	גּוֹלַלְתְּ	גּוֹלַלְתְּ	הִתְגּוֹלַלְתְּ
3ms	סָבַב	תַּם	נָסַב	הֵסֵב	הוּסַב	גּוֹלֵל	גּוֹלַל	הִתְגּוֹלֵל
3fs	סָבְבָה	תַּמָּה	נָסַבָּה	הֵסֵבָּה	הוּסַבָּה	גּוֹלְלָה	גּוֹלְלָה	הִתְגּוֹלְלָה
1cp	סַבּוֹנוּ	תַּמּוֹנוּ	נְסַבּוֹנוּ	הֲסִבּוֹנוּ	הוּסַבּוֹנוּ	גּוֹלַלְנוּ	גּוֹלַלְנוּ	הִתְגּוֹלַלְנוּ
2mp	סַבּוֹתֶם	תַּמּוֹתֶם	נְסַבּוֹתֶם	הֲסִבּוֹתֶם	הוּסַבּוֹתֶם	גּוֹלַלְתֶּם	גּוֹלַלְתֶּם	הִתְגּוֹלַלְתֶּם
2fp	סַבּוֹתֶן	תַּמּוֹתֶן	נְסַבּוֹתֶן	הֲסִבּוֹתֶן	הוּסַבּוֹתֶן	גּוֹלַלְתֶּן	גּוֹלַלְתֶּן	הִתְגּוֹלַלְתֶּן
3cp	סָבְבוּ	תַּמּוּ	נָסַבּוּ	הֵסֵבּוּ	הוּסַבּוּ	גּוֹלְלוּ	גּוֹלְלוּ	הִתְגּוֹלְלוּ
Imf								
1cs	אָסֹב	אֶתַּם	אֶסַּב	אָסֵב	אוּסַב	אֲגוֹלֵל	אֲגוֹלַל	אֶתְגּוֹלֵל
2ms	תָּסֹב	תֵּתַּם	תִּסַּב	תָּסֵב	תּוּסַב	תְּגוֹלֵל	תְּגוֹלַל	תִּתְגּוֹלֵל
2fs	תָּסֹבִּי	תֵּתַּמִּי	תִּסַּבִּי	תָּסֵבִּי	תּוּסַבִּי	תְּגוֹלְלִי	תְּגוֹלְלִי	תִּתְגּוֹלְלִי
3ms	יָסֹב	יֵתַּם	יִסַּב	יָסֵב	יוּסַב	יְגוֹלֵל	יְגוֹלַל	יִתְגּוֹלֵל
3fs	תָּסֹב	תֵּתַּם	תִּסַּב	תָּסֵב	תּוּסַב	תְּגוֹלֵל	תְּגוֹלַל	תִּתְגּוֹלֵל
1cp	נָסֹב	נֵתַּם	נִסַּב	נָסֵב	נוּסַב	נְגוֹלֵל	נְגוֹלַל	נִתְגּוֹלֵל
2mp	תָּסֹבּוּ	תֵּתַּמּוּ	תִּסַּבּוּ	תָּסֵבּוּ	תּוּסַבּוּ	תְּגוֹלְלוּ	תְּגוֹלְלוּ	תִּתְגּוֹלְלוּ
2fp	תְּסֻבֶּינָה	תְּתַמֶּינָה	תִּסַּבֶּינָה	תְּסִבֶּינָה	תּוּסַבֶּינָה	תְּגוֹלֵלְנָה	תְּגוֹלַלְנָה	תִּתְגּוֹלֵלְנָה
3mp	יָסֹבּוּ	יֵתַמּוּ	יִסַּבּוּ	יָסֵבּוּ	יוּסַבּוּ	יְגוֹלְלוּ	יְגוֹלְלוּ	יִתְגּוֹלְלוּ
3fp	תְּסֻבֶּינָה	תְּתַמֶּינָה	תִּסַּבֶּינָה	תְּסִבֶּינָה	תּוּסַבֶּינָה	תְּגוֹלֵלְנָה	תְּגוֹלַלְנָה	תִּתְגּוֹלֵלְנָה
Imv								
2ms	סֹב	תַּם	הִסַּב	הָסֵב		גּוֹלֵל		הִתְגּוֹלֵל
2fs	סֹבִּי	תַּמִּי	הִסַּבִּי	הָסֵבִּי		גּוֹלְלִי		הִתְגּוֹלְלִי
2mp	סֹבּוּ	תַּמּוּ	הִסַּבּוּ	הָסֵבּוּ		גּוֹלְלוּ		הִתְגּוֹלְלוּ
2fp	סֹבְנָה	תַּמְנָה	הִסַּבֶּינָה	הֲסִבֶּינָה		גּוֹלֵלְנָה		הִתְגּוֹלֵלְנָה
IA	סָבוֹב		הִסֵּב	הָסֵב		גּוֹלֵל		הִתְגּוֹלֵל
IC	סֹב	תַּם	הִסֵּב	הָסֵב		גּוֹלֵל		הִתְגּוֹלֵל
Aptc	סֹבֵב	תַּם		מֵסֵב		מְגוֹלֵל	מְגוֹלָל	מִתְגּוֹלֵל
PPtc	סָבוּב				מוּסָב			
W	וַיָּסָב	וַיִּתַּם	וַיִּסַּב	וַיַּסֵב³	וַיּוּסַב			
Jus	יָסֹב	יֵתַם	יִסַּב	יָסֵב	יוּסַב			

---

³ The *dagesh* may be a result of Aramaic influence (cf. Gesenius §67g).

16.1.4 Examples of Geminate Verbs

סָבַב   *to turn, to surround*   הָלַל   *to praise* (P), to glory (Ht)

וַיַּסֵּב אֱלֹהִים אֶת־הָעָם דֶּרֶךְ הַמִּדְבָּר   Exod. 13.18
And God caused the people to **go around** (*H* imf *W* 3m s) the way of the wilderness.

וַנָּסָב אֶת־הַר־שֵׂעִיר יָמִים רַבִּים׃   Deut. 2.1
And we went around (*Q* imf *W* 1c pl) mount Seir many days.

וּבַיּוֹם הַשְּׁבִיעִי תָּסֹבּוּ אֶת־הָעִיר שֶׁבַע פְּעָמִים   Josh. 6.4
And on the seventh day **you shall go around** (*Q* imf 2m pl) the city seven times.

הִתְהַלְלוּ בְּשֵׁם קָדְשׁוֹ   1 Chron. 16.10
Glory (*Ht* pf 3c pl) in his holy name.

כִּי גָדוֹל יְהוָה וּמְהֻלָּל מְאֹד   1 Chron. 16.25
For great is Yahweh, and **praised** (*Pu* ptc m s) exceedingly.

וַיֹּאמְרוּ כָל־הָעָם אָמֵן וְהַלֵּל לַיהוָה   1 Chron. 16.36
And all the people said, Amen, and **praise** (*P* Imv 2m s) to Yahweh.

בַּיהוָה תִּתְהַלֵּל נַפְשִׁי   Ps. 34.3
My soul **will glory** (*Ht* imf 3f s) in Yahweh.

16.2   Vocabulary

גּוּר	*v.* to sojourn	אָחוֹת	*n.f.* sister
עָתַק	*v.* to remove, to move on	אַלּוֹן	*n.f.* oak
הָרַג	*v.* to kill	מִשְׁפָּחָה	*n.f.* clan
אָרַר	*v.* to inflict with a curse	יָפֶה	*n.f.* beautiful
רָכַשׁ	*v.* to gain property, goods	מוֹלֶדֶת	*n.f.* kindred
קָרַב	*v.* to draw near	רְכוּשׁ	*n.* property, goods
קָלַל	*v.* to be small, *Piel* to curse	רָעָב	*n.* famine
כָּבֵד	*v.* to be heavy	יָצַר	*v.* to form
גָּדַל	*v.* to be great	חָשַׂךְ	*v.* to restrain, hold back
בִּגְלַל	*prep.* on account of	נָסָה	*v.* to test, try, prove
בַּעֲבוּר	*prep.* because of	שָׁחַט	*v.* to slaughter
נֶגֶב	Negeb Desert *or figuratively:* south	הִשְׁתַּחֲוָה	*v. hishtafel,* to bow, to worship > חָוָה
אָחַז	*v.* to grasp, seize	חָשַׁךְ	*v.* to restrain, hold back

EXERCISE 16

16.3   Reading Genesis 11.1-9

Translate the following verses; parse the verbs that are indicated; and answer all numbered questions.You are not required to answer the questions that are not numbered. They are intended to direct your analysis in certain directions.

¹ וַיְהִי כָל־הָאָרֶץ שָׂפָה אֶחָת וּדְבָרִים אֲחָדִים: ² וַיְהִי בְּנָסְעָם מִקֶּדֶם
וַיִּמְצְאוּ בִקְעָה בְּאֶרֶץ שִׁנְעָר וַיֵּשְׁבוּ שָׁם: ³ וַיֹּאמְרוּ אִישׁ אֶל־רֵעֵהוּ
הָבָה נִלְבְּנָה לְבֵנִים וְנִשְׂרְפָה לִשְׂרֵפָה וַתְּהִי לָהֶם הַלְּבֵנָה לְאָבֶן
וְהַחֵמָר הָיָה לָהֶם לַחֹמֶר: ⁴ וַיֹּאמְרוּ הָבָה נִבְנֶה־לָּנוּ עִיר וּמִגְדָּל
וְרֹאשׁוֹ בַשָּׁמַיִם וְנַעֲשֶׂה־לָּנוּ שֵׁם פֶּן־נָפוּץ עַל־פְּנֵי כָל־הָאָרֶץ: ⁵ וַיֵּרֶד יְהוָה
לִרְאֹת אֶת־הָעִיר וְאֶת־הַמִּגְדָּל אֲשֶׁר בָּנוּ בְּנֵי הָאָדָם: ⁶ וַיֹּאמֶר יְהוָה הֵן
עַם אֶחָד וְשָׂפָה אַחַת לְכֻלָּם וְזֶה הַחִלָּם לַעֲשׂוֹת וְעַתָּה לֹא־יִבָּצֵר מֵהֶם
כֹּל אֲשֶׁר יָזְמוּ לַעֲשׂוֹת: ⁷ הָבָה נֵרְדָה וְנָבְלָה שָׁם שְׂפָתָם אֲשֶׁר לֹא יִשְׁמְעוּ
אִישׁ שְׂפַת רֵעֵהוּ: ⁸ וַיָּפֶץ יְהוָה אֹתָם מִשָּׁם עַל־פְּנֵי כָל־הָאָרֶץ וַיַּחְדְּלוּ
לִבְנֹת הָעִיר: ⁹ עַל־כֵּן קָרָא שְׁמָהּ בָּבֶל כִּי־שָׁם בָּלַל יְהוָה שְׂפַת כָּל־הָאָרֶץ
וּמִשָּׁם הֱפִיצָם יְהוָה עַל־פְּנֵי כָל־הָאָרֶץ: פ

Genesis 11.1

וַיְהִי כָל־הָאָרֶץ שָׂפָה אֶחָת וּדְבָרִים אֲחָדִים:

Q1: PARSE וַיְהִי (See §12.6.2)

Q2: There are two ways to translate וַיְהִי. It can be simply a paragraph marker, or it can function as a real verb. Should we translate as

1) *And it came to pass . . .*, or

2) *And all the earth was . . .*?

Q3: How do you know which translation is correct? What is the subject of the verb? See Gen. 9.19; Isa. 7.24; but with pl 1Sam. 17.46; 1Chr. 16.23; Ps. 33.8; 66.1, etc. (§26.1.1 #4)

Q4: Is אֶחָת an attributive adj. or predicate adjective? Explain. (§3.1.2.1)

וּדְבָרִים אֲחָדִים

Note that in Hebrew, a singular number can be plural when modifying a plural noun, e.g. אֲחָדִים. The plural אֲחָדִים can also mean *few* (Gen. 27.44; 29.20; Deut. 11.20). However, because of the parallelism within the verse, most versions understand to mean *one*, and translate the phrase accordingly; e.g., *the same words* (NRS), or *a common speech* (NIV).

Genesis 11.2

וַיְהִי בְּנָסְעָם מִקֶּדֶם

Morphemes of בְּנָסְעָם: ם נָסְעָ בְּ

Q5: What two verb forms may accept inseparable prepositions? (§6.5.2)

Q6: What part of speech is the ם?

Q7: Is ם the object or subject of the verbal action?

בְּנָסְעָם (בְּ + IA) introduces a temporal clause (§6.5.2, Williams §504, 505).

מִקֶּדֶם can mean *on the east side* or *eastward* (Williams §323, cf. Gen. 2.8 and 3.24).

וַיִּמְצְאוּ בִקְעָה בְּאֶרֶץ שִׁנְעָר וַיֵּשְׁבוּ שָׁם:

Morphemes of וַיִּמְצְאוּ: וּ מָצָא יִ וַ

Q8: PARSE וַיִּמְצְאוּ (See §13.2.2)

A *wayyiqtol* following a temporal element should be translated *that*. Thus, *And it came to pass, when they journeyed toward the east, that they found.* . . . Another way of translating this verse, omitting some of the Hebrew idiom, would be: *And when they journeyed eastward they found.* . . .

אֶרֶץ שִׁנְעָר is a construct–genitive phrase, a genitive of specification, that gives the proper name for the land – *Shinar* (see §5.3.3.6).

Morphemes of וַיֵּשְׁבוּ: וּ שָׁב יִ וַ

וַיֵּשְׁבוּ *and they dwelled*

Q9: Is the *tsere* under the י the usual vowel for a *qal* imf? (§5.1.1)

Verbs beginning with י will sometimes assimilate the י, and compensate by lengthening the *chireq* to *tsere* under the preformative. We will discuss these verbs in Chapter 17.

Genesis 11.3

וַיֹּאמְרוּ אִישׁ אֶל־רֵעֵהוּ

Morphemes of וַיֹּאמְרוּ: וּ אָמַר יִ וַ

Q10: PARSE וַיֹּאמְרוּ

אִישׁ אֶל־רֵעֵהוּ is an idiom meaning *to one another* (See §11.9 and Williams §132).

הָבָה נִלְבְּנָה לְבֵנִים   (Williams §191)

Morphemes of הָבָה: ה הָב

This is an imperative (from יהב) used as an interjection meaning *Come!* We will study the initial *yod* verbs in Ch. 17.

Q11: What is the הָ ending on הָבָה? (§6.2)

Morphemes of : נ לִבְנֶ ה

Q12: What is the הָ ending on נִלְבְּנָה? (§6.1)

Note: This form could be parsed either as a *qal* or a *nifal*, but the context will determine which parsing is correct here.

Q13: PARSE נִלְבְּנָה

וְנִשְׂרְפָה לִשְׂרֵפָה

Morphemes of וְנִשְׂרְפָה: וְ נ שְׂרָפָ ה

Q14: What is the הָ ending on וְנִשְׂרְפָה? (§6.1, §26.1.1 #54)

Q15: PARSE וְנִשְׂרְפָה

Note the simple *vav* on this cohortative verb.

וַתְּהִי לָהֶם הַלְּבֵנָה לְאָבֶן

Morphemes of וַתְּהִי: וַ תְּ הִי

Q16: PARSE וַתְּהִי (See §12.6.2)

The verb הָיָה followed by לְ indicates possession.

Q17: Why is this verb feminine?

וְהַחֵמָר הָיָה לָהֶם לַחֹמֶר:

This clause is x-*qatal*, contemporary with the previous clause (§26.1.1 #9)

Genesis 11.4

וַיֹּאמְרוּ הָבָה נִבְנֶה־לָנוּ עִיר וּמִגְדָּל

Morphemes of נִבְנֶה: נ בְנֶ ה

Q18: What is the הָ ending on נִבְנֶה? (§6.1)

Q19: PARSE נִבְנֶה (See §12.6.2)

Q20: What part of speech is the נוּ on לָנוּ? (§6.4.3) See also Williams §72.

וְרֹאשׁוֹ בַשָּׁמַיִם See Williams §494

You must supply the verb for this clause.

The concrete meaning of רֹאשׁ was originally *head*, but it developed several extended meanings: *chief, top, leader,* etc.

וְנַעֲשֶׂה־לָנוּ שֵׁם

Morphemes of וְנַעֲשֶׂה: וְ נ עֲשֶׂ ה

Q21: PARSE וְנַעֲשֶׂה

פֶּן־נָפוּץ עַל־פְּנֵי כָל־הָאָרֶץ:

Morphemes of נָפוּץ: נָ פוּץ

Q22: PARSE נָפוּץ

Q23: How would you form the *nifal* imf 1cp of this verb (See §15.1.3)?

פֶּן followed by the imperfect indicates the subjunctive mood.

Remember, the *Nifal* imf always has *chireq* under the preformative, with a *dagesh forte* in the first radical (except for verbs with initial guttural).

Genesis 11.5

וַיֵּרֶד יְהוָה לִרְאֹת אֶת־הָעִיר וְאֶת־הַמִּגְדָּל

Morphemes of וַיֵּרֶד: וַ יֵ רֶד   *and he went down*

Q24: Is the *tsere* under the י the usual vowel for a *qal* imf?

Verbs beginning with י will sometimes assimilate the י, and compensate by lengthening the *chireq* to *tsere* under the preformative. We will discuss these verbs in Chapter 17.

Morphemes of לִרְאֹת: לִ רְאֹ ת

Q25: PARSE לִרְאֹת

Q26: Why does לִרְאֹת end with ת? (See §12.6.2)

This is an infinitive of purpose. See Williams §520

אֲשֶׁר בָּנוּ בְּנֵי הָאָדָם:

Morphemes of בָּנוּ:   בָּנ וּ

Q27: PARSE בָּנוּ (See §12.6.2 and Williams §162)

אֲשֶׁר followed by the perfect is past tense in relation to the previous clause (See §26.1.1 #16).

Genesis 11.6

וַיֹּאמֶר יְהוָה הֵן עַם אֶחָד וְשָׂפָה אַחַת לְכֻלָּם

הֵן is an interjection that means *Behold!*

You must supply two verbs in these clauses.

לְכֻלָּם is made up of three morphemes: לְ כֻל ם

וְזֶה הַחִלָּם לַעֲשׂוֹת   (§7.6)

Morphemes of הַחִלָּם: הַ חִלָּ ם

Q28: Why is there a *dagesh* in the לֹ? (§16.1.2)

Q29: What stem is indicated by the הַ?

Q30: PARSE הַחִלָּם

Without the suffix, this verb form would be הָחֵל. Cf. §16.1.3

Morphemes of לַעֲשׂוֹת: לַ עֲשׂ וֹת

Q31: PARSE לַעֲשׂוֹת   (See §12.6.2)

וְעַתָּה לֹא־יִבָּצֵר מֵהֶם כֹּל אֲשֶׁר יָזְמוּ לַעֲשׂוֹת:

Q32: PARSE יִבָּצֵר

Q33: What stem is characterized by a *dagesh* in the first radical of the imperfect, with a *qamets* under the same radical?

Morphemes of יָזְמוּ: יָ זְמ וּ

You have only two root letters. If you do not immediately recognize the form, you may want to follow these observations. 1) יָזְמוּ looks similar to a *qal* pf 3cp from יָזַם. However, that form would be accented thus: יָזְמוּ ; 2) If this is not a pf 3cp, then the י must be the imf preformative. In that case, there are only two types of the imf 3mp that have *qamets* under the preformative: the hollow verbs and the geminate verbs. 3) The hollow verbs, however, always restore the middle radical in the *yiqtol* (imf). Thus if this were a hollow verb, it would be either יָזִימוּ, יָזוּמוּ, or יָזֵמוּ. 4) Therefore, this must be a geminate root זָמַם (Cf. § 16.1.3). Although the usual paradigm of the imf includes a *dagesh* in the second root letter, the *dagesh* is sometimes omitted. The lexicon will confirm this analysis.

Q34: PARSE יָזְמוּ   (§26.1.1 #39)

Q35: PARSE לַעֲשׂוֹת   (See §12.6.2)

Genesis 11.7

הָבָה נֵרְדָה וְנָבְלָה שָׁם שְׂפָתָם Williams §191

Note the repetition of הָבָה *Come!*

Morphemes of נֵרְדָה: נֵ רְדָ ה from ירד.

נֵרְדָה *let us go down*

Morphemes of וְנָבְלָה: וְ נָ בְלָ ה

Q36: PARSE וְנָבְלָה   (See §16.1.3)

Q37: What part of speech is the הָ ending on נֵרְדָה, הָבָה and וְנָבְלָה? (§6.1)

Q38: Is the *tsere* under the נ of נֵרְדָה the usual vowel for a *qal* imf?

Verbs beginning with י will sometimes assimilate the י, and compensate by lengthening the *chireq* to *tsere* under the preformative. We will discuss these verbs in Chapter 17.

Q39: Why does וְנָבְלָה have a *qamets* under the preformative? Consult the notes on the previous verse.

Do you suppose that שָׁם is a play on words with שֵׁם in verse 4.

שְׂפָתָם is the construct of שָׂפָה with the pronominal suffix ם.

אֲשֶׁר לֹא יִשְׁמְעוּ אִישׁ שְׂפַת רֵעֵהוּ:   See Williams §132

In this context, you should translate אֲשֶׁר as *so that* (Holladay, p. 30).

Q40: PARSE יִשְׁמְעוּ

Genesis 11.8

וַיָּפֶץ יְהוָה אֹתָם מִשָּׁם עַל־פְּנֵי כָל־הָאָרֶץ

Morphemes of וַיָּפֶץ: וַ יָ פֶץ

The *wayyiqtol* is usually shortened in the hollow verbs (See §15.1.3). In this case וַיָּפֶץ is shortened from וַיָּפִיץ.

Q41: PARSE וַיָּפֶץ

וַיַּחְדְּלוּ לִבְנֹת הָעִיר:

Morphemes of וַיַּחְדְּלוּ:   וַ יַ חְדְּל וּ

Q42: PARSE וַיַּחְדְּלוּ

Morphemes of לִבְנֹת: ל בְנֹ ת

Q43: PARSE לִבְנֹת

Q44: What weak verbs end with ת in the infinitive? (See §12.6.2)

Note that the city is mentioned more times than the tower.

Genesis 11.9

עַל־כֵּן קָרָא שְׁמָהּ בָּבֶל   Williams §160

כִּי־שָׁם בָּלַל יְהוָה שְׂפַת כָּל־הָאָרֶץ

וּמִשָּׁם הֱפִיצָם יְהוָה עַל־פְּנֵי כָּל־הָאָרֶץ:

Morphemes of הֱפִיצָם: הֱ פִ י צָ ם

Q45: PARSE הֱפִיצָם

Q46: What part of speech is the ם on הֱפִיצָם?

The pronominal suffix causes the reduction to *sheva* under the ה.

Q47: What stem is indicated by a prefixed ה and an infixed י? (See §15.1.3, but this vowel pattern is unusual. Consult the lexicon.)

Ashkenazi Haggadah—c. 1450 CE

Chapter 17

Initial *Yod* Verbs and Reading Genesis 12.1-13

In this chapter you will learn:

- Forms of weak verbs that begin with י (called פ"י verbs).
- Syntax from inductive study of Genesis 12

17.1 Initial *Yod* Verbs

17.1.1 Prominent פ"י Verbs

Verbs that begin with י are divided into two classes, based upon their origin: 1) Verbs that begin with י and 2) Verbs that originally began with ו, but the ו manifests itself as י when it is not preceded by a preformative or prefix.

These two classes of verbs are similar in their inflections, but they exhibit distinct differences as well.

Some prominent פ"י verbs (with frequency in parentheses) are:

יָמַן	to go to the right (*Hifil*) (139)
יָשַׁר	to be straight (118)
יָטַב	to be well (101)
יָבֵשׁ	to be dry (61)
יָצַר	to form (40)
יָלַל	to groan (*Hifil*) (27)

Some prominent פ"ו verbs are:

יָצָא	to go out (1067)
יָדַע	to know (940)
יָשַׁב	to dwell (815)
יָלַד	to give birth (468)
יָרַד	to go down (379)
יָרֵא	to fear (293)
יָרַשׁ	to take possession (231)
יָסַף	to add (212)
יָשַׁע	to save (*Hifil*) (205)
יָכֹל	to be able (193)
יָדָה	to praise (111)

Verbs with initial yod have two distinct ori-

17.1.2   Characteristics of the פ"י/ו Verbs

1. ***Qal* Perfect** is regular (note the differences, however between יָשַׁב, a fientive verb and יָרֵא and יָכֹל, which are stative verbs.)

2. ***Qal* Imperfect** has several variations, depending on type of verb and its lexical form.

   a. Fientive verbs like יָשַׁב lose the י and have double *tsere* throughout, e.g. אֵשֵׁב.

   b. Stative verbs like יָרֵא, retain the י.

   c. Stative verbs like יָכֹל revert to original ו.

3. ***Nifal*** reverts to the original ו in both perfect (where vowel is וֹ) and imperfect (where the forms have the usual *dagesh* with qamets and *tsere*).

4. ***Hifil*** and **Hofal** also have the original ו in both perfect and imperfect (where vowel is וֹ in the *Hifil* and וּ in the *hofal*).

5. **Original י verbs** will have *patach* in the *qal* imperfect and *tsere* in the *Hifil*.

17.1.3   The Verb הלך

The verb הָלַךְ (occurring 1549 times) usually behaves like a פ"ו verb in the imperfect, dropping the ה and lengthening the *chireq* to *tsere* under the imperfect preformative. Therefore, the *qal* imf. 3ms is יֵלֵךְ (there are exceptions, however, and these exceptions are easy to identify). For the entire paradigm, see §22.13.

17.1.4   Examples of Initial פ"י/ו Verbs and הָלַךְ

וַיֵּצֵא קַיִן מִלִּפְנֵי יְהוָה וַיֵּשֶׁב בְּאֶרֶץ־נוֹד Gen. 4.16
And Cain **went out** (*Q* Imf *W* 3m s >יצא) from the presence of Yahweh, and **he dwelt** (*Q* imf *W* 3m s >יָשַׁב) in the land of Nod.

וּסְפֹר הַכּוֹכָבִים אִם־תּוּכַל לִסְפֹּר אֹתָם Gen. 15.5
And count the stars if **you are able** (*Q* imf 2m s>יָכֹל) to count them.

וַיֵּלֶךְ אִתּוֹ לוֹט Gen. 12.4
And Lot **went** (*Q* imf *W* 3m s >הָלַךְ) with him.

עַל־גְּחֹנְךָ תֵלֵךְ Gen. 3.14
Upon your belly **you will go** (*Q* imf 2m s>הָלַךְ).

לֵךְ וְאָסַפְתָּ אֶת־זִקְנֵי יִשְׂרָאֵל Exod. 3.16
Go! (*Q* imv 2m s>הָלַךְ) and gather the elders of Israel.

17.1.5 פ״י/ו Verb Paradigm[4]

	Orig. ו						Orig. י	
	Qal	**Qal**	**Qal**	**Nifal**	**Hifil**	**Hofal**	**Qal**	**Hifil**
Pf	*sit / dwell*	*fear*	*be able*	*inhabited*	*made to sit*	*made inhab.*	*be well*	*made well*
1cs	יָשַׁבְתִּי	יָרֵאתִי	יָכֹלְתִּי	נוֹשַׁבְתִּי	הוֹשַׁבְתִּי	הוּשַׁבְתִּי	יָטֹב	הֵיטַבְתִּי
2ms	יָשַׁבְתָּ	יָרֵאתָ	יָכֹלְתָּ	נוֹשַׁבְתָּ	הוֹשַׁבְתָּ	הוּשַׁבְתָּ		הֵיטַבְתָּ
2fs	יָשַׁבְתְּ	יָרֵאת	יָכֹלְתְּ	נוֹשַׁבְתְּ	הוֹשַׁבְתְּ	הוּשַׁבְתְּ		הֵיטַבְתְּ
3ms	יָשַׁב	יָרֵא	יָכֹל	נוֹשַׁב	הוֹשִׁיב	הוּשַׁב		הֵיטִיב
3fs	יָשְׁבָה	יָרְאָה	יָכְלָה	נוֹשְׁבָה	הוֹשִׁיבָה	הוּשְׁבָה		הֵיטִיבָה
1cp	יָשַׁבְנוּ	יָרֵאנוּ	יָכֹלְנוּ	נוֹשַׁבְנוּ	הוֹשַׁבְנוּ	הוּשַׁבְנוּ		הֵיטַבְנוּ
2mp	יְשַׁבְתֶּם	יְרֵאתֶם	יְכָלְתֶּם	נוֹשַׁבְתֶּם	הוֹשַׁבְתֶּם	הוּשַׁבְתֶּם		הֵיטַבְתֶּם
2fp	יְשַׁבְתֶּן	יְרֵאתֶן	יְכָלְתֶּן	נוֹשַׁבְתֶּן	הוֹשַׁבְתֶּן	הוּשַׁבְתֶּן		הֵיטַבְתֶּן
3cp	יָשְׁבוּ	יָרְאוּ	יָכְלוּ	נוֹשְׁבוּ	הוֹשִׁיבוּ	הוּשְׁבוּ		הֵיטִיבוּ
Imf								
1cs	אֵשֵׁב	אִירָא	אוּכַל	אִוָּשֵׁב	אוֹשִׁיב	אוּשַׁב	אִיטַב	אֵיטִיב
2ms	תֵּשֵׁב	תִּירָא	תּוּכַל	תִּוָּשֵׁב	תּוֹשִׁיב	תּוּשַׁב	תֵּיטַב	תֵּיטִיב
2fs	תֵּשְׁבִי	תִּירְאִי	תּוּכְלִי	תִּוָּשְׁבִי	תּוֹשִׁיבִי	תּוּשְׁבִי	תֵּיטְבִי	תֵּיטִיבִי
3ms	יֵשֵׁב	יִירָא	יוּכַל	יִוָּשֵׁב	יוֹשִׁיב	יוּשַׁב	יֵיטַב	יֵיטִיב
3fs	תֵּשֵׁב	תִּירָא	תּוּכַל	תִּוָּשֵׁב	תּוֹשִׁיב	תּוּשַׁב	תֵּיטַב	תֵּיטִיב
1cp	נֵשֵׁב	נִירָא	נוּכַל	נִוָּשֵׁב	נוֹשִׁיב	נוּשַׁב	נֵיטַב	נֵיטִיב
2mp	תֵּשְׁבוּ	תִּירְאוּ	תּוּכְלוּ	תִּוָּשְׁבוּ	תּוֹשִׁיבוּ	תּוּשְׁבוּ	תֵּיטְבוּ	תֵּיטִיבוּ
2fp	תֵּשַׁבְנָה	תִּירֶאנָה	תּוּכַלְנָה	תִּוָּשַׁבְנָה	תּוֹשֵׁבְנָה	תּוּשַׁבְנָה	תֵּיטַבְנָה	תֵּיטֵבְנָה
3mp	יֵשְׁבוּ	יִירְאוּ	יוּכְלוּ	יִוָּשְׁבוּ	יוֹשִׁיבוּ	יוּשְׁבוּ	יֵיטְבוּ	יֵיטִיבוּ
3fp	תֵּשַׁבְנָה	תִּירֶאנָה	תּוּכַלְנָה	תִּוָּשַׁבְנָה	תּוֹשֵׁבְנָה	תּוּשַׁבְנָה	תֵּיטַבְנָה	תֵּיטֵבְנָה
Imv								
2ms	שֵׁב	יְרָא		הִוָּשֵׁב	הוֹשֵׁב			הֵיטֵב
2fs	שְׁבִי	יְרְאִי		הִוָּשְׁבִי	הוֹשִׁיבִי			הֵיטִיבִי
2mp	שְׁבוּ	יְרְאוּ		הִוָּשְׁבוּ	הוֹשִׁיבוּ			הֵיטִיבוּ
2fp	שֵׁבְנָה	יְרֶאנָה		הִוָּשַׁבְנָה	הוֹשֵׁבְנָה			הֵיטֵבְנָה
IA	יָשׁוֹב	יָרוֹא		הִוָּשֵׁב	הוֹשֵׁב			הֵיטֵב
IC	שֶׁבֶת	יְרֹא		הִוָּשֵׁב	הוֹשִׁיב	הוּשַׁב		הֵיטִיב
APtc	יֹשֵׁב	יָרֵא			מוֹשִׁיב		יֹטֵב	מֵיטִיב
PPtc	יָשׁוּב			נוֹשָׁב		מוּשָׁב		
W	וַיֵּשֶׁב	וַיִּירָא	וַיּוּכַל	וַיִּוָּשֶׁב	וַיּוֹשֶׁב	וַיּוּשַׁב	וַיִּיטַב	וַיֵּיטֶב
Jus	יֵשֵׁב			יִוָּשֵׁב	יוֹשֵׁב	יוּשַׁב	יֵיטַב	יֵיטֵב

---

[4] *Piel*, *Pual*, and *Hitpael* follow the pattern of the strong verb.

17.2   Vocabulary

עָקַד	v. to bind, tie	אַיֵּה	interr. Where?
עָרַךְ	v. to arrange, prepare	יַחְדָּו	adv. together
חָבַשׁ	v. to tie, restrain, saddle	פֹּה	adv. here
בָּקַע	v. to split, cleave, break open	רָחוֹק	adj. remote, far, distant
הִשְׁכִּים	v. Hifil to arise early > שכם	יָחִיד	adj. only
סְבַךְ	n. thicket	יָרֵא	adj. afraid
אַיִל	n. ram	לְמַעַן	prep. in order that
מַלְאָךְ	n. messenger, angel	מָגוֹר	n.m. sojourning place
נַעַר	n. lad, youth, servant	דִּבָּה	n.f. whispering, evil report
מַאֲכֶלֶת	n. knife	זָקוּן	n.m. old age
קֶרֶן	n. f. horn	שָׂנֵא	v. to hate
חֲמוֹר	n. donkey	שָׁלוֹם	n.m. peace, wholeness
מְאוּמָה	n. anything		

EXERCISE 17

Translate the following verses; parse the verbs that are indicated; and answer all questions. You are not required to answer the questions that are not numbered. They are intended to direct your analysis in certain directions.

17.3 Reading Genesis 12.1-13

¹ וַיֹּאמֶר יְהוָה אֶל־אַבְרָם לֶךְ־לְךָ מֵאַרְצְךָ וּמִמּוֹלַדְתְּךָ וּמִבֵּית אָבִיךָ
אֶל־הָאָרֶץ אֲשֶׁר אַרְאֶךָּ: ² וְאֶעֶשְׂךָ לְגוֹי גָּדוֹל וַאֲבָרֶכְךָ וַאֲגַדְּלָה שְׁמֶךָ
וֶהְיֵה בְּרָכָה: ³ וַאֲבָרֲכָה מְבָרְכֶיךָ וּמְקַלֶּלְךָ אָאֹר וְנִבְרְכוּ בְךָ
כֹּל מִשְׁפְּחֹת הָאֲדָמָה: ⁴ וַיֵּלֶךְ אַבְרָם כַּאֲשֶׁר דִּבֶּר אֵלָיו יְהוָה וַיֵּלֶךְ
אִתּוֹ לוֹט וְאַבְרָם בֶּן־חָמֵשׁ שָׁנִים וְשִׁבְעִים שָׁנָה בְּצֵאתוֹ מֵחָרָן: ⁵ וַיִּקַּח אַבְרָם
אֶת־שָׂרַי אִשְׁתּוֹ וְאֶת־לוֹט בֶּן־אָחִיו וְאֶת־כָּל־רְכוּשָׁם אֲשֶׁר רָכָשׁוּ וְאֶת־הַנֶּפֶשׁ
אֲשֶׁר־עָשׂוּ בְחָרָן וַיֵּצְאוּ לָלֶכֶת אַרְצָה כְּנַעַן וַיָּבֹאוּ אַרְצָה כְּנָעַן: ⁶ וַיַּעֲבֹר
אַבְרָם בָּאָרֶץ עַד מְקוֹם שְׁכֶם עַד אֵלוֹן מוֹרֶה וְהַכְּנַעֲנִי אָז בָּאָרֶץ: ⁷ וַיֵּרָא
יְהוָה אֶל־אַבְרָם וַיֹּאמֶר לְזַרְעֲךָ אֶתֵּן אֶת־הָאָרֶץ הַזֹּאת וַיִּבֶן שָׁם מִזְבֵּחַ
לַיהוָה הַנִּרְאֶה אֵלָיו: ⁸ וַיַּעְתֵּק מִשָּׁם הָהָרָה מִקֶּדֶם לְבֵית־אֵל וַיֵּט אָהֳלֹה
בֵּית־אֵל מִיָּם וְהָעַי מִקֶּדֶם וַיִּבֶן־שָׁם מִזְבֵּחַ לַיהוָה וַיִּקְרָא בְּשֵׁם יְהוָה:
⁹ וַיִּסַּע אַבְרָם הָלוֹךְ וְנָסוֹעַ הַנֶּגְבָּה: פ ¹⁰ וַיְהִי רָעָב בָּאָרֶץ וַיֵּרֶד אַבְרָם

מִצְרַיְמָה לָגוּר שָׁם כִּי־כָבֵד הָרָעָב בָּאָרֶץ: ¹¹ וַיְהִי כַּאֲשֶׁר הִקְרִיב לָבוֹא מִצְרָיְמָה וַיֹּאמֶר אֶל־שָׂרַי אִשְׁתּוֹ הִנֵּה־נָא יָדַעְתִּי כִּי אִשָּׁה יְפַת־מַרְאֶה אָתְּ: ¹² וְהָיָה כִּי־יִרְאוּ אֹתָךְ הַמִּצְרִים וְאָמְרוּ אִשְׁתּוֹ זֹאת וְהָרְגוּ אֹתִי וְאֹתָךְ יְחַיּוּ: ¹³ אִמְרִי־נָא אֲחֹתִי אָתְּ לְמַעַן יִיטַב־לִי בַעֲבוּרֵךְ וְחָיְתָה נַפְשִׁי בִּגְלָלֵךְ:

Genesis 12.1

וַיֹּאמֶר יְהוָה אֶל־אַבְרָם

לֶךְ־לְךָ מֵאַרְצְךָ וּמִמּוֹלַדְתְּךָ וּמִבֵּית אָבִיךָ

Q1: Only two radicals remain on לֵךְ. What is the third radical? (See §17.1.3)

Q2: PARSE לֵךְ (§26.1.1 #56)

Morphemes of וּמִמּוֹלַדְתְּךָ: ךָ דְת מוֹלַ מִ ו

Q3: What part of speech is ךָ?

לְךָ is redundant in English, but it is found in the KJV: *Go thou.* See Gesenius §119*s.*

Q4: Is אָבִיךָ *father* or *fathers*?

אֶל־הָאָרֶץ אֲשֶׁר אַרְאֶךָּ:

Morphemes of אַרְאֶךָּ: ךָ אֶ רְ אַ

Q5: What stem is indicated by the *patach* under the preformative?

Q6: What part of speech is ךָ?

Whenever the form ךָּ occurs instead of ךָ, it indicates the assimilation of *energic nun* (§12.1.1). These forms are usually found *in pause*, that is, when the verb comes at the end of a verse or is strongly accented. Cf. Gesenius §58*i.*

Q7: PARSE אַרְאֶךָּ (See §12.6.2) *Cause you to see = show you* (§26.1.1 #39)

Genesis 12.2

וְאֶעֶשְׂךָ לְגוֹי גָּדוֹל

Morphemes of וְאֶעֶשְׂךָ: ךָ שְׂ עֶ אֶ וְ

Q8: Is this a *wayyiqtol*?

Q9: PARSE וְאֶעֶשְׂךָ (See §12.6.2)

Q10: Is this a simple future (*I shall make you*), or a cohortative (*I will make you*)? See §5.1.2

The cohortative of ל"ה verbs does not have the cohortative ה. See Seow, p. 168 and Joüon §116*h*.

The prep. לְ, when following the verb עָשָׂה may introduce the indirect object.
See Williams §278

וַאֲבָרֶכְךָ וַאֲגַדְּלָה שְׁמֶךָ וֶהְיֵה בְּרָכָה:

Morphemes of וַאֲבָרֶכְךָ: וַ אֲ בָרֵךְ ךָ

Q11: Piel requires a *dagesh* in the middle radical, so why is there no *dagesh* in the *resh*? (§2.1.2 and §14.2)

Q12: PARSE וַאֲבָרֶכְךָ

Morphemes of וַאֲגַדְּלָה: וַ אֲ גַדְּל ה

Q13: What is the ה on וַאֲגַדְּלָה? (§6.1)

Q14: PARSE וַאֲגַדְּלָה (§3.3.3)

Q15: Are these two verbs (וַאֲבָרֶכְךָ וַאֲגַדְּלָה) *wayyiqtols*? (§3.3.3 & §7.2)

What is וֶהְיֵה? It cannot be an imperfect, because there is no preformative. It
cannot be an infinitive, because all לה"ה verbs have ת at the end of the infin.
(e.g. הֱיוֹת). There is no participle of היה, but if there were, it would be הוֹיֶה. If
it were a perfect, it would be pointed וְהָיָה, and the translation would be *and he
shall be*. The only thing left is the imperative, which is usually הֱיֵה, but with *vav*,
it becomes וֶהְיֵה. See Seow, p. 170; and Gesenius §163q.

The imv with *vav* expresses purpose or result (Williams §189, Joüon §116, Seow
p. 175). The translation, therefore, is *so that you may be a blessing*.

Genesis 12.3

וַאֲבָרְכָה מְבָרְכֶיךָ וּמְקַלֶּלְךָ אָאֹר

Morphemes of וַאֲבָרְכָה: וַ אֲ בָרֵךְ ה

Q16: What is the ה?

Q17: PARSE וַאֲבָרְכָה (See §14.2.2)

Morphemes of מְבָרְכֶיךָ: מְ בָרֵךְ י ךָ

Q18: What form of the verb does the מְ indicate?

Q19: PARSE מְבָרְכֶיךָ (See §14.2.2)

Q20: PARSE וּמְקַלֶּלְךָ

Q21: Why is there a י in מְבָרְכֶיךָ, but not in וּמְקַלֶּלְךָ?

The word וּמְקַלֶּלְךָ is a good example where the textual evidence suggests a
scribal error. See the textual apparatus at the bottom of the page of BHS, which
reads: 'verse 3, note a, one copy of the Hebrew Codex Cairensis, a few manuscripts of the Samaritan Pentateuch, the Septuagint, the Syriac, and the Latin

Vulgate have the plural form יּמְקַלֶּלְךָ.

Q22: PARSE אָאֹר

The *qamets* indicates a hollow verb or a geminate verb, but a hollow verb retains its middle vowel in the imperfect.

וְנִבְרְכוּ בְךָ כֹּל מִשְׁפְּחֹת הָאֲדָמָה:

Morphemes of וְנִבְרְכוּ: וְ נ בְרְכ וּ

Q23: What stem is suggested by נ? (See §14.2.2)

Q24: What part of speech is וּ?

Q25: PARSE וְנִבְרְכוּ

Genesis 12.4

וַיֵּלֶךְ אַבְרָם כַּאֲשֶׁר דִּבֶּר אֵלָיו יְהוָה

Morphemes of וַיֵּלֶךְ: וַ יֵ לֶךְ

Q26: Is this a *wayyiqtol*?

Q27: PARSE וַיֵּלֶךְ (See §17.1.3)

Q28: PARSE דִּבֶּר

וַיֵּלֶךְ אִתּוֹ לוֹט

Q29: What is the difference between אֹתוֹ and אִתּוֹ?

וְאַבְרָם בֶּן־חָמֵשׁ שָׁנִים וְשִׁבְעִים שָׁנָה

This clause is an x-*qatal*. Thus it does not advance the action in the narrative. It is parenthetical and is connected to the previous *wayyiqtol* (§26.1.1 #19).

The phrase *son of X years* is an idiomatic way of expressing age.

בְּצֵאתוֹ מֵחָרָן:

Morphemes of בְּצֵאתוֹ: בְּ צֵא ת וֹ

Q30: What are the only two forms of the verb to which a prep. may be attached?

Q31: Does this word begin a temporal clause? (§6.5.2)

Q32: PARSE בְּצֵאתוֹ (See §17.1.5)

Why does בְּצֵאתוֹ have the letter ת?

Genesis 12.5

וַיִּקַּח אַבְרָם אֶת־שָׂרַי אִשְׁתּוֹ

Morphemes of וַיִּקַּח: וַ יִ קַּח

Q33: Why is there a *dagesh* in the קּ? (See §14.1.1)

Q34: PARSE וַיִּקַּח

וְאֶת־לוֹט בֶּן־אָחִיו

וְאֶת־כָּל־רְכוּשָׁם אֲשֶׁר רָכָשׁוּ

Q35: Into what English tense would you translate רָכָשׁוּ?

Q36: PARSE רָכָשׁוּ

וְאֶת־הַנֶּפֶשׁ אֲשֶׁר־עָשׂוּ בְחָרָן

Q37: PARSE עָשׂוּ   (See §12.6.2)

Is הַנֶּפֶשׁ singular or plural?

וַיֵּצְאוּ לָלֶכֶת אַרְצָה כְּנַעַן

Morphemes of וַיֵּצְאוּ: וַ יֵּ צָא וּ

Q38: Why is there a *tsere* under the י? (See §17.1.5)

Q39: PARSE וַיֵּצְאוּ

Morphemes of לָלֶכֶת: לָ לֶכֶ ת   (See §17.1.3)

Q40: PARSE לָלֶכֶת

Q41: What is the ה on אַרְצָה?   (§7.5)

וַיָּבֹאוּ אַרְצָה כְּנַעַן:

Morphemes of וַיָּבֹאוּ: וַ יָ בֹא וּ

Q42: Hollow verbs retain the middle radical in the imperfect. If וַיָּבֹאוּ is imf., why does it not have the middle radical?

Q43: PARSE וַיָּבֹאוּ   (See §15.1.3)

Genesis 12.6

וַיַּעֲבֹר אַבְרָם בָּאָרֶץ עַד מְקוֹם שְׁכֶם עַד אֵלוֹן מוֹרֶה

Q44: Why is there a *patach* under the י in וַיַּעֲבֹר? (See §13.1.2)

Q45: Classify the construct–genitive phrase אֵלוֹן מוֹרֶה according to §5.3.3.

וְהַכְּנַעֲנִי אָז בָּאָרֶץ:

This verbless clause functions as parenthetical, background explanation (§26.1.1 #19).

Morphemes of וְהַכְּנַעֲנִי: וְ הַ כְּנַעֲנִ י

The י is a tribal (gentilic) ending. See Seow, p. 266. For example, Exod. 33.2:

וְשָׁלַחְתִּי לְפָנֶיךָ מַלְאָךְ וְגֵרַשְׁתִּי אֶת־הַכְּנַעֲנִי הָאֱמֹרִי
וְהַחִתִּי וְהַפְּרִזִּי הַחִוִּי וְהַיְבוּסִי:

Genesis 12.7

וַיֵּרָא יְהוָה אֶל־אַבְרָם

Q46: וַיֵּרָא How do you know that this is *nifal*? (§13.1 and §22.11)

Q47: PARSE וַיֵּרָא (See §12.6.2)

וַיֹּאמֶר לְזַרְעֲךָ אֶתֵּן אֶת־הָאָרֶץ הַזֹּאת

Q48: PARSE אֶתֵּן (See §14.1.2)

וַיִּבֶן שָׁם מִזְבֵּחַ לַיהוָה הַנִּרְאֶה אֵלָיו:

Q49: וַיִּבֶן What is the third radical?

Q50: PARSE וַיִּבֶן (See §12.6.2)

Q51: הַנִּרְאֶה What part of speech is the initial ה?

Q52: PARSE הַנִּרְאֶה (See §12.6.2)

Genesis 12.8

וַיַּעְתֵּק מִשָּׁם הָהָרָה מִקֶּדֶם לְבֵית־אֵל

Morphemes of וַיַּעְתֵּק: וַ יַ עְתֵּק

Q53: PARSE וַיַּעְתֵּק (See §13.1.2)

וַיֵּט אָהֳלֹה בֵּית־אֵל מִיָּם וְהָעַי מִקֶּדֶם

Q54: וַיֵּט Two radicals are missing, what are they?

Q55: PARSE וַיֵּט

Ketiv/Qere: In your BHS text, the small circle above the word אָהֳלֹה refers to a note in the margin, placed there by the scribes (Masoretes) who copied the text. In the margin we see the letter קְ, and above it the word אהלו. The קְ stands for the word Qere, which means 'that which is read'. The word in the text (אָהֳלֹה) is called the Ketiv ('that which is written'). *The word in the margin, marked with* קְ, *is consided by the scribes to be the correct form of the word.* Therefore, we read אָהֳלוֹ instead of אָהֳלֹה. Some Ketiv/Qere readings are so common that they are not marked. For example, the word יְהוָה is always read as 'Adonai' (not 'Yahweh'), in order to avoid saying the divine name; and the word הוּא is always read as הִיא ('she'). See Gesenius §17, Joüon §16e-f, and https://youtu.be/U0Fde88fQmU.

וַיִּ֫בֶן שָׁם מִזְבֵּ֫חַ לַיהוָה וַיִּקְרָא בְּשֵׁם יְהוָה׃

Q56: וַיִּ֫בֶן What third radical is dropped from the *wayyiqtol?*

Q57: PARSE וַיִּ֫בֶן (See §12.6.2)

Genesis 12.9

וַיִּסַּע אַבְרָם הָלוֹךְ וְנָסוֹעַ הַנֶּֽגְבָּה׃

Morphemes of וַיִּסַּע: וַ יִ סַּע

Q58: PARSE וַיִּסַּע (See §14.1.2)

Q59: PARSE הָלוֹךְ

The infinitive of הָלַךְ is sometimes used idiomatically to indicate continuation
of an action, Cf. Holladay, *Lexicon*, pp. 79-80. *He journeyed farther and farther towards the south.*

Morphemes of וְנָסוֹעַ: וְ נָסוֹעַ

Q60: PARSE וְנָסוֹעַ (See §14.1.2)

Genesis 12.10

וַיְהִי רָעָב בָּאָרֶץ

רָעָב is the subject of the verb וַיְהִי (§26.1.1 #6)

וַיֵּ֫רֶד אַבְרָם מִצְרַיְמָה לָגוּר שָׁם

Morphemes of וַיֵּ֫רֶד: וַ יֵ רֶד

Q61: PARSE וַיֵּ֫רֶד (See §17.1.5)

Morphemes of לָגוּר: לָ גוּר

Q62: PARSE לָגוּר (See §15.1.3)

כִּי־כָבֵד הָרָעָב בָּאָֽרֶץ׃ (§3.1.2.2)

Genesis 12.11

וַיְהִי כַּאֲשֶׁר הִקְרִיב לָבוֹא מִצְרָיְמָה

וַיְהִי has no subject; therefore, it is a macrosyntactic marker (§26.1.1 #4).

Morphemes of הִקְרִיב: הִ קְרִ י ב

Q63: PARSE הִקְרִיב

The verb קָרַב means *to draw near*. The *Hifil* of קָרַב followed by לְ + inf. means *be about to*. Thus, *When he was about to come to Egypt* . . . See Holladay, *Lexicon*, p. 324.

Q64: PARSE לָבוֹא (See §15.1.3)

וַיֹּאמֶר אֶל־שָׂרַי אִשְׁתּוֹ

הִנֵּה־נָא יָדַעְתִּי כִּי אִשָּׁה יְפַת־מַרְאֶה אָתְּ:

Morphemes of יָדַעְתִּי: יָדַע תִּי

Q65: PARSE יָדַעְתִּי

יְפַת־מַרְאֶה is a construct–genitive phrase made up of an adjective and a noun, *beautiful of appearance*. See §5.3.4.

Genesis 12.12

וְהָיָה כִּי־יִרְאוּ אֹתָךְ הַמִּצְרִים (§26.1.1 #41)

Morphemes of יִרְאוּ: יִ רְא וּ

Q66: PARSE יִרְאוּ (See §12.6.2)

וְאָמְרוּ אִשְׁתּוֹ זֹאת וְהָרְגוּ אֹתִי וְאֹתָךְ יְחַיּוּ: (§26.1.1 #47)

Q67: PARSE וְהָרְגוּ

Q68: PARSE יְחַיּוּ (See §12.6.2)

Genesis 12.13

אִמְרִי־נָא אֲחֹתִי אָתְּ

Q69: PARSE אִמְרִי

For a discussion of the particle נָא, see Seow, p. 173.

Brother is אָח , and *sister* is אָחוֹת.

לְמַעַן יִיטַב־לִי בַעֲבוּרֵךְ

Q70: PARSE יִיטַב (See §17.1.5)

בַעֲבוּרֵךְ has three morphemes בְּ עֲבוּר ךְ and means *on account of you*. See Williams §522 and Holladay, *Lexicon*, p.262.

וְחָיְתָה נַפְשִׁי בִּגְלָלֵךְ:

Q71: PARSE וְחָיְתָה (See §12.6.2)

בִּגְלָלֵךְ: has three morphemes: בְּ גלל ךְ and means *for your sake*.

Chapter 18

Final Guttural Verbs and Reading Genesis 22.1-14

In this chapter you will learn:

- Forms of weak verbs ending with the guttural letters ה, ח, ע
- Syntax from inductive study of Genesis 22.1-14

18.1   Prominent Final ה, ח, and ע Verbs

Verbs that end with the guttural letters ה, ח, ע exhibit special characteristics. Examples of prominent verbs in this category are (frequency in parentheses):

שָׁמַע	to hear (1159)	נָסַע	to depart (146)
לָקַח	to take (966)	נוּחַ	to rest (143)
יָדַע	to know (940)	זָבַח	to slaughter (*qal*), sacrifice (*piel*) (134)
שָׁלַח	to send (846)	בָּטַח	to trust (120)
יָשַׁע	to save (*Hifil*) (205)	שָׁכַח	to forget (102)
שָׁבַע	to swear (*nifal*) (185)	מָשַׁח	to anoint (70)
שָׂמַח	to be glad (154)	בָּרַח	to flee (65)
נָגַע	to touch (150)		

18.2   Final ה, ח, and ע Verbs

18.2.1   Characteristics of the Final Guttural Verbs

The paradigm for final ה, ח, ע verbs varies very little from the strong verb. Note the following peculiarities of these verbs.

> The vowel *patach* is prominent in this paradigm.

1- Furtive *patach* (See the chart below.)

2- *Patach* replaces *cholem*

Qal imf 3ms is not יִשְׁלֹח , but is יִשְׁלַח

3- *Patach* replaces *tsere*

4- *Patach* replaces all occurrences of *tsere*, except in the participle and the infinitive absolute.

Piel perfect 3ms is not שִׁלֵּח , but is שִׁלַּח

Reminder: Whenever a verb begins with a sibilant (ס, ז, שׁ, שׂ, or צ), the first root letter will switch places with the ת in the *hitpael*. This transposition of letters for euphony is called *metathesis*.

18.2.2 Final ע, ח, ה Verb Paradigm

		Qal	Nifal	Hifil	Hofal	Piel	Pual	Hitpael
		send	sent	set loose	let loose	send	sent	
Pf	1cs	שָׁלַחְתִּי	נִשְׁלַחְתִּי	הִשְׁלַחְתִּי	הָשְׁלַחְתִּי	שִׁלַּחְתִּי	שֻׁלַּחְתִּי	הִשְׁתַּלַּחְתִּי[5]
	2ms	שָׁלַחְתָּ	נִשְׁלַחְתָּ	הִשְׁלַחְתָּ	הָשְׁלַחְתָּ	שִׁלַּחְתָּ	שֻׁלַּחְתָּ	הִשְׁתַּלַּחְתָּ
	2fs	שָׁלַחַתְּ	נִשְׁלַחַתְּ	הִשְׁלַחַתְּ	הָשְׁלַחַתְּ	שִׁלַּחַתְּ	שֻׁלַּחַתְּ	הִשְׁתַּלַּחַתְּ
	3ms	שָׁלַח	נִשְׁלַח	הִשְׁלִיחַ	הָשְׁלַח	שִׁלַּח	שֻׁלַּח	הִשְׁתַּלַּח
	3fs	שָׁלְחָה	נִשְׁלְחָה	הִשְׁלִיחָה	הָשְׁלְחָה	שִׁלְּחָה	שֻׁלְּחָה	הִשְׁתַּלְּחָה
	1cp	שָׁלַחְנוּ	נִשְׁלַחְנוּ	הִשְׁלַחְנוּ	הָשְׁלַחְנוּ	שִׁלַּחְנוּ	שֻׁלַּחְנוּ	הִשְׁתַּלַּחְנוּ
	2mp	שְׁלַחְתֶּם	נִשְׁלַחְתֶּם	הִשְׁלַחְתֶּם	הָשְׁלַחְתֶּם	שִׁלַּחְתֶּם	שֻׁלַּחְתֶּם	הִשְׁתַּלַּחְתֶּם
	2fp	שְׁלַחְתֶּן	נִשְׁלַחְתֶּן	הִשְׁלַחְתֶּן	הָשְׁלַחְתֶּן	שִׁלַּחְתֶּן	שֻׁלַּחְתֶּן	הִשְׁתַּלַּחְתֶּן
	3cp	שָׁלְחוּ	נִשְׁלְחוּ	הִשְׁלִיחוּ	הָשְׁלְחוּ	שִׁלְּחוּ	שֻׁלְּחוּ	הִשְׁתַּלְּחוּ
Imf	1cs	אֶשְׁלַח	אֶשָּׁלַח	אַשְׁלִיחַ	אָשְׁלַח	אֲשַׁלַּח	אֲשֻׁלַּח	אֶשְׁתַּלַּח
	2ms	תִּשְׁלַח	תִּשָּׁלַח	תַּשְׁלִיחַ	תָּשְׁלַח	תְּשַׁלַּח	תְּשֻׁלַּח	תִּשְׁתַּלַּח
	2fs	תִּשְׁלְחִי	תִּשָּׁלְחִי	תַּשְׁלִיחִי	תָּשְׁלְחִי	תְּשַׁלְּחִי	תְּשֻׁלְּחִי	תִּשְׁתַּלְּחִי
	3ms	יִשְׁלַח	יִשָּׁלַח	יַשְׁלִיחַ	יָשְׁלַח	יְשַׁלַּח	יְשֻׁלַּח	יִשְׁתַּלַּח
	3fs	תִּשְׁלַח	תִּשָּׁלַח	תַּשְׁלִיחַ	תָּשְׁלַח	תְּשַׁלַּח	תְּשֻׁלַּח	תִּשְׁתַּלַּח
	1cp	נִשְׁלַח	נִשָּׁלַח	נַשְׁלִיחַ	נָשְׁלַח	נְשַׁלַּח	נְשֻׁלַּח	נִשְׁתַּלַּח
	2mp	תִּשְׁלְחוּ	תִּשָּׁלְחוּ	תַּשְׁלִיחוּ	תָּשְׁלְחוּ	תְּשַׁלְּחוּ	תְּשֻׁלְּחוּ	תִּשְׁתַּלְּחוּ
	2mp	תִּשְׁלַחְנָה	תִּשָּׁלַחְנָה	תַּשְׁלַחְנָה	תָּשְׁלַחְנָה	תְּשַׁלַּחְנָה	תְּשֻׁלַּחְנָה	תִּשְׁתַּלַּחְנָה
	3mp	יִשְׁלְחוּ	יִשָּׁלְחוּ	יַשְׁלִיחוּ	יָשְׁלְחוּ	יְשַׁלְּחוּ	יְשֻׁלְּחוּ	יִשְׁתַּלְּחוּ
	3fp	תִּשְׁלַחְנָה	תִּשָּׁלַחְנָה	תַּשְׁלַחְנָה	תָּשְׁלַחְנָה	תְּשַׁלַּחְנָה	תְּשֻׁלַּחְנָה	תִּשְׁתַּלַּחְנָה
Imv	2ms	שְׁלַח	הִשָּׁלַח	הַשְׁלַח		שַׁלַּח		הִשְׁתַּלַּח
	2fs	שִׁלְחִי	הִשָּׁלְחִי	הַשְׁלִיחִי		שַׁלְּחִי		הִשְׁתַּלְּחִי
	2mp	שִׁלְחוּ	הִשָּׁלְחוּ	הַשְׁלִיחוּ		שַׁלְּחוּ		הִשְׁתַּלְּחוּ
	2fp	שְׁלַחְנָה	הִשָּׁלַחְנָה	הַשְׁלַחְנָה		שַׁלַּחְנָה		הִשְׁתַּלַּחְנָה
Inf	Ab	שָׁלוֹחַ	נִשְׁלוֹחַ הִשָּׁלֵחַ	הַשְׁלֵחַ		שַׁלֵּחַ		הִשְׁתַּלֵּחַ
	Cs	שְׁלֹחַ	הִשָּׁלַח	הַשְׁלִיחַ		שַׁלַּח		הִשְׁתַּלַּח
Ptc	Act	שֹׁלֵחַ		מַשְׁלִיחַ		מְשַׁלֵּחַ		מִשְׁתַּלֵּחַ
	Pass	שָׁלוּחַ	נִשְׁלָח		מֻשְׁלָח		מְשֻׁלָּח	

---

[5] Observe the *metathesis* (see §11.2.4.1).

18.3   Vocabulary

חָלַם	*v.* to dream	עֵמֶק	*n.m.* valley, lowland
חֲלוֹם	*n.m.* a dream	תָּעָה	*v.* to wander
עוֹד	*adv.* again, still, yet	שָׁאַל	*v.* to ask
אָלַם	*v.* to bind	קָנָא	*v. piel* to be jealous
אֲלֻמָּה	*n.f.* sheaf (something bound)	סָפַר	*v. qal* to count, *piel* to relate
נִצְּבָה	*v. nifal* to station oneself	אֵיפֹה	*interr.* where? what kind?
סָבַב	*v.* to surround	טֶרֶם	*adv.* before, not yet
מָשַׁל	*v.* to rule	נָכַל	*v.* to act cunningly, deceitfully
אַחֵר	*adj.* another, following	בַּעַל	*n. m.* lord, master
גָּעַר	*v.* to rebuke	הַלָּזֶה	*adj.* this
שֶׁמֶשׁ	*n.* sun	שָׁלַךְ	*v.* to cast, throw
יָרֵחַ	*n.m.* moon	בּוֹר	*n.m.* pit, cistern. *pl* בֹּרוֹת
עֶשֶׂר	*adj.* ten, *f.* עֲשָׂרָה	הִצִּיל	*v. Hifil* to deliver
כּוֹכָב	*n.m.* star	מִדְבָּר	*n.m.* wilderness

EXERCISE 18

18.4   Reading Genesis 22.1-14

Translate the following verses; parse the verbs that are indicated; and answer all numbered questions. You are not required to answer the questions that are not numbered. They are intended to direct your analysis in certain directions.

וַיְהִי אַחַר הַדְּבָרִים הָאֵלֶּה וְהָאֱלֹהִים נִסָּה אֶת־אַבְרָהָם וַיֹּאמֶר אֵלָיו ¹
אַבְרָהָם וַיֹּאמֶר הִנֵּנִי: ² וַיֹּאמֶר קַח־נָא אֶת־בִּנְךָ אֶת־יְחִידְךָ אֲשֶׁר־אָהַבְתָּ
אֶת־יִצְחָק וְלֶךְ־לְךָ אֶל־אֶרֶץ הַמֹּרִיָּה וְהַעֲלֵהוּ שָׁם לְעֹלָה עַל אַחַד הֶהָרִים
אֲשֶׁר אֹמַר אֵלֶיךָ: ³ וַיַּשְׁכֵּם אַבְרָהָם בַּבֹּקֶר וַיַּחֲבֹשׁ אֶת־חֲמֹרוֹ וַיִּקַּח אֶת־שְׁנֵי
נְעָרָיו אִתּוֹ וְאֵת יִצְחָק בְּנוֹ וַיְבַקַּע עֲצֵי עֹלָה וַיָּקָם וַיֵּלֶךְ אֶל־הַמָּקוֹם
אֲשֶׁר־אָמַר־לוֹ הָאֱלֹהִים: ⁴ בַּיּוֹם הַשְּׁלִישִׁי וַיִּשָּׂא אַבְרָהָם אֶת־עֵינָיו
וַיַּרְא אֶת־הַמָּקוֹם מֵרָחֹק: ⁵ וַיֹּאמֶר אַבְרָהָם אֶל־נְעָרָיו שְׁבוּ־לָכֶם פֹּה
עִם־הַחֲמוֹר וַאֲנִי וְהַנַּעַר נֵלְכָה עַד־כֹּה וְנִשְׁתַּחֲוֶה וְנָשׁוּבָה אֲלֵיכֶם: ⁶ וַיִּקַּח
אַבְרָהָם אֶת־עֲצֵי הָעֹלָה וַיָּשֶׂם עַל־יִצְחָק בְּנוֹ וַיִּקַּח בְּיָדוֹ אֶת־הָאֵשׁ
וְאֶת־הַמַּאֲכֶלֶת וַיֵּלְכוּ שְׁנֵיהֶם יַחְדָּו: ⁷ וַיֹּאמֶר יִצְחָק אֶל־אַבְרָהָם אָבִיו וַיֹּאמֶר
וְאֵת

אָבִי וַיֹּאמֶר הִנֶּנִּי בְנִי וַיֹּאמֶר הִנֵּה הָאֵשׁ וְהָעֵצִים וְאַיֵּה הַשֶּׂה לְעֹלָה:

⁸ וַיֹּאמֶר אַבְרָהָם אֱלֹהִים יִרְאֶה־לּוֹ הַשֶּׂה לְעֹלָה בְּנִי וַיֵּלְכוּ שְׁנֵיהֶם יַחְדָּו:

⁹ וַיָּבֹאוּ אֶל־הַמָּקוֹם אֲשֶׁר אָמַר־לוֹ הָאֱלֹהִים וַיִּבֶן שָׁם אַבְרָהָם אֶת־הַמִּזְבֵּחַ וַיַּעֲרֹךְ אֶת־הָעֵצִים וַיַּעֲקֹד אֶת־יִצְחָק בְּנוֹ וַיָּשֶׂם אֹתוֹ עַל־הַמִּזְבֵּחַ מִמַּעַל לָעֵצִים: ¹⁰ וַיִּשְׁלַח אַבְרָהָם אֶת־יָדוֹ וַיִּקַּח אֶת־הַמַּאֲכֶלֶת לִשְׁחֹט אֶת־בְּנוֹ: ¹¹ וַיִּקְרָא אֵלָיו מַלְאַךְ יְהוָה מִן־הַשָּׁמַיִם וַיֹּאמֶר אַבְרָהָם׀ אַבְרָהָם וַיֹּאמֶר הִנֵּנִי: ¹² וַיֹּאמֶר אַל־תִּשְׁלַח יָדְךָ אֶל־הַנַּעַר וְאַל־תַּעַשׂ לוֹ מְאוּמָה כִּי׀ עַתָּה יָדַעְתִּי כִּי־יְרֵא אֱלֹהִים אַתָּה וְלֹא חָשַׂכְתָּ אֶת־בִּנְךָ אֶת־יְחִידְךָ מִמֶּנִּי: ¹³ וַיִּשָּׂא אַבְרָהָם אֶת־עֵינָיו וַיַּרְא וְהִנֵּה־אַיִל אַחַר נֶאֱחַז בַּסְּבַךְ בְּקַרְנָיו וַיֵּלֶךְ אַבְרָהָם וַיִּקַּח אֶת־הָאַיִל וַיַּעֲלֵהוּ לְעֹלָה תַּחַת בְּנוֹ: ¹⁴ וַיִּקְרָא אַבְרָהָם שֵׁם־הַמָּקוֹם הַהוּא יְהוָה׀ יִרְאֶה אֲשֶׁר יֵאָמֵר הַיּוֹם בְּהַר יְהוָה יֵרָאֶה:

Genesis 22.1

וַיְהִי אַחַר הַדְּבָרִים הָאֵלֶּה וְהָאֱלֹהִים נִסָּה אֶת־אַבְרָהָם

This verse begins with a temporal clause, providing a setting for the story which follows. The verb וַיְהִי means here, *and it came to pass.* (§26.1.1 #4)

Although הַדְּבָרִים is usually translated *words*, it also can be translated *things, events, matters,* etc.

Q1: Should the *vav* on וְהָאֱלֹהִים be translated 1) *and*, 2) *but*, or 3) *that*?

The second clause is x-*qatal*, indicating that it is a continuation of the first clause, providing more background (§26.1.1 #1).

Q2: Why is there a *dagesh* in נִסָּה?

Q3: Why is the last vowel of נִסָּה a *qamets* instead of *tsere*?

Q4: PARSE נִסָּה

וַיֹּאמֶר אֵלָיו אַבְרָהָם וַיֹּאמֶר הִנֵּנִי:

This clause begins with *wayyiqtol*; therefore, it is the beginning of the actual narrative.

Q5: Does the accent above אֵלָיו indicate pause or continuation? (§28.1)

Q6: What is the name of the accent mark?

Genesis 22.2

וַיֹּאמֶר קַח־נָא אֶת־בִּנְךָ אֶת־יְחִידְךָ

Q7: What is the missing radical in קַח? (§14.1.1)

Q8: Is this a geminate verb?

Q9: PARSE קַח

Q10: What part of speech is ךָ on בִּנְךָ?

אֲשֶׁר־אָהַבְתָּ אֶת־יִצְחָק

Q11: PARSE אָהַבְתָּ

Q12: Into what tense should we translate אָהַבְתָּ? See Williams §163

וְלֶךְ־לְךָ אֶל־אֶרֶץ הַמֹּרִיָּה

Q13: PARSE וְלֶךְ

This form is usually spelled לֵךְ, (§22.13) but the *maqqef* moves the accent forward making לֶךְ a closed unaccented syllable, which must have a short vowel (§2.1.5.1 and §2.1.5.2).

The לְ in לְךָ is reflexive. See Williams §272

וְהַעֲלֵהוּ שָׁם לְעֹלָה עַל אַחַד הֶהָרִים   (§26.1.1 #62)

Morphemes of וְהַעֲלֵהוּ:   וְ הַ עֲלֵ הוּ

Q14: What stem has a prefixed הַ?

The לְ on לְעֹלָה marks the indirect object. See Williams §269

In a series of imperatives, the final imperative is the most important, with the preceeding imperatives pointing to actions that lead up to it. In this case, Abram is commanded to *take* his son, to *go* to Moriah—two actions that culminate in a third command: *offer him there for a whole burnt offering.*

אֲשֶׁר אֹמַר אֵלֶיךָ:

The ptc. of אָמַר is אוֹמֵר. You may want to check אָמַר in the lexicon.

Q15: PARSE אֹמַר   (§13.1.2)

Q16: Into what tense should we translate אֹמַר? (§26.1.1 #39)

Genesis 22.3

וַיַּשְׁכֵּם אַבְרָהָם בַּבֹּקֶר

Morphemes of וַיַּשְׁכֵּם: וַ יַ שְׁכֵּם

Q17: What stem is indicated by the *patach* under the preformative יְ?

Q18: PARSE וַיַּשְׁכֵּם

וַיַּחֲבֹשׁ אֶת־חֲמֹרוֹ

Q19: Is וַיַּחֲבֹשׁ *Hifil*? Why or why not?

Q20: PARSE וַיַּחֲבֹשׁ

וַיִּקַּח אֶת־שְׁנֵי נְעָרָיו אִתּוֹ וְאֵת יִצְחָק בְּנוֹ

Q21: Why is there a *dagesh* in the ק of וַיִּקַּח?

Q22: PARSE וַיִּקַּח

וַיְבַקַּע עֲצֵי עֹלָה

Q23: What stem is suggested by the *sheva* under the preformative in וַיְבַקַּע?

Q24: What stem is suggested by the *dagesh* in the ק of וַיְבַקַּע?

Q25: Classify the construct–genitive עֲצֵי עֹלָה according to §5.3.3.

וַיָּקָם וַיֵּלֶךְ אֶל־הַמָּקוֹם אֲשֶׁר־אָמַר־לוֹ הָאֱלֹהִים׃

Q26: What two weak verb patterns have *qamets* under the preformative of the imperfect?

Q27: PARSE וַיָּקָם

Q28: What weak verb pattern is characterized by *tsere* under the preformative of the imperfect?

Q29: PARSE וַיֵּלֶךְ

Genesis 22.4

בַּיּוֹם הַשְּׁלִישִׁי וַיִּשָּׂא אַבְרָהָם אֶת־עֵינָיו

Note the beginning of this verse with a temporal indicator.

Q30: Why is there a *dagesh* in the שׂ of וַיִּשָּׂא?

Q31: PARSE וַיִּשָּׂא

It is not necessary to translate the *vav* in this case. The *wayyiqtol* is used here because the action is part of the main line of narrative. The use of a perfect would have suggested background.

וַיַּרְא אֶת־הַמָּקוֹם מֵרָחֹק׃

Q32: PARSE וַיַּרְא

Genesis 22.5

וַיֹּאמֶר אַבְרָהָם אֶל־נְעָרָיו שְׁבוּ־לָכֶם פֹּה עִם־הַחֲמוֹר

Q33: PARSE שְׁבוּ

וַאֲנִי וְהַנַּעַר נֵלְכָה עַד־כֹּה

Q34: What part of speech is the ה on the end of נֵלְכָה?

Notice the *tsere* under the נ of נֵלְכָה.

Q35: PARSE נֵלְכָה

וְנִשְׁתַּחֲוֶה וְנָשׁוּבָה אֲלֵיכֶם:

Q36: What tense is וְנִשְׁתַּחֲוֶה?

Morphemes of וְנִשְׁתַּחֲוֶה: וְ נ שׁתַּ חֲוֶה

See §11.7.3. See also Holladay, *Lexicon*, p. 97, חוה

Q37: PARSE וְנִשְׁתַּחֲוֶה

Q38: What part of speech is the ה on וְנָשׁוּבָה?

Q39: PARSE וְנָשׁוּבָה

Genesis 22.6

וַיִּקַּח אַבְרָהָם אֶת־עֲצֵי הָעֹלָה

Q40: PARSE וַיִּקַּח

וַיָּשֶׂם עַל־יִצְחָק בְּנוֹ

Q41: What weak verb pattern is suggested by the *qamets* in וַיָּשֶׂם?

Q42: PARSE וַיָּשֶׂם

The nouns יִצְחָק בְּנוֹ are in apposition, Williams §70.

וַיִּקַּח בְּיָדוֹ אֶת־הָאֵשׁ וְאֶת־הַמַּאֲכֶלֶת

וַיֵּלְכוּ שְׁנֵיהֶם יַחְדָּו:

Notice the *tsere* in וַיֵּלְכוּ?

Q43: PARSE וַיֵּלְכוּ

Genesis 22.7

וַיֹּאמֶר יִצְחָק אֶל־אַבְרָהָם אָבִיו וַיֹּאמֶר אָבִי

וַיֹּאמֶר הִנֶּנִּי בְנִי וַיֹּאמֶר הִנֵּה הָאֵשׁ וְהָעֵצִים וְאַיֵּה הַשֶּׂה לְעֹלָה:

Find הַשֶּׂה and לְעֹלָה in your lexicon.

Genesis 22.8

וַיֹּאמֶר אַבְרָהָם אֱלֹהִים יִרְאֶה־לּוֹ הַשֶּׂה לְעֹלָה בְּנִי

We find a *dagesh forte* in לֹ because of its position after the vowel
הָ . For the rule governing this use of *dagesh*, see Gesenius §20.2. The *dagesh* in
לֹ appears 95 times in the Hebrew Bible (cf. §2.1.1.2).

Q44: Into what tense should we translate יִרְאֶה? (§26.1.1 #45)

Q45: PARSE יִרְאֶה

וַיֵּלְכוּ שְׁנֵיהֶם יַחְדָּו:

Q46: PARSE וַיֵּלְכוּ

Genesis 22.9

וַיָּבֹאוּ אֶל־הַמָּקוֹם אֲשֶׁר אָמַר־לוֹ הָאֱלֹהִים

Q47: PARSE וַיָּבֹאוּ

Q48: Into what tense should we translate אָמַר?

וַיִּבֶן שָׁם אַבְרָהָם אֶת־הַמִּזְבֵּחַ

Q49: What root letter is usually dropped from the *wayyiqtol*, as in וַיִּבֶן? See §12.6.2.

Q50: PARSE וַיִּבֶן

וַיַּעֲרֹךְ אֶת־הָעֵצִים וַיַּעֲקֹד אֶת־יִצְחָק בְּנוֹ

Q51: Why is there a *patach* under the preformative in וַיַּעֲרֹךְ?

Q52: PARSE וַיַּעֲרֹךְ

PARSE וַיַּעֲקֹד

וַיָּשֶׂם אֹתוֹ עַל־הַמִּזְבֵּחַ מִמַּעַל לָעֵצִים:

Q53: Why does the preformative of וַיָּשֶׂם have *qamets*?

Q54: PARSE וַיָּשֶׂם

Genesis 22.10

וַיִּשְׁלַח אַבְרָהָם אֶת־יָדוֹ

Q55: Why is there a *patach* under the ל of וַיִּשְׁלַח?

Q56: PARSE וַיִּשְׁלַח

וַיִּקַּח אֶת־הַמַּאֲכֶלֶת לִשְׁחֹט אֶת־בְּנוֹ:

Q57: What radical is missing from וַיִּקַּח?

Q58: PARSE וַיִּקַּח

Q59: What verb form is usually indicated by a prefixed לְ?

Q60: PARSE לִשְׁחֹט

Genesis 22.11

וַיִּקְרָא אֵלָיו מַלְאַךְ יְהוָה מִן־הַשָּׁמַיִם

Q61: PARSE וַיִּקְרָא

וַיֹּאמֶר אַבְרָהָם אַבְרָהָם וַיֹּאמֶר הִנֵּנִי:

Genesis 22.12

וַיֹּאמֶר אַל־תִּשְׁלַח יָדְךָ אֶל־הַנַּעַר

Regarding אַל see §6.3.

Q62: PARSE תִּשְׁלַח

וְאַל־תַּעַשׂ לוֹ מְאוּמָּה

Note that the *dagesh* in מְאוּמָּה is probably a scribal error. According to the text critical note at the bottom of the page, many manuscripts have מְאוּמָה.

Q63: PARSE תַּעַשׂ

כִּי עַתָּה יָדַעְתִּי כִּי־יְרֵא אֱלֹהִים אַתָּה

Q64: PARSE יָדַעְתִּי

Q65: Is יְרֵא a ptc. or adj.? As to function, see §5.3.

וְלֹא חָשַׂכְתָּ אֶת־בִּנְךָ אֶת־יְחִידְךָ מִמֶּנִּי:

Q66: PARSE חָשַׂכְתָּ

Q67: What tense is חָשַׂכְתָּ?

Regarding מִמֶּנִּי see §8.4.1.3.

Genesis 22.13

וַיִּשָּׂא אַבְרָהָם אֶת־עֵינָיו וַיַּרְא

Q68: PARSE וַיִּשָּׂא

Q69: PARSE וַיַּרְא

וְהִנֵּה־אַיִל אַחַר נֶאֱחַז בַּסְּבַךְ בְּקַרְנָיו

Q70: PARSE נֶאֱחַז

See §8.2.4 and §13.1.2

וַיֵּלֶךְ אַבְרָהָם וַיִּקַּח אֶת־הָאַיִל

Q71: PARSE וַיֵּלֶךְ

See §22.13.

Q72: PARSE וַיִּקַּח

See §14.1.1.

וַיַּעֲלֵהוּ לְעֹלָה תַּחַת בְּנוֹ:

Q73: PARSE וַיַּעֲלֵהוּ

See §22.3.

Genesis 22.14

וַיִּקְרָא אַבְרָהָם שֵׁם־הַמָּקוֹם הַהוּא יְהוָה יִרְאֶה

אֲשֶׁר יֵאָמֵר הַיּוֹם בְּהַר יְהוָה יֵרָאֶה:

Q74: PARSE יֵאָמֵר

See §22.3.

Q75: PARSE יֵרָאֶה

See §22.3.

Commentary on Habakkuk—c. 150 BCE

Chapter 19

Reading Genesis 37.1-18

In this chapter you will:

- Learn inductively by translating Genesis 37.1-18
- Review material from previous chapters

19.1 Vocabulary for Job 1.1-12

The following vocabulary consists of words found at least 50 times in the Hebrew Bible.

סוּר	*v.* to turn aside, depart	חָרַשׁ	*v.* to plow
קָרַע	*v.* to tear	מָלַט	*v.* to escape
מִסְפָּר	*n.m.* number	שָׁתָה	*v.* to drink
מִקְנֶה	*n.m.* livestock	בָּעַר	*v.* to burn
בְּכוֹר	*n.m.* firstborn	כַּשְׂדִּים	*n.p.* Chaldeans
גָּמָל	*n.m.* camel	יַיִן	*n.m.* wine
עֹלָה	*n.f.* whole burnt offering	בָּקָר	*n.m.* oxen, cattle
יָשָׁר	*adj.* upright	בֶּטֶן	*n.f.* womb
יָצַב	*v.* to stand, in the sense of assuming a post or place (same as נָצַב)	בַּד	*n.m.* a piece, לְבַדִּי = I alone

EXERCISE 19

19.2 Reading Genesis 37.1-18

Translate the following verses; parse the verbs that are indicated; and answer all numbered questions. You are not required to answer the questions that are not numbered. They are intended to direct your analysis in certain directions.

¹ וַיֵּשֶׁב יַעֲקֹב בְּאֶרֶץ מְגוּרֵי אָבִיו בְּאֶרֶץ כְּנָעַן: ² אֵלֶּה| תֹּלְדוֹת יַעֲקֹב יוֹסֵף
בֶּן־שְׁבַע־עֶשְׂרֵה שָׁנָה הָיָה רֹעֶה אֶת־אֶחָיו בַּצֹּאן וְהוּא נַעַר אֶת־בְּנֵי בִלְהָה
וְאֶת־בְּנֵי זִלְפָּה נְשֵׁי אָבִיו וַיָּבֵא יוֹסֵף אֶת־דִּבָּתָם רָעָה אֶל־אֲבִיהֶם:
³ וְיִשְׂרָאֵל אָהַב אֶת־יוֹסֵף מִכָּל־בָּנָיו כִּי־בֶן־זְקֻנִים הוּא לוֹ וְעָשָׂה לוֹ כְּתֹנֶת
פַּסִּים: ⁴ וַיִּרְאוּ אֶחָיו כִּי־אֹתוֹ אָהַב אֲבִיהֶם מִכָּל־אֶחָיו וַיִּשְׂנְאוּ אֹתוֹ

וְלֹא יָכְלוּ דַּבְּרוֹ לְשָׁלֹם: ⁵ וַיַּחֲלֹם יוֹסֵף חֲלוֹם וַיַּגֵּד לְאֶחָיו וַיּוֹסִפוּ עוֹד
שְׂנֹא אֹתוֹ: ⁶ וַיֹּאמֶר אֲלֵיהֶם שִׁמְעוּ־נָא הַחֲלוֹם הַזֶּה אֲשֶׁר חָלָמְתִּי: ⁷ וְהִנֵּה
אֲנַחְנוּ מְאַלְּמִים אֲלֻמִּים בְּתוֹךְ הַשָּׂדֶה וְהִנֵּה קָמָה אֲלֻמָּתִי וְגַם־נִצָּבָה וְהִנֵּה
תְסֻבֶּינָה אֲלֻמֹּתֵיכֶם וַתִּשְׁתַּחֲוֶיןָ לַאֲלֻמָּתִי: ⁸ וַיֹּאמְרוּ לוֹ אֶחָיו הֲמָלֹךְ תִּמְלֹךְ
עָלֵינוּ אִם־מָשׁוֹל תִּמְשֹׁל בָּנוּ וַיּוֹסִפוּ עוֹד שְׂנֹא אֹתוֹ עַל־חֲלֹמֹתָיו
וְעַל־דְּבָרָיו: ⁹ וַיַּחֲלֹם עוֹד חֲלוֹם אַחֵר וַיְסַפֵּר אֹתוֹ לְאֶחָיו וַיֹּאמֶר הִנֵּה
חָלַמְתִּי חֲלוֹם עוֹד וְהִנֵּה הַשֶּׁמֶשׁ וְהַיָּרֵחַ וְאַחַד עָשָׂר כּוֹכָבִים מִשְׁתַּחֲוִים לִי:
¹⁰ וַיְסַפֵּר אֶל־אָבִיו וְאֶל־אֶחָיו וַיִּגְעַר־בּוֹ אָבִיו וַיֹּאמֶר לוֹ מָה הַחֲלוֹם הַזֶּה
אֲשֶׁר חָלָמְתָּ הֲבוֹא נָבוֹא אֲנִי וְאִמְּךָ וְאַחֶיךָ לְהִשְׁתַּחֲוֺת לְךָ אָרְצָה:
¹¹ וַיְקַנְאוּ־בוֹ אֶחָיו וְאָבִיו שָׁמַר אֶת־הַדָּבָר: ¹² וַיֵּלְכוּ אֶחָיו לִרְעוֹת אֶת־צֹאן
אֲבִיהֶם בִּשְׁכֶם: ¹³ וַיֹּאמֶר יִשְׂרָאֵל אֶל־יוֹסֵף הֲלוֹא אַחֶיךָ רֹעִים בִּשְׁכֶם לְכָה
וְאֶשְׁלָחֲךָ אֲלֵיהֶם וַיֹּאמֶר לוֹ הִנֵּנִי: ¹⁴ וַיֹּאמֶר לוֹ לֶךְ־נָא רְאֵה
אֶת־שְׁלוֹם אַחֶיךָ וְאֶת־שְׁלוֹם הַצֹּאן וַהֲשִׁבֵנִי דָּבָר וַיִּשְׁלָחֵהוּ מֵעֵמֶק חֶבְרוֹן
וַיָּבֹא שְׁכֶמָה: ¹⁵ וַיִּמְצָאֵהוּ אִישׁ וְהִנֵּה תֹעֶה בַּשָּׂדֶה וַיִּשְׁאָלֵהוּ הָאִישׁ לֵאמֹר
מַה־תְּבַקֵּשׁ: ¹⁶ וַיֹּאמֶר אֶת־אַחַי אָנֹכִי מְבַקֵּשׁ הַגִּידָה־נָּא לִי אֵיפֹה הֵם
רֹעִים: ¹⁷ וַיֹּאמֶר הָאִישׁ נָסְעוּ מִזֶּה כִּי שָׁמַעְתִּי אֹמְרִים נֵלְכָה דֹּתָיְנָה
וַיֵּלֶךְ יוֹסֵף אַחַר אֶחָיו וַיִּמְצָאֵם בְּדֹתָן: ¹⁸ וַיִּרְאוּ אֹתוֹ מֵרָחֹק וּבְטֶרֶם יִקְרַב
אֲלֵיהֶם וַיִּתְנַכְּלוּ אֹתוֹ לַהֲמִיתוֹ:

Genesis 37.1

וַיֵּשֶׁב יַעֲקֹב בְּאֶרֶץ מְגוּרֵי אָבִיו בְּאֶרֶץ כְּנָעַן:

Q1: What weak verb pattern is indicated by the *tsere* under the preformative in
the verb וַיֵּשֶׁב? (§22.9)

Q2: PARSE וַיֵּשֶׁב

Q3: What would the root be if the spelling had been וַיִּישַׁב? (§22.7)

Q4: Is מְגוּרֵי a definite noun? If so, why does it not have the article?

Q5: Is אָבִיו *his father* or *his fathers*?

Genesis 37.2

אֵלֶּה תֹּלְדוֹת יַעֲקֹב

Q6: Could אֵלֶּה תֹּלְדוֹת be translated *these generations*?   (§3.1.2)

Q7: This is a verbless clause; what is its syntactical function? (§26.1.1 #3)

יוֹסֵף בֶּן־שְׁבַע־עֶשְׂרֵה שָׁנָה הָיָה רֹעֶה אֶת־אֶחָיו בַּצֹּאן

The phrase *son of x years* is an idiomatic way of expressing age.

The masoretic accent on שָׁנָה is disjunctive, while all others are conjunctive, suggesting that the subject of the verb consists of the whole phrase 'Joseph, seventeen years old' (See §26.1.1 #1).

Q8: Is שָׁנָה singular or plural?

Q9: PARSE הָיָה

Q10: Does the perfect suggest the beginning of a new narrative? (§26.1.1 #1)

The בְּ in בַּצֹּאן is locative, *among the flock*. Williams §240

Q11: Is רֹעֶה a ptc. or a noun? Does it have an object? If so, then it functions as a verb.

Q12: How do you translate אֶת?

וְהוּא נַעַר אֶת־בְּנֵי בִלְהָה וְאֶת־בְּנֵי זִלְפָּה נְשֵׁי אָבִיו

Q13: This sentence begins with a *vav* attached to a pronoun. Therefore, is the sentence sequential or non-sequential with the previous clause? Also, this is a verbless clause (§26.1.1 #3).

וַיָּבֵא יוֹסֵף אֶת־דִּבָּתָם רָעָה אֶל־אֲבִיהֶם:

Q14: What weak verb patterns are suggested by the *qamets* under the preformative of וַיָּבֵא?

Q15: PARSE וַיָּבֵא

Q16: What stem is suggested by the *tsere*?

Q17: What part of speech is ם on דִּבָּתָם?

Q18: What part of speech is the הֶם on אֲבִיהֶם?

Genesis 37.3

וְיִשְׂרָאֵל אָהַב אֶת־יוֹסֵף מִכָּל־בָּנָיו

This clause is x-*qatal* (§26.1.1 #1, §26.1.2 #3).

Q19: Is the action of this clause subsequent to the action of the previous clause, or is it contemporaneous?

Q20: PARSE אָהַב

In מִכָּל־בָּנָיו, note the superlative usage of the prep. מִן (§8.4.2 and Williams §317).

כִּי־בֶן־זְקֻנִים הוּא לוֹ

בֶּן־זְקֻנִים is a construct–genitive phrase that expresses an adverbial genitive of time (see §5.3.3.5).

וְעָשָׂה לוֹ כְּתֹנֶת פַּסִּים:

Q21: PARSE וְעָשָׂה

This *vav* + pf is unusual. Cf. Gen. 15.6. A single *weqatal* is usually an important, climactic event. See Niccacci §158, who argues that *weqatal* can be a single action, denoting a shift from narrative to comment by the narrator. (§26.1.1 #13)

Do you see any reason for the traditional translation *colors*? Find פַּסִּים in your lexicon.

Genesis 37.4

וַיִּרְאוּ אֶחָיו כִּי־אֹתוֹ אָהַב אֲבִיהֶם מִכָּל־אֶחָיו

Q22: What radical is missing from וַיִּרְאוּ?

Note diff. spellings of imf, vc: וַיִּרְאוּ וַיִּרָא וַיִּרְאֶה וַתֵּרֶא וַיַּרְא

Q23: PARSE וַיִּרְאוּ

Q24: Is אֹתוֹ in an emphatic position?

Regarding מִכָּל, see §8.4.2.

וַיִּשְׂנְאוּ אֹתוֹ וְלֹא יָכְלוּ דַּבְּרוֹ לְשָׁלֹם:

Q25: PARSE וַיִּשְׂנְאוּ

Q26: PARSE יָכְלוּ

Q27: PARSE דַּבְּרוֹ

The לְ on לְשָׁלֹם is an adverbial usage, *peacefully*. Williams §274.

Genesis 37.5

וַיַּחֲלֹם יוֹסֵף חֲלוֹם וַיַּגֵּד לְאֶחָיו

וַיַּחֲלֹם has a *patach* under the י preformative because the first root letter is a guttural letter. This is a *Qal* imf *wayyiqtol* 3m s.

Q28: Why is there a *dagesh* in the ג of וַיַּגֵּד?

Q29: What stem is suggested by the *patach* under the preformative of וַיַּגֵּד (note also the *tsere*)?

Q30: PARSE וַיַּגֵּד

וַיּוֹסִפוּ עוֹד שְׂנֹא אֹתוֹ:

Q31: What is the only stem that has וֹ following the imperfect preformative?

Q32: PARSE וַיּוֹסִפוּ

Is this a pun on the name *Joseph*?

Q33: PARSE שְׂנֹא

Q34: What verb form is characterized by the *cholem* after the second root letter?

Genesis 37.6

וַיֹּאמֶר אֲלֵיהֶם שִׁמְעוּ־נָא הַחֲלוֹם הַזֶּה אֲשֶׁר חָלָמְתִּי:

Q35: PARSE שִׁמְעוּ

Q36: PARSE חָלָמְתִּי

Genesis 37.7

וְהִנֵּה אֲנַחְנוּ מְאַלְּמִים אֲלֻמִּים בְּתוֹךְ הַשָּׂדֶה

Q37: What verb form and stem is characterized by מְ?

מְאַלְּמִים The masc. pl ending suggests a participle. The *sheva* under the מ and the *dagesh* in the ל indicate a *Piel*.

How does this ptc. function in the sentence? (§3.4.1.1 and §26.1.1 #21)

וְהִנֵּה קָמָה אֲלֻמָּתִי וְגַם־נִצָּבָה

Q38: What part of speech is the ה on קָמָה?

Notice that this clause does not begin with the verb; it is x-*qatal*. See Niccacci §§22-23 for the perfect (*qatal*) in **reporting** events as opposed to the *wayyiqtol* in **narrating** events. (§26.1.1 #23)

Q39: PARSE קָמָה

Q40: PARSE נִצָּבָה

וְהִנֵּה תְסֻבֶּינָה אֲלֻמֹּתֵיכֶם וַתִּשְׁתַּחֲוֶיןָ לַאֲלֻמָּתִי:

Q41: PARSE תְסֻבֶּינָה

The *dagesh* in the the ב should help you determine the root, and the *sheva* plus *qibbutz* should tell you the *binyan* (stem).

See Holladay, *Lexicon*, p. 251-52, *polel*. Is ֶיןָ the same morpheme as ֶ־נָה?

Q42: PARSE וַתִּשְׁתַּחֲוֶיןָ   See §11.7.3. See also Holladay, *Lexicon*, p. 97

Genesis 37.8

וַיֹּאמְרוּ לוֹ אֶחָיו הֲמָלֹךְ תִּמְלֹךְ עָלֵינוּ

Q43: What is the הֲ on הֲמָלֹךְ? (§12.7)

Q44: What verb forms are characterized by the *cholem* after the second root letter? (§5.1 and §6.5)

Q45: PARSE הֲמָלֹךְ

On the grammatical function of הֲמָלֹךְ see §6.5.1.

Q46: PARSE תִּמְלֹךְ

אִם־מָשׁוֹל תִּמְשֹׁל בָּנוּ

This clause is an oath formula. The protasis begins with אִם, but the apodosis is unexpressed: *If you rule over us (may God strike us dead).*

This idiom explains a few passages in Greek of the NT, e.g. Mark 8.12; Heb. 3.11; 4.3, 5

Q47: PARSE מָשׁוֹל

On the grammatical function of מָשׁוֹל see §6.5.1.

Q48: PARSE תִּמְשֹׁל

וַיּוֹסִפוּ עוֹד שְׂנֹא אֹתוֹ עַל־חֲלֹמֹתָיו וְעַל־דְּבָרָיו: (Repeated, cf. v. 5)

Q49: What stem has ו following the imperfect preformative? (§17.1.5)

Q50: PARSE וַיּוֹסִפוּ

Genesis 37.9

וַיַּחֲלֹם עוֹד חֲלוֹם אַחֵר וַיְסַפֵּר אֹתוֹ לְאֶחָיו

Q51: PARSE וַיְסַפֵּר

Q52: What stem is characterized by *sheva* under the imperfect preformative? (§10.3.2)

וַיֹּאמֶר הִנֵּה חָלַמְתִּי חֲלוֹם עוֹד

וְהִנֵּה הַשֶּׁמֶשׁ וְהַיָּרֵחַ וְאַחַד עָשָׂר כּוֹכָבִים מִשְׁתַּחֲוִים לִי:

Note the use of the participle in this sentence indicating durative action.

Q53: PARSE מִשְׁתַּחֲוִים   (See §11.7.3 and Holladay, *Lexicon*, p. 97)

Genesis 37.10

וַיְסַפֵּר אֶל־אָבִיו וְאֶל־אֶחָיו

וַיִּגְעַר־בּוֹ אָבִיו וַיֹּאמֶר לוֹ

Q54: PARSE וַיְגַעַר

מָה הַחֲלוֹם הַזֶּה אֲשֶׁר חָלָמְתָּ

Q55: PARSE חָלָמְתָּ

הֲבוֹא נָבוֹא אֲנִי וְאִמְּךָ וְאַחֶיךָ לְהִשְׁתַּחֲוֹת לְךָ אָרְצָה:

Q56: PARSE הֲבוֹא

Q57: What part of speech is the הֲ prefix? (§12.7)

Q58: PARSE נָבוֹא

Q59: PARSE לְהִשְׁתַּחֲוֹת prefix? (§11.7.3)

Observe the directive ה on אָרְצָה (§7.5).

Genesis 37.11

וַיְקַנְאוּ־בוֹ אֶחָיו וְאָבִיו שָׁמַר אֶת־הַדָּבָר:

Q60: PARSE וַיְקַנְאוּ

Q61: What stem is indicated by the *sheva* under the preformative?
The *dagesh* is missing in the middle letter because of the sheva underneath
(§10.3.2.1).

Genesis 37.12

וַיֵּלְכוּ אֶחָיו לִרְעוֹת אֶת־צֹאן אֲבִיהֶם בִּשְׁכֶם:

Q62: PARSE וַיֵּלְכוּ

Q63: PARSE לִרְעוֹת

Genesis 37.13

וַיֹּאמֶר יִשְׂרָאֵל אֶל־יוֹסֵף

הֲלוֹא אַחֶיךָ רֹעִים בִּשְׁכֶם

Q64: What part of speech is the הֲ on הֲלוֹא? (§12.7)

לְכָה וְאֶשְׁלָחֲךָ אֲלֵיהֶם וַיֹּאמֶר לוֹ הִנֵּנִי:

Q65: PARSE לְכָה   See §22.13 and Holladay, *Lexicon*, p. 79.

Q66: What part of speech is the ה on לְכָה? (§6.2)

Genesis 37.14

וַיֹּאמֶר לוֹ לֶךְ־נָא רְאֵה אֶת־שְׁלוֹם אַחֶיךָ
וְאֶת־שְׁלוֹם הַצֹּאן

Q67: PARSE לֶךְ

This form is usually spelled לֵךְ (§22.13) but the *maqqef* moves the accent forward making לֶךְ a closed unaccented syllable, which must have a short vowel (§2.1.5.1 and §2.1.5.2).

Q68: PARSE רְאֵה

וַהֲשִׁבֵנִי דָּבָר

Morphemes of וַהֲשִׁבֵנִי: וַ הֲ שִׁב נִי

The הֲ and the *chireq* under the שׁ should tell you the stem (§15.1). Regarding the function of this verb, see (§26.1.1 #57).

Q69: PARSE וַהֲשִׁבֵנִי

וַיִּשְׁלָחֵהוּ מֵעֵמֶק חֶבְרוֹן וַיָּבֹא שְׁכֶמָה:

(NOTE: You may need to use your lexicon for verses 14-18.)

Morphemes of וַיִּשְׁלָחֵהוּ:   וַ יִּ שְׁלָח הוּ

Q70: PARSE וַיִּשְׁלָחֵהוּ

Q71: What part of speech is the הוּ suffix on וַיִּשְׁלָחֵהוּ?

Q72: PARSE וַיָּבֹא

Q73: What part of speech is the ה on שְׁכֶמָה?

Genesis 37.15

וַיִּמְצָאֵהוּ אִישׁ וְהִנֵּה תֹעֶה בַּשָּׂדֶה

Q74: PARSE תֹעֶה

וַיִּשְׁאָלֵהוּ הָאִישׁ לֵאמֹר מַה־תְּבַקֵּשׁ:

Genesis 37.16

וַיֹּאמֶר אֶת־אַחַי אָנֹכִי מְבַקֵּשׁ
הַגִּידָה־נָּא לִי אֵיפֹה הֵם רֹעִים:

Morphemes of הַגִּידָה: הַ גִּי(ֹ)ד ָה

Q75: PARSE הַגִּידָה

Genesis 37.17

וַיֹּאמֶר הָאִישׁ נָסְעוּ מִזֶּה

Q76: PARSE נָסְעוּ

כִּי שָׁמַעְתִּי אֹמְרִים נֵלְכָה דֹּתָיְנָה

Q77: PARSE נֵלְכָה

וַיֵּלֶךְ יוֹסֵף אַחַר אֶחָיו וַיִּמְצָאֵם בְּדֹתָן:

Morphemes of וַיִּמְצָאֵם: ם מְצָא י וַ

Q78: PARSE וַיִּמְצָאֵם

Genesis 37.18

וַיִּרְאוּ אֹתוֹ מֵרָחֹק וּבְטֶרֶם יִקְרַב אֲלֵיהֶם

Q79: PARSE וַיִּרְאוּ (While you would expect *patach* before the guttural ר, this is the spelling for the 3mp (occurs 48 times).

וַיִּתְנַכְּלוּ אֹתוֹ לַהֲמִיתוֹ:

Morphemes of וַיִּתְנַכְּלוּ: ו נכל ת י וַ

Q80: PARSE וַיִּתְנַכְּלוּ

Morphemes of לַהֲמִיתוֹ: ו מ(ו)ת הֲ לַ

Q81: PARSE לַהֲמִיתוֹ

burnt offering, in the stead of his sonne.

14 And Abraham called the name of that place ‖ Iehouah-ijreh, as it is said to this day, In the Mount of the LORD it shalbe seene.

15 ¶ And the Angel of the LORD called vnto Abraham out of heauen the

‖ That is, *The LORD will see, or, prouide.*

1611 King James Version (Gen. 22.14)

Chapter 20

Reading Job 1.1-12

In this chapter you will:

- Learn inductively by translating Job 1.1-12
- Review material from previous chapters
- Learn to describe the Hebrew verb syntax

20.1 Vocabulary for 1 Samuel 1.1-14

The following vocabulary consists of words found at least 50 times in the Hebrew Bible.

כָּעַס	*v.* be irritated, angry	בָּכָה	*v.* weep
רָעַע	*v.* be evil	צָרָה	*n.f.* distress, rival
עָנָה	*v.* I- to answer, II- be humble	אָמָה	*n.f.* maidservant
הָרָה	*v.* conceive	פִּחָה	*n.f.* maidservant
שָׁכַח	*v.* forget	נֶדֶר	*n.m.* a vow
פָּלַל	*v.* pray	עֳנִי	*n.m.* affliction, poverty
חָשַׁב	*v.* to think	יֶלֶד	*n.m.* boy
צָבָא	*n.m/f.* army	נֵבֶל	*n.m.* wine-skin
אַף	*n.m.* nostril, face, anger, double	פַּר	*n.m.* young bull
אַךְ	*particle.* indeed (157)	בַּעַד	*prep.* behind, around
חָנַן	*v.* to be gracious, to favor (*Note the paradox in the name 'Hannah'. Hannah means 'favored', but she is barren.*)	נָא	*particle of entreaty.* please, surely, now

SUPPLEMENTAL DICTIONARY FOR JOB 1.1-12

These words occur fewer than 50 times in the Hebrew Bible.

תָּם	*adj.* perfect	שָׂטָן	*n.m.* accuser
צֶמֶד	*n.m.* team & *v.* צָמַד	שׁוּט	*v.* to go about
אָתוֹן	*n.f.* female donkey	חִנָּם	*adv.* freely
מִשְׁתֶּה	*n.m.* feast	שׂוּךְ	*v.* to fence or hedge
נָקַף	*v.* to go around	בַּעַד	*prep.* behind or around

אוּלַי   *adv.* perhaps   פָּרַץ   *v.* to burst or break through

                              אוּלָם   *adv.* but indeed

EXERCISE 20

Translate the Hebrew text of Job 1.1-12; parse the verbs; and study the syntactical analysis that follows.

20.2 Reading Job 1.1-12

אִישׁ הָיָה בְאֶרֶץ־עוּץ אִיּוֹב שְׁמוֹ וְהָיָה| הָאִישׁ הַהוּא תָּם וְיָשָׁר וִירֵא ¹
אֱלֹהִים וְסָר מֵרָע: ² וַיִּוָּלְדוּ לוֹ שִׁבְעָה בָנִים וְשָׁלוֹשׁ בָּנוֹת: ³ וַיְהִי מִקְנֵהוּ
שִׁבְעַת אַלְפֵי־צֹאן וּשְׁלֹשֶׁת אַלְפֵי גְמַלִּים וַחֲמֵשׁ מֵאוֹת צֶמֶד־בָּקָר וַחֲמֵשׁ מֵאוֹת
אֲתוֹנוֹת וַעֲבֻדָּה רַבָּה מְאֹד וַיְהִי הָאִישׁ הַהוּא גָּדוֹל מִכָּל־בְּנֵי־קֶדֶם: ⁴ וְהָלְכוּ
בָנָיו וְעָשׂוּ מִשְׁתֶּה בֵּית אִישׁ יוֹמוֹ וְשָׁלְחוּ וְקָרְאוּ לִשְׁלֹשֶׁת אַחְיֹתֵיהֶם לֶאֱכֹל
וְלִשְׁתּוֹת עִמָּהֶם: ⁵ וַיְהִי כִּי הִקִּיפוּ יְמֵי הַמִּשְׁתֶּה וַיִּשְׁלַח אִיּוֹב וַיְקַדְּשֵׁם
וְהִשְׁכִּים בַּבֹּקֶר וְהֶעֱלָה עֹלוֹת מִסְפַּר כֻּלָּם כִּי אָמַר אִיּוֹב אוּלַי חָטְאוּ בָנַי
וּבֵרֲכוּ אֱלֹהִים בִּלְבָבָם כָּכָה יַעֲשֶׂה אִיּוֹב כָּל־הַיָּמִים: פ ⁶ וַיְהִי הַיּוֹם וַיָּבֹאוּ
בְּנֵי הָאֱלֹהִים לְהִתְיַצֵּב עַל־יְהוָה וַיָּבוֹא גַם־הַשָּׂטָן בְּתוֹכָם: ⁷ וַיֹּאמֶר יְהוָה
אֶל־הַשָּׂטָן מֵאַיִן תָּבֹא וַיַּעַן הַשָּׂטָן אֶת־יְהוָה וַיֹּאמַר מִשּׁוּט בָּאָרֶץ
וּמֵהִתְהַלֵּךְ בָּהּ: ⁸ וַיֹּאמֶר יְהוָה אֶל־הַשָּׂטָן הֲשַׂמְתָּ לִבְּךָ עַל־עַבְדִּי אִיּוֹב כִּי
אֵין כָּמֹהוּ בָּאָרֶץ אִישׁ תָּם וְיָשָׁר יְרֵא אֱלֹהִים וְסָר מֵרָע: ⁹ וַיַּעַן הַשָּׂטָן
אֶת־יְהוָה וַיֹּאמַר הַחִנָּם יָרֵא אִיּוֹב אֱלֹהִים: ¹⁰ הֲלֹא־אַתְּ שַׂכְתָּ בַעֲדוֹ
וּבְעַד־בֵּיתוֹ וּבְעַד כָּל־אֲשֶׁר־לוֹ מִסָּבִיב מַעֲשֵׂה יָדָיו בֵּרַכְתָּ וּמִקְנֵהוּ פָּרַץ
בָּאָרֶץ: ¹¹ וְאוּלָם שְׁלַח־נָא יָדְךָ וְגַע בְּכָל־אֲשֶׁר־לוֹ אִם־לֹא עַל־פָּנֶיךָ יְבָרֲכֶךָּ:
¹² וַיֹּאמֶר יְהוָה אֶל־הַשָּׂטָן הִנֵּה כָל־אֲשֶׁר־לוֹ בְּיָדֶךָ רַק אֵלָיו אַל־תִּשְׁלַח
יָדֶךָ וַיֵּצֵא הַשָּׂטָן מֵעִם פְּנֵי יְהוָה:

Syntactical Analysis of Job 1.1-22

(This analysis is according to appendix: *The Hebrew Verb System in Prose* (§26.1).

V	Verb type	Syntax[6]	Translation
1	x-qatal	antecedent	There was a man in the land of Utz,
	verbless	circ. to prev.	Job was his name;
	weqatal	habitual /	and that man was perfect and upright,
		descriptive	and fearing (ptc/adj) God, and turning (ptc) from evil.
2	wayyiqtol	narrative	And there were born unto him seven sons and three daughters.
3	wayyiqtol	narrative	His property also was seven thousand sheep,
			and three thousand camels, and five hundred yoke . . . [7]
			and five hundred she asses, and a very great household;
	wayyiqtol	narrative	so that man was the greatest of all the men of the east.
4	weqatal	habitual/	And his sons would go and make a feast . . . his day;
	weqatal	shift to	and they would send
	weqatal	description	and they would call for their three sisters . . . with them.
5	wayyiqtol	new paragr.	And it was,
	כִּי-qatal	subord. cl.	when the days of *their* feasting were gone about,
	wayyiqtol	narrative	that Job sent
	wayyiqtol	narrative	and sanctified them,
	weqatal	habitual	He would rise up early in the morning,
	weqatal	habitual	and he would offer burnt offerings . . . .
	x-qatal	reason	for Job said, (כִּי + pf is = "when" or "because")
	x-qatal	past	It may be that my sons have sinned,
	weqatal	habitual	and cursed God in their hearts.
	x-yiqtol	habitual /	Thus Job would do all the days.
		summary	
6	wayyiqtol	new paragr.	Now there was a day
	wayyiqtol	narrative	the sons of God came to present themselves before the LORD,
	wayyiqtol	narrative	and Satan came also among them.
7	wayyiqtol	narrative	And the LORD said unto Satan,
	x-yiqtol	present	Whence comest thou?
	wayyiqtol	narrative	Then Satan answered the LORD,
	wayyiqtol	narrative	and said,
	inf const	response	From going to and fro in the earth,
	inf const	response	and from walking up and down in it.
8	wayyiqtol	narrative	And the LORD said unto Satan,
	x-qatal	begin report	Have you set your heart upon my servant Job,
	verbless	present	that *there is* none like him in the earth,
	verbless	present	a perfect and an upright man,
			one fearing of (adj) God, and turning from . . . ?
9	wayyiqtol	narrative	Then Satan answered the LORD,
	wayyiqtol	narrative	and said,
	x-qatal	begin report	Has Job feared God without compensation?
10	x-qatal	neg. wayyiq.	Hast not thou made an hedge about him,
			and about his house . . . .
	x-qatal	specification	It is the work of his hands, thou hast blessed

---

[6] See definitions at the end of the chart.

[7] Because of space limitations on the page, the English translation is abbreviated.

11	x-qatal	specification	and it is his substance that is increased in the land.
	imv	volitive	But put forth thine hand now,
	imv	volitive	and touch all that he hath,
	yiqtol	future	and he will curse thee to thy face (oath formula).

Antecedent refers to actions that occurred previous to the *wayyiqtol* that follows.

Begin report is the beginning of a narrative within quoted material.

Contrast refers to the use of x-*qatal* to set one idea off against another.

Future refers to the imperfect used as future tense in quoted material.

Habitual refers to events that were repeated in the past.

Narrative refers to the events that make up the primary story line.

Negative refers to the use of the negative particle with a verb.

New Paragr. specifies וַיְהִי as a paragraph marker within a discourse.

Past refers to the perfect used as past tense in quoted material.

Present refers to the imperfect used as present tense in quoted material.

Setting refers to antecedent material that introduces a narrative.

Volitive refers to a statement of the speaker's desire.

X means any element, except *vav*, that comes before the verb.

Some of the decisions in the syntactical analysis are open to question.

Qumran Psalms Scroll
Psalm 142.4–143.8

Chapter 21

Reading 1 Samuel 1.1-14

In this chapter you will:

- Learn inductively by translating 1 Samuel 1.1-14
- Review material from previous chapters
- Learn to describe the Hebrew verb syntax

21.1 Vocabulary

The following vocabulary consists of words found at least 50 times in the Hebrew Bible.

נָטָה	*v.* to stretch out, extend (*e.g. a tent*)	נוּס	*v.* to flee
רוּם	*v.* to be high, exalted	רָדַף	*v.* to pursue, persecute
גָּאַל	*v.* to redeem	רוּץ	v. to run
הָרַג	*v.* to kill	שָׂמַח	*v.* to be glad, rejoice
חָנָה	*v.* to encamp	שַׁעַר	*n.* gate
טָמֵא	*v.* to be unclean (ceremonially)	שָׂדֶה	*n.* field
נוֹתַר	*v.* to be left, remain (*nifal* > יָתַר)	מַטֶּה	*n.* tribe
כָּסָה	*v.* to cover, conceal	חֹק	*n.* statute
שָׁכֵן	*v.* to dwell, settle down		

SUPPLEMENTAL DICTIONARY FOR 1 SAMUEL 1.1-14

These words occur fewer than 50 times in the Hebrew Bible.

מָנָה	*n.f.* portion	מַר	*adj.* bitter
רֶחֶם	*n.m/f.* womb	נדר	*v.* to vow
כַּעַס	*n.m.* vexation	מוֹרָה	*n.m.* razor
עֲבוּר	*particle* in order that	נוּעַ	*v.* to quiver, shake
רעם	*v.* thunder, tremble	שִׁכּוֹר	*adj.* drunken
דַּי	*n.m.* enough	מָתַי	*particle.* when?
מְזוּזָה	*n.f.* doorpost, gatepost	שָׁכַר	*v.* become drunk

EXERCISE 21

Translate the Hebrew text of 1 Samuel 1.1-14; parse the verbs; and study the analysis of the the verb syntax that follows.

21.2   Reading 1 Samuel 1.1-14

¹ וַיְהִי אִישׁ אֶחָד מִן־הָרָמָתַיִם צוֹפִים מֵהַר אֶפְרָיִם וּשְׁמוֹ אֶלְקָנָה
בֶּן־יְרֹחָם בֶּן־אֱלִיהוּא בֶּן־תֹּחוּ בֶן־צוּף אֶפְרָתִי: ² וְלוֹ שְׁתֵּי נָשִׁים שֵׁם אַחַת
חַנָּה וְשֵׁם הַשֵּׁנִית פְּנִנָּה וַיְהִי לִפְנִנָּה יְלָדִים וּלְחַנָּה אֵין יְלָדִים: ³ וְעָלָה הָאִישׁ
הַהוּא מֵעִירוֹ מִיָּמִים יָמִימָה לְהִשְׁתַּחֲוֺת וְלִזְבֹּחַ לַיהוָה צְבָאוֹת בְּשִׁלֹה וְשָׁם
שְׁנֵי בְנֵי־עֵלִי חָפְנִי וּפִנְחָס כֹּהֲנִים לַיהוָה: ⁴ וַיְהִי הַיּוֹם וַיִּזְבַּח אֶלְקָנָה וְנָתַן
לִפְנִנָּה אִשְׁתּוֹ וּלְכָל־בָּנֶיהָ וּבְנוֹתֶיהָ מָנוֹת: ⁵ וּלְחַנָּה יִתֵּן מָנָה אַחַת אַפָּיִם
כִּי אֶת־חַנָּה אָהֵב וַיהוָה סָגַר רַחְמָהּ:⁶ וְכִעֲסַתָּה צָרָתָהּ גַּם־כַּעַס בַּעֲבוּר
הַרְּעִמָהּ כִּי־סָגַר יְהוָה בְּעַד רַחְמָהּ: ⁷ וְכֵן יַעֲשֶׂה שָׁנָה בְשָׁנָה מִדֵּי עֲלֹתָהּ
בְּבֵית יְהוָה כֵּן תַּכְעִסֶנָּה וַתִּבְכֶּה וְלֹא תֹאכַל: ⁸ וַיֹּאמֶר לָהּ אֶלְקָנָה אִישָׁהּ
חַנָּה לָמֶה תִבְכִּי וְלָמֶה לֹא תֹאכְלִי וְלָמֶה יֵרַע לְבָבֵךְ הֲלוֹא אָנֹכִי טוֹב לָךְ
מֵעֲשָׂרָה בָּנִים: ⁹ וַתָּקָם חַנָּה אַחֲרֵי אָכְלָה בְשִׁלֹה וְאַחֲרֵי שָׁתֹה וְעֵלִי הַכֹּהֵן
יֹשֵׁב עַל־הַכִּסֵּא עַל־מְזוּזַת הֵיכַל יְהוָה: ¹⁰ וְהִיא מָרַת נָפֶשׁ וַתִּתְפַּלֵּל
עַל־יְהוָה וּבָכֹה תִבְכֶּה: ¹¹ וַתִּדֹּר נֶדֶר וַתֹּאמַר יְהוָה צְבָאוֹת אִם־רָאֹה תִרְאֶה׀
בָּעֳנִי אֲמָתֶךָ וּזְכַרְתַּנִי וְלֹא־תִשְׁכַּח אֶת־אֲמָתֶךָ וְנָתַתָּה לַאֲמָתְךָ זֶרַע אֲנָשִׁים
וּנְתַתִּיו לַיהוָה כָּל־יְמֵי חַיָּיו וּמוֹרָה לֹא־יַעֲלֶה עַל־רֹאשׁוֹ: ¹² וְהָיָה כִּי הִרְבְּתָה
לְהִתְפַּלֵּל לִפְנֵי יְהוָה וְעֵלִי שֹׁמֵר אֶת־פִּיהָ: ¹³ וְחַנָּה הִיא מְדַבֶּרֶת עַל־לִבָּהּ
רַק שְׂפָתֶיהָ נָּעוֹת וְקוֹלָהּ לֹא יִשָּׁמֵעַ וַיַּחְשְׁבֶהָ עֵלִי לְשִׁכֹּרָה: ¹⁴ וַיֹּאמֶר אֵלֶיהָ
עֵלִי עַד־מָתַי תִּשְׁתַּכָּרִין הָסִירִי אֶת־יֵינֵךְ מֵעָלָיִךְ:

Syntactical Analysis of 1 Samuel 1.1-14[8]

(This analysis is according to appendix: *The Hebrew Verb System in Prose* (§26.1).

	Verb Type	Syntax	Translation
1	wayyiqtol	Beginning of New Narrative	There was a certain man . . .
	verbless	Explanatory/setting	and his name was Elqanah.
2	verbless	Explanatory/setting	He had two wives
	verbless	setting continued	The name of one was Hannah
	verbless	contrast	while the name of the other was . . .
	wayyiqtol	narrative, new parag	And it happened that Peninah. had children
	אֵין	contrast	But Hannah had no children.
3	weqatal	habitual	That man would go up . . .
	verbless	parenthetical	(Now the two sons of Eli were priests there . . .)
4	wayyiqtol	narrative	There came the day . . .
	wayyiqtol	narrative	that Elqanah sacrificed . . .
	weqatal	habitual	Now he would give to Peninah . . .
5	x-yiqtol	contrast & habitual	But to Hannah he would give . . .
	כִּי-qatal	circumstance	because Hannah he loved
	x-qatal	circumstance/coordination	and Yahweh had shut her womb.
6	weqatal	habitual	Here adversary would vex her. . .
	כִּי-qatal	circumstance	because Yahweh had shut . . .
7	x-yiqtol	habitual	And thus he would do . . .
	x-yiqtol	habitual	Thus she would vex her . . .
	wayyiqtol	narrative	So she wept
	x-yiqtol	repeated/negative	and she would not eat.
8	wayyiqtol	narrative	And Elqanah said to her . . .
	x-yiqtol	present/future	Hannah, why do you weep?
	x-yiqtol	coordination	And why won't you eat?
	x-yiqtol	coordination	And why are you sad?
	verbless	present durative	Am I not better to you than . . .
9	wayyiqtol	narrative	After they had eaten and drunk…Hannah arose
	ptc	explanatory	(Now Eli the priest was sitting . . .
10	verbless	explanatory	and she was bitter of soul. . .)
	wayyiqtol	narrative	And she prayed unto Yahweh
	x-yiqtol	repeated	And she wept profusely
11	wayyiqtol	narrative	And she vowed a vow
	wayyiqtol	narrative	And she said, 'Yahweh . . .
	x-yiqtol	future	if you will surely see . . .
	weqatal	future	and you will remember me
	x-yiqtol	negative	and not forget
	weqatal	future	and you will give seed
	weqatal	future	then I will give him to Yahweh
	x-yiqtol	negative	a razor shall not go up on his head

---

[8] Because of space limitation on the page, the English translation is abbreviated.

12	weqatal	repeated	So it continued
	כִּי-qatal	past tense	that she prolonged her praying
	ptc	explanatory	and Eli was watching her mouth
13	ptc	explanatory	Now Hannah, she was speaking
	ptc	durative	only her lips were quivering
	x-yiqtol	contrast	but her voice was not audible
	wayyiqtol	narrative	And Eli though her to be drunk.
14	wayyiqtol	narrative	And he said to her
	x-yiqtol	future	How long will you be drunk?
	imperative	volitive/command	Put away your wine.

Setting refers to antecedent material that introduces a narrative.

Compound means a compound sentence. The first element cannot stand alone as a sentence.

Antecedent refers to actions that occurred previous to the *wayyiqtol* that follows.

Contrast refers to the use of x-*qatal* or *vav*-x to set one idea off against another.

Future refers to the imperfect used as future tense in quoted material.

Habitual refers to actions that were customary in the past.

Repeated refers to events or actions that were repeated in the past.

Narrative refers to the events that make up the primary story line.

New Paragr. specifies וַיְהִי as a paragraph marker within a discourse.

Past refers to the perfect used as past tense in quoted material.

Present refers to the imperfect used as present tense in quoted material.

Negative refers to the use of the negative particle with a verb to form a negative sentence.

Volitive refers to a statement of the speaker's desire.

X means any element, except *vav*, that comes before the verb.

Coordination refers to the use of the conjunction to join parallel statements.

Some of the syntactical decisions in the analysis are debatable.

22.1   PARADIGM OF THE STRONG VERB

	Qatal	Qatel	Qatol	Nifal	Hifil	Hofal	Piel	Pual	Hitpael
Pf									
1cs	קָטַלְתִּי	כָּבַדְתִּי	קָטֹנְתִּי	נִקְטַלְתִּי	הִקְטַלְתִּי	הָקְטַלְתִּי	קִטַּלְתִּי	קֻטַּלְתִּי	הִתְקַטַּלְתִּי
2ms	קָטַלְתָּ	כָּבַדְתָּ	קָטֹנְתָּ	נִקְטַלְתָּ	הִקְטַלְתָּ	הָקְטַלְתָּ	קִטַּלְתָּ	קֻטַּלְתָּ	הִתְקַטַּלְתָּ
2fs	קָטַלְתְּ	כָּבַדְתְּ	קָטֹנְתְּ	נִקְטַלְתְּ	הִקְטַלְתְּ	הָקְטַלְתְּ	קִטַּלְתְּ	קֻטַּלְתְּ	הִתְקַטַּלְתְּ
3ms	קָטַל	כָּבֵד	קָטֹן	נִקְטַל	הִקְטִיל	הָקְטַל	קִטֵּל	קֻטַּל	הִתְקַטֵּל
3fs	קָטְלָה	כָּבְדָה	קָטְנָה	נִקְטְלָה	הִקְטִילָה	הָקְטְלָה	קִטְּלָה	קֻטְּלָה	הִתְקַטְּלָה
1cp	קָטַלְנוּ	כָּבַדְנוּ	קָטֹנּוּ	נִקְטַלְנוּ	הִקְטַלְנוּ	הָקְטַלְנוּ	קִטַּלְנוּ	קֻטַּלְנוּ	הִתְקַטַּלְנוּ
2mp	קְטַלְתֶּם	כְּבַדְתֶּם	קְטָנְתֶּם	נִקְטַלְתֶּם	הִקְטַלְתֶּם	הָקְטַלְתֶּם	קִטַּלְתֶּם	קֻטַּלְתֶּם	הִתְקַטַּלְתֶּם
2fp	קְטַלְתֶּן	כְּבַדְתֶּן	קְטָנְתֶּן	נִקְטַלְתֶּן	הִקְטַלְתֶּן	הָקְטַלְתֶּן	קִטַּלְתֶּן	קֻטַּלְתֶּן	הִתְקַטַּלְתֶּן
3cp	קָטְלוּ	כָּבְדוּ	קָטְנוּ	נִקְטְלוּ	הִקְטִילוּ	הָקְטְלוּ	קִטְּלוּ	קֻטְּלוּ	הִתְקַטְּלוּ
Imf									
1cs	אֶקְטֹל	אֶכְבַּד	(Same	אֶקָּטֵל	אַקְטִיל	אָקְטַל	אֲקַטֵּל	אֲקֻטַּל	אֶתְקַטֵּל
2ms	תִּקְטֹל	תִּכְבַּד	as כבד)	תִּקָּטֵל	תַּקְטִיל	תָּקְטַל	תְּקַטֵּל	תְּקֻטַּל	תִּתְקַטֵּל
2fs	תִּקְטְלִי	תִּכְבְּדִי		תִּקָּטְלִי	תַּקְטִילִי	תָּקְטְלִי	תְּקַטְּלִי	תְּקֻטְּלִי	תִּתְקַטְּלִי
3ms	יִקְטֹל	יִכְבַּד		יִקָּטֵל	יַקְטִיל	יָקְטַל	יְקַטֵּל	יְקֻטַּל	יִתְקַטֵּל
3fs	תִּקְטֹל	תִּכְבַּד		תִּקָּטֵל	תַּקְטִיל	תָּקְטַל	תְּקַטֵּל	תְּקֻטַּל	תִּתְקַטֵּל
1cp	נִקְטֹל	נִכְבַּד		נִקָּטֵל	נַקְטִיל	נָקְטַל	נְקַטֵּל	נְקֻטַּל	נִתְקַטֵּל
2mp	תִּקְטְלוּ	תִּכְבְּדוּ		תִּקָּטְלוּ	תַּקְטִילוּ	תָּקְטְלוּ	תְּקַטְּלוּ	תְּקֻטְּלוּ	תִּתְקַטְּלוּ
2fp	תִּקְטֹלְנָה	תִּכְבַּדְנָה	תִּקְטֶנָּה	תִּקָּטַלְנָה	תַּקְטֵלְנָה	תָּקְטַלְנָה	תְּקַטֵּלְנָה	תְּקֻטַּלְנָה	תִּתְקַטֵּלְנָה
3mp	יִקְטְלוּ	יִכְבְּדוּ		יִקָּטְלוּ	יַקְטִילוּ	יָקְטְלוּ	יְקַטְּלוּ	יְקֻטְּלוּ	יִתְקַטְּלוּ
3fp	תִּקְטֹלְנָה	תִּכְבַּדְנָה	תִּקְטֶנָּה	תִּקָּטַלְנָה	תַּקְטֵלְנָה	תָּקְטַלְנָה	תְּקַטֵּלְנָה	תְּקֻטַּלְנָה	תִּתְקַטֵּלְנָה
Imv									
2ms	קְטֹל	כְּבַד	(Same	הִקָּטֵל	הַקְטֵל		קַטֵּל		הִתְקַטֵּל
2fs	קִטְלִי	כִּבְדִי	as כבד)	הִקָּטְלִי	הַקְטִילִי		קַטְּלִי		הִתְקַטְּלִי
2mp	קִטְלוּ	כִּבְדוּ		הִקָּטְלוּ	הַקְטִילוּ		קַטְּלוּ		הִתְקַטְּלוּ
2fp	קְטֹלְנָה	כְּבַדְנָה		הִקָּטַלְנָה	הַקְטֵלְנָה		קַטֵּלְנָה		הִתְקַטֵּלְנָה
IAb	קָטוֹל	(reg.)	(reg.)	הִקָּטֹל נִקְטֹל	הַקְטֵל	הָקְטֵל	קַטֵּל קַטֹּל	קֻטֹּל	הִתְקַטֵּל
ICs	קְטֹל	(reg.)	(reg.)	הִקָּטֵל	הַקְטִיל		קַטֵּל		הִתְקַטֵּל
APtc	קוֹטֵל	כָּבֵד	קָטֹן		מַקְטִיל		מְקַטֵּל		מִתְקַטֵּל
PPtc	קָטוּל			נִקְטָל		מָקְטָל		מְקֻטָּל	
W	וַיִּקְטֹל	וַיִּכְבַּד	וַיִּקְטֹן	וַיִּקָּטֵל	וַיַּקְטֵל	וַיָּקְטַל	וַיְקַטֵּל	וַיְקֻטַּל	וַיִּתְקַטֵּל

22.2   Final ה Verb

		Qal	Nifal	Hifil	Hofal	Piel	Pual	Hitpael
		uncover						
Pf	1cs	גָּלִיתִי	נִגְלֵיתִי	הִגְלֵיתִי	הָגְלֵיתִי	גִּלִּיתִי	גֻּלֵּיתִי	הִתְגַּלֵּיתִי
	2ms	גָּלִיתָ	נִגְלֵיתָ	הִגְלֵיתָ	הָגְלֵיתָ	גִּלִּיתָ	גֻּלֵּיתָ	הִתְגַּלֵּיתָ
	2fs	גָּלִית	נִגְלֵית	הִגְלֵית	הָגְלֵית	גִּלִּית	גֻּלֵּית	הִתְגַּלֵּית
	3ms	גָּלָה	נִגְלָה	הִגְלָה	הָגְלָה	גִּלָּה	גֻּלָּה	הִתְגַּלָּה
	3fs	גָּלְתָה	נִגְלְתָה	הִגְלְתָה	הָגְלְתָה	גִּלְּתָה	גֻּלְּתָה	הִתְגַּלְּתָה
	1cp	גָּלִינוּ	נִגְלֵינוּ	הִגְלֵינוּ	הָגְלֵינוּ	גִּלִּינוּ	גֻּלֵּינוּ	הִתְגַּלֵּינוּ
	2mp	גְּלִיתֶם	נִגְלֵיתֶם	הִגְלֵיתֶם	הָגְלֵיתֶם	גִּלִּיתֶם	גֻּלֵּיתֶם	הִתְגַּלֵּיתֶם
	2fp	גְּלִיתֶן	נִגְלֵיתֶן	הִגְלֵיתֶן	הָגְלֵיתֶן	גִּלִּיתֶן	גֻּלֵּיתֶן	הִתְגַּלֵּיתֶן
	3cp	גָּלוּ	נִגְלוּ	הִגְלוּ	הָגְלוּ	גִּלּוּ	גֻּלּוּ	הִתְגַּלּוּ
Imf	1cs	אֶגְלֶה	אֶגָּלֶה	אַגְלֶה	אָגְלֶה	אֲגַלֶּה	אֲגֻלֶּה	אֶתְגַּלֶּה
	2ms	תִּגְלֶה	תִּגָּלֶה	תַּגְלֶה	תָּגְלֶה	תְּגַלֶּה	תְּגֻלֶּה	תִּתְגַּלֶּה
	2fs	תִּגְלִי	תִּגָּלִי	תַּגְלִי	תָּגְלִי	תְּגַלִּי	תְּגֻלִּי	תִּתְגַּלִּי
	3ms	יִגְלֶה	יִגָּלֶה	יַגְלֶה	יָגְלֶה	יְגַלֶּה	יְגֻלֶּה	יִתְגַּלֶּה
	3fs	תִּגְלֶה	תִּגָּלֶה	תַּגְלֶה	תָּגְלֶה	תְּגַלֶּה	תְּגֻלֶּה	תִּתְגַּלֶּה
	1cp	נִגְלֶה	נִגָּלֶה	נַגְלֶה	נָגְלֶה	נְגַלֶּה	נְגֻלֶּה	נִתְגַּלֶּה
	2mp	תִּגְלוּ	תִּגָּלוּ	תַּגְלוּ	תָּגְלוּ	תְּגַלּוּ	תְּגֻלּוּ	תִּתְגַּלּוּ
	2fp	תִּגְלֶינָה	תִּגָּלֶינָה	תַּגְלֶינָה	תָּגְלֶינָה	תְּגַלֶּינָה	תְּגֻלֶּינָה	תִּתְגַּלֶּינָה
	3mp	יִגְלוּ	יִגָּלוּ	יַגְלוּ	יָגְלוּ	יְגַלּוּ	יְגֻלּוּ	יִתְגַּלּוּ
	3fp	תִּגְלֶינָה	תִּגָּלֶינָה	תַּגְלֶינָה	תָּגְלֶינָה	תְּגַלֶּינָה	תְּגֻלֶּינָה	תִּתְגַּלֶּינָה
Imv	2ms	גְּלֵה	הִגָּלֵה	הַגְלֵה		גַּלֵּה		הִתְגַּלֵּה
	2fs	גְּלִי	הִגָּלִי	הַגְלִי		גַּלִּי		הִתְגַּלִּי
	2mp	גְּלוּ	הִגָּלוּ	הַגְלוּ		גַּלּוּ		הִתְגַּלּוּ
	2fp	גְּלֶינָה	הִגָּלֶינָה	הַגְלֶינָה		גַּלֶּינָה		הִתְגַּלֶּינָה
Inf	Abs	גָּלוֹה	נִגְלֹה	הַגְלֵה	הָגְלֵה	גַּלֵּה		
			הִגָּלֹה			גַּלֹּה		
	Cs	גְּלוֹת	הִגָּלוֹת	הַגְלוֹת		גַּלּוֹת	גֻּלּוֹת	הִתְגַּלּוֹת
Ptc	Act	גֹּלֶה		מַגְלֶה		מְגַלֶּה		מִתְגַּלֶּה
	Pass	גָּלוּי	נִגְלֶה		מָגְלֶה		מְגֻלֶּה	
W		וַיִּגֶל	וַיִּגָּל	וַיַּגֶל		וַיְגַל	וַיְגֻל	וַיִּתְגַּל
Juss		יִגֶל	יִגָּל	יַגֶל		יְגַל	יְגֻל	יִתְגַּל

22.3   Initial Guttural Verb

		Qal ע	Qal ח	Qal א	Nifal	Hifil	Hofal
Pf	1cs	עָמַדְתִּי	חָזַקְתִּי	אָכַלְתִּי	נֶעֱזַבְתִּי	הֶעֱמַדְתִּי	הָעֳמַדְתִּי
	2ms	עָמַדְתָּ	חָזַקְתָּ	אָכַלְתָּ	נֶעֱזַבְתָּ	הֶעֱמַדְתָּ	הָעֳמַדְתָּ
	2fs	עָמַדְתְּ	חָזַקְתְּ	אָכַלְתְּ	נֶעֱזַבְתְּ	הֶעֱמַדְתְּ	הָעֳמַדְתְּ
	3ms	עָמַד	חָזַק	אָכַל	נֶעֱזַב	הֶעֱמִיד	הָעֳמַד
	3fs	עָמְדָה	חָזְקָה	אָכְלָה	נֶעֶזְבָה	הֶעֱמִידָה	הָעֳמְדָה
	1cp	עָמַדְנוּ	חָזַקְנוּ	אָכַלְנוּ¹	נֶעֱזַבְנוּ	הֶעֱמַדְנוּ	הָעֳמַדְנוּ
	2mp	עֲמַדְתֶּם	חֲזַקְתֶּם	אֲכַלְתֶּם	נֶעֱזַבְתֶּם	הֶעֱמַדְתֶּם	הָעֳמַדְתֶּם
	2fp	עֲמַדְתֶּן	חֲזַקְתֶּן	אֲכַלְתֶּן	נֶעֱזַבְתֶּן	הֶעֱמַדְתֶּן	הָעֳמַדְתֶּן
	3cp	עָמְדוּ	חָזְקוּ	אָכְלוּ	נֶעֶזְבוּ	הֶעֱמִידוּ	הָעֳמְדוּ
Imf	1cs	אֶעֱמֹד	אֶחֱזַק	אֹכַל	אֵעָזֵב	אַעֲמִיד	אָעֳמַד
	2ms	תַּעֲמֹד	תֶּחֱזַק	תֹּאכַל²	תֵּעָזֵב	תַּעֲמִיד	תָּעֳמַד
	2fs	תַּעַמְדִי	תֶּחֶזְקִי	תֹּאכְלִי	תֵּעָזְבִי	תַּעֲמִידִי	תָּעֳמְדִי
	3ms	יַעֲמֹד	יֶחֱזַק	יֹאכַל	יֵעָזֵב	יַעֲמִיד	יָעֳמַד
	3fs	תַּעֲמֹד	תֶּחֱזַק	תֹּאכַל	תֵּעָזֵב	תַּעֲמִיד	תָּעֳמַד
	1cp	נַעֲמֹד	נֶחֱזַק	נֹאכַל	נֵעָזֵב	נַעֲמִיד	נָעֳמַד
	2mp	תַּעַמְדוּ	תֶּחֶזְקוּ	תֹּאכְלוּ	תֵּעָזְבוּ	תַּעֲמִידוּ	תָּעֳמְדוּ
	2fp	תַּעֲמֹדְנָה	תֶּחֱזַקְנָה	תֹּאכַלְנָה	תֵּעָזַבְנָה	תַּעֲמֵדְנָה	תָּעֳמַדְנָה
	3mp	יַעַמְדוּ	יֶחֶזְקוּ	יֹאכְלוּ	יֵעָזְבוּ	יַעֲמִידוּ	יָעֳמְדוּ
	3fp	תַּעֲמֹדְנָה	תֶּחֱזַקְנָה	תֹּאכַלְנָה	תֵּעָזַבְנָה	תַּעֲמֵדְנָה	תָּעֳמַדְנָה
Imv	2ms	עֲמֹד	חֲזַק	אֱכֹל	הֵעָזֵב	הַעֲמֵד	
	2fs	עִמְדִי	חִזְקִי	אִכְלִי	הֵעָזְבִי	הַעֲמִידִי	
	2mp	עִמְדוּ	חִזְקוּ	אִכְלוּ	הֵעָזְבוּ	הַעֲמִידוּ	
	2fp	עֲמֹדְנָה	חֲזַקְנָה	אֱכֹלְנָה	הֵעָזַבְנָה	הַעֲמֵדְנָה	
Inf	Abs	עָמוֹד		אָכוֹל	נַעֲזוֹב הֵאָכֵל	הַעֲמֵד	הָעֳמֵד
	Cs	עֲמֹד		אֱכֹל	הֵעָזֵב	הַעֲמִיד	
Ptc	Act	עֹמֵד		אֹכֵל		מַעֲמִיד	
	Pass	עָמוּד		אָכוּל	נֶעֱזָב		מָעֳמָד

---

¹ There are variations on this that you must learn from the lexicon.

² Note that because of the *alef*, the *cholem* is farther to the left than would be expected.

22.4   Final *Alef* Verb

	Qal	Qal	Nifal	Hifil	Hofal	Piel	Pual	Hitpael
Pf								
1cs	מָצָאתִי	שָׂנֵאתִי	נִמְצֵאתִי	הִמְצֵאתִי	הָמְצֵאתִי	מִצֵּאתִי	מֻצֵּאתִי	הִתְמַצֵּאתִי
2ms	מָצָאתָ	שָׂנֵאתָ	נִמְצֵאתָ	הִמְצֵאתָ	הָמְצֵאתָ	מִצֵּאתָ	מֻצֵּאתָ	הִתְמַצֵּאתָ
2fs	מָצָאת	שָׂנֵאת	נִמְצֵאת	הִמְצֵאת	הָמְצֵאת	מִצֵּאת	מֻצֵּאת	הִתְמַצֵּאת
3ms	מָצָא	שָׂנֵא	נִמְצָא	הִמְצִיא	הָמְצָא	מִצֵּא	מֻצָּא	הִתְמַצֵּא
3fs	מָצְאָה	שָׂנְאָה	נִמְצְאָה	הִמְצִיאָה	הָמְצְאָה	מִצְּאָה	מֻצְּאָה	הִתְמַצְּאָה
1cp	מָצָאנוּ	שָׂנֵאנוּ	נִמְצֵאנוּ	הִמְצֵאנוּ	הָמְצֵאנוּ	מִצֵּאנוּ	מֻצֵּאנוּ	הִתְמַצֵּאנוּ
2mp	מְצָאתֶם	שְׂנֵאתֶם	נִמְצֵאתֶם	הִמְצֵאתֶם	הָמְצֵאתֶם	מִצֵּאתֶם	מֻצֵּאתֶם	הִתְמַצֵּאתֶם
2fp	מְצָאתֶן	שְׂנֵאתֶן	נִמְצֵאתֶן	הִמְצֵאתֶן	הָמְצֵאתֶן	מִצֵּאתֶן	מֻצֵּאתֶן	הִתְמַצֵּאתֶן
3cp	מָצְאוּ	שָׂנְאוּ	נִמְצְאוּ	הִמְצִיאוּ	הָמְצְאוּ	מִצְּאוּ	מֻצְּאוּ	הִתְמַצְּאוּ
Imf								
1cs	אֶמְצָא	אֶשְׂנָא	אֶמָּצֵא	אַמְצִיא	אָמְצָא	אֲמַצֵּא	אֲמֻצָּא	אֶתְמַצֵּא
2ms	תִּמְצָא	תִּשְׂנָא	תִּמָּצֵא	תַּמְצִיא	תָּמְצָא	תְּמַצֵּא	תְּמֻצָּא	תִּתְמַצֵּא
2fs	תִּמְצְאִי	תִּשְׂנְאִי	תִּמָּצְאִי	תַּמְצִיאִי	תָּמְצְאִי	תְּמַצְּאִי	תְּמֻצְּאִי	תִּתְמַצְּאִי
3ms	יִמְצָא	יִשְׂנָא	יִמָּצֵא	יַמְצִיא	יָמְצָא	יְמַצֵּא	יְמֻצָּא	יִתְמַצֵּא
3fs	תִּמְצָא	תִּשְׂנָא	תִּמָּצֵא	תַּמְצִיא	תָּמְצָא	תְּמַצֵּא	תְּמֻצָּא	תִּתְמַצֵּא
1cp	נִמְצָא	נִשְׂנָא	נִמָּצֵא	נַמְצִיא	נָמְצָא	נְמַצֵּא	נְמֻצָּא	נִתְמַצֵּא
2mp	תִּמְצְאוּ	תִּשְׂנְאוּ	תִּמָּצְאוּ	תַּמְצִיאוּ	תָּמְצְאוּ	תְּמַצְּאוּ	תְּמֻצְּאוּ	תִּתְמַצְּאוּ
2fp	תִּמְצֶאנָה	תִּשְׂנֶאנָה	תִּמָּצֶאנָה	תַּמְצֶאנָה	תָּמְצֶאנָה	תְּמַצֶּאנָה	תְּמֻצֶּאנָה	תִּתְמַצֶּאנָה
3mp	יִמְצְאוּ	יִשְׂנְאוּ	יִמָּצְאוּ	יַמְצִיאוּ	יָמְצְאוּ	יְמַצְּאוּ	יְמֻצְּאוּ	יִתְמַצְּאוּ
3fp	תִּמְצֶאנָה	תִּשְׂנֶאנָה	תִּמָּצֶאנָה	תַּמְצֶאנָה	תָּמְצֶאנָה	תְּמַצֶּאנָה	תְּמֻצֶּאנָה	תִּתְמַצֶּאנָה
Imv								
2ms	מְצָא	שְׂנָא	הִמָּצֵא	הַמְצֵא		מַצֵּא		הִתְמַצֵּא
2fs	מִצְאִי	שִׂנְאִי	הִמָּצְאִי	הַמְצִיאִי		מַצְּאִי		הִתְמַצְּאִי
2mp	מִצְאוּ	שִׂנְאוּ	הִמָּצְאוּ	הַמְצִיאוּ		מַצְּאוּ		הִתְמַצְּאוּ
2fp	מְצֶאנָה	שְׂנֶאנָה	הִמָּצֶאנָה	הַמְצֶאנָה		מַצֶּאנָה		הִתְמַצֶּאנָה
IA	מָצוֹא	שָׂנוֹא	נִמְצֹא	הַמְצֵא	הָמְצֵא	מַצֵּא		הִתְמַצֵּא
IC	מְצֹא	שְׂנֹא	הִמָּצֵא	הַמְצִיא	הָמְצִיא	מַצֵּא		הִתְמַצֵּא
APtc	מֹצֵא	שֹׂנֵא		מַמְצִיא		מְמַצֵּא		מִתְמַצֵּא
PPtc	מָצוּא		נִמְצָא		מָמְצָא		מְמֻצָּא	
W	וַיִּמְצָא		וַיִּמָּצֵא	וַיַּמְצֵא	וַיָּמְצָא	וַיְמַצֵּא	וַיְמֻצָּא	וַיִּתְמַצֵּא

22.5   Initial *Nun* Verb (When Assimilation Occurs)

		Qal	Qal	Qal	Nifal	Hifil	Hofal
		fall	*touch*	*give*	*delivered*	*deliver*	*deliver*
Pf	1cs	נָפַלְתִּי	נָגַעְתִּי	נָתַתִּי	נִצַּלְתִּי	הִצַּלְתִּי	הֻצַּלְתִּי
	2ms	נָפַלְתָּ	נָגַעְתָּ	נָתַתָּ	נִצַּלְתָּ	הִצַּלְתָּ	הֻצַּלְתָּ
	2fs	נָפַלְתְּ	נָגַעְתְּ	נָתַתְּ	נִצַּלְתְּ	הִצַּלְתְּ	הֻצַּלְתְּ
	3ms	נָפַל	נָגַע	נָתַן	נִצַּל	הִצִּיל	הֻצַּל
	3fs	נָפְלָה	נָגְעָה	נָתְנָה	נִצְּלָה	הִצִּילָה	הֻצְּלָה
	1cp	נָפַלְנוּ	נָגַעְנוּ	נָתַנּוּ	נִצַּלְנוּ	הִצַּלְנוּ	הֻצַּלְנוּ
	2mp	נְפַלְתֶּם	נְגַעְתֶּם	נְתַתֶּם	נִצַּלְתֶּם	הִצַּלְתֶּם	הֻצַּלְתֶּם
	2fp	נְפַלְתֶּן	נְגַעְתֶּן	נְתַתֶּן	נִצַּלְתֶּן	הִצַּלְתֶּן	הֻצַּלְתֶּן
	3cp	נָפְלוּ	נָגְעוּ	נָתְנוּ	נִצְּלוּ	הִצִּילוּ	הֻצְּלוּ
Imf	1cs	אֶפֹּל	אֶגַּע	אֶתֵּן	אֶנָּצֵל	אַצִּיל	אֻצַּל
	2ms	תִּפֹּל	תִּגַּע	תִּתֵּן	תִּנָּצֵל	תַּצִּיל	תֻּצַּל
	2fs	תִּפְּלִי	תִּגְּעִי	תִּתְּנִי	תִּנָּצְלִי	תַּצִּילִי	תֻּצְּלִי
	3ms	יִפֹּל	יִגַּע	יִתֵּן	יִנָּצֵל	יַצִּיל	יֻצַּל
	3fs	תִּפֹּל	תִּגַּע	תִּתֵּן	תִּנָּצֵל	תַּצִּיל	תֻּצַּל
	1cp	נִפֹּל	נִגַּע	נִתֵּן	נִנָּצֵל	נַצִּיל	נֻצַּל
	2mp	תִּפְּלוּ	תִּגְּעוּ	תִּתְּנוּ	תִּנָּצְלוּ	תַּצִּילוּ	תֻּצְּלוּ
	2mp	תִּפֹּלְנָה	תִּגַּעְנָה	תִּתֵּנָּה	תִּנָּצַלְנָה	תַּצֵּלְנָה	תֻּצַּלְנָה
	3mp	יִפְּלוּ	יִגְּעוּ	יִתְּנוּ	יִנָּצְלוּ	יַצִּילוּ	יֻצְּלוּ
	3fp	תִּפֹּלְנָה	תִּגַּעְנָה	תִּתֵּנָּה	תִּנָּצַלְנָה	תַּצֵּלְנָה	תֻּצַּלְנָה
Imv	2ms	נְפֹל	גַּע	תֵּן	הִנָּצֵל	הַצֵּל	
	2fs	נִפְלִי	גְּעִי	תְּנִי	הִנָּצְלִי	הַצִּילִי	
	2mp	נִפְלוּ	גְּעוּ	תְּנוּ	הִנָּצְלוּ	הַצִּילוּ	
	2fp	נְפֹלְנָה	גַּעְנָה	תֵּנָּה	הִנָּצַלְנָה	הַצֵּלְנָה	
Inf	Abs	נָפוֹל	נָגוֹעַ	נָתוֹן	הִנָּצֵל	הַצֵּל	הֻצֵּל
	Cs	נְפֹל	גַּעַת	תֵּת	הִנָּצֵל	הַצִּיל	הֻצַּל
	Alt		נְגֹעַ	נְתֹן			
Ptc	Act	נֹפֵל	נֹגֵעַ	נֹתֵן		מַצִּיל	
	Pass	נָפוּל	נָגוּעַ	נָתוּן	נִצָּל		מֻצָּל
W		וַיִּפֹּל	וַיִּגַּע	וַיִּתֵּן	וַיִּנָּצֵל	וַיַּצֵּל	וַיֻּצַּל

22.6   Medial Guttural Verb

		Qal *choose*	Nifal *be chosen*	Piel *refuse*	Piel *hasten*	Pual *blessed*	Hitpael *bless oneself*
Pf	1cs	בָּחַרְתִּי	נִבְחַרְתִּי	מֵאַנְתִּי	מִהַרְתִּי	בֹּרַכְתִּי	הִתְבָּרַכְתִּי
	2ms	בָּחַרְתָּ	נִבְחַרְתָּ	מֵאַנְתָּ	מִהַרְתָּ	בֹּרַכְתָּ	הִתְבָּרַכְתָּ
	2fs	בָּחַרְתְּ	נִבְחַרְתְּ	מֵאַנְתְּ	מִהַרְתְּ	בֹּרַכְתְּ	הִתְבָּרַכְתְּ
	3ms	בָּחַר	נִבְחַר	מֵאֵן	מִהַר	בֹּרַךְ	הִתְבָּרֵךְ
	3fs	בָּחֲרָה	נִבְחֲרָה	מֵאֲנָה	מִהֲרָה	בֹּרְכָה	הִתְבָּרְכָה
	1cp	בָּחַרְנוּ	נִבְחַרְנוּ	מֵאַנּוּ	מִהַרְנוּ	בֹּרַכְנוּ	הִתְבָּרַכְנוּ
	2mp	בְּחַרְתֶּם	נִבְחַרְתֶּם	מֵאַנְתֶּם	מִהַרְתֶּם	בֹּרַכְתֶּם	הִתְבָּרַכְתֶּם
	2fp	בְּחַרְתֶּן	נִבְחַרְתֶּן	מֵאַנְתֶּן	מִהַרְתֶּן	בֹּרַכְתֶּן	הִתְבָּרַכְתֶּן
	3cp	בָּחֲרוּ	נִבְחֲרוּ	מֵאֲנוּ	מִהֲרוּ	בֹּרְכוּ	הִתְבָּרְכוּ
Imf	1cs	אֶבְחַר	אֶבָּחֵר	אֲמָאֵן	אֲמַהֵר	אֲבֹרַךְ	אֶתְבָּרֵךְ
	2ms	תִּבְחַר	תִּבָּחֵר	תְּמָאֵן	תְּמַהֵר	תְּבֹרַךְ	תִּתְבָּרֵךְ
	2fs	תִּבְחֲרִי	תִּבָּחֲרִי	תְּמָאֲנִי	תְּמַהֲרִי	תְּבֹרְכִי	תִּתְבָּרְכִי
	3ms	יִבְחַר	יִבָּחֵר	יְמָאֵן	יְמַהֵר	יְבֹרַךְ	יִתְבָּרֵךְ
	3fs	תִּבְחַר	תִּבָּחֵר	תְּמָאֵן	תְּמַהֵר	תְּבֹרַךְ	תִּתְבָּרֵךְ
	1cp	נִבְחַר	נִבָּחֵר	נְמָאֵן	נְמַהֵר	נְבֹרַךְ	נִתְבָּרֵךְ
	2mp	תִּבְחֲרוּ	תִּבָּחֲרוּ	תְּמָאֲנוּ	תְּמַהֲרוּ	תְּבֹרְכוּ	תִּתְבָּרְכוּ
	2fp	תִּבְחַרְנָה	תִּבָּחַרְנָה	תְּמָאֵנָה	תְּמַהֵרְנָה	תְּבֹרַכְנָה	תִּתְבָּרַכְנָה
	3mp	יִבְחֲרוּ	יִבָּחֲרוּ	יְמָאֲנוּ	יְמַהֲרוּ	יְבֹרְכוּ	יִתְבָּרְכוּ
	3fp	תִּבְחַרְנָה	תִּבָּחַרְנָה	תְּמָאֵנָה	תְּמַהֵרְנָה	תְּבֹרַכְנָה	תִּתְבָּרַכְנָה
Imv	2ms	בְּחַר	הִבָּחֵר	מָאֵן	מַהֵר		הִתְבָּרֵךְ
	2fs	בַּחֲרִי	הִבָּחֲרִי	מָאֲנִי	מַהֲרִי		הִתְבָּרְכִי
Inf	2mp	בַּחֲרוּ	הִבָּחֲרוּ	מָאֲנוּ	מַהֲרוּ		הִתְבָּרְכוּ
	2fp	בְּחַרְנָה	הִבָּחַרְנָה	מָאֵנָה	מַהֵרְנָה		הִתְבָּרַכְנָה
	Abs	בָּחוֹר	נִבְחוֹר	מָאֵן	מַהֵר		הִתְבָּרֵךְ
	Cs	בְּחֹר	הִבָּחֵר	מָאֵן	מַהֵר		הִתְבָּרֵךְ
Ptc	Act	בֹּחֵר	נִבְחָר	מְמָאֵן	מְמַהֵר		מִתְבָּרֵךְ
	Pass	בָּחוּר				מְבֹרָךְ	
W		וַיִּבְחַר	וַיִּבָּחֵר	וַיְמָאֵן	וַיְמַהֵר		וַיִּתְבָּרֵךְ

22.7   Hollow Verb

	Qal	Qal	Nifal	Hifil	Hofal	Polel	Polal	Hitpolel
Pf	*return*	*die*	*be firm*	*raise*				
1cs	שַׁבְתִּי	מַתִּי	נְכוּנוֹתִי	הֲקִימוֹתִי	הוּקַמְתִּי	קוֹמַמְתִּי	קוֹמַמְתִּי	הִתְקוֹמַמְתִּי
2ms	שַׁבְתָּ	מַתָּה	נְכוּנוֹתָ	הֲקִימוֹתָ	הוּקַמְתָּ	קוֹמַמְתָּ	קוֹמַמְתָּ	הִתְקוֹמַמְתָּ
2fs	שַׁבְתְּ	מַתְּ	נְכוּנוֹת	הֲקִימוֹת	הוּקַמְתְּ	קוֹמַמְתְּ	קוֹמַמְתְּ	הִתְקוֹמַמְתְּ
3ms	שָׁב	מֵת	נָכוֹן	הֵקִים	הוּקַם	קוֹמֵם	קוֹמַם	הִתְקוֹמֵם
3fs	שָׁבָה	מֵתָה	נָכוֹנָה	הֵקִימָה	הוּקְמָה	קוֹמְמָה	קוֹמֲמָה	הִתְקוֹמְמָה
1cp	שַׁבְנוּ	מַתְנוּ	נְכוּנוֹנוּ	הֲקִימוֹנוּ	הוּקַמְנוּ	קוֹמַמְנוּ	קוֹמַמְנוּ	הִתְקוֹמַמְנוּ
2mp	שַׁבְתֶּם	מַתֶּם	נְכוּנוֹתֶם	הֲקִימוֹתֶם	הוּקַמְתֶּם	קוֹמַמְתֶּם	קוֹמַמְתֶּם	הִתְקוֹמַמְתֶּם
2fp	שַׁבְתֶּן	מַתֶּן	נְכוּנוֹתֶן	הֲקִימוֹתֶן	הוּקַמְתֶּן	קוֹמַמְתֶּן	קוֹמַמְתֶּן	הִתְקוֹמַמְתֶּן
3cp	שָׁבוּ	מֵתוּ	נָכוֹנוּ	הֵקִימוּ	הוּקְמוּ	קוֹמְמוּ	קוֹמְמוּ	הִתְקוֹמְמוּ
Imf								
1cs	אָשׁוּב	אָמוּת	אֶכּוֹן	אָקִים	אוּקַם	אֲקוֹמֵם	אֲקוֹמַם	אֶתְקוֹמֵם
2ms	תָּשׁוּב	etc.	תִּכּוֹן	תָּקִים	תּוּקַם	תְּקוֹמֵם	תְּקוֹמַם	תִּתְקוֹמֵם
2fs	תָּשׁוּבִי		תִּכּוֹנִי	תָּקִימִי	תּוּקְמִי	תְּקוֹמְמִי	תְּקוֹמְמִי	תִּתְקוֹמְמִי
3ms	יָשׁוּב		יִכּוֹן	יָקִים	יוּקַם	יְקוֹמֵם	יְקוֹמַם	יִתְקוֹמֵם
3fs	תָּשׁוּב		תִּכּוֹן	תָּקִים	תּוּקַם	תְּקוֹמֵם	תְּקוֹמַם	תִּתְקוֹמֵם
1cp	נָשׁוּב		נִכּוֹן	נָקִים	נוּקַם	נְקוֹמֵם	נְקוֹמַם	נִתְקוֹמֵם
2mp	תָּשׁוּבוּ		תִּכּוֹנוּ	תָּקִימוּ	תּוּקְמוּ	תְּקוֹמְמוּ	תְּקוֹמְמוּ	תִּתְקוֹמְמוּ
2fp	תְּשׁוּבֶינָה		תִּכּוֹנָה	תְּקִמֶינָה	תּוּקַמְנָה	תְּקוֹמֵמְנָה	תְּקוֹמַמְנָה	תִּתְקוֹמֵמְנָה
3mp	יָשׁוּבוּ		יִכּוֹנוּ	יָקִימוּ	יוּקְמוּ	יְקוֹמְמוּ	יְקוֹמְמוּ	יִתְקוֹמְמוּ
3fp	תְּשׁוּבֶינָה		תִּכּוֹנָה	תְּקִמֶינָה	תּוּקַמְנָה	תְּקוֹמֵמְנָה	תְּקוֹמַמְנָה	תִּתְקוֹמֵמְנָה
Imv								
2ms	שׁוּב		הִכּוֹן	הָקֵם		קוֹמֵם		הִתְקוֹמֵם
2fs	שׁוּבִי		הִכּוֹנִי	הָקִימִי		קוֹמְמִי		הִתְקוֹמְמִי
2mp	שׁוּבוּ		הִכּוֹנוּ	הָקִימוּ		קוֹמְמוּ		הִתְקוֹמְמוּ
2fp	שֹׁבְנָה		הִכּוֹנָה	הָקֵמְנָה		קוֹמֵמְנָה		הִתְקוֹמֵמְנָה
IA	שׁוֹב		הִכּוֹן	הָקֵם				הִתְקוֹמֵם
IC	שׁוּב		הִכּוֹן	הָקִים	הוּקֵם	קוֹמֵם		הִתְקוֹמֵם
APtc	שָׁב	מֵת	נָכוֹן	מֵקִים		מְקוֹמֵם		מִתְקוֹמֵם
PPtc					מוּקָם		מְקוֹמָן	
W	וַיָּשָׁב		וַיִּכּוֹן	וַיָּקֶם	וַיּוּקַם	וַיְקוֹמֵם	וַיְקוֹמַם	
Juss	יָשֹׁב		יִכּוֹן	יָקֵם	יוּקַם	יְקוֹמֵם	יְקוֹמַם	

22.8   Geminate Verb

	Qal	Qal	Nifal	Hifil	Hofal	Polel	Polal	Hitpolel
Pf	*surround*	*finished*				*to roll*		
1cs	סַבּוֹתִי	תַּמּוֹתִי	נְסַבּוֹתִי	הֲסִבּוֹתִי	הוּסַבּוֹתִי	גּוֹלַלְתִּי	גּוֹלַלְתִּי	הִתְגּוֹלַלְתִּי
2ms	סַבּוֹתָ	תַּמּוֹתָ	נְסַבּוֹתָ	הֲסִבּוֹתָ	הוּסַבּוֹתָ	גּוֹלַלְתָּ	גּוֹלַלְתָּ	הִתְגּוֹלַלְתָּ
2fs	סַבּוֹת	תַּמּוֹת	נְסַבּוֹת	הֲסִבּוֹת	הוּסַבּוֹת	גּוֹלַלְתְּ	גּוֹלַלְתְּ	הִתְגּוֹלַלְתְּ
3ms	סָבַב	תַּם	נָסַב	הֵסֵב	הוּסַב	גּוֹלֵל	גּוֹלַל	הִתְגּוֹלֵל
3fs	סָבְבָה	תַּמָּה	נָסַבָּה	הֵסַבָּה	הוּסַבָּה	גּוֹלְלָה	גּוֹלְלָה	הִתְגּוֹלְלָה
1cp	סַבּוֹנוּ	תַּמּוֹנוּ	נְסַבּוֹנוּ	הֲסִבּוֹנוּ	הוּסַבּוֹנוּ	גּוֹלַלְנוּ	גּוֹלַלְנוּ	הִתְגּוֹלַלְנוּ
2mp	סַבּוֹתֶם	תַּמּוֹתֶם	נְסַבּוֹתֶם	הֲסִבּוֹתֶם	הוּסַבּוֹתֶם	גּוֹלַלְתֶּם	גּוֹלַלְתֶּם	הִתְגּוֹלַלְתֶּם
2fp	סַבּוֹתֶן	תַּמּוֹתֶן	נְסַבּוֹתֶן	הֲסִבּוֹתֶן	הוּסַבּוֹתֶן	גּוֹלַלְתֶּן	גּוֹלַלְתֶּן	הִתְגּוֹלַלְתֶּן
3cp	סָבְבוּ	תַּמּוּ	נָסַבּוּ	הֵסֵבּוּ	הוּסַבּוּ	גּוֹלְלוּ	גּוֹלְלוּ	הִתְגּוֹלְלוּ
Imf								
1cs	אָסֹב	אֵתַּם	אֶסַּב	אָסֵב	אוּסַב	אֲגוֹלֵל	אֲגוֹלַל	אֶתְגּוֹלֵל
2ms	תָּסֹב	תֵּתַּם	תִּסַּב	תָּסֵב	תּוּסַב	תְּגוֹלֵל	תְּגוֹלַל	תִּתְגּוֹלֵל
2fs	תָּסֹבִּי	תֵּתַּמִּי	תִּסַּבִּי	תָּסֵבִּי	תּוּסַבִּי	תְּגוֹלְלִי	תְּגוֹלְלִי	תִּתְגּוֹלְלִי
3ms	יָסֹב	יֵתַּם	יִסַּב	יָסֵב	יוּסַב	יְגוֹלֵל	יְגוֹלַל	יִתְגּוֹלֵל
3fs	תָּסֹב	תֵּתַּם	תִּסַּב	תָּסֵב	תּוּסַב	תְּגוֹלֵל	תְּגוֹלַל	תִּתְגּוֹלֵל
1cp	נָסֹב	נֵתַּם	נִסַּב	נָסֵב	נוּסַב	נְגוֹלֵל	נְגוֹלַל	נִתְגּוֹלֵל
2mp	תָּסֹבּוּ	תֵּתַּמּוּ	תִּסַּבּוּ	תָּסֵבּוּ	תּוּסַבּוּ	תְּגוֹלְלוּ	תְּגוֹלְלוּ	תִּתְגּוֹלְלוּ
2fp	תְּסֻבֶּינָה	תְּתַמֶּינָה	תִּסַּבֶּינָה	תְּסִבֶּינָה	תּוּסַבֶּינָה	תְּגוֹלֵלְנָה	תְּגוֹלַלְנָה	תִּתְגּוֹלֵלְנָה
3mp	יָסֹבּוּ	יֵתַּמּוּ	יִסַּבּוּ	יָסֵבּוּ	יוּסַבּוּ	יְגוֹלְלוּ	יְגוֹלְלוּ	יִתְגּוֹלְלוּ
3fp	תְּסֻבֶּינָה	תְּתַמֶּינָה	תִּסַּבֶּינָה	תְּסִבֶּינָה	תּוּסַבֶּינָה	תְּגוֹלֵלְנָה	תְּגוֹלַלְנָה	תִּתְגּוֹלֵלְנָה
Imv								
2ms	סֹב	תַּם	הִסַּב	הָסֵב		גּוֹלֵל		הִתְגּוֹלֵל
2fs	סֹבִּי	תַּמִּי	הִסַּבִּי	הָסֵבִּי		גּוֹלְלִי		הִתְגּוֹלְלִי
2mp	סֹבּוּ	תַּמּוּ	הִסַּבּוּ	הָסֵבּוּ		גּוֹלְלוּ		הִתְגּוֹלְלוּ
2fp	סֻבְנָה	תַּמְנָה	הִסַּבֶּינָה	הֲסִבֶּינָה		גּוֹלֵלְנָה		הִתְגּוֹלֵלְנָה
IA	סָבוֹב		הִסֹּב	הָסֵב		גּוֹלֵל		הִתְגּוֹלֵל
IC	סֹב	תַּם	הִסֵּב	הָסֵב	הֻסֵב	גּוֹלֵל		הִתְגּוֹלֵל
Aptc	סֹבֵב	תַּם		מֵסֵב		מְגוֹלֵל	מְגוֹלָל	מִתְגּוֹלֵל
PPtc	סָבוּב				מוּסָב			
W	וַיָּסָב	וַיִּתַּם	וַיִּסַּב	וַיַּסֶּב[3]	וַיּוּסַב			
Jus	יָסֹב	יֵתַּם	יִסַּב	יָסֵב	יוּסַב			

---

[3] The *dagesh* may be a result of Aramaic influence (cf. Gesenius §67g).

22.9   Initial *Yod* Verb

	Orig. ו						Orig. י	
	Qal	*Qal*	*Qal*	*Nifal*	*Hifil*	*Hofal*	*Qal*	*Hifil*
Pf	sit / dwell	fear	be able	inhabited	made to sit	made inhabited	be well	made well
1cs	יָשַׁבְתִּי	יָרֵאתִי	יָכֹלְתִּי	נוֹשַׁבְתִּי	הוֹשַׁבְתִּי	הוּשַׁבְתִּי	יָטַב	הֵיטַבְתִּי
2ms	יָשַׁבְתָּ	יָרֵאתָ	יָכֹלְתָּ	נוֹשַׁבְתָּ	הוֹשַׁבְתָּ	הוּשַׁבְתָּ		הֵיטַבְתָּ
2fs	יָשַׁבְתְּ	יָרֵאת	יָכֹלְתְּ	נוֹשַׁבְתְּ	הוֹשַׁבְתְּ	הוּשַׁבְתְּ		הֵיטַבְתְּ
3ms	יָשַׁב	יָרֵא	יָכֹל	נוֹשַׁב	הוֹשִׁיב	הוּשַׁב		הֵיטִיב
3fs	יָשְׁבָה	יָרְאָה	יָכְלָה	נוֹשְׁבָה	הוֹשִׁיבָה	הוּשְׁבָה		הֵיטִיבָה
1cp	יָשַׁבְנוּ	יָרֵאנוּ	יָכֹלְנוּ	נוֹשַׁבְנוּ	הוֹשַׁבְנוּ	הוּשַׁבְנוּ		הֵיטַבְנוּ
2mp	יְשַׁבְתֶּם	יְרֵאתֶם	יְכָלְתֶּם	נוֹשַׁבְתֶּם	הוֹשַׁבְתֶּם	הוּשַׁבְתֶּם		הֵיטַבְתֶּם
2fp	יְשַׁבְתֶּן	יְרֵאתֶן	יְכָלְתֶּן	נוֹשַׁבְתֶּן	הוֹשַׁבְתֶּן	הוּשַׁבְתֶּן		הֵיטַבְתֶּן
3cp	יָשְׁבוּ	יָרְאוּ	יָכְלוּ	נוֹשְׁבוּ	הוֹשִׁיבוּ	הוּשְׁבוּ		הֵיטִיבוּ
Imf								
1cs	אֵשֵׁב	אִירָא	אוּכַל	אִוָּשֵׁב	אוֹשִׁיב	אוּשַׁב	אִיטַב	אֵיטִיב
2ms	תֵּשֵׁב	תִּירָא	תּוּכַל	תִּוָּשֵׁב	תּוֹשִׁיב	תּוּשַׁב	תִּיטַב	תֵּיטִיב
2fs	תֵּשְׁבִי	תִּירְאִי	תּוּכְלִי	תִּוָּשְׁבִי	תּוֹשִׁיבִי	תּוּשְׁבִי	תִּיטְבִי	תֵּיטִיבִי
3ms	יֵשֵׁב	יִירָא	יוּכַל	יִוָּשֵׁב	יוֹשִׁיב	יוּשַׁב	יִיטַב	יֵיטִיב
3fs	תֵּשֵׁב	תִּירָא	תּוּכַל	תִּוָּשֵׁב	תּוֹשִׁיב	תּוּשַׁב	תִּיטַב	תֵּיטִיב
1cp	נֵשֵׁב	נִירָא	נוּכַל	נִוָּשֵׁב	נוֹשִׁיב	נוּשַׁב	נִיטַב	נֵיטִיב
2mp	תֵּשְׁבוּ	תִּירְאוּ	תּוּכְלוּ	תִּוָּשְׁבוּ	תּוֹשִׁיבוּ	תּוּשְׁבוּ	תִּיטְבוּ	תֵּיטִיבוּ
2fp	תֵּשַׁבְנָה	תִּירֶאנָה	תּוּכַלְנָה	תִּוָּשַׁבְנָה	תּוֹשַׁבְנָה	תּוּשַׁבְנָה	תִּיטַבְנָה	תֵּיטֵבְנָה
3mp	יֵשְׁבוּ	יִירְאוּ	יוּכְלוּ	יִוָּשְׁבוּ	יוֹשִׁיבוּ	יוּשְׁבוּ	יִיטְבוּ	יֵיטִיבוּ
3fp	תֵּשַׁבְנָה	תִּירֶאנָה	תּוּכַלְנָה	תִּוָּשַׁבְנָה	תּוֹשַׁבְנָה	תּוּשַׁבְנָה	תִּיטַבְנָה	תֵּיטֵבְנָה
Imv								
2ms	שֵׁב	יְרָא		הִוָּשֵׁב	הוֹשֵׁב			הֵיטֵב
2fs	שְׁבִי	יִרְאִי		הִוָּשְׁבִי	הוֹשִׁיבִי			הֵיטִיבִי
2mp	שְׁבוּ	יִרְאוּ		הִוָּשְׁבוּ	הוֹשִׁיבוּ			הֵיטִיבוּ
2fp	שֵׁבְנָה	יְרֶאנָה		הִוָּשַׁבְנָה	הוֹשֵׁבְנָה			הֵיטֵבְנָה
IA	יָשׁוֹב	יָרוֹא		הִוָּשֵׁב	הוֹשֵׁב			הֵיטֵב
IC	שֶׁבֶת	יְרֹא		הִוָּשֵׁב	הוֹשִׁיב	הוּשֵׁב		הֵיטִיב
Aptc	יֹשֵׁב	יָרֵא			מוֹשִׁיב		יָטֵב	מֵיטִיב
PPtc	יָשׁוּב			נוֹשָׁב		מוּשָׁב		

22.10   Final ה, ח, or ע Verb

		Qal *send*	Nifal *sent*	Hifil *set loose*	Hofal *let loose*	Piel *send*	Pual *sent*	Hitpael
Pf	1cs	שָׁלַחְתִּי	נִשְׁלַחְתִּי	הִשְׁלַחְתִּי	הָשְׁלַחְתִּי	שִׁלַּחְתִּי	שֻׁלַּחְתִּי	הִשְׁתַּלַּחְתִּי
	2ms	שָׁלַחְתָּ	נִשְׁלַחְתָּ	הִשְׁלַחְתָּ	הָשְׁלַחְתָּ	שִׁלַּחְתָּ	שֻׁלַּחְתָּ	הִשְׁתַּלַּחְתָּ
	2fs	שָׁלַחַתְּ	נִשְׁלַחַתְּ	הִשְׁלַחַתְּ	הָשְׁלַחַתְּ	שִׁלַּחַתְּ	שֻׁלַּחַתְּ	הִשְׁתַּלַּחַתְּ
	3ms	שָׁלַח	נִשְׁלַח	הִשְׁלִיחַ	הָשְׁלַח	שִׁלַּח	שֻׁלַּח	הִשְׁתַּלַּח
	3fs	שָׁלְחָה	נִשְׁלְחָה	הִשְׁלִיחָה	הָשְׁלְחָה	שִׁלְּחָה	שֻׁלְּחָה	הִשְׁתַּלְּחָה
	1cp	שָׁלַחְנוּ	נִשְׁלַחְנוּ	הִשְׁלַחְנוּ	הָשְׁלַחְנוּ	שִׁלַּחְנוּ	שֻׁלַּחְנוּ	הִשְׁתַּלַּחְנוּ
	2mp	שְׁלַחְתֶּם	נִשְׁלַחְתֶּם	הִשְׁלַחְתֶּם	הָשְׁלַחְתֶּם	שִׁלַּחְתֶּם	שֻׁלַּחְתֶּם	הִשְׁתַּלַּחְתֶּם
	2fp	שְׁלַחְתֶּן	נִשְׁלַחְתֶּן	הִשְׁלַחְתֶּן	הָשְׁלַחְתֶּן	שִׁלַּחְתֶּן	שֻׁלַּחְתֶּן	הִשְׁתַּלַּחְתֶּן
	3cp	שָׁלְחוּ	נִשְׁלְחוּ	הִשְׁלִיחוּ	הָשְׁלְחוּ	שִׁלְּחוּ	שֻׁלְּחוּ	הִשְׁתַּלְּחוּ
Imf	1cs	אֶשְׁלַח	אֶשָּׁלַח	אַשְׁלִיחַ	אָשְׁלַח	אֲשַׁלַּח	אֲשֻׁלַּח	אֶשְׁתַּלַּח
	2ms	תִּשְׁלַח	תִּשָּׁלַח	תַּשְׁלִיחַ	תָּשְׁלַח	תְּשַׁלַּח	תְּשֻׁלַּח	תִּשְׁתַּלַּח
	2fs	תִּשְׁלְחִי	תִּשָּׁלְחִי	תַּשְׁלִיחִי	תָּשְׁלְחִי	תְּשַׁלְּחִי	תְּשֻׁלְּחִי	תִּשְׁתַּלְּחִי
	3ms	יִשְׁלַח	יִשָּׁלַח	יַשְׁלִיחַ	יָשְׁלַח	יְשַׁלַּח	יְשֻׁלַּח	יִשְׁתַּלַּח
	3fs	תִּשְׁלַח	תִּשָּׁלַח	תַּשְׁלִיחַ	תָּשְׁלַח	תְּשַׁלַּח	תְּשֻׁלַּח	תִּשְׁתַּלַּח
	1cp	נִשְׁלַח	נִשָּׁלַח	נַשְׁלִיחַ	נָשְׁלַח	נְשַׁלַּח	נְשֻׁלַּח	נִשְׁתַּלַּח
	2mp	תִּשְׁלְחוּ	תִּשָּׁלְחוּ	תַּשְׁלִיחוּ	תָּשְׁלְחוּ	תְּשַׁלְּחוּ	תְּשֻׁלְּחוּ	תִּשְׁתַּלְּחוּ
	2mp	תִּשְׁלַחְנָה	תִּשָּׁלַחְנָה	תַּשְׁלַחְנָה	תָּשְׁלַחְנָה	תְּשַׁלַּחְנָה	תְּשֻׁלַּחְנָה	תִּשְׁתַּלַּחְנָה
	3mp	יִשְׁלְחוּ	יִשָּׁלְחוּ	יַשְׁלִיחוּ	יָשְׁלְחוּ	יְשַׁלְּחוּ	יְשֻׁלְּחוּ	יִשְׁתַּלְּחוּ
	3fp	תִּשְׁלַחְנָה	תִּשָּׁלַחְנָה	תַּשְׁלַחְנָה	תָּשְׁלַחְנָה	תְּשַׁלַּחְנָה	תְּשֻׁלַּחְנָה	תִּשְׁתַּלַּחְנָה
Imv	2ms	שְׁלַח	הִשָּׁלַח	הַשְׁלַח		שַׁלַּח		הִשְׁתַּלַּח
	2fs	שִׁלְחִי	הִשָּׁלְחִי	הַשְׁלִיחִי		שַׁלְּחִי		הִשְׁתַּלְּחִי
	2mp	שִׁלְחוּ	הִשָּׁלְחוּ	הַשְׁלִיחוּ		שַׁלְּחוּ		הִשְׁתַּלְּחוּ
	2fp	שְׁלַחְנָה	הִשָּׁלַחְנָה	הַשְׁלַחְנָה		שַׁלַּחְנָה		הִשְׁתַּלַּחְנָה
Inf	Ab	שָׁלוֹחַ	נִשְׁלוֹחַ הִשָּׁלֵחַ	הַשְׁלֵחַ		שַׁלֵּחַ		הִשְׁתַּלֵּחַ
	Cs	שְׁלוֹחַ	הִשָּׁלַח	הַשְׁלִיחַ		שַׁלַּח		הִשְׁתַּלַּח
Ptc	Act	שֹׁלֵחַ		מַשְׁלִיחַ		מְשַׁלֵּחַ		מִשְׁתַּלֵּחַ
	Pass	שָׁלוּחַ	נִשְׁלָח		מָשְׁלָח		מְשֻׁלָּח	

22.11   Doubly Weak Verbs

	פ"ן & ל Guttural				ל"א & פ"ן		
	Qal	*Nifal*	*Hifil*	*Piel*	*Qal*	*Nifal*	*Hifil*
Perf	נָגַע	נִגַּע	הִגִּיעַ	נִגַּע	נָשָׂא	נִשָּׂא	הִשִּׂיא
Imf	יִגַּע	etc. like III-Gutt.	יַגִּיעַ	יְנַגַּע	יִשָּׂא	etc. Like III-*Alef*	יַשִּׂיא
Jussive			יַגַּע	etc. like III-Gutt.			
Imv	גַּע		הַגַּע		שָׂא		הַשֵּׂא
Ptc	נֹגֵעַ		מַגִּיעַ		נֹשֵׂא		מַשִּׂיא
Inf A	נָגוֹעַ		הַגֵּעַ		נָשׂוֹא		הַשֵּׂא
Inf. C.	נְגֹעַ גַּעַת		הַגִּיעַ		שְׂאֵת		הַשִּׂיא

	ל"ה & פ"ן				פ Guttural & ל"א			
	Qal		*Hifil*	*Hofal*	*Qal*	*Nifal*	*Hifil*	
Perf	נָטָה	הִטָּה הִכָּה הֻטָּה	יִכָּה		חָטָא	נֶחְבָּא	הֶחְטִיא הֶחְבִּיא	
Imf	יִטֶּה	יַטֶּה יַכֶּה	יֻכֶּה	יִכֶּה	יֶחֱטָא	יֵחָבֵא	יַחֲטִיא יַחְבִּיא	
Jussive	יֵט יֵט	יַךְ			יֶחֱטָא			יַחֲטֵא
Imv	נְטֵה	הַכֵּה			חֲטָא	הֵחָבֵא	הַחֲטֵא הַחְבֵּא	
Pt c	נֹטֶה	מַטֶּה מַכֶּה	מֻכֶּה		חֹטֵא	נֶחְבָּא	מַחֲטִיא מַחְבִּיא	
Inf A	נָטֹה	הַטֵּה הַכֵּה	הֻכֵּה		חָטוֹא		הַחֲטֵא הַחְבֵּא	
Inf. C.	נְטוֹת נְטוֹת	הַטּוֹת הַכּוֹת	הֻכּוֹת		חֲטֹא	הֵחָבֵא	הַחֲטִיא הַחְבִּיא	

	פ Guttural & ל"ה				ל"ה & פ"א	
	Qal		*Nifal*	*Hifil*	*Qal*	*Nifal*
Perf	עָשָׂה עָלָה	נַעֲשָׂה נַעֲלָה		הֶעֱלָה	אָפָה	נֶאֱפָה
Imf	יַעֲשֶׂה יַעֲלֶה	יֵעָשֶׂה		יַעֲלֶה	יֹאפֶה	יֵאָפֶה
Jussive	יַעַשׂ יַעַל	יֵעָשׂ		יַעַל		
Imv	עֲשֵׂה עֲלֵה	הֵעָשֵׂה הֵעָלֵה	הַעַל הַעֲלֵה		אֱפֵה	
Ptc	עֹשֶׂה עֹלֶה	נַעֲשֶׂה		מַעֲלֶה	אֹפֶה	
Inf A	עָשֹׂה עָלֹה	נַעֲשֹׂה		הַעֲלֵה	אָפֹה	
Inf. C.	עֲשׂוֹת עֲלוֹת	הֵעָשׂוֹת		הַעֲלוֹת	אֲפוֹה	הֵאָפוֹת

Doubly Weak Verbs, Cont'd

	פ"ו & ל-Guttural					ל"א & פ"ו		
	Qal	*Nifal*	*Hifil*	*Hofal*	*Hitpael*	*Qal*	*Hifil*	*Hofal*
Perf	יָדַע	נוֹדַע	הוֹדִיעַ	הוֹדַע	הִתְוַדַּע	יָצָא	הוֹצִיא	הוּצָא
Imf	יֵדַע	יִוָּדַע	יוֹדִיעַ		יִתְוַדַּע	יֵצֵא	יוֹצִיא	יוּצָא
Jussive			יוֹדַע				יוֹצֵא	
Imv	דַּע	הִוָּדַע	הוֹדַע		הִתְוַדַּע	צֵא	הוֹצֵא	
Ptc	יֹדֵעַ	נוֹדָע	מוֹדִיעַ	מוֹדָע	מִתְוַדֵּע	יֹצֵא	מוֹצִיא	מוּצָא
Inf A	יָדוֹעַ	נַעֲשֹה	הוֹדֵעַ			יָצוֹא	הוֹצֵא	
Inf. C.	דַּעַת	הֵעָשֹוֹת	הוֹדִיעַ		הִתְוַדַּע	צֵאת	הוֹצִיא	

	ל"א & ע"ו		
	Qal	*Hifil*	*Hofal*
Perf	בָּא	הֵבִיא	הוּבָא
Imf	יָבֹא	יָבִיא	יוּבָא
Jussive		יוֹבֵא	
Imv	בֹּא	הָבֵא	
Ptc	בָּא	מֵבִיא	מוּבָא
Inf A	בּוֹא	הָבֵא	
Inf. C.	בֹּא	הָבִיא	הוּבָא

22.12   Pronominal Suffixes

22.12.1 Perfect Verb with Pronominal Suffixes

	Qal								Piel
	1cs	2ms	2fs	3ms	3fs	1cp	2m/fp	3cp	3ms
Suff	קָטַלְתִּי	קָטַלְתָּ	קָטַלְתְּ	קָטַל	קָטְלָה	קָטַלְנוּ	קְטַלְתֶּם/ן	קָטְלוּ	קִטֵּל
1cs		קְטַלְתַּנִי	קְטַלְתִּנִי	קְטָלַנִי	קְטָלַתְנִי		קְטַלְתּוּנִי	קְטָלוּנִי	קִטְּלַנִי
2ms	קְטַלְתִּיךָ			קְטָלְךָ	קְטָלַתְךָ	קְטַלְנוּךָ		קְטָלוּךָ	קִטֶּלְךָ
2fs	קְטַלְתִּיךְ			קְטָלֵךְ	קְטָלַתֶךְ	קְטַלְנוּךְ		קְטָלוּךְ	קִטְּלֵךְ
3ms	קְטַלְתִּיהוּ / קְטַלְתִּיו	קְטַלְתָּהוּ	קְטַלְתִּיהוּ	קְטָלוֹ / קְטָלַתּוּ	קְטָלַתְהוּ / קְטָלַהוּ	קְטַלְנוּהוּ	קְטַלְתּוּהוּ	קְטָלוּהוּ	קִטְּלוֹ
3fs	קְטַלְתִּיהָ	קְטַלְתָּהּ	קְטַלְתִּיהָ	קְטָלָהּ	קְטָלַתָהּ	קְטַלְנוּהָ			קִטְּלָהּ
1cp	קְטַלְתִּנוּ	קְטַלְתָּנוּ	קְטַלְתִּינוּ	קְטָלָנוּ	קְטָלַתְנוּ		קְטַלְתּוּנוּ	קְטָלוּנוּ	קִטְּלָנוּ
2mp	קְטַלְתִּיכֶם					קְטַלְנוּכֶם			
2fp	קְטַלְתִּיכֶן								
3mp	קְטַלְתִּים	קְטַלְתָּם	קְטַלְתִּים	קְטָלָם	קְטָלַתָם	קְטָלוּם			קִטְּלָם
3fp	קְטַלְתִּין	קְטַלְתָּן	קְטַלְתִּין	קְטָלָן	קְטָלַתָן				קִטְּלָן

22.12.2 Imperfect Verb with Pronominal Suffixes

	Qal Imf			Qal Imv		Qal Infin C	Piel Imf	Hifil Imf
	3ms	נ energic see §12.1.1	3mp	Sing.	Plur.		3ms	3ms
Suff	יִקְטֹל			קְטֹל	קִטְלוּ	קְטֹל	יְקַטֵּל	יַקְטִיל
1cs	יִקְטְלֵנִי	יִקְטְלֵנִּי	יִקְטְלוּנִי	קְטָלֵנִי	קְטָלוּנִי	קָטְלֵנִי	יְקַטְּלֵנִי	יַקְטִילֵנִי
2ms	יִקְטָלְךָ		יִקְטְלוּךָ			קָטְלְךָ / קָטְלֶךָ	יְקַטֶּלְךָ	יַקְטִילְךָ
2fs	יִקְטְלֵךְ		יִקְטְלוּךְ			קָטְלֵךְ	יְקַטְּלֵךְ	יַקְטִילֵךְ
3ms	יִקְטְלֵהוּ	יִקְטְלֶנּוּ	יִקְטְלוּהוּ	קְטָלֵהוּ	קְטָלוּהוּ	קָטְלוֹ	יְקַטְּלֵהוּ	etc.
3fs	יִקְטְלֶהָ	יִקְטְלֶנָּה	יִקְטְלוּהָ	קְטָלֶהָ	קְטָלוּהָ	קָטְלָהּ	etc.	
1cp	יִקְטְלֵנוּ		יִקְטְלוּנוּ	קְטָלֵנוּ	קְטָלוּנוּ	קָטְלֵנוּ		
2mp	יִקְטָלְכֶם		יִקְטְלוּכֶם		קְטָלוּכֶם	קָטְלְכֶם		
2fp	יִקְטָלְכֶן		יִקְטְלוּכֶן		קְטָלוּכֶן	קָטְלְכֶן		
3mp	יִקְטְלֵם		יִקְטְלוּם	קְטָלֵם	קְטָלוּם	קָטְלָם		
3fp	יִקְטְלֵן		יִקְטְלוּן		קְטָלָן	קָטְלָן		

22.13 Irregular Verbs הלך and היה

	The Verb היה		The Verb הלך	
	Qal	*Nifal*	*Qal*	*Hifil*
Pf	*he was*		*he went*	
1cs	הָיִיתִי		הָלַכְתִּי	
2ms	הָיִיתָ	נִהְיֵיתָ	הָלַכְתָּ	
2fs	הָיִית		הָלַכְתְּ	
3ms	הָיָה	נִהְיָה	הָלַךְ	הוֹלִיךְ
3fs	הָיְתָה	נִהְיְתָה	הָלְכָה	
1cp	הָיִינוּ		הָלַכְנוּ	
2mp	הֱיִיתֶם		הֲלַכְתֶּם	
2fp	הֱיִיתֶן		הֲלַכְתֶּן	
3cp	הָיוּ		הָלְכוּ	
Imf				
1cs	אֶהְיֶה		אֵלֵךְ	אוֹלִיךְ
2ms	תִּהְיֶה		תֵּלֵךְ	
2fs	תִּהְיִי		תֵּלְכִי	
3ms	יִהְיֶה		יֵלֵךְ	
3fs	תִּהְיֶה		תֵּלֵךְ	יוֹלִיךְ
1cp	נִהְיֶה		נֵלֵךְ	
2mp	תִּהְיוּ		תֵּלְכוּ	
2fp	תִּהְיֶינָה		תֵּלַכְנָה	
3mp	יִהְיוּ		יֵלְכוּ	
3fp	תִּהְיֶינָה		תֵּלַכְנָה	
Imv				
2ms	הֱיֵה		לֵךְ / לְכָה	הוֹלֵךְ
2fs	הֲיִי		לְכִי	הֵילִיכִי
2mp	הֱיוּ		לְכוּ	הוֹלִיכוּ
IA	הָיֹה		הָלוֹךְ	הוֹלִיךְ
IC	הֱיוֹת		לֶכֶת	
APtc		נִהְיֶה	הוֹלֵךְ	מוֹלִיךְ

23.1   Noun Declensions

23.1.1   Masculine Nouns

	Unchangeable Vowels		Changeable *Qamets*				Changeable *Tsere*		
Sing.	*horse*	*just man*	*star*	*tower*	*overseer*	*word*	*wise man*	*heart*	*enemy*
abs.	סוּס	צַדִּיק	כּוֹכָב	מִגְדָּל	פָּקִיד	דָּבָר	חָכָם	לֵב	אֹיֵב
const.	סוּס	צַדִּיק	כּוֹכַב	מִגְדַּל	פְּקִיד	דְּבַר	חֲכַם	לֵב	אֹיֵב
my (c)	סוּסִי	צַדִּיקִי	כּוֹכָבִי	מִגְדָּלִי	פְּקִידִי	דְּבָרִי	חֲכָמִי	לִבִּי	אֹיְבִי
your (m)	סוּסְךָ	צַדִּיקְךָ	כּוֹכָבְךָ	etc.	פְּקִידְךָ	דְּבָרְךָ	חֲכָמְךָ	לְבָבְךָ	אֹיִבְךָ
your (f)	סוּסֵךְ	צַדִּיקֵךְ	כּוֹכָבֵךְ		פְּקִידֵךְ	דְּבָרֵךְ	חֲכָמֵךְ	לְבָבֵךְ	אֹיְבֵךְ
his	סוּסוֹ	צַדִּיקוֹ	כּוֹכָבוֹ		פְּקִידוֹ	דְּבָרוֹ	חֲכָמוֹ	לִבּוֹ	אֹיְבוֹ
her	סוּסָהּ	צַדִּיקָהּ	כּוֹכָבָהּ		פְּקִידָהּ	דְּבָרָהּ	חֲכָמָהּ	לְבָבָהּ	אֹיְבָהּ
our (c)	סוּסֵנוּ	צַדִּיקֵנוּ	כּוֹכָבֵנוּ		פְּקִידֵנוּ	דְּבָרֵנוּ	חֲכָמֵנוּ	לְבָבֵנוּ	אֹיְבֵנוּ
your (m)	סוּסְכֶם	צַדִּיקְכֶם	כּוֹכַבְכֶם	מִגְדַּלְכֶם	פְּקִידְכֶם	דְּבַרְכֶם	חֲכַמְכֶם	לְבַבְכֶם	אֹיִבְכֶם
your (f)	סוּסְכֶן	צַדִּיקְכֶן	כּוֹכַבְכֶן	etc.	פְּקִידְכֶן	דְּבַרְכֶן	חֲכַמְכֶן	לְבַבְכֶן	אֹיִבְכֶן
their (m)	סוּסָם	צַדִּיקָם	כּוֹכָבָם		פְּקִידָם	דְּבָרָם	חֲכָמָם	לְבָבָם	אֹיְבָם
their (f)	סוּסָן	צַדִּיקָן	כּוֹכָבָן		פְּקִידָן	דְּבָרָן	חֲכָמָן	לְבָבָן	אֹיְבָן

	horses	*just men*	*stars*	*towers*	*overseers*	*words*	*wise men*		*enemies*
Plural									
abs.	סוּסִים	צַדִּיקִים	כּוֹכָבִים	מִגְדָּלִים	פְּקִידִים	דְּבָרִים	חֲכָמִים		אֹיְבִים
const	סוּסֵי	צַדִּיקֵי	כּוֹכְבֵי	מִגְדְּלֵי	פְּקִידֵי	דִּבְרֵי	חַכְמֵי		אֹיְבֵי
my (c)	סוּסַי	צַדִּיקַי	כּוֹכְבַי	מִגְדָּלַי	פְּקִידַי	דְּבָרַי	חֲכָמַי		אֹיְבַי
your (m)	סוּסֶיךָ	צַדִּיקֶיךָ	כּוֹכָבֶיךָ	etc.	פְּקִידֶיךָ	דְּבָרֶיךָ	חֲכָמֶיךָ		אֹיְבֶיךָ
your (f)	סוּסַיִךְ	צַדִּיקַיִךְ	כּוֹכָבַיִךְ		פְּקִידַיִךְ	דְּבָרַיִךְ	חֲכָמַיִךְ		אֹיְבַיִךְ
his	סוּסָיו	צַדִּיקָיו	כּוֹכָבָיו		פְּקִידָיו	דְּבָרָיו	חֲכָמָיו		אֹיְבָיו
her	סוּסֶיהָ	צַדִּיקֶיהָ	כּוֹכָבֶיהָ		פְּקִידֶיהָ	דְּבָרֶיהָ	חֲכָמֶהָ		אֹיְבֶיהָ
our (c)	סוּסֵינוּ	צַדִּיקֵינוּ	כּוֹכָבֵינוּ		פְּקִידֵינוּ	דְּבָרֵינוּ	חֲכָמֵינוּ		אֹיְבֵינוּ
your (m)	סוּסֵיכֶם	צַדִּיקֵיכֶם	כּוֹכְבֵיכֶם	מִגְדְּלֵיכֶם	פְּקִידֵיכֶם	דִּבְרֵיכֶם	חַכְמֵיכֶם		אֹיְבֵיכֶם
your (f)	סוּסֵיכֶן	צַדִּיקֵיכֶן	כּוֹכְבֵיכֶן	etc.	פְּקִידֵיכֶן	דִּבְרֵיכֶן	חַכְמֵיכֶן		אֹיְבֵיכֶן
their (m)	סוּסֵיהֶם	צַדִּיקֵיהֶם	כּוֹכְבֵיהֶם		פְּקִידֵיהֶם	דִּבְרֵיהֶם	חַכְמֵיהֶם		אֹיְבֵיהֶם
their (f)	סוּסֵיהֶן	צַדִּיקֵיהֶן	כּוֹכְבֵיהֶן		פְּקִידֵיהֶן	דִּבְרֵיהֶן	חַכְמֵיהֶן		אֹיְבֵיהֶן

Masculine Nouns (*continued*)

	Segholates			Guttural Segholates		
Sing.	*king*	*book*	*holiness*	*lad*	*eternity*	*work*
abs.	מֶלֶךְ	סֵפֶר	קֹדֶשׁ	נַעַר	נֶלַח	פֹּעַל
const.	מֶלֶךְ	סֵפֶר	קֹדֶשׁ	נַעַר	נֶעַח	פֹּעַל
my (c)	מַלְכִּי	סִפְרִי	קָדְשִׁי	נַעֲרִי	נִעְחִי	פָּעֳלִי
your (m)	מַלְכְּךָ	סִפְרְךָ	קָדְשְׁךָ	נַעַרְךָ	נִעְחֶךָ	פָּעֳלְךָ
your (f)	מַלְכֵּךְ	סִפְרֵךְ	etc.	etc.	etc.	etc.
his	מַלְכּוֹ	סִפְרוֹ				
her	מַלְכָּה	etc.				
our (c)	מַלְכֵּנוּ					
your (m)	מַלְכְּכֶם					
your (f)	מַלְכְּכֶן					
their (m)	מַלְכָּם					
their (f)	מַלְכָּן					

	kings	*books*	*holinesses*	*lads*	*eternities*	*work*
Plural						
abs.	מְלָכִים	סְפָרִים	קָדָשִׁים	נְעָרִים	נְצָחִים	פְּעָלִים
const.	מַלְכֵי	סִפְרֵי	קָדְשֵׁי	נַעֲרֵי	נִצְחֵי	פָּעֳלֵי
my (c)	מְלָכַי	סְפָרַי	קָדָשַׁי	נְעָרַי	נְצָחַי	פְּעָלַי
your (m)	מְלָכֶיךָ	סְפָרֶיךָ	קָדָשֶׁיךָ	נְעָרֶיךָ	נְצָחֶיךָ	פְּעָלֶיךָ
your (f)	מְלָכַיִךְ	etc.	etc.	etc.	etc.	
his	מְלָכָיו					
her	מְלָכֶיהָ					
our (c)	מְלָכֵינוּ					
your (m)	מַלְכֵיכֶם	סִפְרֵיכֶם	קָדְשֵׁיכֶם	נַעֲרֵיכֶם	נִצְחֵיכֶם	פָּעֳלֵיכֶם
your (f)	מַלְכֵיכֶן	סִפְרֵיכֶן	etc.	etc.	etc.	etc.
their (m)	מַלְכֵיהֶם	etc.				
their (f)	מַלְכֵיהֶן					

Masculine Nouns (*continued*)

	Double *Ayin*			*Lamed Heh*, ending in הָ		
Sing.	*people*	*arrow*	*statute*	*shepherd*	*field*	*deed*
abs.	עַם	חֵץ	חֹק	רֹעֶה	שָׂדֶה	מַעֲשֶׂה
const.	עַם	חֵץ	חָק־	רֹעֵה	שָׂדֵה	מַעֲשֵׂה
my (c)	עַמִּי	חִצִּי	חֻקִּי	רֹעִי	שָׂדִי	מַעֲשִׂי
your (ms) etc.	עַמְּךָ	חִצְּךָ	חֻקְּךָ	רֹעֲהוּ	שָׂדֵהוּ	מַעֲשֵׂהוּ
your (mp) etc.	עַמְּכֶם	חִצְּכֶם	חָקְּכֶם	רֹעֲכֶם		

Plural	*peoples*	*arrows*	*statues*	*shepherds*	*reeds*	*deeds*
abs	עַמִּים	חִצִּים	חֻקִּים	רֹעִים	קָנִים	מַעֲשִׂים
const	עַמֵּי	חִצֵּי	חֻקֵּי	רֹעֵי	קְנֵי	מַעֲשֵׂי
my (c)	עַמַּי	חִצַּי	חֻקַּי	רֹעַי	קָנַי	מַעֲשַׂי
your (ms) etc.	עַמֶּיךָ	חִצֶּיךָ	חֻקֶּיךָ	רֹעֶיךָ	קָנֶיךָ	מַעֲשֶׂיךָ
your (mp) etc.	עַמֵּיכֶם	חִצֵּיכֶם	חֻקֵּיכֶם	רֹעֵיכֶם	קְנֵיכֶם	מַעֲשֵׂיכֶם

Sing.	*vessel*	*half*	*sickness*	*death*	*olive*
abs.	כְּלִי	חֲצִי	חֳלִי	מָוֶת	זַיִת
const.	כְּלִי	חֲצִי	חֳלִי	מוֹת	זֵית
my (c)	כֶּלְיִי	חֶצְיִי	חָלְיִי	מוֹתִי	זֵיתִי
your (ms) etc.	כֶּלְיְךָ	חֶצְיְךָ	חָלְיְךָ	מוֹתְךָ	זֵיתְךָ
your (mp) etc.	כֶּלְיְכֶם			מוֹתְכֶם	זֵיתְכֶם

Plural	*vessels*	*sicknesses*	*olives*
abs	כֵּלִים	חֳלָיִים	זֵיתִים
const	כְּלֵי	חֳלָיֵי	זֵיתֵי
my (c)	כֵּלַי	חֳלָיַי	זֵיתַי
your (ms) etc.	כֵּלֶיךָ	חֳלָיֶיךָ	זֵיתֶיךָ
your (mp) etc.	כְּלֵיכֶם	חֳלָיֵיכֶם	זֵיתֵיכֶם

23.1.2   Feminine Nouns

	I	II	III	IV	V
Sing.	law	year	righteousness	queen	kingdom
abs.	תּוֹרָה	שָׁנָה	צְדָקָה	מַלְכָּה	מַמְלָכָה
const.	תּוֹרַת	שְׁנַת	צִדְקַת	מַלְכַּת	מַמְלֶכֶת
my (c)	תּוֹרָתִי	שְׁנָתִי	צִדְקָתִי	מַלְכָּתִי	מַמְלַכְתִּי
your (m)	תּוֹרָתְךָ	שְׁנָתְךָ etc.	צִדְקָתְךָ etc.	מַלְכָּתְךָ etc.	מַמְלַכְתְּךָ etc.
your (f)	תּוֹרָתֵךְ				
his	תּוֹרָתוֹ				
her	תּוֹרָתָהּ				
our (c)	תּוֹרָתֵנוּ				
your (m)	תּוֹרַתְכֶם	שְׁנַתְכֶם etc.	צִדְקַתְכֶם etc.	מַלְכַּתְכֶם	
your (f)	תּוֹרַתְכֶן				
their (m)	תּוֹרָתָם				
their (f)	תּוֹרָתָן				

	I	II	III	IV	V
Plural	laws	years	righteous-nesses	queens	king-doms
abs.	תּוֹרוֹת	שָׁנוֹת	צְדָקוֹת	מְלָכוֹת	מַמְלָכוֹת
const.	תּוֹרוֹת	שְׁנוֹת	צִדְקוֹת	מַלְכוֹת	מַמְלְכוֹת
my (c)	תּוֹרוֹתַי	שְׁנוֹתַי	צִדְקֹתַי	מַלְכוֹתַי	מַמְלְכוֹתַי
your (m)	תּוֹרוֹתֶיךָ	שְׁנוֹתֶיךָ etc.	צִדְקֹתֶיךָ etc.	מַלְכוֹתֶיךָ etc.	etc.
your (f)	תּוֹרוֹתַיִךְ				
his	תּוֹרוֹתָיו				
her	תּוֹרוֹתֶיהָ				
our (c)	תּוֹרוֹתֵינוּ				
your (m)	תּוֹרוֹתֵיכֶם	שְׁנוֹתֵיכֶם etc.	צִדְקֹתֵיכֶם etc.	מַלְכוֹתֵיכֶם etc.	
your (f)	תּוֹרוֹתֵיכֶן				
their (m)	תּוֹרוֹתֵיהֶם				
their (f)	תּוֹרוֹתֵיהֶן				

23.2   Irregular Nouns

Sing.	father	brother	sister	son	daughter	mouth	house
abs.	אָב	אָח	אָחוֹת	בֵּן	בַּת	פֶּה	בַּיִת
const.	אַב אֲבִי	אֲחִי	אֲחוֹת	בֶּן־	בַּת	פִּי	בֵּית
my (c)	אָבִי	אָחִי	אֲחוֹתִי	בְּנִי	בִּתִּי	פִּי	בֵּיתִי
your (m)	אָבִיךָ	אָחִיךָ	אֲחוֹתְךָ	בִּנְךָ	בִּתְּךָ	פִּיךָ	בֵּיתְךָ
your (f)	אָבִיךְ	אָחִיךְ	etc.	בְּנֵךְ	etc.	פִּיךְ	etc.
his	אֲבִיהוּ	אֲחִיהוּ	אֲחוֹתָ		בְּנוֹ		פִּיהוּ	
	אָבִיו	אָחִיו		etc.		פִּיו	
her	אָבִיהָ	אָחִיהָ				פִּיהָ	
our (c)	אָבִינוּ	אָחִינוּ				פִּינוּ	
your (m)	אֲבִיכֶם	אֲחִיכֶם		בִּנְכֶם	בִּתְּכֶם	פִּיכֶם	
your (f)	אֲבִיכֶן	אֲחִיכֶן		etc.	etc.	etc.	
their (m)	אֲבִיהֶם	אֲחִיהֶם		בְּנָם	בִּתָּם	פִּיהֶם	
their (f)	אֲבִיהֶן	אֲחִיהֶן			etc.	etc.	

Plural	father	brother	sister	son	daughter	mouth	house
abs.	אָבוֹת	אַחִים	(אֲחָיוֹת)	בָּנִים	בָּנוֹת	פִּיוֹת	בָּתִּים
const.	אֲבוֹת	אֲחֵי	אַחְיוֹת	בְּנֵי	בְּנוֹת		בָּתֵּי
my (c)	אֲבוֹתַי	אַחַי	אַחְיֹתַי	בָּנַי	בְּנוֹתַי		בָּתַּי
your (m)	אֲבוֹתֶיךָ	אַחֶיךָ	etc.	בָּנֶיךָ	בְּנוֹתֶיךָ		etc.
your (f)	אֲבוֹתַיִךְ	אַזַיִךְ			etc.		
his	אֲבוֹתָיו	אֶחָיו					
her	אֲבוֹתֶיהָ	אַחֶיהָ					
our (c)	אֲבוֹתֵינוּ	אַחֵינוּ					
your (m)	אֲבוֹתֵיכֶם	אֲחֵיכֶם	אֲחִיּוֹתֵיכֶם	בְּנֵיכֶם	בְּנוֹתֵיכֶם		בָּתֵּיכֶם
your (f)	אֲבוֹתֵיכֶן	אֲחֵיכֶן	etc.	etc.			etc.
their (m)	אֲבוֹתָם	אֲחֵיהֶם					
their (f)	אֲבוֹתָן	אֲחֵיהֶן					

24.1   Glossary of Terms

ABSOLUTE STATE: The Hebrew absolute is the base form of the noun. It is used together with another noun in the construct state to express the genitive. Not to be confused with the infinitive absolute.

ACTIVE VOICE: In the active voice, the subject is the doer of the action that is expressed by the verb. 'In the beginning God created (active voice) the heavens and the earth' (Gen. 1.1).

ADJECTIVE: An adjective is a word that attributes a quality to another word, usually a noun. In Hebrew, it agrees with the word modified (concord). In the sentence, 'Abraham held a big feast' (Gen. 21.8), the word *big* is an adjective.

ADVERB: An adverb modifies a verb, adjective, or another adverb. In English, adverbs are usually formed with the suffix '-ly'. In the sentence, 'Agag came to him confidently' (1 Sam. 15.32), *confidently* is an adverb.

AFFIX: The inflexional endings that are affixed to Hebrew verbs to indicate person, gender, and number. Also called afformative or sufformative.

AFFORMATIVE: An inflexional ending on a verb.

AKTIONSART: German for 'kind of action'. A verbal action may express an durative activity or as a singular action. For example, the word *fight* expresses a durative activity, but *strike* is a singular action. However, *Aktionsart* is used in some grammars as the equivalent of aspect (see below).

ANARTHROUS: A word that appears without the article is anarthrous. 'Let us make humanity' (Gen. 1.26).

ANTECEDENT: A substantive to which a pronoun refers: personal, demonstrative, and relative pronouns have antecedents. 'a nation whose language you will not understand' (Deut. 28.49).

APOCOPATION: To cut short by apocope, i.e., the rejection of a letter or syllable at the end of a word. The loss of the final ה in many Hebrew words.

APODOSIS: The conclusion in a conditional sentence, expressing the result of a protasis; the independent or 'then' clause. 'If you fully obey the Lord your God... (protasis), the Lord your God will set you high above all the nations on earth (apodosis)' (Deut. 28.1).

ARAMAIC: A branch of the northwest Semitic languages that is closely related to Hebrew. In the OT Masoretic text, Ezra 4.8-6.18; 7.12-26; Dan. 2.4b-7.28; and Jer. 10.11 are in Aramaic rather than Hebrew. Aramaic had become the common language of the Jewish people by NT times.

ARTICULAR: A word that appears with the definite article is articular. 'God saw that the light was good' (Gen. 1.4).

ASPECT: A category used in grammatical analysis of the verb (along with tense and mood) to describe the duration or kind of action. Hebrew utilizes 3 aspects: perfective, imperfective, and durative.

ASSIMILATION: The adaptation of two adjacent sounds (consonant or vowel) to each other, either forward (progressive assimilation) or backward (regressive assimilation) in the word. Generally, a consonant that should close a syllable passes over into another that begins the next syllable and forms with it a strengthened letter or syllable.

ATTRIBUTIVE: An adjective or other adjunct word that qualifies a noun. Ex. white bread. The attributive may also be expressed by the genitive relationship: 'man of strength' = 'strong man'.

BARTH-GINSBURG LAW: A statement of predictable vowel changes in Hebrew. If the thematic vowel of the perfect is a-class, the thematic vowel of the imperfect will be of the u-class. If the perfect thematic vowel is i or u, the imperfect will be a-class.

BEGAD KEFAT LETTERS: A mnemonic device containing the six Hebrew consonants (ת פ כ ד ג ב) whose pronunciation may change by the insertion or omission of a *dagesh lene*.

CAUSATIVE VERB: A transitive verb that can be said to cause the action depicted in a corresponding intransitive verb; e.g. *lay* ('cause to lie') is the causative of *lie*; and *raise* is the causative of *rise*.

CLOSED SYLLABLE: A syllable that ends in a consonant.

COGNATE ACCUSATIVE: A noun, derived from the same root as the verb, that defines, explains, or strengthens (emphasizes) the verbal idea. It is also called the absolute object or the internal object. 'Jerusalem has sinned greatly' (Lam. 1.8), lit., 'Jerusalem has sinned a sin'.

COHORTATIVE: Modal aspect of a verb, expressing desire, will, request, wish, self-encouragement, intention of the speaker for himself. It may be considered a modified imperative and usually appears in the first person. 'Then God said, "Let us make man in our image"' (Gen. 1.26). Indicated in Heb. by appending ה to the end of a 1st person imperfect. Also called hortatory.

COHORTATIVE ה: See VOLITIVE ה.

COMPARATIVE DEGREE: Forms of adjectives and adverbs, or adjectival and adverbial constructions, that express relative increase of quality, quantity, or intensity. In English, the comparative degree is expressed by an adjective with the suffix '-er' (*richer*) or by 'more' with an adverb (*more richly*). In Hebrew, it is expressed by various means (the preposition מִן or the context). 'God made...the greater light...and the lesser light' (Gen. 1.16).

COMPENSATORY LENGTHENING: The lengthening of a short vowel to make up for the loss of one or more consonants.

COMPOSITE *SHEVA*: A form of the *sheva* in the Hebrew language that normally appears with guttural letters.

CONJUGATION: An orderly arrangement or listing of the inflected forms of a verb or verbal according to its person, gender, number, tense, voice, and mode.

CONSTRUCT STATE: A word in Hebrew that is dependent on the following word for meaning and definiteness (also for accent if the words are joined by a *maqqef*); together they make up a compound state that is the equivalent of the genitive in English or Greek. 'God set them in the expanse of (construct) the sky' (Gen. 1.17).

DAGESH FORTE: A dot that may appear in all the Hebrew consonants except the gutturals. It doubles the consonant in which it appears.

DAGESH LENE: A dot that appears only in the *begad kephat* letters in Hebrew. It affects the pronunciation by giving the consonant in which it appears a hard sound.

DECLENSION: An orderly arrangement or listing of the inflection of a noun, pronoun, participle, or adjective according to its case, person, gender, and number.

DEFECTIVE WRITING: When the vowel letter is omitted in Hebrew. Also called *scriptio defectiva*.

DEMONSTRATIVE ADJECTIVE: An adjective that points out particular persons, places, or things. There are two types: near (*this, these*) and remote (*that, those*). The demonstrative adjective is also called a demonstrative pronoun.

DENOMINATIVE VERB: A verb derived from a noun or adjective root.

DIRECT OBJECT: The word, phrase, or clause that is the primary goal or result of the action of the verb (cf. accusative case); the person or thing is directly affected by the action of the verb. 'God created the heavens and the earth' (Gen. 1.1).

DIRECTIVE ה: An old accusative ending appended at the end of a word to indicate motion towards.

DUAL NUMBER: A form denoting two persons or things.

ENERGIC NUN: A verbal form in Hebrew that is strengthened by the insertion of a connecting *nun* between the verbal stem and the suffix. Also called *nun energicum, nun demonstrativum, nun epentheticum*, epenthetic *nun*.

EUPHONIC NUN: A nun placed at the end of a Hebrew word for pleasing sound or ease of pronunciation.

FULL VOWELS: The vowels that are formed by using a consonant as a vowel letter.

FULL WRITING: Another name for *plena* writing.

GENDER: Gender is distinction as to sex. English expresses masculine, feminine, and neuter genders, but Hebrew has only two classes of gender – masculine and feminine. When the same form is used to express both masculine and feminine, it is called common gender.

GENITIVE: The case that expresses possession or specifies a relationship that can be expressed in English by 'of'. In Hebrew this is called a construct relationship: 'the expanse of the sky' (Gen. 1.21).

GUTTURALS: The mute consonants whose sounds are produced when the front of the tongue approaches the palate of the mouth. Four letters in Hebrew, א ה ח and ע are the guttural letters (ר has some guttural characteristics). Hebrew gutturals cannot be doubled, and they prefer a-class vowels and composite *sheva*s. Also called velars, laryngeals, or palatals.

HITPAEL: A verbal form in Hebrew that expresses intensive or emphatic action (classified by some grammars as causative action) and reflexive voice.

HOLLOW VERB: In Hebrew, a biconsonantal root that has a long vowel between the two root letters.

HOFAL: A verbal form in Hebrew that expresses causative action and passive voice. 'Let seven of his male descendants be given [*hofal*] to us' (2 Sam. 21.6).

IMPERATIVE: A verb or verbal mood that expresses command or makes a request. 'Give us water to drink' (Exod. 17.2).

IMPERFECT: In Hebrew, the form of the verb used to express action that is incomplete or unfinished. 'What if they do not believe me' (Exod. 4.1). Other regular uses of the tense include iterative, frequentative, inceptive, and conative.

INFINITIVE: A verbal noun that has characteristics of both verbs and nouns. In English usually introduced by 'to'. Hebrew has both infinitive absolute and infinitive construct forms. 'I am the Lord, who brought you out of Ur of the Chaldeans **to give** you this land' (Gen. 15.7).

INFINITIVE ABSOLUTE: A form of the Hebrew infinitive that may function in a number of ways: to express certainty or intensification ('you will surely die', Gen. 2.17); to express repeated or continued action ('Be ever hearing',

Isa. 6.9); as a finite verb ('They ... broke the jars', Judg. 7.19); to express an emphatic imperative ('Remember the Sabbath day', Exod. 20.8).

INFIX: A letter inserted within a verb root instead of at the beginning (prefix) or at the end (suffix), a characteristic of Semitic languages, where forms of the verb are indicated by infixes in the consonantal root.

INTERROGATIVE PARTICLE: A morpheme that introduces a question.

JUSSIVE: Modal aspect of the verb with the same function as the cohortative, but ordinarily it appears in the second or third person in Hebrew. 'And God said, "Let there be light"' (Gen. 1.3).

MAPPIQ: The dot found in the Hebrew letter ה when it comes at the end of a word.

MAQQEPH: A hyphen-like line joining two Hebrew words.

MASORETES: From Hebrew for 'tradition'. The Jewish scholars who added the vowel points to the Hebrew consonantal text. Also spelled MASSORETES.

MASORETIC TEXT: The vocalized text of the Hebrew Bible, prepared by a group of Jewish scholars around 700 CE to preserve the oral pronunciation of the Hebrew words.

MATRES LECTIONIS: The letters ה ו י (some mss such as the DSS also use א) that represent vowels in an unpointed text of the Hebrew Bible. Also called vowel letters.

METATHESIS: The transposition or reversal of letters (often consonants), words, or sentences.

METHEG: A small, perpendicular stroke written under a Hebrew consonant and to the left of the vowel to indicate the secondary accent of a word, or the secondary accent of words joined with the *maqqef*.

MODAL: A term that refers to some particular attitude (such as wish, possibility) toward the fulfillment of the action or state predicted, which may be expressed by inflectional mood, auxiliary verbs, word order, etc. 'God may yet relent' (Jonah 3.9).

NIFAL: A verbal form (stem) in Hebrew that expresses simple action and passive or reflexive voice. 'She was given in marriage to Adriel of Meholah' (1 Sam. 18.19).

NOMINAL SENTENCE: A sentence is nominal if the predicate does not contain a finite verb. 'For the Lord is our judge' (Isa. 33.22). Cf. Verbless Sentence.

NUMBER: In parsing of words in Hebrew, this term is used to show whether the word refers to one or more than one person, place, or thing. In Hebrew there are three numbers: singular, plural, and dual.

OPEN SYLLABLE: A syllable that ends in a vowel.

PARADIGM: An example or pattern of a conjugation or declension, showing a word in all its inflectional forms.

PARAGOGIC: In Hebrew, the *paragogic nun* ending is found attached to the plural ending over three hundred times. Its meaning is not fully understood. It may be for euphony or for emphasis.

PARSE/PARSING: To describe grammatically a verb by listing its inflectional modifications and/or its syntactic relationships in the sentence.

PARTICIPLE: A verbal form that has characteristics of both noun and verb. In Hebrew it represents characteristic, continual, uninterrupted action. 'The Spirit of God was hovering over the waters' (Gen. 1.2).

PARTICLE: A unit of speech that is ranked as an uninflected word but expresses some kind of syntactical relationship or some general aspect of meaning. Some grammarians classify all conjunctions, prepositions, and negatives as particles.

PASSIVE VOICE: A voice form of the verb that represents the subject as receiver of the action. 'This land was given to us as our possession' (Ezek. 11.15).

PAUSE: A Hebrew word marked by a heavy accent such as *silluq* or *athnach* is said to be in pause. If a word is in pause its short vowel is subject to lengthening.

PERFECT/PERFECT TENSE: In Hebrew, this form of the verb is used to express completed action, whether in reality or in the thought of the speaker or writer.

PIEL: A verbal form in Hebrew that expresses intensive or emphatic action and active voice. 'They destroyed the high places and the altars' (2 Chron. 31.1). p. 131.

PLENE: Latin for 'full'. When the originally long vowel is written with its vowel letters (ו י), it is said to be written fully, (*plene* writing). Also called full writing, *scriptio*, or *plena* writing.

POINTING: A term that refers to the vowels added by the Masoretes to the consonantal text of the OT (Hebrew was originally written without vowels) in order to preserve the pronunciation of the language at a time when it was in danger of being forgotten.

PREFIX: An inflectional affix; one or more letters or syllables placed at the beginning of a root or stem in Hebrew that will modify its meaning. Also called a preformative.

PREFORMATIVE: Another term for prefix.

PREPOSITION: A word that shows relationships between its object and some other word in the sentence. Some common English prepositions are *in*, *to*, *from*, *with*, *above*, *for*, *by*.

PRETONIC: The syllable immediately preceding the tone or tonic syllable, or the vowel that immediately precedes the tonic syllable.

PRONOMINAL: A term used by some grammarians for pronoun, or that which is related to the pronoun. In Hebrew, pronominal suffixes can be added to verbs, nouns, and particles.

PUAL: A verbal form in Hebrew that expresses intensive or emphatic action and passive voice. 'There was Baal's altar, demolished' (Judg. 6.28).

QAL: The ground form of the verb in Hebrew that expresses simple action.

QATAL: A perfect verb with no conjunction attached. Usually past tense in meaning.

QUIESCENT LETTERS: In Hebrew, the letter א is so weak in pronunciation that under certain conditions it loses its consonantal character and quiesces (that is, becomes silent).

RADICAL: One of the consonants belonging to the root of a word.

REFLEXIVE VOICE: Denotes an action that is directed back upon the agent or subject; expressed in Hebrew by the *nifal* and the *hitpael*. 'I have...kept myself from sin' (Ps. 18.23).

ROOT: The consonants (usually three) in Hebrew that ordinarily compose the basic uninflected spelling of a word.

SEGHOLATE: In Hebrew, a term used of words that are characterized by the use of *e* vowels in spelling; these are sometimes called second declension nouns.

SEMITE/SEMITIC: A descendent of Shem, the son of Noah (Gen. 10.21-31). Included Babylonians, Assyrians, and Arameans in ancient times, as well as Arabs and Jews.

SIBILANTS: The consonants that are characterized by the *s* sound. In Hebrew, the sibilants are ז ס צ שׂ and שׁ. Sometimes called spirants.

SILLUQ: The Hebrew accent mark placed on the last word in a verse. See PAUSE.

SIGN OF THE DEFINITE OBJECT: An untranslated sign that points to the object of the verb in Hebrew (אֵת).

STATIVE VERB: A stative verb is one that indicates a state of being or relationship rather than action. In Hebrew, its vowel pattern is different from that of verbs of action or motion.

STEM: In Hebrew, the stem is the verb conjugations that indicate the kinds of action. The seven major verbal stems are *qal*, *nifal*, *piel*, *pual*, *hitpael*, *hifil*, and *hofal*.

STRONG VERB: In Hebrew, the regular verb whose root consonants are not guttural letters or weak letters, in contrast to the weak verb.

SUBSTANTIVE: Any part of speech that is used grammatically as a noun, e.g. an adjective, participle, or infinitive used as the subject of a sentence, e.g., 'to err is human'.

SUFFIX: One or more syllables added to the end of a root or to a stem in Hebrew that will modify its meaning. Also called an afformative or sufformative, pronominal suffixes added to the noun to indicate person, gender, and number.

SUFFORMATIVE: Another name for suffix.

SYLLABLE: A unit of pronunciation in a word. As a general rule, a Hebrew syllable begins with one consonant followed by a vowel and may be closed by another consonant. A Hebrew word has as many syllables as full vowels.

THEMATIC VOWEL: The vowel that characteristically appears with the second root letter of a Hebrew word; helpful in the identification of certain verbal stems.

TONE-LONG VOWEL: In Hebrew, a short vowel may become a long vowel under the influence of the accented (tone) syllable. Also called heightening.

TONE SYLLABLE, TONIC SYLLABLE: The syllable that receives the principal accent of the word in pronunciation.

UNPOINTED TEXT: The Hebrew text written only with consonants; the vowels were omitted in early Hebrew writing and were added by scribes called the Masoretes.

VAV CONJUNCTIVE: In Hebrew a simple connective conjunction (וְ), usually translated as 'and', but may also be translated as 'but', 'yet', 'when', 'so', 'for', 'since', 'that', 'how', 'therefore', 'then'. It is also called the light *vav*, the simple *vav*, and the copulative *vav*.

VAV CONSECUTIVE: In Hebrew, a *vav* that may be prefixed to the perfect and imperfect forms of verbs; it will affect the meaning of the verb. Earlier grammars called it the *vav* conversive. When the *vav* is attached to the perfect it is called the *weqatal*, and when the *vav* (pointed with *patach* plus *dagesh* in the preformative) is attached to the imperfect it is called the *wayyiqtol*.

VOICE: Voice is a modification of a verb that tells whether the subject of the verb acts or is acted upon. There are three voices in English and Hebrew: active, passive, and reflexive.

VOLITIVE ‏ה‎: The addition of ‏ה‎ to the cohortative, jussive, or imperative, indicating volition/will.

VOWEL: A speech sound made by not blocking the oral part of the breath passage. In Hebrew syllables a vowel always follows a consonant (except for a furtive *patach*).

VOWEL LETTER: See *MATRES LECTIONIS*.

VOWEL POINTS: See POINTING.

WAYYIQTOL: See VAV CONSECUTIVE. This is the Hebrew narrative tense.

WEAK VERB: In Hebrew, the verbs with gutturals or weak letters as radicals, which produce modifications in the conjugation, in contrast to the strong verb.

WEQATAL: A perfect verb with conjunction attached. Either future or past habitual in meaning.

WEYIQTOL: The imperfect verb with a simple conjunction attached. Volitive in meaning.

YIQTOL: An imperfect verb with no conjunction attached. Usually future in meaning.

25.1   CHARACTERISTICS OF THE VERB STEMS[4]

(The 'stems' are also בִּנְיָנִים 'formations'.)

Names	Short Description	Fuller Descriptions

Qal	Simple Active	1. Simple fientive (Action verb as opposed to stative verb)
		   a. Transitive (subject acts upon an object)
		   b. Intransitive (subject acts, but not upon an object)
		2. Stative (describes a state of being, condition, quality, circumstance, or characteristic)
		3. Impersonal verbs (may be fientive or stative)
		   e.g. 'all is well', or 'it is raining'.
		4. Denominative verb formed from noun.

Nifal	Passive/reflexive of *Qal*	In all its uses the action or state expressed by the verb affects the subject (mid & pass) or its interests (reflex).
		1. Passive (subject is in the state of being acted upon by an agent, usually stated)
		2. Middle (emphasizes the process of the subject's being acted upon by an unstated agent)
		3. Adjectival: a. Simple: 'The wall is *broken*'.
		                b. Ingressive-stative: 'Naomi *grew sad*'.
		4. Double-status (subject is both agent & recipient)
		   a. Reflexive (subj. acts upon itself: 'washed himself')
		   b. Benefactive (subj. acts for his own interests)
		   c. Reciprocal (plural subj. act with one another, 'they fought together')
		   d. Tolerative (passive/permissive: 'God allowed himself to be asked')

Hifil	Causative fientive	Causes an event; the subject causes the object to participate in the action of the verb. Contrast the *Piel* emphasis on result. 1. Intransitives: 'I will cause you to go out of Egypt'. 2. Transitives: 'They caused Joseph to take off his coat'. 3. Denominatives: light/cause to be light, right/turn right 4. Modal: Permission, Toleration, Compulsion, or bestowal.
Hofal	Passive of *Hifil*	Passive of *Hifil*; the subj. causes the object to be acted upon. E.g., 'He begat Boaz' in *H*, means 'He caused Boaz to be born'.
Piel	Causative Stative	Brings about a state corresponding to the basic meaning of the root, with the object being a passive receiver. 1. Factitive (Intrans. vbs: Brings to a state of being, e.g. 'he set up camp', or 'made the camp to be set up') 2. Resultative (Trans. vbs: 'he broke the jar', that is he 'made the jar broken'. Emph. on result not on process) 3. Denominative (produces, removes, or results in the state of the noun or adjective. e.g. cloud/make clouds, sin/cleanse from sin, blind/make blind) 4. Frequentative (iterative action or repeated actions)
Pual	Passive of *Piel*	Passive counterpart of all four types of *Piel*. The subject is brought into a state of being. 'He was made weak', etc.

Hitpael	Reflexive of *Piel*	Double-Status counterpart of the *Piel*. The subject brings himself into a state or brings about an action for his own interests. (See explanation of Double-status in *Nifal*)
		1. Direct reflexive
		   a. Resultative: *Hitpael* of 'gird' means '*made* himself *girded*'.
		   b. Factitive: 'he *made* himself *happy*'.
		2. Indirect reflexive: 'he removed (from himself) his robe'.
		3. Benefactive reflexive: 'we packed provisions (for ourselves)'
		4. Reciprocal reflexive: 'they looked on one another'.
		5. Middle of *Piel* (cf. *Nifal*): 'he was healed'.

---

[4] Adapted from Waltke and O'Connor, *Introduction to Biblical Hebrew Syntax*.

26.1 HEBREW VERB SYNTAX IN PROSE[5]

The Hebrew verb system develops from only two finite verb forms: perfect and imperfect. Thus, these two forms must be usable in many tenses and moods. The following variations developed.

VERB FORM	NEGATIVE COUNTERPART
qatal (perfect in initial position)	לֹא+*qatal*
yiqtol (imperfect in initial position)	עַל+*yiqtol*
weqatal (vav+perfect)	לֹא+*yiqtol*
weyiqtol (vav+imperfect)	עַל+*yiqtol*
wayyiqtol (vav-consecutive)	וְלֹא+*qatal*
x-*qatal* (x+perfect[6])	x-לֹא+*qatal*
x-*yiqtol* (x+imperfect)	x-לֹא+*yiqtol* (if x-*yiqtol* is volitive it is negated with x-עַל+*yiqtol*)

Each of the seven variations above have particular uses. Verbal ideas are also carried by the infinitive and the participle.

VERB FORM   PURPOSE

wayyiqtol   narrative, main-line events

weqatal   (a) narrative: habitual / repeated actions
            (b) direct speech: continues future tense
            (c) exhortation: continues an exhortation after a *volitive*

weyiqtol (a) volitive in direct speech
            (b) indicates purpose after a cohortative, imperative, or jussive

x-*qatal*   (a) narrative: background in narrative
                (1) provides setting (antecedent action or condition)when coming before a *wayyiqtol*
                (2) circumstance, contrast, specification, or parenthetical when following a *wayyiqtol*
                (3) emphasis on x, when answering the question 'Who?'
            (b) direct speech: beginning of an oral report
            (c) direct speech: background if it is not the initial statement

x-*yiqtol* (a) narrative: habitual/repeated action but sub-ordinate to weqatal
            (b) direct speech: future tense (sometimes present tense)
            (c) direct speech: continues an exhortation after a volitive, with emphasis on x

Initial *qatal*   direct speech: past tense

Initial *yiqtol*   direct speech: volitive (cohortative, jussive, injunctive)

וַיְהִי   (a) Macrosyntactic signal of new information, paragraph, or
              (b) A true verb, indicating a state, *to be*, or a action, *to happen*.

---

[5] Adapted from Niccacci, *Syntax of the Verb* and Rocine, *Learning Biblical Hebrew*.

[6] Where x is any non verbal element except *vav*.

GENRE	TASK	MAINLINE VERB
I. Historical Narrative		
A. Narrative	tell a story	*wayyiqtol*
B. Procedural Discourse	tell how something was done	*weqatal*
II. Direct Speech		
A. Oral Report	report an event	x+*qatal* → *wayyiqtol*
B. Expository Discourse	statements of opinion	nominal clauses
C. Predictive Narrative	state future events	x+*yiqtol* → *weqatal*
D. Exhortations	influence behavior	volitive → *weqatal*
E. Instructional Discourse	tell how to do something	*weqatal*

26.1.1   Detailed Syntactical Chart for Verbs

I. Narrative   Narrates a story (Past tense)

Setting

1 x-*qatal* (x+perfect) Antecedent / x-לֹא+*qatal* (negated x-*qatal*)

2 participle

3 verbless clause

4 Macrosyntactic וַיְהִי (new episode within a narrative).

5 יֵשׁ or אֵין clause

Main Story line

6 *wayyiqtol*: primary story line (includes וַיְהִי when it has an object)

וְלֹא+*qatal* (negated *wayyiqtol*)

7 x-*qatal* (x+perfect) = topicalization / emphasis (in answer to question 'Who?')

8 x-*qatal* (x+perfect) / x-לֹא+*qatal* (negated x-*qatal*)

9 circumstance

10 contrast

11 specification

12 parenthetical / explanatory

13 solitary *weqatal* (*vav*+perfect): climactic, pivotal event

Backgrounded activities

14 *weqatal* (*vav*+perfect) = habitual/repetitive / לֹא+*yiqtol* (negated *weqatal*)

15 x-*yiqtol* (x+imperfect) = habitual/repetitive / x-לֹא+*yiqtol* (negated x-*yiqtol*)

16 אֲשֶׁר+*qatal* (perfect) = past tense in relation to main clause

17 אֲשֶׁר+(imperfect) = future tense in relation to main clause

18 הִנֵּה + participle

19 Verbless Clauses

II. Direct Speech

A. Oral Report (Past Tense) Embedded within a narrative, reporting an event.

Setting

20 nominal clause

21 participle

22 Interjection

Direct Speech, cont'd

Story line

23 x-*qatal*: begins report in past tense

24 x-לֹא+*qatal* (negated x-*qatal*)

25 *wayyiqtol* continues storyline in past tense

26 וְלֹא+*qatal* (negated *wayyiqtol*)

27 x-*qatal* (x+perfect) = topicalization / emphasis

28 x-*qatal* (x+perfect)

29 circumstance

30 contrast

31 specification

32 parenthetical

33 x-לֹא+*qatal* (negated x-*qatal*)

Backgrounded activities

34 *weqatal* = habitual / repetitive

35 לֹא+*yiqtol* (negated *weqatal*)

36 x-*yiqtol* (x+imperfect) = habitual / repetitive

37 x-לֹא+*yiqtol* (negated x-*yiqtol*)

38 אֲשֶׁר+*qatal* (perfect) = past tense in relation to main clause

39 אֲשֶׁר+*yiqtol* (imperfect) = future in relation to main clause

40 הִנֵּה + participle

B. Predictive Narrative (Future Tense)

Setting

41 Macrosyntactic וְהָיָה

42 nominal clause

43 participle

44 יֵשׁ or אֵין clause

Story line

45 x-*yiqtol* (x+imperfect) begins future storyline

46 x-לֹא+*yiqtol* (negated x-*yiqtol*)

47 *weqatal* (*vav*+perfect) continues storyline in future tense

48 לֹא+*yiqtol* (negated weqatal)

49 x-*yiqtol* (x+imperfect): secondary story line w/ x in focus

50 x-לֹא+*yiqtol* (negated x-*yiqtol*)

51 *yiqtol* (imperfect) in dep. clause: secondary story line

52 לֹא+*yiqtol* (negated *yiqtol* in dep.clause)

Backgrounded activities

53 participle (durative)

C. Exhortations (Future tense), Intended to influence behavior

54 Cohortative (1st person)

55 עַל+*yiqtol* (negated volitive)

56 Imperative (2nd person)

57 imv + *weqatal* = immediate command + further instructions

58 imv + imf/coh = immediate command + purpose: *so that* (Lambdin §107)

Exhortations, cont'd

    59 Jussive (3ʳᵈ person)

      60 עַל+*yiqtol* (negated volitive)

    61 *yiqtol* (Imperfect) in initial position

      62 *weqatal* continues the exhortation

      63 *weyiqtol* after a volitive shows purpose

      64 In a series of imperatives, the final one is the main point

      65 עַל+*yiqtol* (negated volitive)

D. Expository Discourse (Present Tense) States and explains truth

  66 Participle

  67 Nominal clauses

26.1.2   Subordinate Clauses Beginning with the Conjunction *vav*.

The discourse approach used above is quite precise and detailed. The traditional approach to syntax, while not as exact, can be helpful to beginning students. The traditional classification of clauses that begin with the conjunction *vav* is one such helpful formulation. When a clause begins with a *vav* that is attached to anything other than a verb, it indicates either:

1. Contrast

The second clause is relates a situation that stands in contrast to the first clause, e.g., *There was famine in all the lands, but in all* (וּבְכָל) *Egypt there was food* (Gen. 41.54).

2. Circumstance

This clause describes a situation or circumstance contemporary with or prior to the action of the preceding clause, e.g., *A man found him (while)* (וְהִנֵּה) *wandering lost in the field* (Gen 37.15).

3. Explanation or parenthesis

This clause breaks into the main narrative to supply information relevant to the narrative. For example, in 1 Sam. 1.9, Hannah performs two actions: 1) she arises, and 2) she prays. Between these two actions, the narrator has inserted an explanatory note that says, *Now Eli* (וְעֵלִי) *the priest was sitting on the seat by the door post of the temple.*

4. Conclusion or Beginning

Sometimes this kind of clause indicates the end of an episode, and at other times, it signals the beginning of an episode, e.g.,

Beginning of an episode: *Now the serpent* (וְהַנָּחָשׁ) *was more subtle* . . . (Gen. 3.1).

An initial clause may also be preceded by a temporal element, e.g.
Now after these things, God (וְהָאֱלֹהִים) *tested Abram* (Gen. 22.1).

NOTE: When the conjunction is attached to a series of like elements, it indicates coordination, e.g. *Hannah, why do you weep? And why* (וְלָמֶה) *do you not eat? And why* (וְלָמֶה) *is your heart sad?* (1 Sam. 1.8).

27.1 GUIDE TO PARSING HEBREW VERBS

1. Identify any **prefixes**.
   - (1) Conjunction (*vav* consecutive = impf)
   - (2) Interrogative (may be on any verb)
   - (3) Prepositions (ptc. or infin. only)
   - (4) Definite article (ptc. only)
2. Identify any **preformatives**
   - (1) Imperfect: א נ י ת
   - (2) Participle: נ   מ
3. Identify any **pronominal suffixes**.

   They may attach to perfect, imperfect, imperative, participle, and infinitive construct.
4. Identify any **Afformatives**
   - (1) Perfect
   - (2) Imperfect
   - (3) Imperatives
   - (4) Infinitives
   - (5) Participles
   - (6) Connective vowel
   - (7) Emphatics
5. Analyze each **Dagesh Forte**
   - (1) In first radical it will indicate either a *Nifal* or a פ"נ verb.
   - (2) In second radical it indicates either a *Piel*, *Pual*, *Hitpael*, or Geminate.

   Watch out, however, for *dagesh lene*.
6. Look for **stem indicators** (6, 9, 10)

   Qal has no special preformative or *dagesh*
   - (1) A *holem* in first syllable is active ptc. (except in פ"א).
   - (2) A ו or ָ in second syllable is passive ptc.

   Nifal has a נ in the perfect and ptc.

   All other forms of *nifal* have a *dagesh forte* in the first radical, except I-Guttural Imf, which have lengthening (ָ). Infin. has ה

   Piel has *dagesh forte* in middle radical with
   - (1) ִ under first radical in the perfect (ֵ) in middle gutturals)
   - (2) ְ י in the imperfect, ַ י in middle gutturals
   - (3) ְ מ in the participle ַ מ in middle gutturals

   Pual has *dagesh forte* in middle radical with
   - (1) ֻ under first radical in the perfect, שׁ in medial guttural
   - (2) ְ י in the imperfect, ׁ י in middle gutturals
   - (3) ְ מ in the participle, מ in middle gutturals

Hifil has

הֵ־ in the perfect,

יַ־ in the imperfect, and

מֵ־ or מַ־ in the ptc.

Hofal has

הָ־ in the perfect,

יָ־ in the imperfect, and

מָ־ or מֳ־ in the ptc.

Hitpael has

הִת־ in the perfect, imperative, and infinitive

יִת־ in the imperfect, and

מִת־ in the ptc.

7. If still uncertain, look for
    (1) Letter dropped or changed. Missing radicals may occur as follows:
        XX?, X?X, ?XX, ?X?, or ??X
    (2) Infix
    (3) If there are no preformatives or afformatives, it will be either a
        - Perfect, 3ms; a
        - Participle, ms or fs; or an
        - infinitive

8. Watch for identical forms:
    (1) In Hollow vbs, *Q* and *N* Perf 3ms/fs are same as the ms/fs ptc.
    (2) In Hollow vbs, *H* imf is same as *Q* imf in middle *yod* vbs, e.g. שִׂים
    (3) *Hitpael* Perf 3ms is identical to the *Hitpael* infinitive.
    (4) *Q* Imv fs & m pl ל"ה are same as פ"י.
    (5) *Q* impf is same as *H* impf in double weak verbs פ"ע / ל"ה.
    (6) *H* impf 1c pl is same as *N* ptc in double weak verbs פ"ע / ל"ה.
    (7) In פ"י, the *H* jussive, 3ms, (if defective) is same as *Q* act. ptc., e.g. Deut. 1.11 יֹסֵף for יוֹסֵף.

28.1   The Hebrew Accent Marks

The Hebrew accent marks (also known as cantillation signs) serve as guides to the reading and the chanting of the Hebrew text. Generally, each word of text has a cantillation mark at its primary accent and associated with that mark is a musical phrase that tells how to chant that word. More specifically, some words have two marks, some have no marks, and the musical meaning of some marks is dependent upon context. There is one set of accent marks associated with the narrative books of the Bible and another associated with the poetical books.

For purposes of exegesis, it should be noted that the placement of the accent marks indicates the grammar and syntax of the verse as understood by the Masoretic scribes. It is often helpful to note whether the accent on a word is disjunctive (separating a word from the one that follows), such as *athnach or zaqqef,* or conjunctive (joining a word with the one that follows).

Important Note: Words that have a strong accent (e.g., *silluq* and *athnach*) often undergo the lengthening of the vowel. These are called pausal forms.

Some prominent accent marks can be identified in the following verse:

וַיְהִ֗י אַחַר֙ הַדְּבָרִ֣ים הָאֵ֔לֶּה וְהָ֣אֱלֹהִ֔ים נִסָּ֖ה אֶת־אַבְרָהָ֑ם
וַיֹּ֣אמֶר אֵלָ֔יו אַבְרָהָ֖ם וַיֹּ֥אמֶר הִנֵּֽנִי׃

(Gen. 22.1)

The end of a verse is marked by the accent *sof pasuq*: הִנֵּֽנִי׃

The accent on the final word of a verse is a small vertical line called *silluq*: הִנֵּֽנִי

The major division within a verse is marked by the accent *athnach*: אַבְרָהָ֑ם

The disjunctive accent over הָאֵ֔לֶּה is called *zaqqef.*

The printed editions of the BHS include a bookmark that lists all of the accent marks, separated into the categories of conjunctive and disjunctive.

See Gesenius §15 and James D. Price. *The Syntax of the Masoretic Accents in the Hebrew Bible* (Lewiston, NY: Edwin Mellen Press, 1990).

29.1 Vocabulary of Hebrew Words Used in the Exercises

Abbreviations

adj.	adjective	m.	masculine		part.	particle	
adv.	adverb	n.	noun		prep.	preposition	
conj.	conjunction	pl	plural		pr.n.	proper noun	
f.	feminine	s.	single		prn.	pronoun	
interr.	interrogative	v.	verb				

א

אָב   *n.m.* father. *pl* אָבוֹת

אָבָה   *v.* be willing

אֶבֶן   *n.f.* stone

אָדוֹן   *n.m.* lord, אֲדוֹנָי = The Lord

אָדָם   *n.m.* man, human

אֲדָמָה   *n.f.* ground, earth

אָהַב   *v.* to love

אוֹר   *n.m.* light

אוּלָם   *adv.* but indeed

אוּלַי   *adv.* perhaps

אָז   *adv.* then

אָח   *n.m.* brother. *pl* אַחִים

אָחוֹת   *n.f.* sister

אֶחָד   *adjective (cardinal number).* one. *fem.* אַחַת

אָחַז   *v.* to grasp, seize

אַחַר   *prep.* after, behind. *construct* אַחֲרֵי

אַחֵר   *adj.* other

אַיֵּה   *interr.* where?

אַיִל   *n.* ram

אֵין   *particle of nonexistence.* There is not . . .

אֵיפֹה   *interr.* where? what kind?

אֵיפָה   *n.f.* ephah

אִישׁ   *n.m.* man, husband. *pl* אֲנָשִׁים

אַךְ   *particle.* indeed

אָכַל   *v.* ate

אֶל   *preposition.* unto

אֱלֹהִים   *n.m.* God

אַלּוֹן   *n.f.* oak

אָלַם   *v.* to bind

אֲלֻמָּה   *n.f.* sheaf (something bound)

אֵם   *n.f.* mother. *pl* אִמּוֹת

אִם   *particle,* if

אָמָה   *n.f.* maidservant

אָמַר   *v.* to say

אָסַף   *v.* gather

אָסַר   *v.* to bind

אַף   *n.m.* nostril, face, anger

אַף   *particle.* Indeed

אֶרֶץ   *n.f.* land. *pl* אֲרָצוֹם

אָרַר   *v.* to inflict with a curse

אִשָּׁה   *n.f.* woman, wife. *pl* נָשִׁים

אֲשֶׁר   *relative pronoun.* who, which, that, what

אָתוֹן   *n.f.* female donkey

ב

בְּ   *inseparable prep.* in, by

בָּבֶל   *n.* Babel

בִּגְלַל   *prep.* on account of

בַּד   *n.m.* a piece, לְבַדִּי = I alone

בָּדַל   *v.* to divide, separate (*Nif.* & *Hif.* only)

בְּהֵמָה   *n.f.* cattle

בּוֹא   *v.* to come

בּוֹר   *n.m.* pit, cistern. *pl* בְּרוֹת

בָּחַר   *v.* to choose

בָּטַח   *v.* to trust

בֶּטֶן   *n.f.* womb

בֵּין   *prep.* between

בַּיִת   *n.m.* house. *pl* בָּתִּים

בָּכָה   *v.* weep

בְּכוֹר   *n.m.* firstborn

בָּלַל   *v.* to mix, confuse

בְּלִיַּעַל   *n.m.* worthlessness

בָּלַע   *v.* to swallow

בֵּן   *n.m.* son. *pl* בָּנִים

בָּנָה   *v.* to build

בַּעֲבוּר   *prep.* because of , in order that

בַּעַד   *prep.* Behind, around

בַּעַל   *n.m.* lord, master

בָּעַר   *v.* to burn

בָּצַר   *v.* to gather together, to restrain

בָּקַע   *v.* split, cleave, break open

בִּקְעָה   *n.f.* plain, valley

בָּקָר   *n.m.* oxen, cattle

בֹּקֶר   *n.m.* morning

בִּקֵּשׁ   *v. Piel* to seek

בָּרָא   *v.* to create

בָּרַח   *v.* to flee

בְּרִית   *n.f.* covenant, = כָּרַת בְּרִית *He made a covenant.*

בְּרָכָה   *n.f.* blessing

בָּרַךְ   *v.* to bless (*usually Piel*)

בָּשָׂר   *n.m.* flesh

בַּת   *n.f.* daughter. *pl* בָּנוֹת

ג

גָּאַל   *v.* to redeem

גִּבּוֹר   *adj.* mighty, strong

גָּדוֹל   *adj.* great, large

גָּדַל   *v.* to be great

גּוֹי   *n.* nation, gentile

גּוּר   *v.* to sojourn

גַּם   *adv.* also, even

גָּמַל   *v.* to deal fully, recompense, wean

גָּמָל   *n.m.* camel

גַּן   *n.m.* garden

גָּעַר   *v.* to rebuke

ד

דִּבָּה   *n.f.* whispering, evil report

דָּבַק   *v.* to cleave

דָּבָר   *n.m.* word, thing

דִּבֶּר   *v.* to speak (*usually Piel*)

דּוֹר   *n.m.* generation

דַּי   *n.m.* enough

דּוּן   *v.* to remain, stay

דָּם   *n.* blood

דַּעַת   *n.f.* knowledge

דֶּרֶךְ   *n.m. or f.* road, way

דָּרַשׁ   *v.* to seek

ה

הוֹדָה   *v.* to praise, confess (*Hifil* > יָדָה)

הָיָה   *v.* to be

הֵיכָל   *n.m.* temple, palace, *sometimes irreg. pl* הֵיכָלוֹת

הִכָּה   *v.* to strike, smite. *Hifil* > נכה

הַלָּזֶה   *adj.* this

הָלַךְ   *v. Qal* to go, *Hitpael* to walk

הִנֵּה   *particle.* behold!

הַר   *noun, m.* mountain. *w. art.* הָהָר *pl* הָרִים

הָרַג   *v.* to kill

הָרָה   *v.* conceive

ו

וַיְהִי   *v.* It came to pass *wayyiqtol form of* הָיָה

ז

זָהָב   *n.* gold

זָבַח   *v. Qal* to slaughter; *Piel* to offer

זֶה   *prn.m.* this. *f.* זֹאת. *pl m., f.* אֵלֶּה these

זָכַר   *v.* to remember, to mention; *Hif* to make known

זָמַם   *v.* to plot, devise, plan

זָעַק   *v.* to cry out

זָקוּן   *n.m.* old age

זָרַע   *v.* to sow

ח

חָבַשׁ	v. tie, restrain, saddle
חָדַל	v. to stop, cease
חָדָשׁ	adj. new
חָוָה	v. Hishtafel to worship (§11.7.3)
חָזָה	v. to see, gaze at
חָזַק	v. to be strong
חָטָא	v. to sin
חַי	life. חַיָּה f. living thing, beast. חַי adj. living. חַיִּים m.p. life.
חָיָה	v. to live
חָלַל	v. Hifil to begin
חָלַם	v. to dream
חֲלוֹם	n.m. a dream
חָם	p.n. Ham
חֲמוֹר	n. donkey
חֵמָר	n.m. slime, pitch, asphalt, bitumen
חֹמֶר	n.m. cement, mortar
חֵן	n.m. grace, favor (cf. the verb חָנַן, to be gracious, to favor)
חָנָה	v. to encamp
חִנָּם	adv. freely
חָנַן	v. to be gracious, to favor
חֶסֶד	n.m. loyalty, favor
חָפֵץ	v. to delight, take pleasure in
חֹק	n. statute
חֶרֶב	n. sword
חָרָה	v. to be hot, to burn, to be angry
חָרַשׁ	v. to plow
חָשַׂךְ	v. to restrain, hold back
חָשַׁב	v. to think
חֹשֶׁךְ	n.m. darkness

ט

טוֹב	adj. good
טֶרֶם	adv. before, not yet

י

יָד	n.f. hand. const. s. יַד. const. pl יְדֵי
יָבֵשׁ	v. to be dry
יָדַע	v. to know. The perf. of יָדַע is often translated present tense.
יָהַב	v. to give
יוֹם	n.m. day. irreg. pl יָמִים
יַחְדָּו	adv. together
יָחִיד	adj. only
יָטַב	v. to be well
יַיִן	n.m. wine
יָכֹל	v. to be able
יֶלֶד	n.m. child, boy, f. girl = יַלְדָּה
יָלַד	v. to beget
יָם	n.m. sea, pl יַמִּים
יָנַק	v. to nurse
יָסַף	v. to add, to do again
יָפֶה	n.f. beautiful
יֶפֶת	p.n. Japheth
יָצָא	v. to go out
יָצַב	v. to stand, in the sense of assuming a post or place (same as נָצַב)
יָצַק	v. to pour out
יָצַר	v. to form
יֵצֶר	n.m. shape, form
יָרֵא	v. to fear
יָרֵא	adj. afraid
יָרַד	v. to go down
יָרֵחַ	n.m. moon
יֵשׁ	particle of existence. There is
יָשַׁב	v. to dwell, to sit
יָשַׁע	v. Nifal to be victorious; Hifil to help, deliver
יָשָׁר	adj. upright

כ

כְּ	inseparable prep. like, as, according to
כָּבֵד	v. to be heavy
כֹּה	part. Thus
כֹּהֵן	n.m. priest
כּוֹכָב	n.m. star

כּוּן   *v.* to stand fast, to be firm

כֹּחַ   *n.* strength, power

כִּי   *particle/conjunction.* because, when, that

כִּי־אִם   *conj. Combined, these words mean* nevertheless, truly, except, rather

כֹּל   *n.m.* the whole, all, every. *also* כָּל־

כֵּן   *adv.* so, thus

כִּסֵּא   *n.m.* throne

כָּסָה   *v.* to cover, conceal

כֶּסֶף   *n.* silver

כָּעַס   *v.* be irritated, angry

כָּרַת   *v.* to cut, cut off

כַּשְׂדִּים   *n.p.* Chaldeans

כָּתַב   *v.* to write

ל

לְ   *inseparable preposition.* to, for

לֵאמֹר   *infinitive construct.* Saying

לֵב   *n.* heart (*also* לֵבָב). *w. suff.* לִבִּי *pl* לִבּוֹת

לְבַד   *n.m.* solitude, alone

לָבֵן   *v.* I-to become white, II-to make brick

לְבֵנָה   *n.f.* brick

לֶחֶם   *n.m.* bread

לַיְלָה   *n.m.* night

לִין   *v.* to remain overnight

לָכַד   *v.* to seize, to capture

לָמָה   *interr.* why?

לְמַעַן   *prep.* in order that

לָקַח   *v.* to take, seize

לָשׁוֹן   *n.* tongue

מ

מְאֹד   *adv.* very

מֵאָה   *adj.* one hundred

מְאוּמָה   *n.* anything

מַאֲכָל   *n.* food

מַאֲכֶלֶת   *n.* knife

מַבּוּל   *n.* flood

מִגְדָּל   *n.m.* tower

מָגוֹר   *n.m.* sojourning place

מִדְבָּר   *n.m.* wilderness

מָה   *interrogative pronoun.* what?

מוֹלֶדֶת   *n.f.* kindred

מוֹרָה   *n.m.* razor

מוּת   *v.* to die

מִזְבֵּחַ   *n.* altar

מְזוּזַת   *n.f.* doorpost, gatepost

מָחָה   *v.* to blot out

מַחֲשָׁבָה   *n.f.* thought

מַטֶּה   *n.* tribe

מִי   *interrogative pronoun.* who?

מַיִם   *n.m.* water, *construct* מֵי

מָלֵא   *v.* to fill

מַלְאָךְ   *n.* messenger, angel

מִלְחָמָה   *n.* war

מָלַט   *v.* to escape

מָלַךְ   *v.* to reign

מֶלֶךְ   *n.m.* king

מִן   *prep.* From

מָנָה   *n.f.* portion

מִנְחָה   *n.m.* offering

מִסְפָּר   *n.m.* number

מָקוֹם   *n.* place

מִקְנֶה   *n.m.* livestock

מַר   *adj.* bitter

מָשַׁל   *v.* to rule

מִשְׁפָּחָה   *n.f.* clan (smaller than tribe)

מִשְׁפָּט   *n.* justice

מִשְׁתֶּה   *n.m.* feast

מָתַי   *particle.* when?

נ

נָא   *interjection* surely

נָבִיא   *n.m.* prophet

נֵבֶל   *n.m.* wine-skin

נֶגֶב   Negeb Desert *or figuratively:* south

נָגַד — v. *Hifil* to report, tell

נֶגֶד — prep. over against, opposite

נָגַע — v. to touch

נָגַשׁ — v. to approach

נדר — v. to vow

נֶדֶר — n.m. a vow

נָהָר — n.m. river, sometimes *irreg.*, pl נְהָרוֹת

נוֹתַר — v. to be left, remain (*Nifal* > יָתַר)

נוּחַ — v. to rest, settle

נוּס — v. to flee

נוּעַ — v. to quiver, move

נֹחַ — p.n. Noah

נָחַל — v. to possess, to inherit

נָחַם — v. to be sorry

נָחָשׁ — n. serpent

נָטָה — v. to stretch out, extend (e.g. a tent)

נָכַל — v. to act cunningly, deceitfully

נָסָה — v. to test, try, prove

נָסַע — v. to journey, to set out on a journey

נַעַר — n. lad, youth, servant

נְפִילִים — n. giants or *pr.n.* Nephilim

נָפַל — v. to fall

נֶפֶשׁ — n.f. soul, life. pl נְפָשׁוֹת

נָצַב — v. to station oneself (*cf.* יצב)

נָצַל — v. to deliver

נָקַף — v. to go around

נָשָׂא — v. to lift, carry

נִשְׁבַּע — v. to swear (*nifal*), > שבע

נָתַן — v. to give

ס

סָבַב — v. to surround

סְבָךְ — n. thicket

סוּר — v. to turn aside, depart

סָפַר — v. *Qal* to count, *Piel* to relate

ע

עָבַד — v. to serve, to work

עֶבֶד — n.m. servant. pl עֲבָדִים

עָבַר — v. to pass over

עַד — prep. until

עוֹד — adv. again, still, while, yet

עוּר — v. To awake, to arouse

עוֹלָם — n.m. eternity, a long time

עַיִן — n. eye, spring

עִיר — n.f. city, pl עָרִים

עַל — prep. upon, over, against

עָלָה — v. to go up

עֹלָה — n.f. whole burnt offering

עַם — n.m. people, pl עַמִּים

עִם — prep. with

עָמַד — v. to stand

עֵמֶק — n.m. valley, lowland

עָנָה — v. I- to answer, II- be humble

עֳנִי — n.m. affliction, poverty 1

עָנָן — n. cloud

עָנַן — v. *Piel* to make clouds

עָצַב — v. to grieve

עָקַד — v. to bind, tie

עֶרֶב — n.m. evening

עָרוּם — adj. 1. cunning; 2. naked

עָרַךְ — v. to arrange, prepare

עָשָׂה — v. to do, make

עֶשֶׂר — adj. ten

עֶשְׂרִים — adj. twenty

עַתָּה — particle. now

עָתַק — v. to remove, to move on

פ

פֶּה — n.m. mouth

פֹּה — adv. Here

פּוּץ — v. to scatter

פָּלַל — v. pray

פֶּן — Particle. lest

פָּנָה — n.m. face. construct פְּנֵי. With prep., לִפְנֵי = before, in front of

פָּקַד   *v. Qal* to visit, to miss or search for, to appoint, *Piel* to muster

פַּר   *n.m.* young bull

פָּרָה   *v.* bear fruit

פְּרִי   *n.* fruit

פָּרַץ   *v.* to burst or break through

צ

צֹאן   *n.m.* flock, sheep

צָבָא   *n.m/f.* army

צַדִּיק   *adj.* righteous

צֶדֶק   *n.* righteousness

צִוָּה   *v. Piel* to command

צֶמֶד   *n.m.* team + *v.* צָמַד =2

צָעַק   *v.* to cry out

צָרָה   *n.f.* distress, rival

ק

קָבַץ   *v.* to gather

קֶדֶם   *n.m.* east

קֹדֶשׁ   *n.* holiness

קוֹל   *n.m.* voice

קוּם   *v. Qal* to rise, stand; *Hifil* to establish

קָלַל   *v. Qal* to be small; *Piel* to curse

קֶמַח   *n.m.* flour

קָנָא   *v.* to be jealous

קֵץ   *n.m.* end, boundary

קָרָא   *v.* to call; *followed by* ל = to name

קָרַב   *v.* to draw near

קֶרֶב   *n.m.* midst, nearness

קֶרֶן   *n.f.* horn

קָרַע   *v.* to tear

קָשֶׁה   *adj.* hard, fierce

קֶשֶׁת   *n.* bow

ר

רָאָה   *v.* to see

רֹאשׁ   *n.* head

רֵאשִׁית   *n.f.* beginning.

רַב   *adj.* much, many, great. plural, רַבִּים

רוּחַ   *n.f.* spirit, wind

רָחַף   *v. Qal* to grow soft; *Piel* to hover

רָבָה   *v.* multiply, become many

רָבַב   by-form of רָבָה above

רָדַף   *v.* to pursue, persecute

רוּם   *v.* to be high, exalted

רוּץ   *v.* to run

רָחוֹק   *adj.* Remote, far, distant

רֶחֶם   *n.m./f.* womb

רְכוּשׁ   *n.* property, goods

רָכַשׁ   *v.* to gain property, goods

רֶמֶשׂ   *n.m.* creeping thing, insect

רַע   *adj.* evil. *f.* רָעָה *m. pl* רָעִים

רֵעַ   *n.m.* friend

רָעָב   *n.* famine

רָעָה   *v.* to shepherd

רָעַם   *v.* thunder, tremble

רָעַע   *v.* be evil

רַק   *adv.* only

רָשָׁע   *adj.* wicked

שׂ

שָׂדֶה   *n.* field

שׂוּךְ   *v.* to fence or hedge

שָׂטָן   *n.m.* accuser

שִׂיחַ   *n.m.* complaint

שִׂים   *v.* to put, to place

שָׂמַח   *v.* to be glad, rejoice

שָׂנֵא   *v.* to hate

שָׂפָה   *n.f.* lip

שַׂר   *n.* leader, official

שָׂרַף   *v.* to burn

שְׂרֵפָה   *n.f.* a burning, conflagration

שׁ

שֶׁ   *rel. prn.* who, which

שָׁאַל   *v.* to ask

שְׁאֵלָה   *n.f.* request

שָׁחַט   *v.* to slaughter

שָׁכַב   *v.* to lie down

שִׁכּוֹר   *adj.* drunken

שׁוּב   *v.* to return

שׁוּט   *v.* to go about

שָׁכַח   *v.* forget

שָׁכַם   *v.* arise / start early (*Hifil only*)

שָׁכֵן   *v.* to dwell, settle down

שָׁכַר   *v.* become drunk

שֵׁכָר   *n.m.* strong drink

שְׁאֵלָה   *n.f.* petition

שָׁלוֹם   *n.m.* peace, wholeness

שָׁלַח   *v.* to send

שָׁלַךְ   *v.* to cast, throw

שָׁלֵם   *v.* to be whole, complete

שָׁלֹשׁ   *adj.* three

שְׁלֹשָׁה   *n.f.* three

שֵׁם   *n.m.* name. *pl* שֵׁמוֹת

שָׁם   *particle.* there

שֶׁמֶן   *n.* oil, fat

שָׁמַיִם   *n.* heaven

שָׁמַע   *v.* to hear

שָׁמַר   *v.* to keep, guard

שֶׁמֶשׁ   *n.* sun

שָׁנָה   *n.* year

שֵׁנִי   *adj.* two

שִׁנְעָר   *n.* Shinar

שַׁעַר   *n.* gate

שִׁפְחָה   *n.f.* maidservant

שָׁפַט   *v.* to judge

שָׁפַךְ   *v.* to pour out

שֶׁקֶר   *n.* falsehood, lie

שָׁרַץ   *v.* to teem, swarm

שֵׁרֵת   *v.* to minister, serve

שָׁתָה   *v.* to drink

ת

תֵּבָה   *n.* ark, box

תָּוֶךְ   *n.* midst, *cs* תּוֹךְ midst of

תּוֹלְדֹת   *n.f.p.* descendents

תּוֹרָה   *n.f.* instruction

תַּחַת   *prep.* under, instead of

תָּם   *adj.* perfect

טָמֵא   *v.* to be unclean (ceremonially)

תָּמִיד   *n.* continually, regular (sacrifice)

תָּמִים   *n.m.p.* blameless

תָּעָה   *v.* to wander

תְּקוּפָה   *n.f.* a coming around, arrival, due time

30.1   Resources for Hebrew Exegesis

The Hebrew Text

Biblia Hebraica Quinta (Stuttgart: Deutsche Bibelgesellschaft, 2004–).

Kittel, Rudolph, *et al.*, *Biblia Hebraica Stuttgartensia* (Stuttgart: Deutsche Bibelgesellshaft, 3rd emended edn, 1987).

Dotan, Aron (ed.), *Biblia Hebraica Leningradensia* (Peabody, MA: Hendrickson Publishers, 2001).

Interlinear Bibles

Green, Jay (ed.), *The Interlinear Bible* (Sovereign Grace Publishers). This edition has both the OT Hebrew and the NT Greek. The Interlinear Bible has the original Hebrew text with the corresponding English words directly underneath.

Kohlenberger, John R. (ed.), *The Interlinear NIV Hebrew-English OT*. Zondervan Publishers. This interlinear is OT only. It is larger than the version by Green (above), and the print is much easier to read.

Parsing Guides

Davidson, B. *Analytical Hebrew-Chaldee Lexicon* (Peabody, MA: Hendrickson Publishers). Hebrew words are listed in alphabetical order.

Owens, John Joseph, *Analytical Key to the Old Testament* (4 vols.; Grand Rapids: Baker Academic Books). Every verse in the Hebrew Bible is analyzed word-by-word.

Concordances

Even-Shoshan, Abraham. *A New Concordance of the Old Testament* (Jerusalem: Kiryat Sefer, 1989). This work includes definitions in modern Hebrew.

Strong, James. *The New Strong's Concordance* (Nashville: Thomas Nelson Publishers, 1996). The index assigns a number to each Hebrew word, and that number can be used to locate the Hebrew word in other reference works listed below.

Wigram, George (ed.), *The New Englishman's Hebrew Concordance* (Peabody, MA: Hendrickson Publishers, 1996. This book lists the biblical verses where each Hebrew word appears. Words are organized according to the Strong's Concordance numbers.

Easy to Use Dictionaries

Gesenius, *The New Brown-Driver-Briggs-Gesenius Hebrew and English Lexicon* (Peabody, MA: Hendrickson Publishers, 1979). Hebrew words are identified with Strong's Concordance numbers.

Harris, R. Laird, Gleason Archer, and Bruce Waltke (eds.), *Theological Wordbook of the Old Testament* (2 vols.; Chicago: Moody Press, 1980). Includes English index and Strong's numbers. This is a very good work with in-depth discussions of the Hebrew words, yet it is quite easy to understand.

Other Dictionaries and Word Books

Botterweck, G. Johannes, and Helmer Ringgren (eds.), *Theological Dictionary of the Old Testament* (Grand Rapids: Eerdmans, 1974-).

Clines, David. *Dictionary of Classical Hebrew* (Sheffield: Sheffield Academic Press, 1993-).

Holladay, William (ed.), *A Concise Hebrew and Aramaic Lexicon of the Old Testament* (Grand Rapids: Eerdmans,1988).

Jenni, Ernst and Claus Westermann (eds.), *Theological Lexicon of the OT* (3 Vols.; Peabody, MA: Hendrickson Publishers, 1997).

Kittel, Gerhard (ed.), *Theological Dictionary of the New Testament* (10 vols.; Grand Rapids: Eerdmans, 1964). Contains a large amount of Hebrew information.

Köhler, Ludwig, *The Hebrew and Aramaic Lexicon of the Old Testament* (2 vols.; Leiden: E.J. Brill, Study edn, 2001).

VanGemeren, Willem A. (ed.), *New International Dictionary of Old Testament Theology and Exegesis* (5 Vols.; Grand Rapids: Zondervan, 1997).

Grammar and Syntax

Gesenius, Wilhelm. *Hebrew Grammar* (ed. E. Kautzsch; trans. A.E. Cowley; Oxford: Clarendon Press, 1910).

Joüon, Paul. *A Grammar of Biblical Hebrew* (2 vols.; trans. and revised by T. Muraoka; Subsidia Biblica-14/II. Rome: Editrice Pontificio Instituto Biblico, Reprint of first edition with corrections, 1993).

Niccacci, Alviero. *The Syntax of the Verb in Classical Hebrew Prose* (trans. Wilfred G.E. Watson; JSOTSup, 86; Sheffield: Sheffield Academic Press, 1990).

Rocine, B.M. *Learning Biblical Hebrew: A New Approach Using Discourse Analysis* (Macon, GA: Smyth & Helwys Publishers, 2000).

Waltke, Bruce K. and M. O'Connor. *An Introduction to Biblical Hebrew Syntax* (Winona Lake, IN: Eisenbrauns Pub., 1990).

Williams, Ronald J. *Hebrew Syntax: An Outline* (Toronto: University of Toronto Press, 2nd edn, 1976).

31.1 Subject Index

Torah Scroll from Germany
700 to 800 years old

HEBREW VERB SLOTS

14	13	12	11	10	9	8
Pronominal Suffixes	Emphatics	Afformatives	Connective Vowel	ל Root Letter	Infix	ע Root Letter
1cs ־נִי 2ms ־ךָ or ־ָ 2fs ־ךְ 3ms ־וֹ or ־וֹ 3fs ־ה or ־ָה 1cp ־נוּ 2mp ־כֶם 3mp ־הֶם or ־ם or ־מוֹ 3fp ־הֶן or ־ן *Signifies:* 1. Object of the verb, or 2. Subj or object of infinitive	*A. Volative* ־ה Cohortative: Attached to 1p imf to express desire, will, or intention Jussive: Added to the jussive for emphasis Imperative: Added to the imperative for emphasis *B. Paragogic* ה Added to 3ms for euphony, and between pf or imf and the pronom. Suff. for euphony *C. Paragogic* נ Added either at the end of a verb, or between verb and pronominal suffix (energic) for: 1. Euphony or 2. Emphasis	*A. Perfect* 1cs ־תִי 2ms ־תָ 3fs ־ת 3ms --- 3fs ־ה 1cp ־נוּ 2mp ־תֶם 2fp ־תֶן 3cp ־וּ *B. Imperfect* 2fs ־י 2mp ־וּ 2fp ־נָה or ־ןָ 3mp ־וּ 3fp ־נָה or ־ןָ *C. Imperative* Same as imperf., but with no prefix *D. Participle* ms --- fs ־ה or ־ת mp ־ים fp ־וֹת *E. Infinitive* ־ת = QIC of פ"י, פ"נ, & (orig. פ"ו)	־וֹ־ Occurs in 1st & 2d p forms of Niphal, and Hiphil pf of Hollow vb e.g. הֲשִׁיבוֹת And in all 1st & 2d person perfects of geminate verbs.	*A. Dropped* Last radical may be omitted in ל"ה or geminates, which usually have a dagesh compensative. ה is always dropped in the vav cons. & jussive of ל"ה *B. Changed* 1- In ל"ה the ה changes to י in pf. 1st & 2d p, & to ת in 3fs. In imf, imv, etc. the ה may drop or change to י 2- ה Changes to ־וֹת in all ל"ה infin. construct and sometimes in קרא *C. Hollow Vbs* Doubles in Polel and Hitpolel e.g. קוֹמַמְתִּי	*A. Hiphil* י = Hiphil Pf 3p and all Imf except f pl *B. Infinitives* וֹ= Infinitive Defective= XXX *C. Participle* וֹ =Qal P Ptc Defective= XXX	*A. Doubled* Dagesh Forte in Piel, Pual, & Hitpael *B. Dropped* Drops out in the Hollow verbs, except for Qal imf and Niphal pf and imperfect

HEBREW VERB SLOTS

7	6	5	4	3	2	1
Infix	פ Root Letter	Verb Pattern Indicators	Imperfect Preformatives	Definite Article	Prepositions	Conj. or Interrog.
A. Participle וֹ Occurs in Qal Active Ptc, qatal. Defective: X̣ *B. As Stem Indicator* וֹ Occurs in all forms of Polel, Polal, Hitpolel of Hollow and geminate verbs. Defective: X̣	*A. In Niphal* Dagesh Forte in N imf, imv, Inf *B. Dropped* 1- Omitted in imf & imv of פ"י & פ"נ (פ"ן), also in vbs לקח & הלך. פ"נ & usually לקח add dagesh 2-Lengthening in imf of פ"י (פ"ר) qatal form יָדַע☞יֵידַע *C. Changed* 1- י goes back to ו in H & N הוֹצִיא = H perf יוֹצִיא = H imf 2-In qatol the י returns to original ו in the imperf: יוּכַל☞יָכֹל (The י may stay in imf of יָרֵשׁ יָרֵא & others) *D. Sibilants* שׁ, ס, צ switch places with the ת in Hitpael: שָׁבַת goes to הִשְׁתַּבֵּת	*A.* נ = Niphal Pf Changes to Dagesh in Imf הַ = Hiphil Pf X̣ in Imf הָ = Hophal שׁ in Imf הִת = Hitp. Pf Xת in Imf *B. Participles:* מְ = Piel מְ or מֻX = Pu מִת = Hitpael מַ or מְ= Hiph מָ or מֻ =Hoph נ = Niphal *C.* Stem indicators that are peculiar to Hollow Verbs and Geminates וֹX= Polel/Polal הוּ = Hophal הִתXוֹ =Hitpol. *Participles:* מְוֹX =Polel or Polal מוּ = Hophal מִתXוֹ =Hitpol	*A.* ALL imperfects have these preformatives. 1cs א 2ms תִ 2fs תִ 3ms יִ 3fs תִ 1cp נִ 2mp תִ 2fp תִ 3mp יִ 3fp תִ *B.* Sheva under the imf prefix = Piel or Pual, except when pronominal suffixes are attached. *C. Pointing* Qal = יִ Piel = יְ Pual = יְ Hiphil = יַ Hophal = יָ Niphal = יִ Hitpael = יִת Hollow and geminate= יָ	הַ plus a Dagesh in the 1st Radical. With gutturals it may be הָ or הֶ Attaches only to the participle.	לְ כְּ בְּ מִן Attach only to Participles or Infinitives Construct. לְ Usually indicates infinitive construct	*A. Conj.* וְ or וַ attaches only to the Imperfect וְ attaches to any verb. May be וּ before פ, מ, ב, & before vocal sheva. Before Composite sheva it will be וַ, וֶ, or וָ. *B. Interrog. Particle* הֲ הֶ before gutturals © 2000 Lee R Martin

Printed in Great Britain
by Amazon

59842912R00161